CONTRASTING PRISONERS' RIGHTS

Contrasting Prisoners' Rights

A Comparative Examination of Germany and England

Liora Lazarus

Fellow and Tutor in Law, St. Anne's College, Oxford
Lecturer in Law, University of Oxford

OXFORD
UNIVERSITY PRESS

OXFORD
UNIVERSITY PRESS

Great Clarendon Street, Oxford OX2 6DP

Oxford University Press is a department of the University of Oxford.
It furthers the University's objective of excellence in research, scholarship,
and education by publishing worldwide in

Oxford New York

Auckland Bangkok Buenos Aires Cape Town Chennai
Dar es Salaam Delhi Hong Kong Istanbul Karachi Kolkata
Kuala Lumpur Madrid Melbourne Mexico City Mumbai Nairobi
São Paulo Shanghai Singapore Taipei Tokyo Toronto

Oxford is a registered trade mark of Oxford University Press
in the UK and in certain other countries

Published in the United States
by Oxford University Press Inc., New York

© L. Lazarus, 2004

The moral rights of the author have been asserted
Database right Oxford University Press (maker)

First published 2004

British Library Cataloguing in Publication Data
Data available

Library of Congress Cataloging in Publication Data
Data available

ISBN 0–19–925983–6

1 3 5 7 9 10 8 6 4 2

Typeset by Hope Services (Abingdon) Ltd.
Printed in Great Britain
on acid-free paper by
Biddles Ltd, King's Lynn

For my mother, Evelyn Dalberg

General Editor's Preface

Recent years have seen increasing discussion and debate about the rights of prisoners, but this monograph contributes in an original and striking way. Dr Lazarus takes a comparative view, focusing on the different legal, social, and constitutional traditions of England and Wales and of Germany in order to explore the way in which questions of prisoners' rights are approached. The result is a sophisticated comparative study that digs deep into the socio-legal culture of each jurisdiction. The analysis raises a range of issues about the foundation and extent of prisoners' rights, and also about the role of the judiciary in relation to the legislature and the executive. This fine monograph therefore constitutes a major contribution to scholarship in relation to the rights of prisoners, the judicial function, and the comparative method.

Andrew Ashworth
Oxford, December 2003

Acknowledgments

I am hugely indebted to Lucia Zedner for encouraging me to write the doctorate upon which this book is based, and for her guidance and support ever since.

While conducting my doctoral research I was privileged to have the support of the Max Planck Gesselschaft and access to the expertise and resources of the Max Planck Institute for Foreign and International Criminal Law, Freiburg, Germany. I would particularly like to thank Professor Albin Eser, Dr Barbara Huber and the library staff at the Institute for their support. Very special thanks must go also to Professor Johannes Feest (University of Bremen) for reading the German part of the manuscript, Professor Klaus Günther (University of Frankfurt) for his helpful ideas on German constitutionalism, and to Professors Nicola Lacey (LSE) and Denis Galligan (Oxford) for their constructive and critical examination of my doctoral thesis.

In the course of writing this book, I was very lucky to have an office at the Centre for British Studies, Humboldt University, Berlin and to receive the warm hospitality of those who worked there. Thanks in particular to Prof. Gerhard Dannemann for arranging my time there.

Fiona Barry, Gwen Booth, John Louth, and the production staff at OUP were all very helpful and I am grateful to them for their assistance.

Finally, thanks must go to my friends, family and colleagues who supported me in their various ways, and to those who read drafts of chapters: Andrew Ashworth, Christopher Boulle, Nigel Bowles, Ruth Deech, Benjamin Goold, Lisa Gourd, Karen Guida, Peter Ghosh, Andrea Huber, Murray Hunt, Penny Hill, Susan James, John Lazarus, Micha Lazarus, Alison McDonald, Kevin Reel, Olaf Roth, Harry Rutter, Harriet Rutter, Otto Rutter and Karen Yeung—and of course, my special thanks to Isabella Moebius.

Contents

I: GERMANY

II: ENGLAND AND WALES

Table of German Cases

Table of German Constitutional and Statutory Provisions

CONSTITUTIONAL PROVISIONS

STATUTORY PROVISIONS

Table of Cases: England and Wales

Table of Statutory Provisions: England and Wales

STATUTORY INSTRUMENTS

BILLS

Table of European Court of Human Rights Cases

Table of International Conventions, Treaties, Instruments and Standards

Citation Conventions

Please note that the citation of German commentaries on the Prison Act will follow the standard German citation method for legal commentaries. This is done by referring to the names of the authors, the relevant paragraph (§) of the German Prison Act and, where applicable, the margin numbers (mn) of the text relevant to that paragraph (e.g. Calliess/Müller Dietz, § 3, mn 4).

The commentaries in question are: R.-P. Calliess and H. Müller-Dietz *Strafvollzugsgesetz* (9th edn, Beck, Munich, 2002); H.-D. Schwind and A. Böhm, *Strafvollzugsgesetz* (3rd edn, Walter de Gruyter, Berlin, 1999); J. Feest (ed.), *Kommentar zum Strafvollzugsgesetz* (4th edn, Luchterhand, Neuwied, 2000).

Abbreviations

AJCL	American Journal of Comparative Law
AC	Appeal Court Reports
AnwBl	Anwaltsblatt
All ER	All England Law Reports
AöR	Archiv für öffentliches Recht
BGB	Bürgerliches Gesetzbuch (Civil Code)
Beck	C.H. Beck Verlag
BGBl	Bundesgesetzblatt (Federal Law Gazette)
BGH	Bundesgerichtshof (Federal Supreme Court)
BGHSt	Sammlung der Entscheidungen des Bundesgerichtshofs in Strafsachen (Decisions of the Federal Supreme Court in Criminal Law Matters)
BJC	British Journal of Criminology
BlGefk	Blätter für Gefängiskunde
BlStVKunde	Blätter für Strafvollzugskunde
BVerfG Beschl.	Beschluß des Bundesverfassungsgericht (Chamber Decisions of the Federal Constitutional Court)
BVerfGE	Sammlung der Entscheidungen des Bundesverfassungsgerichts (Senate Decisions of the Federal Constitutional Court)
Bt - Dr.	Bundestags-Drucksache (Federal Parliament Publications)
Boorberg	Richard Boorberg Verlag
Calliess/Müller-Dietz	R.-P. Calliess and H. Müller Dietz, *Strafvollzugsgesetz* (9th edn, Beck, Munich, 2002)
CEU Press	Central European Press
CLJ	Cambridge Law Journal
CJA	Criminal Justice Act 1991
CJB	Criminal Justice Bill
CJPOA	Criminal Justice and Public Order Act 1994
CLP	Current Legal Problems
CUP	Cambridge University Press
CLR	Criminal Law Review
DuR	Demokratie und Recht
DÖV	Die Öffentliche Verwaltung
ECHR	European Convention on Human Rights
ECtHR	European Court of Human Rights
EuGRZ	Europäische Grundrechte Zeitschrift

EHRLR	European Human Rights Law Review
Feest	J. Feest (ed.), *Kommentar zum Strafvollzugsgesetz* (4th edn, Luchterhand, Neuwied, 2000)
FCC	Federal Constitutional Court
GA	Goltdammer's Archiv für Strafrecht
Heymanns	Carl Heymanns Verlag
Howard Journal	Howard Journal of Criminal Justice
HPT	History of Political Thought
HRA	Human Rights Act
IJSL	International Journal of the Sociology of Law
Imm. A.R.	Immigration Appeal Reports
INFO	Info zum Strafvollzug im Praxis und Rechtsprechung (Zeitschrift)
JA	Juristische Arbeitsblätter
JLS	Journal of Law and Society
JRev	Judicial Review
JR	Juristische Rundschau
JuS	Juristische Schulung
Jura	Juristische Ausbildung
JZ	Juristenzeitung
KG	Kammergericht (Higher Regional Court of Berlin)
KrimJ	Kriminologisches Journal
Kriminalistik	Kriminalistik Verlag
Kluwer	Kluwer Law International
LS	Legal Studies
LG	Landgericht (Regional Court)
LQR	Law Quarterly Review
MDR	Monatsschrift für Deutsches Recht
MLR	Modern Law Review
mn	margin number
MPI	Max Planck Institute for Foreign and International Penal Law
Mohr	J.C.B. Mohr Verlag
MschrKrim	Monatsschrift für Kriminologie und Strafrechts-reform
Müller	C.F. Müller Verlag
NJW	Neue Juristische Wochenschrift
NK	Neue Kriminalpolitik
Nomos	Nomos Verlagsgesellschaft
NStZ	Neue Zeitschrift für Strafrecht
OJLS	Oxford Journal of Legal Studies
OUP	Oxford University Press
OLG	Oberlandesgericht (Higher Regional Court)
PA	Public Administration

PL	Public Law
PSJ	Prison Service Journal
P&S	Punishment & Society
QMWLJ	Queen Mary and Westfield Law Journal
RdA	Recht der Arbeit
SAJC	South African Journal of Criminal Law and Criminology
SAJHR	South African Journal of Human Rights
Schwind/Böhm	H.-D. Schwind and A. Böhm, *Strafvollzugsgesetz* (Walter de Gruyter, Berlin, 1999)
SH	Sonderheft (Special Issue)
S&LS	Social and Legal Studies
Stanford LRev	Stanford Law Review
StV	Strafverteidiger
VVDStRL	Veröffentlichungen der Vereinigung der Deutschen Staatsrechtslehrer
WLR	Weekly Law Reports
ZRP	Zeitschrift für Rechtspolitik
ZfRSoz	Zeitschrift für Rechtssoziologie
ZfRV	Zeitschrift für Rechtsvergleichung
ZfStrVo	Zeitschrift für Strafvollzug und Straffälligenhilfe
ZStW	Zeitschrift für die gesamte Strafrechtswissenschaft

1

Introduction

It is said that no one truly knows a nation until one has been inside its jails. A nation should not be judged by how it treats its highest citizens, but its lowest ones.[1]

It does not require much imagination to understand why society is concerned about the state of its prisons or the treatment which prisoners receive. In the absence of the death penalty, imprisonment is the most severe form of state punishment. It deprives offenders of their freedom of movement, it removes them from the rest of society and subjects them to numerous other restraints which restrict their liberty and erode their 'civic selves'.[2] The coercive potential of imprisonment is heightened by the closed nature of prison institutions. Lack of visibility to the outside world increases the vulnerability of the prisoner to particular risks: 'if people are going to be ill-treated and abused, prison . . . seems to provide fertile soil'.[3]

Given the considerable threat to offenders' liberty and humanity which prisons represent, it is small wonder that the protection and enforcement of prisoners' legal rights has featured regularly in international and regional human rights discourse over the last 30 years.[4] Nor is it surprising that in the debates concerning prison policy in England 'much has been made of the

---

[1] N. Mandela, *Long Walk to Freedom* (Little Brown, London, 1994) 187.

[2] E. Goffmann, 'On the Characteristics of Total Institutions: the Inmate World' in D. Cressey (ed.), *The Prison: Studies in Institutional Organisation and Change* (Holt, Rinehart and Winston, New York, 1961) 16, 23.

[3] V. Stern, *A Sin Against the Future* (Penguin, London, 1998) 195.

[4] See, *inter alia, Declaration on the Protection of All Persons from Being Subjected to Torture and Other Cruel, Inhuman or Degrading Treatment or Punishment* (UN General Assembly Res. 3452, 9 December 1975); *Convention against Torture and Other Cruel, Inhuman or Degrading Treatment or Punishment* (UN General Assembly Res. 39/46, 10 December 1984); *Inter-American Convention to Prevent and Punish Torture* (OAS Treaty Series No. 67, 9 December 1985); *European Convention for the Prevention of Torture and Inhuman and Degrading Treatment or Punishment* (European Treaty Series No. 126, 26 November 1987); *Standard Minimum Rules for the Treatment of Prisoners* (Adopted by the First UN Congress on the Prevention of Crime and the Treatment of Offenders, Geneva 1955, approved by UN Economic and Social Council Res. 663, 31 July 1957; and amended by Economic and Social Council Res. 2076, 13 May 1977); *Body of Principles for the Protection of All Persons under Any Form of Detention or Imprisonment* (UN General Assembly Res. 43/173, 9 December 1988); *Code of Conduct for Law Enforcement Officials* (UN General Assembly Res. 34/169, 17 December 1979). See N. Rodley, *The Treatment of Prisoners under International Law* (2nd edn, Clarendon Press, Oxford, 1999) 1–7; R. Morgan and M. Evans (eds), *Protecting Prisoners: The Standards of the European Committee for the Prevention of Torture in Context* (OUP, Oxford, 1999) 1–9.

notion of prisoners' rights'.[5] Yet, despite international and domestic concern, proponents of prison reform in England still argue that the system of
prisoners' rights protection is inadequate, in terms of the rights which prisoners can claim, the possibilities of enforcement, and the independence of
enforcement bodies.[6] More recently, calls for a new Prison Act which clarifies prisoners' rights and duties have accompanied the Human Rights Act
1998.[7] Given the general concern with prisoners' rights protection and calls
for statutory reform, it is timely to stand back and reflect on the conception
and protection of prisoners' rights in England.[8] This book seeks, through
comparative reflection, to deepen our understanding of prisoners' rights in
England whilst exploring the social and legal cultural context in which they
are shaped.[9] Through juxtaposition with Germany, by distancing ourselves
from our local environment and bringing out the 'strangeness in the familiar',[10] the book explores the method and manner of conceiving of prisoners'
legal rights in England.

To move forward the debate surrounding prisoners' rights we must look
beyond rhetoric and examine the notion of prisoners' rights more closely.
Others have adopted a legal theoretical perspective, explaining the nature
and justification of prisoners' rights.[11] These theories, while varying in
detail, all root the prisoner's normative claim to individual rights protection
in the view of the prisoner as an equal bearer of fundamental human rights,
in their particular view of what these fundamental rights are, and in their
interpretations of the protections afforded by them. While punishment
involves some loss of basic human rights, it should never entirely negate

---

[5] G. Richardson, 'Prisoners and the Law: Beyond Rights' in C. McCrudden and
G. Chambers (eds), *Individual Rights and the Law in the UK* (Clarendon Press, Oxford, 1993)
179.
[6] J. Schone, 'The Short Life and Painful Death of Prisoners' Rights' (2001) 40 *Howard
Journal* 70; S. Livingstone, T. Owen and A. MacDonald, *Prison Law* (3rd edn, OUP, Oxford
2003) 551ff.
[7] Editorial, 'Prisons and the Law' (2002) 142 *Prison Service Journal* 1.
[8] Throughout this book the term England refers to the legal jurisdiction of England and
Wales. While many of the same rules and issues exist in Scotland and Northern Ireland, the
nuances of their legal cultures inevitably differ.
[9] See 1.3 below on legal culture.
[10] M. Lacey and K. Haakonssen, 'History, historicism, and the culture of rights' in M. Lacey
and K. Haakonssen, *A Culture of Rights* (CUP, Cambridge, 1990) 1, 17.
[11] Relatively little theoretical attention is paid to the normative foundation of post-
conviction prisoners' rights in England. The leading English theorist on this is G. Richardson,
'The Case for Prisoners' Rights' in M. Maguire, R. Morgan and J. Vagg (eds), *Accountability
and Prisons* (Tavistock, London, 1985) 19. See, more recently H. Lardy, 'Prisoner
Disenfranchisement: Constitutional Rights and Wrongs' (2002) *Public Law* 524. The relevant
literature in Germany is more extensive: T. Würtenberger, 'Freiheit und Zwang im Strafvollzug'
(1969) *NJW* 1747; H. Schuler-Springorum, *Strafvollzug im Übergang* (Schwartz Verlag,
Göttingen, 1969); H. Müller-Dietz, *Strafvollzugsgesetzgebung und Strafvollzugsreform*
(Heymanns, Cologne, 1970); B. Freudenthal, 'Die staatsrechtliche Stellung des Gefangenen',
Rektoratsrede Jena 1910, printed in (1955) *ZfStrVo* 157; B. Freudenthal, 'Der Strafvollzug als
Rechtsverhältnis des öffentlichen Rechts' (1911) *ZStW* 222. For a recent American perspective,
see R. Lipkke, 'Toward a theory of prisoners' rights' (2002) 15(2) *Ratio Juris* 122.

them. Moreover, while punishment limits human rights, the extent of limitation should depend on the purpose of imprisonment, which in turn should link to a background theory for the justification of punishment. Many theorists also argue that, due to their particular vulnerability and dependence in prisons, prisoners should have special legal rights which protect them against ill-treatment during imprisonment, and compensate for its potential long-term damages.[12]

While these analytical approaches help to shed light on the normative foundations of a prisoners' claim to rights protection, they do not consider how prisoners' legal rights are formed, or not formed, within the social practice of the law. This is the central concern of this book, which operates on the premise that law and legal institutions can usefully be considered in the light of broader social processes. Theories of prisoners' rights protection are of interest here to the extent that they have a formative influence on the conception of the prisoners' legal status in either England or Germany, but this book will not provide a theoretical analysis of prisoners' rights, nor seek to resolve the normative controversies inherent therein, namely the normative foundation of the claim to fundamental rights, the relationship between human rights and punishment, and the justifications of punishment.[13] Rather, this comparison seeks to identify the social, political and cultural dynamics which have shaped the method and manner of conceiving of prisoners' legal rights in both jurisdictions.

England and Germany's respective approaches to prisoners' rights present bold contrasts. In England, despite significant judicial activity in developing a prisoners' rights jurisprudence, prisoners' rights protection remains partial and equivocal. Judges are disinclined to intervene in many areas of prison life, notwithstanding the introduction of the Human Rights Act (HRA) 1998. While the statutory regime furthers political control and accountability of prison administration, there is a strong disinclination in England to provide prisoners with legally enforceable entitlements. This equivocal commitment to prisoners' rights in England is heightened when juxtaposed against Germany's highly articulated rights culture and ambitious system of prisoners' rights protection under the Prison Act 1976. The German Prison

---

[12] A number of theorists argue that prisoners' rights should enjoy legal protection which for Richardson 'implies the ultimate stamp of formal authority and carries considerable political significance'. It is accepted that such legal protection need not involve immediate or constant recourse to legal adjudication. However, the courts should at least act as a mechanism of last resort enforcement and supplement other informal but independent control mechanisms within prisons, which are themselves adequately equipped with proper powers of rights enforcement. See Richardson (n 11) and Würtenberger (n 11). Note that the *Body of Principles for the Protection of All Persons under Any Form of Detention or Imprisonment* (UN General Assembly Res. 43/173, 9 December 1988) calls for the protection of prisoners' rights by a 'judicial body' or 'other authority under the law whose status and tenure affords the strongest possible guarantees of competence, impartiality and independence'.

[13] For attempts to resolve these, see Lipkke (n 11); Lardy (n 11).

Act, underpinned by a considerable constitutional jurisprudence on prisoners' rights, sets out foundational principles of prison administration, affords prisoners' positive rights, defines the limitations of prisoners' constitutional rights, and provides prisoners' recourse to Prison Courts. Moreover, the rights and principles under the German Prison Act have been developed and refined in a substantial body of prison law jurisprudence over the last thirty years.

Through comparison with Germany, this study contributes to the discussion in England on the protection and conception of prisoners' rights. In the light of the possibility of future statutory reform of prisoners' rights in England, there is much to learn from the successes and failures of Germany's long experience of prisoners' rights protection. And there is certainly much revealed about England's conception of the prisoners' legal status through contrast with Germany. But the book also speaks to the broader debate on the protection of fundamental rights in England, which has intensified with the HRA 1998. This debate, as in the case law under the 1998 Act, has been predominantly Anglo-American, with much comparative reference made to the constitutional models and case law of Canada, New Zealand and South Africa. It is curious, however, that with the incorporation of the European Convention on Human Rights (ECHR), there has been relatively little attention to rights traditions on the European Continent itself, notwithstanding the engagement with Convention jurisprudence.[14] Germany is particularly influential in this jurisprudence, with the proportionality doctrine being only one famous example. It is timely therefore to engage more fully with continental models of human rights protection and to make available to an English speaking audience, both in and outside England, a previously inaccessible body of information on German constitutional protection of prisoners' rights.

But if comparison is to provide us with meaningful insights into the manner in which prisoners' rights have been defined and the broader context in which this has taken place, the comparative endeavour must be conducted with care. The remainder of this chapter examines some of the methodological problems facing comparative law and the methodology and structure of this book.

1.1 THE CHALLENGES OF COMPARISON

. . . comparative law has provided a seemingly unending pastime for comparatists and others to discuss its true meaning, historical development, dangers, virtues, scope, functions, aims and purposes, uses and misuses, and method . . .[15]

---

[14] For a notable exception in this respect, see: *Aston Cantlow and Wilmcote with Billesley Parochial Church Council v Wallbank and another* [2003] All ER (D) 360 (HL).

[15] E. Örücü, 'Unde Venit, Quo Tendit Comparative Law?' in A. Harding and E. Örücü (eds), *Comparative Law in the 21st Century* (Kluwer, London, 2002) 1.

... everyone is now a methodologist—to be a comparativist today is to worry about the proper terms, categories, scale, methods and data to be used in comparison.[16]

Comparative law is presently subject to much virulent criticism and growing 'methodological angst'.[17] Legrand argues that comparativists take a narrow view of the comparative endeavour: merely comparing the rules of one jurisdiction with that of another. They have failed, he insists, 'to ask the most fundamental questions about the act of comparison in law'.[18] Comparativists are called to take up the *contrarian challenge* by looking beyond legal rules to the jurisdiction's mentalité, respecting difference, accepting the 'foreignness of languages' and adopting an interdisciplinary and theoretical approach to comparative law.[19] His is a vision of scholarly erudition and self-critical engagement, an endeavour 'ill-suited to clever minds in a hurry'.[20]

Fellow comparativists articulate Legrand's challenges more modestly. Merryman tells us that 'there are professional activities for which rule-comparison is directly useful, but scholarship is supposed to have larger concerns'.[21] Bell requires that we understand the 'context or institutional setting' in which rules operate,[22] and the 'tradition in which a legal text or idea becomes accessible'.[23] Zedner warns of the 'generalising imperatives of the comparative', born of a legal universalism which beguiles comparativists.[24] She criticizes the failure of comparative criminal justice scholarship to refer to 'the broader political or socio-economic or to the cultural context in which ... differences evolved'.[25] Moreover, Nelken tells us that 'merely juxtaposing descriptions of various aspects of criminal process in different cultures does little to advance the goal of explanation or understanding'.[26] It seems that presently 'comparative lawyers are agreed that it is not sufficient just to look at legal texts and rules to explain why legal systems are different'.[27]

---

[16] A. Riles 'Introduction: The Projects of Comparison' in A. Riles (ed.), *Rethinking the Masters of Comparative Law* (Hart, Oxford, 2001) 1, 2.

[17] Riles (n 16) 18; P. Legrand, 'How to Compare Now' (1996) 16(2) *LS* 232, 233–4.

[18] Legrand (n 17) 234.

[19] P. Legrand, *Fragments of Law-as-Culture* (W.E.J. Tjeenk Willink, Deventer, 1999) ch. 1.

[20] Legrand (n 19) 25.

[21] Quoted in P. Legrand, 'John Merryman and Comparative Legal Studies: A Dialogue' (1999) 27(3) *American Journal of Comparative Law* 50.

[22] J. Bell, 'Comparing Public Law' in Harding and Örücü (n 15) ch. 13, 236.

[23] J. Bell, *French Legal Cultures* (Butterworths, London, 2001) 8.

[24] L. Zedner, 'In Pursuit of the Vernacular: Comparing Law and Order Discourses in England and Germany' (1995) 4 *Social and Legal Studies* 517, 518.

[25] L. Zedner, 'Comparative research in criminal justice' in L. Noaks, M. Maguire and M. Levi (eds), *Contemporary Issues in Criminology* (University of Wales Press, Cardiff, 1995) ch. 2, 8.

[26] D. Nelken, 'Comparing Criminal Justice' in M. Maguire, R. Morgan and R. Reiner (eds), *Oxford Handbook of Criminology* (3rd edn, OUP, Oxford, 2002) ch. 6, 180.

[27] Bell (n 23) 11.

But while comparativists might now agree to look beyond formal legal rules or functions, there is little consensus on what the discipline comprises. Concern is expressed about the fragmentation of the discipline with the range of comparative legal methods now in play. We now talk of comparative legal history, comparative jurisprudence, comparative legal cultural studies, and comparative law and economics.[28] But this dissonance is both inevitable and familiar, produced by the open-ended nature of the two central questions 'haunting' comparative law: why we compare and what we should compare.[29] Without conclusive answers to these questions, comparative law is, inevitably, a site of innovation and self-invention. To this extent, perhaps the quest for a cohesive paradigm is illusory.

Paradigmatic fluidity is also an inevitable consequence of the fact that comparative law, despite calls for its recognition as a distinct academic discipline,[30] is a method not a subject: 'it is the common name for a variety of methods of looking at law, and especially of looking at one's own law'.[31] Comparison is thus especially susceptible to becoming the handmaiden of broader disciplinary and political movements in academic law. Its history is not one of consistent paradigmatic development, but of disciplinary and political 'projects'.[32] Perhaps we should embrace this diversity of comparative projects rather than viewing them as a threat which could 'swallow up and change the character of the discipline'.[33] Instead of resisting innovation, we might critically engage with it; there seems 'little point in trying to specify what comparative law should be, because it already is many different things'.[34]

Nevertheless, the aspiring comparativist can be forgiven for quailing in the face of the venture's potential scale, its methodological challenges, and its indistinct disciplinary boundaries. More constructively, however, we could approach with 'sound judgement' and common sense while still recognizing the difficulties of the enterprise.[35] Those who venture into comparison must be wary of its methodological hazards and intellectual temptations, approaching the enterprise fully conscious of both its limits and possibilities. Crucially, comparativists tempted to resolve the uncertainties of their discipline should resist off-the-shelf models of comparative law.[36] Maps may guide our initial conception of the comparative endeavour

---

[28] Örücü (n 15) 2–6.
[29] R. Cotterell, 'Seeking Similarity, Appreciating Difference: Comparative Law and Communities' in Harding and Örücü (n 15) ch. 3, 36.
[30] See P. de Cruz, *Comparative Law in a Changing World* (2nd edn, Cavendish, London, 1999) 2–6.
[31] O. Kahn-Freund, *Comparative Law as an Academic Subject* (Clarendon Press, Oxford, 1965) 4.
[32] Riles (n 16) 5.   [33] Örücü (n 15) 2.   [34] Cotterell (n 29) 36.
[35] P. Leyland, 'Oppositions and Fragmentations: In Search of a Formula for Comparative Analysis?' in Harding and Örücü (n 15) ch. 12, 221.
[36] e.g., M. Van Hoecke and M. Warrington, 'Legal Cultures, Legal Paradigms and Legal Doctrine: Towards a New Model for Comparative Law' (1998) *ICLQ* 47, 495; Leyland (n 35).

and preliminary navigation of foreign jurisdictions,[37] but there are few easy solutions for those who venture beyond formal legal rules or familiar environments. Understanding of the complexity of the law's local setting calls primarily for curiosity, engagement, intuition, and reflection. Without losing the crucial detachment of the foreign observer, the comparativist must unearth the unsaid and the unwritten. This process, of careful discovery and lateral exploration, is not easily systematized. Without a model of the comparative endeavour, the comparativist's aspiration is, to paraphrase Kahn-Freund, a 'consciousness' of her enterprise.[38] We might characterize this as a methodological awareness, rather than a system or model; a *reflective comparison*. Of what, then, is the reflective comparativist conscious?

1.2 GLOBAL PERSPECTIVES AND LOCAL KNOWLEDGE: SEEING SIMILARITY/FINDING DIFFERENCE

By the international exchanges which it requires, comparative law procures the gradual approximation of viewpoints, the abandonment of deadly complacency and the relaxation of fixed dogma. It affords us a glimpse into the form and formation of legal institutions which develop in parallel, possibly in accordance with laws yet to be determined, and permits us to catch sight, through the differences in detail, of the *grand similarities* and so to deepen our belief in the existence of a unitary sense of justice.[39]

It is this imaginative, or constructive, or interpretive power, a power rooted in the collective resources of culture rather than in the separate capacities of individuals . . . upon which the comparative study of law, or justice, or forensics, or adjudication should . . . train its attention. It is there—in the method and manner of conceiving decision situations so that settled rules can be applied to decide them (as well, of course, of conceiving the rules), in what I have been calling legal sensibility—that the *informing contrasts* lie.[40]

Much has been made of the tendency of comparative lawyers to see similarity between legal systems over differences exposed by local explanations.[41] The debate reveals deeper beliefs concerning the comparative study of law. Two distinct visions of law underwrite the claims above about the purpose of legal comparison. The first sees law as an autonomous system ultimately similar in form and content across all cultures. The second view is that, far

---

[37] Bell (n 23) 7.   [38] Kahn-Freund (n 31) 4.

[39] K. Zweigert and H. Kötz, *An Introduction to Comparative Law*, vol. 1 (North-Holland Publishing Co., Amsterdam, 1977) 3. Emphasis added.

[40] C. Geertz, 'Local Knowledge: Fact and Law in Comparative Perspective' in C. Geertz (ed.), *Local Knowledge* (Basic Books, New York, 1983) 167, 215. Emphasis added.

[41] P. Legrand, 'European Legal Systems are Not Converging' (1996) 45 *ICLQ* 52; Cotterell (n 29) 45; V.G. Curran, 'Cultural Immersion, Difference and Categories in US Comparative Law' (1998) 46 *American Journal of Comparative Law* 43.

from being autonomous of it, law *is* culture.[42] Law, like language and art, is a cultural system—an articulation of the common identity of a particular society. These contrasting views influence the way in which comparative law is conducted. Acting on the universalist view, the comparativist sees law in all jurisdictions as different 'species of the same genus',[43] subject to the same questions and the same criteria. Her or his analysis and subject matter is culturally neutral and without 'local substance'.[44] She can iron out legal dissimilarities between different jurisdictions by classifying them as variations on the same theme. Her vision of comparative law is of a 'universal legal science'.[45] Acting on a view of law as culture, the comparative lawyer's task becomes more problematic, but perhaps ultimately more illuminating. To know another legal culture the comparativist must understand its 'local knowledge'.[46] She must illuminate a 'different structure of meaning' through which legal discourse may be understood. [47] Here is a vision of comparative law, not as a science, but as the craft of interpretation.

The difference/similarity debate not only reveals deeper dissent about the comparativist's conception of law and its implications for the comparative exercise, but also reflects our geo-political climate:

The tension between seeking similarity and appreciating difference clearly exists, writ large in major social movements that are still imperfectly understood. Globalization seems pre-eminently to be about seeking similarity by unifying social, economic and often legal arrangements. Localization seems to be about appreciating difference by creating, preserving or rediscovering conditions in which difference (for example, political or cultural) can flourish and be respected.[48]

---

[42] The meaning, content, and boundaries of the concept of legal culture are by no means settled. See 1.3 below.

[43] Zedner (n 24).

[44] B. Puchalska-Tych and M. Salter, 'Comparing legal cultures of Eastern Europe: the need for a dialectical analysis' (1996) 16 *LS* 157, 175.

[45] This notion was developed by Anselm von Feuerbach in his essay 'Idee und Notwendigkeit einer Universaljurisprudenz', cited in W. Hug, 'The History of Comparative Law' [1931/32] XLV *Harvard L Rev* 1027. For further examples see K. Zweigert, 'Rechtsvergleichung als universale Interpretationsmethode' (1949/50) 54 *Rabels Zeitschrift für ausländisches und internationales Privatrecht* 203; H. Jescheck, *Recht und Staat in Geschichte und Gegenwart: Entwicklung, Aufgaben und Methoden der Strafrechtsvergleichung* (Mohr, Tübingen 1955); K. Zweigert and H. Kötz (n 39); F. Ferracuti, 'Possibilities and Limits of Comparative Research in Criminology' in H. Jescheck and G. Kaiser (eds), *Die Vergleichung als Methode der Strafrechtswissenschaft und der Kriminologie* (Duncker and Humblot, Berlin, 1980) 129.

[46] Geertz (n 40), 215.

[47] P. Legrand, 'Comparative Legal Studies and Commitment to Theory' (1995) 58(2) *MLR* 262.

[48] Cotterell (n 29) 45.

This geo-political climate holds risks for the integrity of the comparative endeavour. Comparison, which inevitably constructs the 'other',[49] can also become the instrument of broader social ends. This risk is greatest where the pursuit of such ends legitimates, or rationalizes, comparative projects. Comparative lawyers feed off and into the globalization of law generally and, more specifically, the process of European legal harmonization. One compelling example is the *Ius Commune* project which unearths commonalities between European legal systems, aiming at a common law of Europe.[50] But this trend is also evident in comparative criminal justice.[51]

The comparative examination of human rights generally, and particularly prisoners' rights, is inextricable from the drive towards globalization. For those who champion universal human rights, the defence of local values represents a dilemma.[52] The protection of cultural diversity is a recognized human rights goal. But human rights (involving belief in universally shared values) and cultural diversity (demanding the recognition of difference) can seem antithetical.[53] Comparative human rights researchers have to navigate this environment carefully, ensuring that their normative commitment to human rights does not lead them either to downplay the complexity and diversity of local environments, or represent (or re-construct) cultural differences in opposition to human rights values.

Comparison for broader social or policy objectives does not always favour similarity, however. Critics seeking to effect policy change at home are sometimes tempted to overstate difference abroad. In their attempt to change domestic policy, comparativists can sometimes blur the line between the view of Europe as a *locus* of comparison, and the idea of Europe as an ideal standard to which to aspire. As Douglas and Moerings argued, 'European approaches to imprisonment are the yardstick against which the English system is found wanting'.[54] Thus, comparativists' concerns with

---

[49] 'Comparative analysis of law is a serious political act—does it not ascertain the other for me and inscribe him to the point where what I write becomes the other's legal identity?' Legrand (n 19) 84.

[50] See Hart Publishing's series *Ius Commune Casebooks for the Common Law of Europe*. See also B. Markesinis, 'Learning from Europe and Learning in Europe' in B. Markesinis (ed.), *The Gradual Convergence* (OUP, Oxford, 1994); B. Markesinis *Bridging the Channel* (OUP, Oxford, 1996).

[51] e.g., U. Sieber (ed.), *Europäische Einigung und Europäisches Strafrecht* (Carl Heymanns, Cologne, 1993); G. Kaiser, *Strafvollzug im Europäischen Vergleich* (Wissenschaftliche Buchgesellschaft, Darmstadt, 1983); C. Harding *et al.* (eds), *Criminal Justice in Europe: A Comparative Study* (Clarendon Press, Oxford, 1995); F. Heidensohn and M. Farrell (eds), *Crime in Europe* (Routledge, London, 1991); J Muncie and R Sparks, (eds), *Imprisonment: European Perspectives* (Harvester Wheatsheaf, Hemel Hempstead, 1991); J. Dine, 'European Community Criminal law?' (1993) *CLR* 163; J. Bengoetxea and H. Jung, 'Towards a European Criminal Jurisprudence?' (1991) 11 *LS* 239; S. Field and N. Jörg, 'Corporate Liability and Manslaughter: Should We Be Going Dutch?' (1991) *CLR* 156.

[52] K. Hastrup (ed.), *Legal Cultures and Human Rights* (Kluwer, The Hague, 2001) 1.

[53] Cotterell (n 29) 45.

[54] G. Douglas and M. Moerings, 'Prisoners' Rights in the Netherlands and England and Wales' in Harding *et al.* (n 51) 341.

their domestic environment can also lead them to emphasize difference using simplified or idealized constructions of foreign comparators.

We cannot therefore call for comparison merely for difference's sake. Even a sophisticated understanding of the law's local setting may perceive parallels between systems. Rather, we might strive to avoid making comparison the mere instrument of our defence of a particular hypothesis or normative position, the quest to further broader social goals or change domestic policy. We could be conscious not to overlook the complexity of the local, or to construct the local, so as to produce a skewed understanding of the other, or even of ourselves. Misperceptions, or misconstructions, of both difference and similarity are both potential outcomes of what might be termed 'instrumental' comparison. The idealization of Europe in opposition to ourselves may be just as helpful in promoting domestic legal reform, as the assumption of similarity might be to the furtherance of European convergence.

A commitment to local knowledge need not negate the possibility of arriving at generalized or abstracted conclusions in the comparative endeavour, however. There is the danger that 'both universalism and relativism tend to reproduce the dichotomy of the self and other; they are non dialectical in the sense that they either come up with "bad abstractions or with no abstractions at all" '.[55] Yet a focus on local knowledge in comparative legal analysis can escape die-hard cultural relativism,[56] as it should also be possible to draw from localities general conclusions regarding the relationship between legal culture, legal reasoning, and law. At the same time, however, it is important not to skew the local by viewing it through the lens of abstract and generalized criteria.[57] This is a difficult balance to strike. The comparativist must walk a tightrope between respect for local variation and the assertion of generalizable truths.

Finally, it is worth remembering that a focus on law's local environment need not refute the proposition that law displays universal features (such as rights and duties, obligations, rules, norms). As Craig acknowledges, 'every democratic society will have some ideas of rights . . . but these will differ depending upon the nature of that society'.[58] Thus, legal concepts can have both universal and parochial qualities, as Raz concedes:

The truth of the theses of a general theory of law is not contingent on existing political, social, economic or cultural conditions, institutions or practices. To be sure such social facts determine whether legal institutions of one kind or another exist in this

[55] G. Frankenberg, 'Critical Comparisons: Re-thinking Comparative Law' (1985) 26 *Harvard Intl Law J* 411, 415.

[56] P. Beirne, 'Cultural Relativism and Comparative Criminology' (1983) 7 *Contemporary Crises* 371.

[57] A tendency amongst those who use comparison to advance 'the agenda of scientific criminology'. Nelken (n 26) 176. See, e.g., Ferracuti (n 45).

[58] P. Craig, *Administrative Law* (4th edn, Sweet & Maxwell, London, 1999) 3.

country or that. But they do not determine the nature of law, they only affect its instantiation. But its instantiation, the determination whether or another legal institution or practice exists in one country or another is not itself a philosophical question. The universality of the theses of the general theory of law is a result of the fact that they claim to be necessary truths, and there is nothing less that they can claim. In as much as the general theory of law is about the nature of law it strives to elucidate law's essential features, i.e. those features which are possessed by every legal system just in virtue of its being legal, by every legislative institution in virtue of its being legislative, by every practice of legal reasoning in virtue of its being a practice of legal reasoning, and so on.[59]

To this extent, there is no necessary conflict between the local specificity of law and the universality of legal concepts. What is crucial, however, is the extent to which the comparativist remains conscious of this duality.

1.3 UNDERSTANDING CULTURE

Like sailing, gardening, politics, and poetry, law and ethnography are crafts of place: they work by the light of local knowledge.[60]

Unravelling the local environment that shapes prisoners' rights invokes the notion of culture in various contexts: legal culture, rights culture, constitutional culture, penal culture, and political culture.[61] This book therefore follows a number of comparativists who have turned to the notion of culture in their scholastic endeavour.[62] Indeed, culture is used beyond comparative analysis, such as in recent criminal justice and human rights studies.[63] Its ubiquity indicates that culture, and associated concepts such as legal culture or rights culture, is useful in capturing a broad set of interlinked variables which shape the social practice of the law and legal institutions. In brief, it offers a 'contextual matrix' which embraces the nuances of the local environment in which law and legal institutions are situated.[64]

---

[59] J. Raz, 'On the Nature of Law' (1996) 82(1) *Archives for Philosophy of Law and Social Philosophy* 1.

[60] Geertz (n 40), 167.

[61] This book does not pretend to be a comprehensive account of German or English legal culture or 'cultures'. For an excellent account of this kind on France, see Bell (n 23).

[62] See, *inter alia*, Legrand (n 19); D Nelken, (ed.), *Comparing Legal Cultures* (Dartmouth, Aldershot, 1997); L. Friedman, 'Is There a Modern Legal Culture?' (1994) 7 *Ratio Juris* 117; V. Gessner *et al.* (eds), *European Legal Culture* (Dartmouth, Aldershot, 1996); R. Abel, 'Comparative Law and Social Theory' (1978) 26 *AJCL* 219; D. Downes, *Contrasts in Tolerance* (Clarendon Press, Oxford, 1993); L.-J. Constantinesco, 'Die Kulturkreise als Grundlage der Rechtskreise' (1981) 22 *ZfRV* 161; B. Großfeld, *Kernfragen der Rechtsvergleichung* (Mohr, Tübingen, 1996).

[63] See, *inter alia*, D. Garland, *The Culture of Control* (OUP, Oxford, 2001); M. Hunt, 'The Human Rights Act and Legal Culture: The Judiciary and the Legal Profession' (1999) *JLS* 86.

[64] L. Friedman, *The Legal System: A Social Science Perspective* (Russell Sage Foundation, New York, 1975) 201.

Whilst the power of culture as an explanatory tool lies in the potential breadth and depth of its descriptive reach, it is also in this that its weakness lies. The concepts of culture and legal culture[65] generate continuous definitional controversy.[66] There are 'almost as many definitions of the term (culture) as there are anthropologists'.[67] This clamour is unsurprising, ' "culture" is said to be one of the two or three most complex words in the English language'.[68] As a result of this opacity, the notion of culture invites more methodological questions than answers. This is no less the case for the notion of legal culture, as Nelken's sobering questions reveal:

What about legal culture? Are we interested in the definitions of law used by politicians, legal officials, legal scholars or more in lay or popular definitions of law? How do all these relate to sociological definitions of law? How should we go about studying (legal) culture? Are we aiming to learn more about other cultures or more about what we take for granted about our own? What sources shall we use to make sense of culture? Does behaviour count more than words? Should we rely on what people can tell us, or search for the assumptions that make sense of their world views?[69]

Given this complexity, one can see why Cotterell finds the concept of culture and legal culture 'lacking in rigour' and 'theoretically incoherent'; and that he doubts whether these concepts can gain any theoretical insights useful in the comparative sociology of law.[70]

But to pin down culture, to construct a phenomenological or causal concept of culture and associated concepts such as legal culture, to identify measurable cultural variables,[71] is, when looked at in another way, to impoverish the idea of culture. Friedman defends culture and legal culture arguing that it is not a precisely measurable social variable.[72] For him, the beauty of the concept is its capacity to encompass diverse variables or elements.[73] Equally, Nelken questions whether 'empirical specificity and concreteness', while enhancing 'the possibilities of measurement', may hinder understanding of 'unmeasurable aspects of cultural ideas and meanings'.[74] For Legrand, the problem is one of disciplinary attitudes:

[65] See Nelken (n 62).

[66] For a list of possible definitions, see C. Geertz, 'Thick Description: Toward an Interpretive Theory of Culture' in C. Geertz (ed.), *The Interpretation of Cultures* (Basic Books, New York, 1973) 3, 4–5.

[67] D. Garland, *Punishment and Modern Society* (Clarendon Press, Oxford, 1990) 195.

[68] T. Eagleton, *The Idea of Culture* (Blackwell, Oxford, 2000) 1.

[69] D. Nelken, 'Comparing Legal Cultures: An Introduction' in Nelken (n 62), 1, 1–2.

[70] R. Cotterell, 'The Concept of Legal Culture' in Nelken (n 62) 13, 14.

[71] e.g., E. Blankenburg, 'Civil Litigation Rates as Indicators for Legal Cultures' in Nelken (n 62), 41; Van Hoecke and Warrington (n 36); A. Ogus, 'The Economic Basis of Legal Culture: Networks and Monopolization' (2002) 22 *OJLS* 419.

[72] L. Friedman, 'The Concept of Legal Culture: A Reply' in Nelken (n 62) 33.

[73] D. Nelken, 'Puzzling Out Legal Culture: A Comment on Blankenburg' in Nelken (n 62) 69, 74.

[74] Nelken (n 73).

... the indeterminacy of 'culture' or, if you will, the impossibility of distinguishing between 'culture' and 'non-culture' in a way that would allow the identification of empirically verifiable causal relationships through which control over social life could be effectively attained ought to be a handicap only for the positivist.[75]

So perhaps the very search to define culture is to miss the point of culture: 'culture is not a power, something to which social events, behaviours, institutions, or processes can be causally attributed; it is a context, something within which they can be intelligibly—that is thickly—described'.[76] To describe a culture, to describe thickly, is for Geertz to describe the 'socially established structures of meaning' which can render social practice intelligible.[77] Or, in Legrand's language, it is to describe 'the framework of intangibles within which an interpretive community operates'.[78] Culture is irreducible to a set of measurable social variables. In inviting us to address the 'immediacies' of the local, it resists theoretical definition and efforts to create logical coherence. Culture is 'unseverable from the immediacies thick description presents, its freedom to shape itself in terms of its own internal logic is rather limited. What generality it contrives to achieve grows out of the delicacy of its distinctions, not the sweep of its abstractions'.[79]

The longstanding, seemingly intractable discussion of the meaning and boundaries of 'culture' and legal culture is not easily resolved. The opacity of culture gives rise not merely to differences of opinion as to its meaning, but also to dispute between those who argue that culture is a blunt tool of social analysis because it eludes clarification and those who argue that the very power of culture lies in its inherent immunity to theoretical definition or logical coherence. Notwithstanding the clamour surrounding the concept, this book agrees with Legrand, Nelken, Friedman, and Geertz,[80] that cultural analysis, if for its very fluidity, can identify the local nuances of the social context of the law. Moreover, it can capture the intricate web of attitudes, beliefs, values, understandings, and practices which render intelligible the objects of social enquiry. This need not be a controversial assertion: even sceptics like Cotterell concede that culture is useful for its capacity to

---

[75] Legrand (n 19) 28–9.

[76] Geertz (n 66) 14. See also Legrand (n 19) 32–4.

[77] Geertz (n 66) 13. This hermeneutical view of cultural analysis, as 'thick description', stems from linguistic philosophy: namely that the meaning of language can only be understood in a broader structure of shared meaning. Thus, Geertz borrows from Gilbert Ryle's theory of meaning and from Wittgenstein's philosophy of language (see pp. 6–7, 13). In this theory of meaning, and focus on meaning as a path to understanding social practice, Geertz's theory of culture resembles Hart's theory of law (*The Concept of Law* (2nd edn, Clarendon Press, Oxford, 1994)).

[78] Legrand (n 19) 27.

[79] Geertz (n 66) 25.

[80] Legrand (n 19); Friedman (n 72); Geertz (n 66); Nelken (n 73). I do not suggest that these authors agree on the meaning of culture, rather that they embrace it as a useful interpretive (as opposed to phenomenological) concept in the comparative endeavour.

characterize a complex web of social factors which can act as a 'preliminary to more specific enquiries'.[81]

This book's understanding of culture can be broadly described at best. Cultural analysis here embraces the legal, constitutional, penal, political, and rights systems and institutions in their formal sense, and the practices, beliefs, and convictions of those operating and exerting influence within these systems and of those viewing, criticising, and influencing them from without. Regarding law in particular, it encompasses what can be termed 'internal legal culture': the organizational culture and traditions of legal institutions,[82] and the professional sensibilities, legalistic habits of mind and intellectual reflexes, interpretive styles, and styles of argument of legal actors.[83] However, it also encompasses the relationship between law and wider culture. For 'just as legal culture would surely form part of any definition of the wider culture, so it is difficult to imagine any extensive project of comparing legal cultures which did not show the way they were directly or indirectly shaped by larger political, economic and intellectual aspects of the culture(s) of which they formed a part'.[84] Thus, this book views the relationship between law, legal culture, and wider culture reflexively, embracing the cultural environment of law's conception, interpretation, and execution while also registering law's bearing on this environment. The law is thus viewed as responding to and constructing the environment from which it arises.

The core focus of this comparative enquiry is the formal law (statutory law and legal judgments) and legal, rights, political, and penal discourse. Legal and rights discourse includes academic, political, and popular arguments about law and rights. Such discourse may be viewed as externally observable, conscious attempts to construct or interpret the meaning of social practice or to construct a system of meaning in which social practice can be understood.[85] Most arguments in this book are based on published texts, whether academic sources, case law, or media reporting. But the intuitions which guided my research and framed my arguments were formed through long immersion in the cultures of both Germany and England. Behind my explanations, are numerous informal legal discussions and political debates with German and English lawyers, judges, academics, and anyone else who was kind and knowledgeable enough to answer my questions. Equally, living for many years in both countries[86] has provided me with

---

[81] Friedman (n 72) 29–30.

[82] Bell (n 23) ch. 1, particularly pp. 6–7 and 10–11.

[83] K. Klare, 'Legal Culture and Transformative Constitutionalism' (1988) 14 *SAJHR* 146, 166–7.

[84] Nelken (n 73) 83.   [85] Geertz (n 40) 215; Zedner (n 24) 519.

[86] I was born and raised in South Africa, but am also of English and German descent. I studied law in London, England, whereafter I completed a year's fellowship at the Max Planck Institute for International and Comparative Criminal Law, Freiburg, Germany. Since beginning my doctoral research, on which this book is based, I have commuted between England and Germany for eight years, dividing my time between both countries.

opportunities to observe and reflect on the language, sensibilities, habits, beliefs, and opinions of the people in both jurisdictions. These discussions and reflections enabled me to gain further insight into local knowledge, to guess at the 'intangible framework of meanings' within English and German culture. They form the invisible background to the conclusions I draw in this book.

1.3.1 Rights and Rights Culture

... 'a culture of rights' is a seamless garment. The habit of arguing in terms of rights and their protection is not likely to be confined to one area of political debate, and it is not likely to be confined to one set of institutions.[87]

The notion of a rights culture can be distinguished from the substantive law which protects fundamental rights. In its analysis of rights culture in Germany and England, therefore, this book adopts the valuable distinctions of Eric Feldman,[88] namely the distinctions between 'rights', 'rhetoric about rights', and 'rights rhetoric'.[89]

Formally, an individual asserts a legal 'right' when she or he makes a claim to performance, either action or forbearance, on the part of another which is asserted in law.[90] This right might be enshrined in a constitution, a code, a statute, or held to be part of the common law. As this book will show, England and Germany both have formal legal expressions of special rights and fundamental rights, although the rights protected and the bodies against which these can be enforced differ significantly. The book will also show that while fundamental rights have had an impact on the special rights which prisoners hold in both Germany and England, the results are very different indeed. This is attributed to wider factors than differences in the formal law. Rather the book seeks to anchor this discussion in a broader concept of rights culture which includes the notions of 'rhetoric about rights' and 'rights rhetoric'.

'Rhetoric about rights' refers to the 'relative importance attributed to rights in a particular society by popular and academic writers, as well as laypersons. The power rights are imagined to possess, the frequency with which they are supposedly invoked, and how they are thought to define the identity of people'.[91] 'Rhetoric about rights' thus refers to the attitudes and beliefs which a society, or influential actors within that society, reflects when

[87] A. Ryan, 'The British, the Americans and rights' in M. Lacey and K. Haakonssen (eds), *A Culture of Rights* (CUP, Cambridge, 1991) 435.

[88] E. Feldman, 'Patients' Rights, Citizens' Movements and Japanese Legal Culture' in Nelken (n 62) 215.

[89] Feldman (n 88) 216.

[90] This definition encompasses the Hohfeldian notion of a 'claim right' and a 'liberty right'. See W. Hohfeld, *Fundamental Legal Conceptions as Applied in Judicial Reasoning* (Yale University Press, New Haven, 1919).

[91] Feldman (n 88) 216.

engaging in talk about rights. This book argues that 'rhetoric about rights' can have a different tone in different legal cultures; particularly, that England and Germany's contrasting histories and traditions have produced different conceptions of the weight and role of fundamental rights, as displayed within 'rhetoric about rights'.

Finally, rights culture analysis involves attention to 'rights rhetoric', which requires 'an examination of how rights are used to frame, discuss and debate issues relevant to social policy; paying attention to the language of actors engaged in social movements, particularly the context and timing of rights assertion; determining the efficacy of invoking rights rhetoric for mobilizing like-minded individuals; and evaluating success of those who use rights in pursuit of social ends'.[92] Applying this analysis to the nature of criminal justice discourse in Germany and England yields interesting insights. In Germany criminal justice reformers drew heavily on 'rights rhetoric' when advancing arguments about the reform of prison law, and despite the growth of competing discourses within the criminal justice environment, Germany remains characterized by a strong and defining 'rights rhetoric' as regards prison law and policy. This is less the case in England, however, where 'rights rhetoric' competes with a strong managerialist and 'law and order' rhetoric and holds no such dominance in the conception and definition of prison law and policy.

There is a complex and reflexive relationship between the legal protection of fundamental rights, the tone of 'rhetoric about rights', and the efficacy of 'rights rhetoric'. The extent of judicial activism when interpreting constitutional rights relates to society's faith in fundamental rights and general acceptance of the court's role in interpreting those rights. This relationship is difficult to pin down, as it combines judicial perceptions of a society's receptivity to constitutional rights, and the judiciary's own political preconceptions regarding the importance of fundamental rights and the judge's role in that society. Social and political receptivity to fundamental rights will also impact on use of 'rights rhetoric'. Use of this rhetoric by pressure groups or social critics normally makes sense if it can influence those who wield political influence (directly or indirectly) and thereby constitute a platform for social reform. Moreover, 'rights rhetoric' will be linked to its persuasive legal force in judicial proceedings. All of these associations will be displayed in this comparison of prisoners' rights.

1.4 BEING HERE AND THERE

If comparativists accept that law is culture, then they might also accept that, as lawyers, they are part of a legal culture. This acceptance raises difficulties

---

[92] Feldman (n 88) 216.

in our examination of other legal cultures, for how are we to transcend our own legal cultural perceptions? How are we to find a neutral or culture-free place from which to observe our subject matter? Thus, 'comparativists, acting as cultural intermediaries, must determine how to convey their acquired understanding of another legal culture within the inconsistent parameters of their own'.[93]

A constructive approach to this problem could be that the acceptance of our legal conditioning can inform rather than limit our possibility of understanding another legal culture. We might then abandon the comparativist's pretence of neutrality. Rather, the comparative lawyer might place herself within her own analysis—juxtaposing her own legal conceptions against those of her chosen system. Doing this can form an important element of reflective comparison. Insight into our preconceptions can arise through identifying their dissonance with an alien environment, and may in turn lead us to reflect back on our own cultural environment.

But, the comparativist's status as an 'outsider' to a system should not preclude the possibility of gaining 'insider' knowledge; handled correctly, it may even heighten it. As Downes suggests, 'to be a foreigner may confer certain privileges, in particular a licence to naïveté'.[94] This naivety can unearth the implicit presumptions, beliefs, and attitudes within a particular legal culture. The outsider knowledge may therefore be 'privileged': 'by the benefits of distance and perspective, and by the insights which present themselves only when appreciation is fresh and free from the accumulated assumptions of long-learned familiarity'.[95] Hence, while retaining the foreigner's crucial distance, the comparativist need not forego the prospect of unravelling the local.

Finally, reflective comparison might include consideration of the relationship between the comparativist and her or his intended audience. This relationship is inextricable from the comparative endeavour generally, and from the exercise of legal translation more specifically. The comparativist has to find a language in which to explain a legal culture to a foreign audience. Similarly, she cannot assume linguistic and conceptual equivalency between languages and cultures; linguistic 'selecting' and 'purging' can erode the connotation that a legal concept evokes in its original linguistic context.[96] Thus, comparativists must know when 'not to translate', to convey 'the strangeness of language' in words her audience understands;[97]

---

[93] Legrand (n 47).   [94] Downes (n 63) 2.

[95] N. Lacey and L. Zedner, 'Community in German Criminal Justice: A Significant Absence?' (1998) 7 *S&LS* 7, 9.

[96] Legrand (n 47) 269. For general linguistic problems in comparative law see B. Großfeld, *Kernfragen der Rechtsvergleichung* (Mohr/Siebeck, Tübingen, 1996); Zedner (n 25), 13; P. Sack, 'Law and Custom: Reflections on the Relation between English Law and the English Language' in V. Gessner, A. Hoeland and C. Varga (eds), *European Legal Culture* (Dartmouth, Aldershot, 1996) 66.

[97] Legrand (n 19), 4.

her subject matter must be both foreign and intelligible. But to be successful in these aims, the comparativist must accept her role as cultural intermediary. The comparativist translating an alien environment must know her audience. She must anticipate the implicit cultural expectations or preconceptions (*Vorverständnis*) of her readers.[98]

In short, when unravelling the insider knowledge of a foreign environment and when translating a foreign environment to a local audience, the reflective comparativist must always be both here, and there.

1.5 IMPLICIT AND EXPLICIT COMPARISON

The structure of this book is bound up with the criticisms and reflections on comparative law set out in this chapter; particularly in the adoption of two different styles of exposition on Germany and England, which I call implicit and explicit comparison.

1.5.1 Implicit Comparison

Part I of this book provides a 'thick description' of the prisoner's legal status in the context of German legal, penal and constitutional culture. Here little explicit comparative reference is made to England. The object is to provide a full, nuanced account of the prisoners' legal status in Germany and its broader cultural context. The chapters on Germany therefore contain more background information than those on England. They are written with the intention of translating a foreign legal culture for an audience outside that culture. This exercise could perhaps equally be termed translation. But, as argued at 1.4 above, the comparativist is not simply transposing a legal or cultural term into another language. She or he is constantly juxtaposing a variety of frameworks of meaning, including her own. Hence the term implicit comparison was chosen to convey the complexity of rendering a legal culture intelligible to a foreign audience.

1.5.2 Explicit Comparison

While Part I is predominantly intended to provide a foreign audience with the full, formative context of German prisoners' legal rights, this is not its only purpose. An allied purpose is to distance readers from their own legal culture, providing a comparative foil for the analysis of England in Part II of the book. Thus, following implicit comparison, the second part of the book will undertake explicit comparison with respect to England, asking the reader to consider England in the light of the German chapters. Explicit

---

[98] H.G. Gadamer, *Truth and Method* (Sheed & Ward, London, 1975).

comparison, is essentially an exercise in distancing. It invites the reader to stand back from their own local context, by looking at England through a German lens. It seeks, through juxtaposition, to uncover the 'strangeness in the familiar' and thereby to gain insights into the domestic environment's legal cultural dynamics.

Other mechanisms, such as historical analysis, might achieve distancing. Perhaps one could gain equal distance by asking 'was it always thus?' But distancing is also achieved through explicit comparative questions: why is A like A and not like B? Or, why is A like B? It is crucial not to read this process as comparative evaluation. This book does not ask, through explicit comparison, is A better than B? Answering such a question requires a prior standard by which to judge the better legal system or culture. That is not the enquiry here. Rather this book seeks in Part II, through the process of explicit comparison, to explore the method and manner of conceiving of the prisoner's legal status in England and the broader cultural dynamics surrounding this conception.

PART I

GERMANY

2

Prisoners in a Constitutional State

The modern West German code of prison law owes its emergence, more than in most countries, to the application of constitutional principles in the sphere of prison law reform.[1]

Observing the complicated and long drawn-out introduction of the German Prison Act we conclude that the presence of a written constitution was the pivotal point, the mechanism that could be activated against the odds of diverse attitudes to punishment.[2]

This comparative analysis of prisoners' rights in Germany and England is rooted in the broader make-up of the constitutional and legal cultures of each country. Until recently, these jurisdictions diverged in that Germany had, and England lacked, a legally entrenched Bill of Rights. Since the Human Rights Act (HRA) 1998 came into effect, this aspect of German and English legal culture can no longer be said to be so markedly divergent. But for our analysis of the development of prisoners' rights over the last thirty years, it remains highly relevant. In England, rights protections in prisons have been developed in the absence of a local Bill of Rights: their conception has not been grounded in 'rational adherence to an authoritative and coherent legal text'.[3] In Germany, conversely, the prisoner's legal status, and prison law in general, is underpinned by the rights and principles of the Basic Law. To understand Germany's conception of prisoners' rights, therefore, we need to know more about her constitution.

2.1 THE BASIC LAW—THE HEART OF GERMAN LEGAL CULTURE

The Germans' reverential respect for constitutional law, its insistence that major political fault lines be closed by judicial arbitration and its acceptance of the

---

[1] D. van Zyl Smit, 'Leave of Absence for West German Prisoners' (1988) 28 *BJC* 1, 2.
[2] R. Prowse *et al.*, 'Rights and Prisons in Germany: Blueprint for Britain?' (1992) 20 *IJSL* 111, 117.
[3] P. Legrand, 'European Systems are Not Converging' (1996) 45 *ICLQ* 52.

judiciary's presence in every facet of life, is the product of a nation that has looked over the abyss.[4]

Democracies require tradition. For this, twenty-five years are too few. But enough time has elapsed to say that the Germans of the Federal Republic of Germany can be content with their constitution.[5]

In German legal and political culture, a commitment to constitutionalism has grown since the introduction of the Basic Law in 1949; 'by the 1980s . . . the political system and its constitution enjoyed such prestige for the term constitutional patriotism (*Verfassungspatriotismus*) . . . to have entered into political debate'.[6] The strength of German constitutionalism is in part a reflection of local anxiety about Germany's frail democratic tradition, is partly born of faith in law, rather than politics, as the successful mediator of social relations, and is partly due to the success of the Federal Constitutional Court (FCC) in maintaining its own legitimacy and that of the Constitution. The German Constitution, by entrenching the Federal, Democratic, Social and *Rechtsstaat* principles, has comprehensively shaped the entire political order.[7] Equally, the Constitution sits at the apex of the German legal hierarchy of norms.[8] At the heart of German constitutionalism is a profound belief in basic rights (*Grundrechte*). In Germany, unlike Britain, fundamental rights occupy a central place in the legal order. As symbols of a rejection of Germany's recent totalitarian past, their political weight and meaning are unique. Those who assume that rights evoke a common significance across different legal traditions, cultures, and languages should take note. Rights may embody different things in different legal cultures: they have a particular 'social and historical substance'.[9]

The legal substance and symbolic meaning of basic rights in Germany has been moulded by recent German history.[10] Germany's Basic Law was

---

[4] J. Steinberg, 'Constitutional Court can take cue from foreign experiences' *Business Day* (11 November 1999).

[5] Comment on the Saar Radio on the 25th anniversary of the German Basic Law quoted in G. Craig, *The Germans* (Penguin, London, 1991) 60.

[6] S. Parkes, *Understanding Contemporary Germany* (Routledge, London, 1997) 34.

[7] K. Hesse, 'Bestand und Bedeutung der Grundrechte in der Bundesrepublik Deutschland' (1978) *EuGRZ* 427, 428.

[8] Hesse (n 7).

[9] B. Puchalska-Tych and M. Salter, 'Comparing legal cultures of Eastern Europe: the need for a dialectical analysis' (1996) *LS* 157, 175.

[10] The immediate factors which led to the introduction of the Basic Law should not, however, be confused with its legal historical origins. German constitutional historians locate the historical roots of the Basic Law in the ferment of democratic libertarian ideas in American and Western European political philosophy during the 18th century. In Germany, this political movement found brief public expression in the *Paulskirche* assembly in 1848 and the resultant Frankfurt Constitution of 1849. It was later represented in the Prussian Constitution of 1850, the North German Federal Constitutions of 1867 and 1871, and the Weimar Imperial Constitution of 1919. See H. Hofmann, 'Die Grundrechte 1789–1949–1989' (1989) *NJW* 3177; H. Hofmann, 'Zur Herkunft der Menschenrechtserklärungen' (1988) *JuS* 841; B. Pieroth, 'Geschichte der Grundrechte' (1984) *Jura* 568; J.-D. Kühne, 'Die französische Menschen- und

drafted in the shadow of the failed Weimar Constitution and the horrific consequences of its breakdown.[11] The drafters of the Basic Law, and the German Parliamentary Council, were acutely 'conscious of their responsibility before God and humankind'.[12] They had to deliver a constitution that would not only safeguard against a repetition of the systematic human rights violations of the Third Reich, but would also restore faith, both nationally and internationally, in a State that had forfeited any claim to legitimacy. The constitution was to define 'the spirit (*Geist*) of the new State in total opposition to that of the State system destroyed in May 1945'.[13] This historical mission was central to the legal construction of the document, particularly in its emphasis on basic rights. In aiming to avoid the mistakes of the Weimar Constitution, in which rights were articulated as 'declarations of intent',[14] the drafters of the Basic Law placed basic rights at the head of the text of the Constitution,[15] declaring as unamendable the right to human dignity and the Democratic, Social, Federal and *Rechtsstaat* principles,[16] and ensuring that all state institutions were unambiguously obliged to safeguard basic rights.[17] In addition, they vested the FCC with the guardianship of the Basic Law, affording it extensive powers of legislative review and giving citizens direct access to this Court.[18] Thus, the German Constitution

Bürgerrechtserklärung im Rechtsvergleich mit den Vereinigten Staaten und Deutschland' (1990) *Jahrbuch des öffentlichen Rechts der Gegenwart* 1; J. Ziekow, 'Deutsche Verfassungsentwicklung und sozialer Liberalismus' (1989) *JuS* 107.

[11] Pieroth (n 10). It is not possible here to engage fully with the historical and jurisprudential discussion on the breakdown of the Weimar Constitution. See further P. Stirk, 'Hugo Preuss, German political thought and the Weimar constitution' (2002) 23(3) *HPT* 497; J. McCormick, 'The Crisis of Constitutional Social Democracy in the Weimar Republic' (2002) 1(1) *European Journal of Political Theory* 121; A. Jacobsen and B. Schlink (eds), *Weimar: A Jurisprudence of Crisis* (University of California Press, Berkeley, 2000); D. Dyzenhaus, *Legality and Legitimacy* (OUP, Oxford, 1997); P.C. Caldwell, *Popular Sovereignty and the Crisis of German Constitutional Law* (Duke University Press, Durham, 1997); B. Scheuerman, 'The rule of law under siege: Carl Schmitt and the death of the Weimar Republic' (1993) 14(2) *HPT* 265; J. Muller, 'Carl Schmitt, Hans Freyer and the radical conservative critique of liberal democracy in the Weimar republic' (1991) 12(4) *HPT* 695; E. Kennedy, 'The Politics of Toleration in Late Weimar' (1985) 5 *HPT* 109; W. Schluchter, *Entscheidung für den sozialen Rechtsstaat* (Nomos, Baden-Baden, 1983); M. Friedrich, 'Die Grundlagendiskussion in der Weimarer Staatsrechtlehre' (1972) 13 *Politische Vierteljahresschrift* 582; K. Sontheimer, 'Zur Grundlagenproblematik der deutschen Staatsrechtlehre in der Weimarer Republik' (1960) 46 *ARSP* 39.

[12] See Basic Law, Preamble.

[13] H. von Mangoldt, 'Grundrechte und Grundsatzfragen des Bonner Grundgesetzes' (1949) *AöR* 273, 279.

[14] Von Mangoldt (n 13): a drafter of the Basic Law, repeatedly sets its constitutional rights provisions against the weaker constitutional rights provisions of the Weimar Constitution.

[15] Basic Law, arts 1–19. For further basic rights, see Basic Law, arts 20(4), 33, 38, 101, 103, 104. Despite the exclusion of these rights from the first chapter of the Constitution, they are still considered to be fundamental. Hesse (n 7) 427.

[16] Basic Law, art. 79(3): 'Amendments to this Basic Law affecting the division of the Federation into *Länder*, their participation in the legislative process, or the principles laid down in arts 1 and 20 shall be prohibited'.

[17] Basic Law, art. 1(3): 'The following basic rights shall bind the legislature, the executive and the judiciary as directly enforceable law'.

[18] Basic Law, arts 19(4), 93(1)(4a).

was to mark a clean break with Germany's recent past. As Hesse explains:

. . . the fact that, in the Federal Republic of Germany, basic rights are not only constitutionally guaranteed, but are generally ensured and protected, is . . . above all historically explicable: these guarantees, safeguards and extensive protections are to be understood as being created, in the first instance, as a response to modern Germany history.[19]

The historical imperative which produced the provisions of the Basic Law continues to underline its symbolic and normative force within the German legal community. This is evident not only in the case law of the FCC, but also in the tone of influential constitutional commentary.[20] For constitutional commentators, the failure of the Weimar Constitution and the rise and fall of Nazism were not just national catastrophes. This history spawned a profound suspicion of unfettered democratic processes, a deep consensus that political processes must be limited by constitutional rights and principles, and a perception of the FCC as a legitimate and necessary safeguard against the dangers of democracy. This history led, moreover, to a self-perception of the FCC as not only the 'guardians of the Constitution', but as pioneers of a new opposition to totalitarianism. It is hardly surprising then, that German rhetoric about rights post-1945 very rarely displays the self-assured scepticism of entrenched constitutional rights present in England.[21]

This does not imply that there is agreement in Germany over the meaning and interpretation of constitutional rights, or how their protections are best reconciled with other constitutional goals, not least democracy.[22] Nor does this imply that the decisions of the FCC are immune to criticism and controversy.[23] On the contrary, post-war Germany has produced a rich constitutional rights literature which critically engages with FCC jurispru-

---

[19] Hesse (n 7) 427.

[20] Constitutional commentary is mainly the province of the legal academy, but is also heard from political theorists, constitutional court judges arguing extra-curially, former constitutional court judges, and politicians. FCC members are chosen from the academy, the judiciary and the executive. This academic component of the FCC, coupled with the general influence of the legal academy within German legal culture (see further chs 3 and 4), ensures that the FCC usually examines published arguments of constitutional commentators. The influence is not one-way: many FCC judges contribute to the constitutional debate during and after their term of service, some examples being Ernst Friesenhahn, Gerhard Leibholz, Ernst-Wolfgang Böckenförde, Winfried Hassemer, and Jutta Limbach.

[21] A recent example is T. Campbell, K.D. Ewing and A. Tomkins, *Sceptical Essays on Human Rights* (OUP, Oxford, 2001). See further ch. 6.

[22] See Postscript in R. Alexy, *A Theory of Constitutional Rights* (trans. Julian Rivers, OUP, Oxford, 2002) on the current debate in German constitutional theory.

[23] e.g., The controversy surrounding the 'Crucifix' judgment (*BVerfG* (1995) *NJW* 2477) which held that placing crucifixes in school classrooms violated Basic Law, art. 4 (freedom of faith, conscience and creed).

dence.[24] But the controversy in German constitutional commentary post-1945 cannot be attributed, as it might be in England,[25] to a *culture* of rights scepticism. While critically engaging with constitutional rights interpretations, constitutional commentary is unlikely to question the constitutional rights project *per se*, or the FCC's competence to declare on the meaning of these rights. As Alexy argues, 'the question of whether the constitutional court has controlling powers in the field of legislation is not open for discussion; the only question is as to their extent'.[26] Thus, German rhetoric about rights is concerned less with *whether* to take constitutional rights seriously than with *how* to take them seriously.

While this commitment to the constitutional rights project is one factor important in our analysis of prisoners' rights, the broad conception of constitutional rights developed since 1945 is another. Of course, these two aspects are not unrelated, as the activism of the FCC cannot be viewed in isolation from the normative and symbolic depth of its constitutional legitimacy. What then of the German conception of basic rights? The classical liberal understanding of basic rights, as subjective and negative rights (*Abwehrrechte*) protecting the individual against the State, enjoys wide recognition in the provisions of the Basic Law, the jurisprudence of the FCC, and German constitutional theory.[27] This is to be expected in a constitutional culture founded on a rejection of the Third Reich's total negation of individual and political freedoms.[28] But by the early 1970s it had become clear that constitutional commentary and FCC jurisprudence had gone beyond the classical conception of the negative subjective right of the individual.[29]

In Germany, basic rights are viewed both as subjectively held and also as a 'system of values' or 'objective norms' which radiate through the whole legal system.[30] This has been asserted by the FCC since its earliest

---

[24] See, e.g., Alexy (n 22); H. Siekmann (ed.), *Der Staat des Grundgesetzes* (Heymanns, Cologne, 1993); E.-W. Böckenförde, *Staat, Verfassung, Demokratie* (Suhrkamp, Frankfurt am Main, 1991); J. Habermas, *Faktizität und Geltung* (Suhrkamp, Frankfurt am Main, 1992); J. Isensee and P. Kirchhoff (eds), *Handbuch des Staatsrechts der Bundesrepublik Deutschland, Band IV: Allgemeine Grundrechtslehren* (Müller, Heidelberg, 1992); C. Starck, 'Die Grundrechte des Grundgesetzes' (1981) *JuS* 237; Hesse (n 7).

[25] See 6.1.1.

[26] Alexy (n 22), 367.

[27] *BVerfGE* 7, 198, 204; H.-D. Jarass and B. Pieroth, *Grundgesetz für die Bundesrepublik Deutschland* (6th edn, Beck, Munich, 2002) 18.

[28] T. Ramm, 'Die sozialen Grundrechte im Verfassungsgefüge' in E.-W. Böckenförde, J. Jekewitz and T. Ramm (eds), *Soziale Grundrechte* (Müller, Heidelberg, 1980) (n 56) 17, 21.

[29] E. Friesenhahn, 'Der Wandel des Grundrechtsverständnisses' in *Verhandlungen des 50. Deutschen Juristentages* (Beck, Munich, 1974) G1; H.H. Rupp, 'Vom Wandel der Grundrechte' (1976) *AöR* 161.

[30] Jarass and Pieroth (n 27) 18; R. Alexy, 'Grundrechte als subjektive Rechte und als objektive Normen' (1990) *Der Staat* 49; E.-W. Böckenförde, 'Grundrechte als Grundsatznormen' (1990) *Der Staat* 1; H. Jarass, 'Grundrechte als Wertentscheidungen bzw. objektivrechtliche Prinzipien in der Rechtsprechung des Bundesverfassungsgerichts' (1985) *AöR* 363.

jurisprudence.[31] It has been linked, *inter alia*, with the constitutional protection of private social institutions[32] and with constitutional standards in the development and organization of state institutions.[33] The conception of basic rights as objective norms also underlines the view that basic rights 'radiate' their intrinsic value outside the public law sphere and over legal relationships between individual parties in civil law.[34]

Alongside the notion of constitutional rights as 'objective norms and values' is the view of basic rights as not only negative limits to state intervention, but also as positive justifications for state action. The State is viewed as both a threat to rights and a protector of rights. The positive, objective aspect of constitutional rights is associated with the FCC's 'protective duties' (*Schutzpflichten*) which place positive duties on the State to protect against the violation of individuals' rights by other individuals.[35] Equally, the notion of positive rights is linked to the FCC's recent development of procedural and organizational entitlements,[36] which are grounded in the positive constitutional duty of the State to give *de facto* effect to constitutional rights protections.[37]

From a formal theoretical perspective, the positive conception of constitutional rights in Germany stems from Jellinek's classic argument that rights bearers may be vested with either a *status negativus*, a *status positivus* or a *status activus*.[38] But this conception is also grounded in the language of the Basic Law. The FCC,[39] and constitutional commentary,[40] roots this notion in the first and most fundamental article of the Constitution:

---

[31] See the Lüth judgment, *BVerfGE* 7, 198.

[32] e.g., marriage and property. See *BVerfGE* 6, 55, 72. Originally developed by Carl Schmitt and Martin Wolff in relation to the Weimar Constitution, the FCC continued after 1945 to link the protection of private law institutions with the notion of basic rights as 'objective norms'. Critics have argued, however, that these can now be derived from subjective rights under the Basic Law (Alexy (n 22) 157, 324–5).

[33] *BVerfGE* 35, 79; 47, 327.

[34] Commonly referred to as the 'third party effect' (*Drittwirkung*): see *BVerfGE* 7, 198; 39, 1, 41; H.-U. Erichsen, 'Die Drittwirkung der Grundrechte' (1996) *Jura* 527.

[35] *Schutzpflichten* are often used to justify extension of the criminal law. Most controversially, *Schutzpflichten* have been used to protect the unborn foetus (*BVerfGE* 39, 1). See J. Isensee, 'Das Grundrecht als Abwehrrecht und als staatliche Schutzpflicht' in Isensee and Kirchhoff (n 24) 143. As the FCC is equivocal on this matter, I will not here enter the ongoing debate over whether *Schutzpflichten* should be seen as objective state duties or as correlative duties derived from subjective individual rights to state protection; see Alexy (n 22) 301ff.

[36] *BVerfGE* 33, 303; 35, 79.

[37] P. Häberle, 'Grundrechte im Leistungsstaat' (1972) 30 *VVDStRL* 75; Hesse (n 7) 434.

[38] G. Jellinek, *System der subjektiven öffentlichen Rechte* (2nd edn, Tübingen, 1905; reprinted Scientia Verlag, Aalen, 1964).

[39] *BVerfGE* 27, 344, 351; 6, 32, 41; 12, 45, 53; 27, 1, 6; 30, 1, 39; 30, 173, 193; 32, 98; 106, 108; 37, 57, 65ff.; 45, 187, 227, and 50, 166, 175; K. Stern, 'Menschenwürde als Wurzel der Menschen- und Grundrechte' in Siekmann (n 24) 224.

[40] C. Starck, 'Menschenwürde als Verfassungsgarantie im modernen Staat' (1981) *JZ* 457; Stern (n 39); K. Sontheimer, 'Principles of Human Dignity in the Federal Republic' in K. Stern (ed.), *Germany and its Basic Law* (Nomos, Baden-Baden, 1993) 213; Jarass and Pieroth (n 27), 46.

The dignity of man is inviolable. To respect and protect it shall be the duty of all public authority.

The FCC views article 1(1) of the Basic Law as the 'highest value' (*oberster Wert*) and 'foundational principle' (*tragendes Konstitutionsprinzip*) of the Constitution.[41] From this article all basic rights are said to flow.[42] Importantly, article 1(1) is taken to embody the notion of basic rights as 'pre-State': 'the State is there for the sake of the people and not the other way round'.[43] German constitutional thinking also takes this to mean that the State must not merely refrain from violating human dignity; its activity must be guided by the purpose of upholding it. This is an important constitutional legitimation for positive constitutional rights: 'human dignity is not only the limit of, but also the responsibility of, state activity'.[44]

The departure from classical liberal conceptions of basic rights in Germany is also evident in Germany's social conception of rights, and the ideal of the *soziale Rechtsstaat*.[45] This has two aspects: it legitimizes state restrictions of basic rights, and empowers individual claims to social assistance. On the one hand, the FCC emphasizes the social context in which individual rights are interpreted and balanced and rejects the view of constitutional rights as instruments of egoistic individualism. As the Court has frequently maintained, the 'image of man under the Basic Law is not that of the isolated sovereign individual, rather, the Basic Law resolves the conflict between the individual and the community by binding the citizen to the community without detracting from his intrinsic value'.[46] This reinforces the FCC's now well-known 'balancing' approach to fundamental rights which manifests in a clearly articulated and widely applied doctrine of proportionality.[47]

On the other hand, despite their notable absence in the Constitution's text,[48] the Court has drawn on a number of constitutional arguments to develop social constitutional rights (*soziale Grundrechte*) or, in the language of Jellinek and Hohfeld,[49] positive claim rights (*Leistungsrechte/Leistungsansprüche*) to social assistance. Evidently, the development of social rights is connected to the notions of positive constitutional rights and correlative positive State duties, as embodied in article 1(1) of the Basic Law.

---

[41] *BVerfGE* 32, 98, 108; 50, 166, 175; 54, 341, 357; 87, 209, 228.
[42] Jarass and Pieroth (n 27) 43.   [43] Jarass and Pieroth (n 27) 42.
[44] B. Pieroth and B. Schlink, *Grundrechte: Staatsrecht II* (2nd edn, Müller, Heidelberg, 1986) 87.
[45] *BVerfGE* 4, 7, 15; 5, 85, 198; C. Degenhart, *Staatsrecht I* (13th edn, Müller, Heidelberg, 1997) 145; K. Stern, 'Sozialstaat' and 'Menschenwürde als Wurzel der Menschen- und Grundrechte' in Siekmann (n 24) 123 and 224.
[46] *BVerfGE* 12, 45, 51; 28, 175, 189.
[47] Starck (n 24).
[48] J. Isensee, 'Verfassung ohne soziale Grundrechte' (1980) *Der Staat* 19, 374.
[49] Jellinek (n 38), W. Hohfeld, *Fundamental Legal Conceptions as Applied in Judicial Reasoning* (Yale University Press, New Haven, 1919).

But the Court can also invoke the constitutional Social State principle (*Sozialstaatsprinzip*) entrenched, alongside the Democratic and Federal State principles, in article 20(1) of the Basic Law. The Social State principle represents constitutional acknowledgement that the State is, in some way, bound to ensure the achievement of social justice.[50] But although clearly of normative importance,[51] the FCC and constitutional commentators view it as too vague to generate individual rights and duties on its own. Rather it is said to represent a general goal of the State (*Staatszielbestimmung*), directed primarily at the legislature, to pursue social justice without indicating the concrete means by which this might be achieved.[52] Few FCC cases, and only in conjunction with other basic rights, see the Social State principle as generating subjective constitutional entitlements to social assistance.[53] Nevertheless, it is accepted that the Social State principle in conjunction with article 1(1) of the Basic Law and/or the protection of equality under article 3 of the Basic Law, place a positive constitutional duty on the State to guarantee the basic material and social existence necessary for human dignity.[54] Equally, the FCC has held that individuals enjoy certain benefits or demand certain action from the State to ensure the 'factual prerequisites' necessary for the enjoyment of their basic rights.[55]

Social constitutional rights and the notion of the *soziale Rechtsstaat* are not new in German constitutional history. In 1848, attempts to include the 'right to work and income' in the *Paulskirche* Constitution failed.[56] The social constitutional rights debate continued in social democratic circles during the late nineteenth century, although their support was often undermined by the rights scepticism associated with followers of Marx and Lassalle.[57] Notwithstanding, the social-liberal founders of the Weimar Republic, facing the immediate threat of socialist revolution in 1919, sought a politically expedient compromise between 'capitalism and socialism' and

---

[50] Degenhart (n 45), 140–5; P. Kunig, 'The Principle of Social Justice' in U. Karpen (ed.), *The Constitution of the Federal Republic of Germany: Essays on the Basic Rights and Principles of the Basic Law* (Nomos, Baden-Baden, 1988) 187.

[51] This is underlined by the fact that, like art. 1, art. 20 has been made immune from constitutional amendment under Basic Law, art. 79(3).

[52] Jarass and Pieroth (n 27) 541ff.; Kunig (n 50), 187; Stern (n 45) 123; K. Koepsel *Strafvollzug im Sozialstaat* (Doctoral Dissertation, Hamburg, 1985) 13ff.

[53] For an exceptional decision here see *BVerfG* (1990) *NJW* 2869, 2871.

[54] *BVerfGE* 82, 60; 87, 153; 91, 93; Degenhart (n 45) 143; Jarass and Pieroth (n 27) 541ff.

[55] e.g., *BVerfGE* 33, 303.

[56] K. Lange, 'Soziale Grundrechte in der deutschen Verfassungsentwicklung und in den derzeitigen Länderverfassungen' in E.-W. Böckenförde, J. Jekewitz and T. Ramm (eds), *Soziale Grundrechte* (Müller, Heidelberg, 1980) 49.

[57] S. Miller, 'Soziale Grundrechte in der Tradition der deutschen Sozialdemokratie' in E.-W. Böckenförde, J. Jekewitz and T. Ramm (eds), *Soziale Grundrechte* (Müller, Heidelberg, 1980) 35. See, in general, B. Russell, *German Social Democracy* (Simon and Schuster, New York, 1965).

included a number of social rights provisions groundbreaking for their time.[58]

One of the leading constitutional theorists of the Weimar period, Hermann Heller, highlighted the link between constitutional democracy and the protection of social justice.[59] Defending the Weimar Constitution at a time of severe economic depression and growing political intolerance, Heller viewed the attainment of social justice as a precondition of a sustainable liberal and democratic state, and a necessary bulwark against anti-democratic forces in German politics. Heller's writing was openly political and, whilst operating at a more abstract level, was representative of the convictions of social democrats and social liberals at the time.[60] His arguments remain influential within social democratic thinking and constitutional commentary post-1945,[61] and have been linked to the progress of the Social State principle under the Basic Law.[62]

Reflecting the social-liberal tradition of Weimar, a number of state (*Länder*) constitutions, drafted immediately after 1945, included catalogues of social constitutional rights. Despite this, similar rights were not codified in the text of the Basic Law passed in 1949, and the FCC was initially slow to develop them by implication.[63] Unlike the total negation of political and civil liberties under the Nazi regime, social rights were generally promoted during the Third Reich. The Court's immediate priority in post-war Germany was therefore the constitutional assertion of negative rights against the State.[64] Nevertheless, by the early 1970s, the movement towards promoting social constitutional rights, particularly within social democratic circles,[65] was palpable.[66] Constitutional commentators were quick to invoke the history of social rights protection in the Weimar period, and the FCC had already begun to adopt a more activist approach in developing social constitutional rights and the *soziale Rechtsstaat*.[67]

---

[58] Although the legal effect of these provisions were seriously undermined by the approach of the courts at this time. Lange (n 56) 52; P. Badura, 'Das Prinzip der sozialen Grundrechte und seine Verwirklichung im Recht der Bundesrepublik Deutschland' (1975) 14 *Der Staat* 17, 20.

[59] Dyzenhaus (n 11), chs. 1, 4, 5; C. Müller and I. Staff (eds), *Der Soziale Rechtsstaat: Gedächtnisschrift für Hermann Heller 1981–1933* (Nomos, Baden-Baden, 1984); Schluchter (n 11); Kennedy (n 11); Friedrich (n 11); Sontheimer (n 11).

[60] Dyzenhaus (n 11) chs 1 and 3, particularly p. 163.

[61] Häberle (n 37) 30.　　　　[62] Kunig (n 50) 187.　　　　[63] Lange (n 56) 59.

[64] Ramm (n 28).

[65] See further 3.1.2.

[66] P. Saladin, 'Die Funktion der Grundrechte in einer revidierten Verfassung' (1968) 87 *Zeitschrift für Sozialreform (Neue Fassung)* 531; W. Daum, 'Soziale Grundrechte' (1968) RdA 81; U. Scheuner, 'Die Funktion der Grundrechte im Sozialstaat' (1971) DÖV 505; P. Saladin and L. Wildhaber, *Der Staat als Aufgabe, Gedenkschrift für M. Imboden* (Helbing & Lichtenhahn, Basle and Stuttgart, 1972); Häberle (n 37); Friesenhahn (n 29); Rupp (n 29); Badura (n 58).

[67] P. Haberle, 'Das Bundesverfassungsgericht im Leistungsstaat' (1972) DÖV 729; W. Schmidt, 'Soziale Grundrechte im Verfassungsrecht der Bundesrepublik Deutschland' (1981) 5 *Der Staat* (Beiheft) 9.

To sum up at this point, two characteristics particularly relevant to our analysis of prisoners' rights have been identified within German constitutional culture. The first is the German faith in the constitutional rights project which underpins the symbolic and normative legitimacy of the FCC. The second is the broad conception of constitutional rights developed in Germany, which goes beyond a notion of rights as regulating bipolar and uni-directional relationships between State as aggressor and individual as victim. Rather, rights are viewed as multifaceted (negative and positive, subjective and objective) and as regulating a complex network of social relations between the State and the individual: between individuals within society, and for the development of society as a whole.

The broad conception of fundamental rights in Germany, and the commitment to the fundamental rights project has made rights highly constitutive of legal and political culture. Few social and legal relations are expressed without recourse to basic rights language. 'Rights rhetoric' dominates most processes of political and legal change, and judges of the FCC are called upon to determine the constitutionality of many central social issues.[68] This level of 'rights rhetoric' has overloaded the FCC,[69] and recently attracted criticisms that 'rights fundamentalism' has undermined German legal culture.[70] This has in turn led to the FCC reconsidering its own role in German politics and measures have been implemented to limit immediate access to the Court.[71] Yet while significant, these recent doubts have not succeeded in radically undermining the social and cultural weight of constitutional rights and the FCC in Germany. At present, basic rights remain the cornerstone of modern German democracy and a defining feature of its political, legal, and constitutional culture. In Germany, 'basic rights have become the heart of the free democratic and legal state'.[72]

---

[68] J. Limbach, 'Das Bundesverfassungsgericht als politischer Machtfaktor' (1996) *Humboldt Forum Recht* Beitrag 12; A. Stone-Sweet, *Governing With Judges: Constitutional Politics in Europe* (OUP, Oxford, 2000) 78.

[69] E.-W. Böckenförde, 'Die Überlastung des Bundesverfassungsgerichts' (1996) *ZRP* 281; J. Rivers, 'Stemming the flood of constitutional complaints in Germany' (1993) *PL* 553.

[70] K. Redecker, 'Der moderne Fluch der Versuchung zur Totalität' (1995) *NJW* 3369; Alexy (n 22) 213. More recently, serious doubts have been expressed about the political checks and balances built into the Basic Law. These have been blamed for the German Government's inability to bring about economic reform and avoid recession. See 'Die enthauptete Republik' and 'Die Konsens-Falle' *Der Spiegel*, 25 June 2003; D. Von Kyaw, 'Germany's problem is federalism' *Financial Times*, 29 July 2003.

[71] Rivers (n 69).

[72] K. Stern, 'Staatsrecht und Verfassungsrecht in ihrer Wechselbezüglichkeit' in Siekmann (n 24) 133.

2.2 The Constitutional Foundations of the Prison Act and the Prisoner's Legal Status

While the German Basic Law gives the State competence to imprison criminal offenders,[73] asserts a right to personal liberty[74] and habeas corpus,[75] and lays out criteria by which a person may be punished,[76] detained, or sentenced to imprisonment,[77] it does not make explicit how prisons should be administered or which rights prisoners should hold post-conviction.[78] The existence and shape of the legislation that governs the prisoner's legal status today is determined by the FCC's interpretation of constitutional rights and principles. These constitutional foundations were set out in the decisive and creative interventions of the FCC in the early 1970s.[79]

The FCC is not solely responsible for the conception of the prisoner's legal status. Recognition must also be given to the work and arguments of those academics and politicians involved in an ongoing prison reform process at the time. Although the FCC's decisive interventions in the early 1970s were pivotal in the development of the prisoner's fundamental rights status and the ultimate enactment of the Prison Act 1976, their arguments were nevertheless significantly shaped by the concerns and expertise of these reformers and the rights arguments they invoked.[80]

But the existence of prior rights arguments should not lead us to underestimate the role of the Basic Law and the FCC in this reform process. The reform debate was clearly framed by the ambient legal culture. The imperatives of constitutional law and the dynamics of rights culture in Germany made talk of legal reform unlikely to occur without evidence of its basis in, and accordance with, the Basic Law. Recourse to constitutional rights and principles was an important rhetorical tool in a political culture which, while united by a belief in constitutionalism, did not display consensus as to punishment. The FCC furthered the pre-existing prison reform project by explicating how the proposed foundations of a future Act would be anchored in the Constitution. Through its unequivocal support, the FCC gave the proposed Act legal and political legitimacy of the highest order, and by declaring existing prison law unconstitutional and setting a deadline for the enactment of new legislation, it crucially eliminated any possible delay in implementing these penal reforms.[81] Thus, while the prisoner's fundamental rights status and the Prison Act 1976 were established in Germany

---

[73] Basic Law, art. 74, point 1.
[74] Basic Law, art. 2(2), sentence 2.
[75] Basic Law, art. 104(2) and (3).
[76] Basic Law, art. 103(2).
[77] Basic Law, art. 104.
[78] C. Gusy, 'Freiheitsentziehung und Grundgesetz' (1992) *NJW* 457, 461.
[79] *BVerfGE* 33,1; 35, 202; 40, 276.
[80] See 3.1.
[81] The landmark decision of the FCC (*BVerfGE* 33, 1) set a one-year deadline for introducing new constitutionally legitimate legislation, later extended by three years in *BVerfGE* 40, 276, 284.

through an intricate combination of judicial, academic and political interventions, these interventions were ultimately framed by a legal culture dominated by constitutional rights and rights rhetoric.

2.2.1 Prisoners, Basic Rights and the *Rechtsstaatsprinzip*

In 1972, prisoners were a legal anomaly. They were not seen as full bearers of basic rights,[82] and no primary or secondary legislation determined their legal status. As a result, the prisoner's legal status violated two central tenets of the *Rechtsstaatsprinzip*:[83] the 'legal proviso' (*Gesetzesvorbehalt*)[84] and the principle that all state authorities are bound by basic rights (*Grundrechtsbindung*). The 'legal proviso' stipulates that a primary statute, or clearly and narrowly defined secondary legislation, must authorize administrative action wherever such action relates to a matter of 'substantial importance for the citizen or the public'.[85] The principle of 'binding basic rights' derives from article 1(3) of the Basic Law which states that 'basic rights shall bind the legislature, the executive and the judiciary as directly enforceable law'. Given that they are unamendable,[86] these principles are central provisions of the German Constitution and therefore foundational principles of the entire legal order.

Despite these fundamental principles, however, prisoners were governed by the Service and Administration Ordinance of 1962 (*Dienst- und Vollzugs-Ordnung 1962*). As an administrative regulation this Ordinance was, strictly speaking, classified as 'internal law' ('*Innenrecht*').[87] It neither

---

[82] The prisoner's right of recourse to law (*Rechtsschutzgewährleistung*) under Basic Law, art. 19(4) and the *Rechtsstaatsprinzip* had, however, been recognized in 1961 in the Introductory Act to the Constitution of the Courts Act, §§ 23ff. H. Müller-Dietz, *Strafvollzugsrecht* (Walter de Gruyter, Berlin, 1977) 49.

[83] The *Rechtsstaatsprinzip* is central to German constitutional law and culture. It is equivalent to, though differs significantly from, the Rule of Law in England. For an explanation of its significance, see K. Stern, 'Der Rechtsstaat' in Siekmann (n 24) 3.

[84] H. Maurer, *Allgemeines Verwaltungsrecht* (11th edn, Beck, Munich 1997) 105; Degenhart (n 44) 116.

[85] This is known as the theory of 'substantiality' (*Wesentlichkeitstheorie*) which holds that legislation is always necessary if the issue is one of 'substantial' importance for the citizen or the public. A 'substantial interest' may be a basic right or other significant interests. H.-U. Schwarze, *European Administrative Law* (Sweet & Maxwell, London, 1992) 216; Degenhart (n 44) 113.

[86] As explained previously, these principles are tenets of the *Rechtsstaatsprinzip* explicit in Basic Law, art. 20. Arts 1 and 20 are declared unamendable under Basic Law, art. 79(3).

[87] German administrative law distinguishes external law (*Außenrecht*) from internal law (*Innenrecht*). External law regulates the relationship between individual and State, and has a direct impact on citizens and other legal persons outside the administrative structure (*unmittelbare Rechtswirkung nach außen*). Acts classified as, or based on, external law are in general legally binding and can be challenged by citizens. In opposition thereto, internal law regulates the activity of administrative officials only and is not binding on citizens outside the administration. Citizens cannot normally challenge a rule or act classified as internal law, unless they can be shown to violate the equality principle (*Gleichheitssatz*) under art. 3 of the Basic Law. Maurer (n 84) 36, 598.

created prisoners' rights nor was legally binding on the prison administration.[88] Importantly, it did not qualify as primary statute law for the purpose of fulfilling the 'legal proviso'. Reformers consequently argued that, under the Ordinance, limitations of prisoners' rights were without constitutional legitimacy:[89] 'in a *Rechtsstaat*, the prison as a State institution and social entity may never be outside the remit of law and statute' (*Recht und Gesetz*).[90]

The justification given for the anomalous position of the prisoner was the 'special authority relationship' (*besonderes Gewaltverhältnis*) doctrine, a product of nineteenth-century administrative legal theory[91] allied to the distinction between 'internal' and 'external' law.[92] It stipulated that categories of persons who were in an unusually close relationship to the State, such as prisoners, school students, and members of the armed forces, were not protected by the full range of basic rights. The original logic of the doctrine was that these groups of individuals were considered 'internal' to the State and in a 'sphere unregulated by law' (*rechtsfrei erachteter Bereich*).[93] These persons were viewed as exempt from the protections of the 'legal proviso' (*Gesetzesvorbehalt*) as they were without the full range of basic rights to be protected by 'external law'. Inevitably, with the introduction of the Basic Law in 1948 and the growing influence of the *Rechtsstaatsprinzip*, the negation of the 'legal proviso' through the 'special authority relationship' came under increasing criticism.[94]

If the original rationale which underpinned the 'special authority relationship' doctrine was being questioned in the late 1960s and early 1970s, it was clearly discredited by the groundbreaking decision of the FCC in 1972. Here, the *Rechtsstaatsprinzip* was strongly invoked: prisoners were to be protected in the same way as all citizens under the Basic Law.[95] This was the FCC's first important intervention into matters of prison reform, and its close relationship with the reform movement showed in direct references to the proposals of the Prison Administration Commission of the Federal Ministry (*Strafvollzugskommission des Bundesministeriums*)[96] and relevant leading academic publications.[97] The judgment, concerning the power of a

---

[88] Müller-Dietz (n 82) 49.

[89] H. Müller-Dietz, *Strafvollzugsgesetzgebung und Strafvollzugsreform* (Heymanns, Cologne, 1970) 33.

[90] T. Würtenberger, 'Freiheit und Zwang im Strafvollzug' (1969) *NJW* 1747, 1748.

[91] D. Merten, 'Grundrechte und besonderes Gewaltverhältnis' in B. Börne *et al.* (eds), *Einigkeit und Recht und Freiheit—Festschrift für Karl Carstens* (Heymanns, Cologne, 1984) 721.

[92] See n 87.   [93] Maurer (n 84) 166.

[94] Müller-Dietz (n 89) 33; Würtenberger (n 90) 1748.   [95] *BVerfGE* 33, 1.

[96] Bundesministerium der Justiz, *Entwurf eines Gesetzes über den Vollzug der Freiheitsstrafe und der freiheitsentziehenden Maßregeln der Besserung und Sicherung—Strafvollzugsgesetz* (Müller, Karlsruhe, 1971).

[97] H. Schüler-Springorum, *Strafvollzug im Übergang* (Schwartz Verlag, Göttingen, 1969); Müller-Dietz (n 89) 33. On the prison reform movement see 3.1.

prison governor to intercept a prisoner's correspondence,[98] ended the legal anomaly that prisoners represented at the time.

The FCC noted that the 'special authority relationship' had been used as an 'independent and implicit limitation of the basic rights of the prisoner',[99] and insisted that all basic rights and the 'legal proviso' applied to prisoners. It thereby dismissed the doctrine as inadequate justification for the prisoner's unconstitutional status, describing it as 'qualifying' prisoners' basic rights 'in an intolerably vague manner'.[100] Its position on the prisoner's legal status was unequivocal:

> The Basic Law is a value-bound order, which recognises the protection of the freedom and dignity of persons as the uppermost aim of all law; the image of humanity is not however one of an egotistical individual, but rather one of a socially bound figure with manifold obligations . . . article 1(3) Basic Law declares that basic rights bind the legislature, the administration and the judiciary as directly enforceable law. This comprehensive binding of all organs of the State is contradicted when in the administration of prisons, prisoners' basic rights are limited in an arbitrary or discretionary manner. Such a limitation is only possible when it is essential to the achievement of a socially related constitutional purpose and occurs in a constitutionally recognised form. The basic rights of prisoners can therefore only be limited on the basis of, or through, a law which while unable to avoid the use of general clauses should be as limited as possible.[101]

Thus, prisoners were to be afforded full and equal rights under the Basic Law, and limitations of these rights could only be constitutionally legitimate if they were made pursuant to a primary 'external' law which itself fulfilled a 'constitutional purpose'. Only thus could prison law accord with the 'legal proviso' and thereby the *Rechtsstaatsprinzip*.[102] Having declared the extant law on prisons unconstitutional, the FCC set a deadline for a new legal regime to be introduced. The result was the Prison Act 1976.

The significance of this decision lies not only in its hastening of legislative reform, its assertion of the *Rechtsstaatsprinzip*, or its categorical support of prisoners' rights. It is also important for its explicit grounding of prisoners'

---

[98] The Service and Administration Ordinance 1962 permitted the prison governor to monitor and intercept post in the interests of security. The FCC asserted that the provision in question violated the prisoner's fundamental right under Basic Law, art. 5(1) (freedom of expression), and declared that, in the absence of primary legislation setting out constitutionally legitimate limitations of these rights, these actions were unconstitutional. As this legislation did not exist at the time, the FCC acknowledged that for an interim period certain violations of basic rights would have to be tolerated.

[99] *BVerfGE* 33, 1, 10.   [100] *BVerfGE* 33, 1, 10.

[101] *BVerfGE* 33, 1, 11.

[102] The doctrine of *besonderes Gewaltverhältnis* was discredited in general by this decision. While a notion of a 'special administrative relationship' (*verwaltungsrechtliche Sonderbeziehung*) now exists, it is clear from the decision that basic rights and the 'legal proviso' applies in these cases. It is, however, acknowledged on pragmatic grounds, regarding such relationships, that the extent of the 'legal proviso' is more restricted than in normal administrative relationships. However, there is no doubt that with respect to infringements of basic rights the 'legal proviso' applies. Maurer (n 84) 113–17, 166–71; Degenhart (n 44) 115.

rights within a social context. This was in line with the FCC's approach to fundamental rights in general.[103] In this regard, it is significant that the FCC insisted that the constitutional purpose of imprisonment be 'socially related'. Equally it is noteworthy that before pronouncing on the subject of prisoners' rights, the FCC reminded us again that basic rights are premised on the notion of the individual as a 'socially bound figure with manifold obligations'.

The use of this language hinted at two interconnected issues: first, reference to the individual's 'manifold obligations' signalled that prisoners should not only bear rights but should also be placed under obligations and duties ultimately justifiable by the protection of the social interest. Secondly, the FCC's allusion to a 'socially related constitutional purpose' reflected its concern that new prison legislation should serve the interests of society as well as the prisoner. It thereby averred that prisoners' rights should be balanced against the social rationale for their limitation or protection. This relationship between the social interest and the prisoner's individual interest was not necessarily seen as one of conflict. To a great extent, the FCC has viewed the social interest as being served by vesting prisoners with basic rights.[104] On the other hand, the FCC has invoked the social interest, in particular in being protected from crime, as justification for the limitation of prisoners' rights.[105] Both tendencies are evident in its development of the purpose of prison administration.

2.2.2 The Federal Constitutional Court and the Purpose of Imprisonment

To recapitulate briefly: by vesting prisoners with full and equal basic rights and asserting the protections of the *Rechtsstaatsprinzip*, the FCC placed the onus on the State to justify any rights limitations where they occurred. Without legal authority to limit individual rights, explained in legal terms as *Eingriffsbefugnisse* (power to encroach on rights), state limitations would be struck down as rights violations. Furthermore, as the FCC explained, limitations cannot simply be justified through the legislative process, as they must accord with the fundamental principles of the Basic Law.[106] In other words, the basic rights of prisoners can be limited, but such limitations are themselves subject to constitutional limitations.[107] It was therefore essential that the proposed legislation state explicitly the purpose, function, and extent of legal limitations of prisoners' basic rights.

---

[103] See 2.1 above.   [104] See 2.2.2.2 below.   [105] See 2.2.3.2 below.

[106] Under Basic Law, art. 20(3) the legislature is bound by the constitutional order and is therefore duty bound to respect basic rights in the content and shape of legislation.

[107] Known as the doctrine of 'limits of limits' (*Schranken-Schranken*). B. Pieroth and B. Schlink, *Grundrechte—Staatsrecht II* (13th edn, Müller, Heidelberg, 1997) 64. See further 2.2.2.4 below.

The demand for a clear, overarching legislative purpose was reinforced by a further substantive principle of the *Rechtsstaatsprinzip*: the doctrine of proportionality (*Verhältnismäßigkeitsgrundsatz*). This stipulates that state measures be 'suitable' and 'necessary' for attaining a legitimate (i.e. constitutional or legal) purpose, and 'proportionate' in the narrow sense. A measure is 'suitable' where it clearly relates to achieving the purpose in question; it is 'necessary' when shown to be the least restrictive measure which achieves that end 'as effectively'. In its narrow sense, the measure must be 'proportionate': it should strike a proper balance between the rights protected by the measure and the protection of the individuals' rights being affected by the measure in question.[108] Without a clear legislative purpose by which a measure could be judged 'necessary' and 'suitable', the doctrine of proportionality in its wide sense would be undermined. Such is the centrality of the doctrine of proportionality to the fulfilment of the 'legal proviso' requirement, that Schlink has argued for a separate constitutional principle called 'the proportionate law proviso' (*Vorbehalt des verhältnismäßigen Gesetzes*).[109]

Given this constitutional framework, the Prison Act 1976 was expected to define clearly a constitutionally legitimate purpose of prison administration and set out a homogenous and coherent legal basis, in line with this purpose, upon which administrative action with regard to prisoners is justified. It is important to recognize, at this stage, that the Prison Act was as much about justifying and setting out limitations of prisoners' basic rights as it was about giving prisoners special rights, if not more so.[110] The central problem of the Act was, therefore, to find a justificatory purpose in line with the values of the Constitution. The FCC was in a central position to give guidance on this point.

2.2.2.1 The Purpose of Punishment and the Purpose of Imprisonment

Before showing how the purpose of imprisonment was constitutionally defined, a brief clarification must be made. The German Prison Act 1976 forms part of the criminal law in its broad sense,[111] but regulates prison administration only. The purpose of imprisonment refers here to the purpose of prison administration alone, not to the purpose of punishment in general. The general part of the Penal Code (*Strafgesetzbuch*) regulates the latter, stipulating in paragraph 46 that the primary basis upon which the

---

[108] Degenhart (n 44) 128–33. See also L. Hirschberg, *Der Grundsatz der Verhältnismäßigkeit* (Schwarz, Göttingen, 1981).

[109] Pieroth and Schlink (n 107) 63. See further 2.2.2.4 below.

[110] See further 2.2.2.3 below.

[111] The controversy over whether prison law is procedural (*formelles*) or substantive (*materielles*) criminal law, or whether it forms a third part of the criminal law, is reported in G. Kaiser and H. Schöch, *Strafvollzug* (5th edn, Müller, Heidelberg, 2002) 171.

sentence is to be awarded is the extent of the offender's criminal guilt (*Schuldausgleich*),[112] and that within these limits the effect of the sentence on the offender's future life in society can be taken into account.[113] Only after the sentence is set (*Strafzumessung*) and officially executed (*Strafvollstreckung*) does the administration of the prison sentence (*Strafvollzug*) become governed by the provisions and purpose of the Prison Act.

Historically, the relationship between prison law and criminal law has been articulated as the 'three-pillar theory' (*Drei-Säulen-Theorie*).[114] This argues that the criminal law in its broader sense is composed of three stages: the material criminal law threatens punishment, the criminal judge determines punishment, and the administration executes and administers punishment. Complementing this theory, Roxin's widely-accepted 'dialetical-unification-theory' (*dialektische Vereinigungstheorie*)[115] and the 'step-theory' (*Stufentheorie*)[116] argue that different purposes of punishment predominate at different stages of the criminal justice system. In brief, the criminal law and resultant 'legislative threat of punishment' is aimed primarily at general deterrence; conviction, predominantly,[117] at retribution; and the execution and administration of punishment at special prevention (*Spezialprävention*) which emphasizes prisoner resocialization. Despite acknowledgement that the separate stages of the criminal justice system are intrinsically interconnected, it is argued that a specific aim of the criminal law and of punishment should predominate at each stage.

Prison reform campaigners and authors of preliminary drafts of the Prison Act 1976 aimed to set a clear distinction between the aims of criminal punishment and the aims of prison administration.[118] These reformers were concerned to remedy the problems of prior prison regulations, particularly the Service and Administration Ordinance 1961, which set out multiple purposes of imprisonment and thereby did not provide a clear substantive basis for the exercise of discretion in prisons. In solving these problems, they attempted both to distinguish the aims of the criminal punishment from those of the administration of punishment, and to settle on a unitary purpose of prison administration.[119] According to majority opinion, this is what paragraph 2 of the Prison Act was meant to achieve.[120]

---

[112] Penal Code, § 46(1), sentence 1.   [113] Penal Code, § 46(1), sentence 2.

[114] Kaiser and Schöch (n 111) 179.

[115] C. Roxin, 'Sinn und Grenzen staatlicher Strafe' (1966) *JuS* 377.

[116] Kaiser and Schöch (n 111) 247.

[117] As stated above, Penal Code, § 46(2) allows consideration of the resocialization effects of the sentence on the offender within the limits of the proportionality guarantee of Penal Code, § 46(1).

[118] J. Baumann *et al.* (eds), *Alternativ-Entwurf eines Strafvollzugsgesetzes* (Arbeitskreis deutscher und schweizerischer Strafrechtslehrer, Tübingen, 1973); *Regierungsentwurf eines Strafvollzugsgesetzes* (BT-Dr. 7/918, 1972/73).

[119] On prison reform movement in Germany see 3.1.   [120] See 4.2.1.1.

Decisions taken at the sentencing stage and at the punishment administration stage are distinguished as 'status' decisions (*Status: entscheidungen*) and 'administrative' decisions (*Gestaltung: sentsscheidungen*).[121] Status decisions, directed by the Penal Code, determine 'which' sentence (i.e. type and length) should be given. This includes decisions regarding early release taken by the higher chamber of the Prison Courts (*Strafvollstreckungskammer*)[122] under the Penal Code.[123] Administrative decisions are governed by the Prison Act and determine 'how' the prisoner should be treated in prison. In practice, status and administrative decisions have a 'reflexive influence' on one another. The length of the prison sentence, set at the sentencing stage, indirectly determines the content of the sentence plan as well as the timing and implementation of particular measures stipulated in the Prison Act; decisions made during the administration of the prison sentence, such as whether to relax the prisoner's sentence regime, often influence the prisoner's later eligibility for early release. German criminal and penal theorists argue, however, that the two types of decisions are distinct in both the applicable legislation and the punishment aim to be followed.[124] As Van Zyl Smit argues, the German distinction reflects the Anglo-American *dictum*: 'people are sent to prison as punishment and not for punishment'.[125]

Though the distinction between the aims of criminal punishment and the aim of prison administration has been challenged,[126] the law continues to distinguish between a primary retributive justification for punishment as explicated in the Penal Code, and the primarily resocialisative purpose of imprisonment of the Prison Act.[127] Equally the law distinguishes between 'status' decisions, regulated by the Penal Code, and 'administrative' decisions regulated by the Prison Act. The following section will examine the constitutional basis for the resocialisation purpose of prison administration.

2.2.2.2 Resocialization as 'Verfassungsgebot des Sozialstaats'[128]

The FCC first gave explicit guidance on the purpose of imprisonment in the *Lebach* decision of 1973,[129] where it determined that resocialization was the purpose of imprisonment most in line with the basic principles of the Constitution.[130] The decision dealt with a prisoner's claim that his constitutional rights to human dignity (Basic Law, article 1(1)) and personal free-

---

[121] R.-P. Callies and H. Müller-Dietz, *Strafvollzugsgesetz* (9th edn, Beck, Munich, 2002) § 2 mn 9 (henceforth Calliess/Müller-Dietz).

[122] Criminal Procedure Code, § 462a.

[123] Penal Code, §§ 57–58. Parole procedure is regulated in Criminal Procedure Code, §§ 454 and 454a.

[124] Calliess/Müller-Dietz, § 2, mn 10; K. Laubenthal, *Strafvollzug* (2nd edn, Springer, Berlin, 1998) 76.

[125] Van Zyl Smit (n 1). [126] See 4.2.1.1.

[127] Calliess/Müller-Dietz, § 2, mn 8ff.

[128] 'A constitutional requirement of a Social State'. [129] *BVerfGE* 35, 202.

[130] *BVerfGE* 35, 202, 203.

dom (Basic Law, article 2(2)) would be violated if a documentary on his involvement in a group which murdered four soldiers was screened on national television. The documentary was to be broadcast shortly before the prisoner's release and, in addition to reminding viewers of his criminal act, insinuated that the prisoner had had homosexual relations with his criminal partners. The conflict in the case was therefore between the prisoner's afore-mentioned rights and the television broadcaster's right to freedom of expression (Basic Law, article 5(1), sentence 2).[131]

The starting point of the FCC was that the public's information interest in knowing about serious crimes generally took precedence over protection of the personal reputation of the offender. However, it then argued that, in assessing infringements of basic rights, the doctrine of proportionality was central: the invasion of the prisoner's personal sphere should not go beyond that required to fulfil the public's interest in information about crime and criminals in general.[132] Constitutional protection of the personality there-fore limited television broadcasters to reporting the facts of serious crimes, and not irrelevant aspects of the offender's personality or any other facts which could be said to belong to his private sphere. One central argument supporting the prisoner's case was the negative effect of the content and timing of the documentary on his chances of social reintegration. The refer-ence to the prisoner's homosexual relations was regarded as particularly damaging to the prisoner's chances of reintegration into his conservative home town. The FCC drew upon specialist opinion in forming its conviction that the documentary would seriously disadvantage the prisoner's chances of resocialization.[133] It considered this deleterious effect to be a major factor in tipping the proportional balance between the public interest in knowing about crimes committed and the prisoner's right to dignity (Basic Law, article 1(1)) and the free exercise of his personality (Basic Law, article 2(1)). The FCC therefore upheld the prisoner's rights over those of the broadcaster.

Through this reasoning, the FCC developed what came to be referred to as the prisoner's 'right' to resocialization,[134] and more recently the 'constitutional resocialization requirement' (*verfassungsrechtliches*

---

[131] See analysis in Alexy (n 22) 54–56. The television broadcaster, ZDF, was a private cor-poration. This case therefore involved the *Drittwirkung* (horizontal application) of basic rights.

[132] See *BVerfGE* 35, 202, 232.

[133] Prof. Dr Lüscher, a social psychologist and media specialist, argued that the content of the film would create social prejudice against the claimant. Dr Einsele, a prison administration specialist, argued (1) that the purpose of imprisonment could only be that of resocialization and (2) that the timing and content of the film would particularly damage the prisoner's chances of reintegration by undermining the potential support of his community. Mr Possehl, the pris-oner's own prison psychologist, showed that the prisoner was prone to isolating himself from society and that social prejudice against him would raise the chances of this occurring.

[134] While implicit in the FCC's reasoning in the *Lebach* decision, explicit reference to a 'right to resocialisation' (*Anspruch auf Resozialisierung*) was first made in *BVerfGE* 45, 187, 239. Jarass and Pieroth (n 27) 81; Calliess/Müller-Dietz, § 2, mn 6.

Resozialisierungsgebot).[135] It began by quoting paragraph 2 of the Federal Government Draft Proposal for a Prison Act,[136] which favoured resocialization as the primary purpose of imprisonment, and the Response of the Federal Council (*Bundesrat*),[137] which categorically supported this point. It went on, however, to anchor this resocialization purpose in the fundamental principles of the Basic Law:

> Constitutionally this claim [to resocialization] corresponds to the self image of a society that places human dignity at the centre of its value order and that is bound by the Social State principle. As the holder of human dignity and the rights which guarantee it, the criminal offender must have the chance, after serving his sentence, to integrate into society. From the position of the offender this interest in resocialisation grows out of his basic right under article 2(1) in connection with article 1(1) Basic Law. From the vantage point of society, the Social State principle demands State assistance for groups in society who, through personal weakness, guilt, inability or social deprivation are hindered in their social and personal development. Prisoners and released prisoners also belong to this group. Not least, resocialisation serves the protection of society itself which has a direct interest in the prisoner not re-offending and once more damaging his fellow citizens or society in general.[138]

While the FCC's 1972 decision was designed to reconcile prison law with the imperatives of the *Rechtsstaatsprinzip*,[139] the *Lebach* decision was a creative application of the Social State principle (*Sozialstaatsprinzip*) to prison law reform. The FCC interpreted the Social State principle as establishing a 'right to resocialization' by combining it with the fundamental rights of human dignity (Basic Law, article 1(1)) and freedom of the personality (Basic Law, article 2(1)). Its reasoning made explicit a belief that a socially isolated existence violates human dignity, and implied that the chance to start afresh is guaranteed by the freedom to develop one's personality.[140] Allied to this, the Social State principle placed a positive duty on the State to assist socially vulnerable groups in their 'social and personal development',[141] the correlative of which was the prisoner's claim to be resocialized.

In line with its decision in 1972, the FCC was concerned here to invoke the social interest in order to bolster the prisoner's substantive claim to resocialization. This was evident in two ways. On an abstract level, the FCC developed the prisoner's right to resocialization by recourse to an 'image of society which placed human dignity at the centre of its value order and was bound by the Social State principle'.[142] Implicit in this statement was the value judgment that German society would have to pursue the aim of

---

[135] *BVerfGE* 98, 169. See also 'Gefangene müssen bei Pflichtarbeit besser entlohnt werden' *Frankfurter Allgemeine Zeitung*, 2 July 1998, 1.
[136] *Regierungsentwurf eines Strafvollzugsgesetzes* (BT-Dr. 7/918, 1972/73).
[137] *Gesetzesvorschlag des Bundesrates* 1973 (BT-Dr. 7/918).
[138] *BVerfGE* 35, 202, 235–6.   [139] See 2.1 above.
[140] Jarass and Pieroth (n 27) 81.   [141] *BVerfGE* 35, 202, 235.
[142] See *BVerfGE* 35, 202, 235.

resocializing its criminal offenders if it was to fulfil its stated social and constitutional ideals. On a more concrete level, the FCC highlighted the practical benefits to society that could be derived from such a penal strategy. It thus concluded that society would benefit from resocialization in being protected from the damage caused by future crimes.[143]

2.2.2.3 *Resocialization: A Mixed Blessing?*

To the extent that the prisoner benefits from this substantive claim to resocialization, the FCC allied the 'social interest' with that of the prisoner. Its insistence on a unitary purpose of imprisonment was an advance, as it delimited the State to a clear substantive basis for the exercise of prison administration. Moreover, 'the constitutional resocialization requirement' and its realization in the Prison Act 1976 has led to important rights for prisoners in Germany.[144] Yet resocialization could potentially work against the prisoner's individual interests, as the FCC's next decision on prison law in 1975 showed.[145]

In the *St. Pauli-Nachrichten* case the FCC had to consider whether refusing a prisoner access to a magazine containing pornographic and sado-masochistic materials violated his basic rights to human dignity, personal development, and freedom of expression under the Basic Law, articles 1, 2(1) and 5(1) respectively. The FCC first reiterated that the basic rights of prisoners could only be limited by primary legislation which reflected a 'contemporary understanding of basic rights' and respect for the Social State and *Rechtsstaat* principles.[146] It insisted that it was the State's function to introduce all legislative measures that were necessary and suitable to the resocialization of the prisoner, but immediately qualified this by claiming that these actions were to be undertaken 'within reason' (*im Rahmen des Zumutbaren*). This qualification represented the first weakening of the ambitions voiced in the *Lebach* decision, as it indicated that the fulfilment of the resocialization aim by the federal legislature could be curtailed by considerations of affordability, political acceptability and general administrative constraints. Concerned not to usurp Parliament, the FCC allowed for some margin of interpretation regarding the imperatives of the constitutional resocialization principle.

The FCC's subsequent reasoning was sobering for those who viewed resocialization as a key to prisoner empowerment alone:

The refusal to hand over the *St. Pauli-Nachrichten* to the complainant is a measure which is indispensable to the proper maintenance and organisation of the prison. Indispensable are those measures without which the administration of prisons would break down or the aim of imprisonment would be seriously endangered . . . Particularly indispensable are attempts to reintegrate the offender into society. The

---

[143] *BVerfGE* 35, 202, 235.
[145] *BVerfGE* 40, 276.

[144] See 4.2 and 4.4.1.
[146] *BVerfGE* 40, 276, 283.

ability and will to conduct his life in a responsible manner should be conveyed to the offender. He should learn to live in a free society, maintaining a crime-free existence, using the chances offered to him while withstanding the risks presented. *A prison administration understood in this way cannot only establish the rights of the prisoner, but, under certain circumstances, should justify those rights limitations which are necessary for the promotion of a crime-free existence for the prisoner in the future.*[147]

What had always been implicit in the reasoning of the FCC was here brought home: that it required a purpose of prison administration not only to empower prisoners, but also to legitimize state limitations of prisoners' basic rights. The decision vividly displayed the double-edged nature of a 'constitutional resocialization requirement' or a 'right to resocialization'. In one sense, the right to resocialisation could be seen in German constitutional terms as a 'negative right' (*Abwehrrecht*) which delimits state intervention in prisons to one particular constitutional purpose. From this perspective the State has the correlative duty not to pursue other prison administrative aims, such as retribution, alongside resocialization. Strictly speaking, prison administrators may therefore not consider other punishment aims when exercising their discretion under the Prison Act. For example, when considering the risks involved in giving a prisoner leave from prison, prison officials may not take the gravity of the prisoner's original offence into account as this would be a retributive consideration.[148]

In another sense, a right to resocialization in German constitutional terms is also a 'positive right' (*Leistungsrecht*) which obliges the State to assist the prisoner's resocialization, and can generate special rights to state action that would enhance the prisoner's chances of resocialization. Rights to home leave, to be placed in an open prison, or to family visits are examples of such special rights. Conversely, in fulfilling the 'constitutional resocialization requirement' the State can place prisoners under certain duties, such as the duty to work, that would enhance their chances of resocialization and give effect to society's interest in their resocialization. Here the State is justified in limiting prisoners' negative basic rights pursuant to the aim of resocializing them.

Implicit also in the FCC's statement was the acknowledgement that limitations of basic rights are inherent to imprisonment. The creation of a substantive constitutional purpose for prison administration was not meant to wipe away such limitations, but rather to provide a constitutional justification for their use. While it was clear that imprisonment would abrogate rights, it was moot whether the purpose of resocialization in Germany's new prison law would involve a greater abrogation of rights than any other

---

[147] *BVerfGE* 40, 276, 285. Emphasis added.
[148] Van Zyl Smit (n 1) 7. The Prison Act reflects this notion although it has not been without controversy (See 4.2.1.1).

possible purpose. Theoretically, resocialization had clear invasive potential: it could comprise not only a mere deprivation of liberty but also a closer analysis of the offender's personality.[149] Equally, as the substantive basis of prison administration, resocialization had greater invasive potential due to its lack of conceptual clarity.[150] Although the FCC indicated, in both the *Lebach* and *St. Pauli-Nachrichten* decisions, that resocialization measures should aim at reintegrating the offender into society, it left the legislature to decide which measures were viewed as pursuing this aim.

2.2.2.4 *The Constitutional Limits of Resocialization*

The Federal Parliament could not, however, limit the rights of prisoners however it chose. Like the administration and judiciary, the legislature remains bound by article 1(3) of the Basic Law, which entrenches basic rights as directly enforceable law. Accordingly, it had to abide by the substantive limits in the Constitution when limiting the prisoner's basic rights in the name of resocialization. Basic rights may be limited where the Basic Law provides for legal reservations (*Gesetzesvorbehalte*),[151] which exist where the constitution expressly stipulates that a basic right may be limited in law. Moreover, the FCC has developed a doctrine of 'constitutional limitations' (*verfassungsimmanente Schranken*), whereby basic rights may be limited by other basic rights or further constitutional norms. Though some basic rights are not subject to any limitation, such as the right to human dignity (Basic Law, article 1(1)) and the right to equality (Basic Law, article 3), most basic rights are subject to some kind of legal or constitutionally immanent limitation.

Where the Constitution foresees the limitation of a basic right, a number of principles must be followed. Many of these principles stem from the *Rechtsstaatsprinzip*, but are referred to independently under the umbrella term of 'limits of limits' (*Schranken-Schranken*).[152] Included in the notion of *Schranken-Schranken* are five important limitations: two have substantive implications and three act as formal limits on rights-limiting legislation. The first substantive limitation, the 'essence guarantee' (*Wesensgehalt-garantie*), is set out in article 19(2) of the Basic Law, and sets an absolute limit beyond which no basic right can be restricted by asserting that each right has an inviolable essence or core. No general definition of this guarantee has been set beyond the basic conditions that individuals cannot be deprived of the protections of their basic rights entirely and that the extent of the protection differs according to rights, actions, individuals, and

---

[149] W. Hassemer, 'Resozialisierung und Rechtsstaat' (1982) *KrimJ* 161. On the academic view of resocialization in Germany, see 3.1.2.

[150] H. Schellhoss in G. Kaiser *et al.* (eds), *Kleines Kriminologisches Wörterbuch* (Müller, Heidelberg, 1993) 429.

[151] Calliess/Müller-Dietz Einleitung, mn 27.　　　　[152] Pieroth and Schlink (n 107) 73.

context.[153] Furthermore, commentators argue that the 'essence guarantee' offers little practical protection beyond that inherent to article 1(1) of the Basic Law, which declares human dignity inviolable and from which all other basic rights are said to follow. Attempts at defining the inviolable core of every right as equal to the protection offered under article 1(1) have therefore been criticized for redundancy.[154] The case law has also shown that the 'essence guarantee' is not a strong legal tool in practice.[155]

The vagueness of the 'essence guarantee' notwithstanding, it would have placed at least one important limit on the legislature had it been defined either as a core protection of each particular right or as a re-affirmation of article 1(1) of the Basic Law. Statutory provisions which attempted to make prisoners into 'mere or passive objects' (*bloße Objekte staatlichen Handelns*) of treatment measures aimed at resocialization would clearly have been problematic because of their total denial of the prisoner's free will.[156] This would have violated article 1(1) and the essence of article 2(1) of the Basic Law, which protects a person's ability to determine her or his own actions. It would therefore have been problematic to force the prisoner to take part in therapeutic or treatment programmes by creating an absolute duty to abide by them.[157] As Feest argued, '. . . it conflicts with our legal culture to change people against their will, even if this . . . were to be possible'.[158]

Rights restrictions short of those which infringed upon the 'essence' of a right are also subject to limitation. The principle of proportionality would have placed a substantive limit on the legislature's power. As explained above,[159] it would have been prohibited from producing a law which excessively limited the rights of individuals beyond that which was 'necessary', 'suitable', and 'proportional' to the attainment of a 'legitimate' purpose. It is therefore often known as the 'prohibition of excess' principle (*Übermaßverbot*). Inherent in this principle is a check on both the 'purpose' of prison administration and the 'means' of attaining this purpose. It would have had bearing on the basic and specific provisions of the Prison Act 1976. For example, a provision in the legislation which justified giving prison administrators broad powers to use solitary confinement as a resocialization measure would have fallen foul of the proportionality principle.[160] It would

---

[153] Pieroth and Schlink (n 107) 70; Jarass and Pieroth (n 27) 471.
[154] Pieroth and Schlink (n 107) 70.   [155] Jarass and Pieroth (n 27) 471.
[156] *BVerfGE* 5, 85, 204; 27, 1, 6. See also *BVerfGE* 22, 219; Würtenberger (n 90) 1751; H. von Schewick, 'Verfassungsrechtliche Grenzen der Resozialisierung' (1985) *Bewährungshilfe* 3; B. Haffke, 'Gibt es ein verfassungsrechtliches Besserungsverbot' (1975) *MschrKrim* 246, 251; M. Walter, *Strafvollzug* (2nd edn, Boorberg, Stuttgart, 2002) 56.
[157] See Prison Act, § 4(1) and commentary thereon at 4.2.3.1.
[158] J. Feest (ed.), *Kommentar zum Strafvollzugsgesetz* (3rd edn, Luchterhand, Neuwied, 1990) § 2, mn 3.
[159] See 2.2.2 above.
[160] Solitary confinement is permitted under the Prison Act, § 88, but is drafted in line with a strict proportionality requirement: it would have to be justified that the measure was clearly indispensable to the security aim to be achieved.

either have been 'unsuitable', as there is no evidence that solitary confinement promotes resocialization, 'unnecessary', as there are many other, less invasive, measures which are 'as effective' in promoting resocialization, and/or 'disproportionate', as it would not have balanced the rights of the prisoner and the rights of those protected by the measures chosen (e.g. potential future victims of crime). Clearly, therefore, the legislature's power was restricted in that it had, in practical terms, to reconcile the resocialization purpose in the Prison Act with the proportionality requirement.

Finally, the legislature had to fulfil three formal requirements when limiting basic rights through legislation: the 'clarity principle' (*Bestimmtheitsgebot*); the 'specification principle' (*Zitiergebot*);[161] and the 'generality principle' (*Verbot des Einzelfallgesetzes*).[162] The 'clarity principle' would have affected the drafting of the legislation in requiring that legal provisions be 'clearly defined' so that the bearers of rights know what to do, what behaviour is prohibited or inhibited, or what kinds of rights they have.[163] It was therefore important that the legislation followed the FCC's stipulations by avoiding the use of 'general clauses' giving broad powers to infringe basic rights 'as much as possible'.[164] In particular, it would have been problematic to create a broad power to encroach upon basic rights (*Eingriffsbefugnis*) in the name of resocialization.[165] Rather, the limitations justified by resocialization would have had to be clear and specific. Under the 'specification principle' it would not have been possible to limit all basic rights through the legislation, but only those which had been particularly specified.[166] The 'generality principle' stipulated that rights-limiting legislation must apply generally (i.e. to all prisoners), thus prohibiting the singling out of a particular group of prisoners for resocialization at the expense of others.

To summarize, though the FCC had given the legislature authority to limit basic rights in the name of resocialization and some discretion to define what resocialization could mean or include, it did so in the context of a constitutionalized legal system, in which the legislature was already bound by pre-existing substantive and formal constitutional limits on the legislative process. In this system, the word 'limit' (*Schranke*) neither evoked a total negation, or disproportionate invasion, of basic rights, nor permitted broad, undefined powers to encroach unequally or inconsistently upon unspecified basic rights.

---

[161] Basic Law, art. 19(1), sentence 2.
[163] Degenhart (n 45) 117.
[164] *BVerfGE* 33, 1, 11. See quotation at 2.2.1.
[166] See Prison Act, § 196.

[162] Basic Law, art. 19(1), sentence 1.

[165] Haffke (n 156) 251.

2.3 CONCLUSION

The German Prison Act 1976 was to be infused with the ideals of the Constitution from start to finish. It had to deliver a constitutionally legitimate, coherent legislative basis for state limitation and protection of prisoners' basic rights at the 'administrative' level. The protection and limitation of these rights had to be commensurate with the constitutional ideal of resocialization. The FCC had inextricably linked prisoners' rights to the resocialization purpose of imprisonment, arguing that the basic rights to personality and human dignity, with the Social State principle, gave rise to this purpose. Basic rights and principles therefore became constitutive of the very purpose of imprisonment and prison administration. In realizing these constitutional ideals, however, the legislature had to resolve the tension between what Würtenberger referred to as '*Freiheit und Zwang*' (freedom and coercion).[167] It had to draw a line between state limitations of prisoners' rights and constitutional restrictions on state intervention.

To elucidate: the Prison Act had to provide a mechanism by which prison administration could be limited and held to legal account. Its limitation to those acts stipulated in the Act was reinforced by the *Rechtsstaat* principle of the 'legality of administration' (*Gesetzmäßigkeit der Verwaltung*). This provides that the administration shall (1) respect the priority of primary statute law over any other secondary source of law (*Gesetzesvorrang*); (2) apply the law (*Anwendungsgebot*); and (3) neither deviate from nor contravene the law (*Abweichungsverbot*).[168] The extent to which this could be effectively achieved, however, depended on the clarity and particularity of the provisions in question and thereby the extent of the discretion (*Ermessen*) granted by them. It was therefore imperative that the legislation followed the 'clarity principle' (*Bestimmtheitsgrundsatz*), which required that legal provisions be as clearly defined as possible. Equally, the Act had to specify explicitly which rights were to be limited and ensure that these limitations applied generally and not to one particular case.[169] Furthermore, the granting of substantive powers to encroach upon prisoners' basic rights had to be in line with the 'proportionality principle'.[170] Article 19(4) of the Basic Law also required that the Prison Act provide sufficient legal avenues to challenge the prison administration's actions under the Act and thereby fulfil the principle of legal protection (*Rechtsschutzgewährleistung*) by protecting the prisoner's access to a court of law.[171] In short, the Act was to be designed to protect the negative aspect of prisoners' rights by providing

---

[167] Würtenberger (n 90) 1748ff.
[168] F. Ossenbühl, 'Rechtsbindung der Verwaltung' in H.-U. Erichsen, *Allgemeines Verwaltungsrecht* (10th edn, Walter de Gruyter, Berlin, 1995) 172, 174.
[169] See 2.2.2.4 above.   [170] See 2.2.2.3 above.   [171] See n 82.

a clear legal limit to state action and an effective legal mechanism to enforce it.

In following the Social State principle and the prisoners' basic rights under articles 1(1) and 2(1) of the Basic Law, the Prison Act had to breathe life into the 'constitutional resocialisation requirement' and the prisoner's positive claim rights to a prison regime which promoted the prisoner's chances of resocialization.[172] In this sense the Act had to provide substantive provisions which could make up the kind of prison regime best suited to the resocialization aim. But the provision of substantive prisoners' rights, as the FCC had indicated in the *St. Pauli-Nachrichten* decision, was not the only object of the resocialization purpose: prisoners' basic rights could also be limited by measures aimed at their resocialization. The State was justified in doing this in pursuance of society's interest in the prisoner being resocialized. To summarize, the Prison Act needed to do three things in order to fulfil the 'constitutional resocialization requirement'. First, it had to provide a clear and unitary statement on the purpose of imprisonment; secondly, in the special provisions of the Act it had to entrench substantive positive rights for prisoners which further concretized the 'right to resocialization'; and thirdly, it could impose on prisoners specific duties which accorded with the resocialization aim.[173]

In fulfilling its constitutional duty to give legal form to the ideals enunciated by the FCC, Parliament had a significant margin of appreciation. This was evident from the explicit statements made in the *St. Pauli-Nachrichten* case, and was also a necessary concomitant of the process of legal concretization from broad constitutional principles. For all its lofty constitutional aspirations, the Prison Act was nevertheless to be indelibly marked by the politics surrounding its realisation. Chapter 3 will examine the broader legal and political context of the prison reform process and the legislative drafting of the Prison Act.

[172] See 2.2.2.2 above.
[173] Koepsel, (n 52) 44ff.

3

Reform Ideals and Political Compromise

The groundbreaking decisions of the Federal Constitutional Court (FCC) in the 1970s were deeply embedded in a broader process of prison reform. There was a direct relationship between the Court's interpretation of the Basic Law and the arguments of the prison reform movement. This movement drew on constitutional and criminal justice arguments resonant with Germany's legal and political culture and history. Its ideals were a key influence not only in the reasoning of the FCC, but also in the make-up of the Prison Act 1976. While the prisoner's legal status is embedded in Germany's constitutional environment, it is also a product of the 'rights rhetoric' of prison reformers.

The political forces in play during the final stages of legislative drafting were equally fundamental to the content of the Prison Act. The imperatives of German federalism gave rise to substantial tension between the Federal Parliament (*Bundestag*), committed to far-reaching reforms, and the Federal Council (*Bundesrat*), concerned to protect the administrative and fiscal interests of the states (*Länder*). The composition of the Prison Act thus reflects the compromise between reform ideals and political imperatives. This chapter examines the context in which prison reform ideals were shaped as well as the political and institutional imperatives which undercut their realization.

3.1 Reform Ideals

Penal reform in Germany encompassed movements for the codification of prison law on the one hand and the achievement of the resocialization purpose of imprisonment on the other. The Prison Act represented the achievement of both aspirations.

3.1.1 Prison Administration and the Codification Impulse

Calls for the codification of prison law significantly predate the enactment of the Penal Code of the German Reich in 1871.[1] Prominent in the early nineteenth century were the views of Hirzel, Mittermaier, and Von Holtzendorff, who argued that the basic principles of prison administration should be defined by Parliament and taken out of the province of administrative discretion. These arguments flowed from the imperatives of the *Rechtsstaatsprinzip*. It was contended that prison authorities and judges must be bound by clear principles concerning the execution of criminal judgments, judges should have clear control of the content of the punishment, punished persons should be protected by law against arbitrary administrative treatment, and the public must be informed of the extent of the hardship imposed by the prison authorities and of the steps being taken towards the rehabilitation of the prisoner. On the basis of the 'separation of powers doctrine' (*Gewaltenteilungsprinzip*), reformers maintained that Parliament should determine the content and administration of the punishment and the judge should enforce Parliament's will.[2]

Importantly, an Act regulating the administration of the criminal sanction was viewed as central to the achievement of the 'unity of the criminal law' (*Strafrechtseinheit*). The theory behind *Strafrechtseinheit*, which later came to be identified as the *Drei-Säulen-Theorie*,[3] saw the criminal law as a three-stage process whereby the material criminal law threatened punishment, the criminal judge imposed punishment, and the administration executed and administered punishment. Already at this early stage, prison and criminal law were conceptually linked in an 'internal relationship' (*Innere Zusammenhang*) concerning imprisonment. The material criminal law formed the legal conditions under which prison sanctions could be imposed, while prison law provided the substantive basis of the administration and execution of the sanction. In short, reformers argued that prison sanctions imposed under criminal law could only be properly executed through a law regulating prisons. Prison regulations thus became infamously branded as the 'last piece of customary criminal law'.[4]

These arguments were present in the debate surrounding the codification of the criminal law in the North German Federation of the 1860s,[5] and intensified with the introduction of the Penal Code in 1871. Moreover, with German unification, prison law codification was promoted as eliminating

---

[1] H. Müller-Dietz, *Strafvollzugsgesetzgebung und Strafvollzugsreform* (Heymanns, Cologne, 1970) 1ff.; B. Huber, 'Safeguarding of Prisoners' Rights Under the New West German Prison Act' (1978) *SAJC* 229; G. Kaiser and H. Schöch, *Strafvollzug* (5th edn, Müller, Heidelberg, 2002) 41.

[2] Müller-Dietz (n 1) 2.   [3] See 2.2.2.1.

[4] Wirth, 'Beiträge zur Frage über die gesetzliche Regelung des Strafvollzugs' (1873) 8 *BlGefk* 36.

[5] G. Kaiser, H.-J. Kerner, and H. Schöch, *Strafvollzug* (Müller, Heidelberg, 1992) 89–90.

differential treatment of prisoners across states and thereby achieving legal unity (*Rechtseinheit*) and equality before the law (*Rechtsgleichheit*).[6] Hence, 'the necessity for a Prison Act was widely acknowledged' in this period.[7] This was manifest in two proposals for prison law reform, namely the 'Bill on the Execution of the Prison Sentences 1879' and the 'Bill regarding the Administration of Prisons' in 1892.

Resistance to a Prison Act came from state executives, represented in the powerful Federal Council,[8] who were concerned about infringements of their executive independence and the costs involved in prison reform.[9] Instead of an Act, the Federal Council agreed in 1897 to the 'Basic Principles Applicable to Court-Imposed Prison Sentences until the Enactment of a Common Prison Regulation', an executive agreement widely criticized for reinforcing the discretion of states.[10] The impetus for codification of prison law thus faltered in the face of German-style federalism: a central element of her political structure borne out of the careful compromise necessary for German unification.[11] From this point on it was clear that any successful prison legislation would have to allow for substantial administrative autonomy at state level.

Calls for the codification of prison law continued after the turn of the century. Practitioners argued that 'the best Criminal Code remains incomplete without a good Prison Act'.[12] Objecting to the fact that the content of the prison sentence (*Strafinhalt*) was determined by administrative customary practice, the Society of German Prison Administrators published 'Proposals for a Law on the Administration of the Prison Sentence and other Security Measures' in 1913. While, in Parliament, the unsuccessful 'Preliminary Draft of a German Criminal Code' (1909); 'Alternative Draft of a German Criminal Code (1911); and 'Draft of the German Criminal Code (1913)' all incorporated provisions on the basic principles of prison administration.[13]

At the forefront of academic opinion were the views of Berthold Freudenthal, Rector of the *Akademie für Sozial- und Handelswissenschaft* and Professor of Public and Criminal Law at the University of Frankfurt am Main.[14] In his 1909 inaugural lecture, he argued that a Prison Act was a

---

[6] Wirth, 'Soll der Strafvollzug auf dem Wege der Gesetzgebung geregelt werden?' (1875) *BlGefk* 359, 362; K. Krohne, *Die gesetzliche Regelung des Strafvollzugs im Deutschen Reiche* (Schulze, Oldenburg, 1875) 2.

[7] K. Krohne, 'Der gegenwärtige Stand der Gefängniswissenschaft' (1881) 1 *ZStW* 53, 71.

[8] The powers of the Federal Council were enshrined in the Constitution of the German Reich of 1871.

[9] Müller-Dietz (n 1) 8.

[10] P.F. Aschrott, 'Die neuen Grundsätze über den Vollzug von Freiheitsstrafen in Deutschland' (1898) 18 *ZStW* 384; von Engelberg, 'Zur Frage des Strafvollzugs' (1898) 3 *DJZ* 195.

[11] See, in depth, D. Blackbourn, *The Fontana History of Germany: The Long Nineteenth Century, 1780–1918* (Fontana, London, 1997) ch. 5.

[12] Müller-Dietz (n 1) 15.   [13] Müller-Dietz (n 1) 11–12.

[14] F. Geerds, 'Berthold Freudenthal' (1969) *ZfStrVo* 251.

legal requirement of the *Rechtsstaat* principles of 'equality before the law' (*Gleichheitsgrundsatz*) and the 'legal proviso' (*Gesetzesvorbehalt*). The prisoner's legal status, he argued, had to be defined in law:

In the legal relationship between the State and the prisoner, nothing may be imposed on the prisoner which has not been included in the legal definition of the judicially imposed prison sentence.[15]

Freudenthal's lecture is still viewed as the classic exposition of the legal status of the prisoner, and his arguments were as influential in the prison reform debate after 1945 as they were at the beginning of the century.[16] His exposition, centred on defining the prisoners' legal status, was rooted both in the 'internal relationship' between criminal law and prison law and in broader constitutional principles.

Interrupted by the First World War, the movement towards the codification of prison law received new impetus in the reform climate of the Weimar Republic.[17] Proposals for a Prison Act were bound up with the criminal law reforms inspired by Gustav Radbruch, Professor of Law and Social Democrat Minister of Justice in the early 1920s. The primary aims of these reforms were the reinforcement of offender rehabilitation and,[18] in line with Freudenthal's views, the strengthening of the legal guarantees of the prisoner.[19] In 1923 the states agreed, in anticipation of a General Prison Act, to the 'Basic Principles of the Administration of the Prison Sentence' which enhanced the standardization of prison administration across states and highlighted the aims of prisoner correction. This was followed by the Prison Bill in 1927, which was presented alongside the Bill for a General Criminal Code. The simultaneous drafting and presentation of these two Bills reflected the continuing acknowledgement of the 'internal relationship' between criminal sanctions and the regulation of prison administration. The Bills would certainly have become law were it not for the dissolution of Parliament in 1930 and the demise of the Social Democratic Government three years later.[20]

Between 1933 and 1945, criminal law and prison administration became a tool of National Socialist ideology.[21] Punishment was aimed 'in the first

[15] B. Freudenthal, 'Die staatsrechtliche Stellung des Gefangenen', Rektoratsrede Jena 1910, printed in (1955) *ZfStrVo* 157. See also B. Freudenthal, 'Der Strafvollzug als Rechtsverhältnis des öffentlichen Rechts' (1911) *ZStW* 222; Kaiser *et al.* (n 5) 7.

[16] Müller-Dietz (n 1) 15.

[17] H. Müller-Dietz, 'Der Strafvollzug in der Weimarer Zeit und im Dritten Reich' in M. Busch and E. Krämer (eds), *Strafvollzug und Schuldproblematik* (Centaurus, Pfaffenweiler, 1988) 15.

[18] Radbruch was influenced by Franz von Liszt and the Modern Criminological School in this respect. See further 3.1.2 below.

[19] Müller-Dietz (n 1) 15.

[20] M. Fulbrook, *The Fontana History of Germany: 1918–1990—The Divided Nation* (Fontana, London, 1991) ch. 3.

[21] Kaiser and Schöch (n 1) 27–33; B. Olechinski, 'Strafvollzug in Deutschland vor und nach 1945' (1992) 2 *Neue Justiz* 65; P. O'Brien 'The Prison on the Continent: Europe, 1865–1965'

instance at deterrence' (*Abschreckung*), a policy to be maintained 'until the world of crime was wiped out'.[22] National Socialists also saw punishment as serving the secondary aims of prisoner atonement (*Sühne*) and retribution (*Vergeltung*).[23] Thus, in 1934 the executive amended the Basic Principles of the Administration of the Prison Sentence of 1923 to emphasize the deterrent and retributive elements of the prison sentence. A year later, the administration of prisons was placed under the central control of the Minister of Justice, a move later entrenched in the Ordinance for the Standardization of Prison Administration Provisions of 1940.[24] It hardly needs saying that during this time any notion of prisoners' rights was entirely eliminated: 'the prisoner can claim no rights, but must submit'.[25] Rather, under the National Socialist regime, prisons and concentration camps,[26] became synonymous with 'systematic repression and extermination'.[27]

The history of prison reform post-1945 was indelibly marked by its immediate past.[28] The extremes of the Third Reich provoked widespread calls for the 'rehumanization' of the prison system and for the 'total reform' of the criminal law. In this time of 'restoration', the immediate purpose was the denazification of criminal and penal law through fundamental reform.[29] While prompted by the Allied powers,[30] calls for denazification came also from Social Democrat academics, politicians, and prison administrators who had suffered under the Nazi regime and had come together in the Working Group for Prison Reform (*Arbeitsgemeinschaft für Reform des Strafvollzugs*).[31] Their first instinct was to call for a return to the criminal political ideals of the Weimar period. This meant three things: a recognition of the 'internal relationship' between the definition of criminal sanctions under the Penal Code and the administration of punishment under a Prison Act; a commitment to the notion of prisoner correction (*Erziehungsgedanke/Kriminalpädagogik/Spezialprävention*); and, importantly, a belief in the codification of prison law centring on the definition and protection

---

in N. Morris and D. Rothman (eds), *The Oxford History of the Prison* (OUP, Oxford, 1998) 178, 216ff.; Müller-Dietz (n 17).

[22] H. Frank, 'Der Sinn der Strafe' (1935) *BlfGefK* 191.

[23] K. Laubenthal, *Strafvollzug* (2nd edn, Springer, Berlin, 1998) 43.

[24] Kaiser and Schöch (n 1) 28–30.

[25] Christians, 'Die Sicherung gerechter Behandlung der Gefangen im deutschen Recht' (1935) 66 *BlGefk* 232, 242.

[26] W. Sofsky, *Die Ordnung des Terrors: Das Konzentrationslager* (Fischer, Frankfurt am Main, 1993).

[27] O'Brien (n 21) 217.

[28] Legislative change came immediately after the fall of the Third Reich, when, in 1945, the Control Council issued Directive No. 19 on the Basic Principles for the Administration of German Penitentiaries and Prisons. This Ordinance, while an interim measure, signalled a clear move from the practices of National Socialism.

[29] G. Blau, 'Die Entwicklung des Strafvollzugs seit 1945—Tendenzen und Gegentendenzen' in H.-D. Schwind and G. Blau (eds), *Strafvollzug in der Praxis* (2nd edn, Walter de Gruyter, Berlin, 1988) 19.

[30] Fulbrook (n 20) 141–50.   [31] Müller-Dietz (n 1) 24.

of prisoners' rights.[32] The latter had special resonance both domestically and internationally in the light of the horrors of the Nazi concentration camps.[33]

Despite this vocal reform movement, legislative initiatives towards the creation of a Prison Act were not forthcoming. Much of this was due to the belief, remaining predominant until the mid-1960s, that the 'total reform' of the criminal law had to be completed before a Prison Act could be properly discussed.[34] It was argued that the content and hierarchy of criminal sanctions had to be determined by the Penal Code before a law regulating prison administration could be enacted. Legislative initiatives regarding prison law were thereby stalled until the completion of the work of the Criminal Law Commission (*Große Strafrechtskommission*) which began in the early 1950s. Moreover, judicial development of prisoners' rights was hindered by the persistence of the administrative law 'special authority relationship' (*besonderes Gewaltverhältnis*) which continued to apply to prisoners for almost thirty years after the enactment of the Basic Law.[35] Thus, despite much talk of prison reform, the only legal change after the Control Council Directive of 1945[36] was the Service and Administration Ordinance of 1962 (*Dienst- und Vollzugs-Ordnung 1962*), an administrative agreement between the states which was heavily criticized by promoters of a Prison Act.[37]

Early work on criminal law reform was not without significance for prison reform, however. In the 1950s, the Ministry of Justice commissioned comparative research which included reports on prison reform developments in countries such as the Netherlands, Scandinavia and the USA.[38] The ideas in these reports were to have a strong influence on the proposals tabled in Germany in the early 1970s, and ultimately included in the Prison Act. In particular, exposure to penological thinking in Scandinavia and the USA shifted academic thinking from a traditional Weimar agenda, with its focus on prisoner correction (*Erziehung*) associated with the moral improvement of the criminal offender, to a more 'humane and social science-oriented' notion of prisoner treatment (*Behandlungsvollzug*).[39] More generally, by placing academic research and opinion at the centre of the reform debate, the report intensified an ongoing trend of academic dominance over penal thinking, known as the *Verwissenschaftlichung* of prison reform.[40]

Debate on the content of the Prison Act began in earnest after the publication of the first Draft Penal Code in 1962. The Draft Penal Code

---

[32] Blau (n 29) 19.   [33] O'Brien (n 21) 218.
[34] Müller-Dietz (n 1) 25.
[35] Blau (n 29) 20; T. Würtenberger, 'Freiheit und Zwang im Strafvollzug' (1969) *NJW* 1747, 1748. See 2.2.1.
[36] See n 28.   [37] See 2.2.1.
[38] *Materialien zur Strafrechtsreform: rechtsvergleichende Gutachten zur Strafvollzugsreform* (Bundesministerium der Justiz, Bonn, 1969) vol. 8.
[39] Laubenthal (n 23) 44.   [40] Blau (n 29) 21.

acknowledged that criminal law reform would only be complete once a Prison Act had been enacted, in so doing it restricted itself to determining only the 'type, duration and incidental consequences (*Nebenfolgen*) of custodial sentences (paragraphs 43ff.)'.[41] It left it to a future Prison Act to elaborate on the substantive aims and content of custodial sanctions. For this, the Draft Penal Code was heavily criticized by the Working Group of German and Swiss Criminal Law Professors (*Arbeitskreis deutscher und schweizerischer Strafrechtslehrer*), progressive penologists and criminal lawyers who came together privately to publish an Alternative Draft Penal Code in 1966.[42] These academics argued that the Draft Penal Code lacked a 'modern criminal political conception', restricted as it was to eliminating the doctrinal inconsistencies of the old Criminal Code.[43] The Alternative Code sought to create a coherent sanctions system in line with the aim of resocialization. This classified sanctions and set out substantive principles for their execution and administration.[44] The Alternative Code was picked up by the Free Democratic Party (*Freie Demokratische Partei*) in 1966 as their official legislative counter-proposal. This represented a 'turning point' in the politics of German criminal law reform in that it placed the resocialization ideal at the centre of the discussion on custodial sanctions.[45] The influence of the Alternative Code demonstrated, once more, the weight of academic opinion in the penal reform debate.

The Alternative Code was echoed by the Special Committee for Criminal Law Reform (*Sonderausschuß für die Strafrechtsreform*). This Committee was set up in 1963 to advise government on the reform of the Criminal Code and the 'criminal political problems of prison administration'.[46] The Committee heard a number of detailed representations by eminent penologists on the question of the content of a future Prison Act. Influenced strongly by these representations, it reiterated the view that the criminal law would only be complete once a Prison Act had been introduced and, importantly, that resocialization should be the aim of prison administration. Furthermore, it recommended instituting an expert Prison Administration Reform Committee (*Strafvollzugskommission*). This was achieved in 1967 when the Federal Ministry of Justice brought practitioners and academics together to work in committee on a Draft Prison Administration Act.[47]

---

[41] Müller-Dietz (n 1) 26.

[42] J. Baumann *et al.* (eds), *Alternativ-Entwurf eines Strafgesetzbuches (Allgemeiner Teil)* (Arbeitskreis deutscher und schweizerischer Strafrechtslehrer, Tübingen, 1966).

[43] A. Schönke and H. Schröder, *Strafgesetzbuch, Kommentar* (25th edn, Beck, Munich, 1997) 1.

[44] Schönke and Schröder (n 43) 1.

[45] G. Blau, 'Die Kriminalpolitik der deutschen Strafrechtsreformgesetze' (1977) *ZStW* 511, 534; C. Roxin, 'Zur Entwicklung der Kriminalpolitik seit den Alternativ-Entwürfen' (1980) *JA* 545, 547.

[46] Müller-Dietz (n 1) 38.   [47] Laubenthal (n 23) 46; Müller-Dietz (n 1) 38–40.

The establishment of the Prison Administration Reform Committee represented a breakthrough in the prison reform process, as this was the first time since 1945 that the content of the Prison Act could be discussed in an officially sanctioned forum. Given the widespread currency of views on a future Prison Act,[48] backed up by a substantial academic literature, the Committee was able to deliver a Draft Act with relative speed. It drew on the ideas contained in the Alternative Draft Penal Code in 1966 and was influenced by the views of eminent penologists such as Würtenberger, Schüler-Springorum and Müller-Dietz.[49] In 1971 the Commission Draft of a Prison Act was presented, and it was adopted in 1972 by the Government as their own legislative draft proposal.[50]

The speed with which the Committee's proposals were picked up by Government in the early 1970s was due, in no small measure, to the reformist political climate which had characterized German society from the mid-1960s. Beginning with the inclusion of the Social Democratic Party (SDP) in the governing 'Great Coalition' with the Christian Democratic Union (CDU) and Christian Social Union (CSU) in 1966, this tide of reformism intensified when the Social-Liberal coalition, made up of the majority Social Democratic Party (SDP) and the minority Free Democratic Party (FDP), was elected to government in 1969. The express Social Democratic (later to become the Social-Liberal) agenda was widespread reform of the legal system.[51] This included the five fundamental Penal Code Reform Laws,[52] the Introductory Act to the Penal Code,[53] the Prison Act (*Strafvollzugsgesetz*) 1976, as well as numerous smaller Acts changing specific offences in the Criminal Code.[54]

The reforms implemented by the Social-Liberal alliance were by no means limited to the sphere of criminal justice: also targeted were family law,

---

[48] Summarized in the well-timed report of the Criminal Division of the 48th German Lawyers' Conference (*Deutsche Juristentag*) in 1970 (a prestigious annual conference attended by practising lawyers, judges, and academics). See *Verhandlungen des 48. Deutschen Juristentages* (Beck, Munich, 1970).

[49] Würtenberger (n 35); T. Würtenberger, *Kriminalpolitik im sozialen Rechtsstaat* (Enke, Stuttgart, 1970); H. Schüler-Springorum, *Strafvollzug im Übergang* (Schwartz Verlag, Göttingen, 1969); Müller-Dietz (n 1).

[50] Bundesministerium der Justiz, *Entwurf eines Gesetzes über den Vollzug der Freiheitsstrafe und der freiheitsentziehenden Maßregeln der Besserung und Sicherung—Strafvollzugsgesetz* (Müller, Karlsruhe, 1971); *Regierungsentwurf eines Strafvollzugsgesetzes* (BT-Dr. 7/918, 1972/73).

[51] 31% of the criminal law reforms introduced between 1945 and 1982 took place between 1969 and 1977. The impact of the 1968 student demonstrations here is unclear from the literature. H.-J. Vogel, '10 Jahre sozialliberale Rechtspolitik' (1980) *ZRP* 1; K. Rogall, 'Stillstand oder Fortschritt der Strafrechtsreform' (1982) *ZRP* 124.

[52] 1 *Strafrechtsreformgesetz vom 25.6.1969* (BGBl I 645); 2 *Strafrechtsreformgesetz vom 4.7.1969* (BGBl I 717); 3 *Strafrechtsreformgesetz vom 20.5.1970* (BGBl 505); 4 *Strafrechtsreformgesetz vom 23.11.1973* (BGBl I 1725); 5 *Strafrechtsreformgesetz vom 18.6.1974* (BGBl 1287).

[53] *Einführungsgesetz zum Strafgesetzbuch vom 2.3.1974* (BGBl I 469).

[54] See overview in Schönke and Schröder (n 43) 2–3.

consumer protection law, and civil procedure.[55] With respect to criminal justice, however, the Social-Liberal programme included three fundamental aims. First, the Government continued the endeavours of the Criminal Law Commission and built on the Draft Criminal Code of 1962 by perfecting doctrinal criminal law in line with the constitutional ideal of *nulla crimen, nulla poena sine lege* (no crime and punishment without a law).[56] Focused mainly on the precision of offence construction (*Tatbestand*),[57] this work had originated primarily in response to National Socialist abuse of criminal law doctrine.[58] Secondly, the Social-Liberal Government was committed to 'humanizing' the criminal law by respecting the highest possible individual freedom. This was reflected in the attempt to restrict the scope of the criminal law only to those acts which were seriously damaging to society and only when other forms of legal intervention were not appropriate for such a social aim.[59] Frequently expressed as the ideal of *ultima ratio Strafrecht* (criminal law of last resort) or in the maxim *in dubio pro libertate* (in doubt favour liberty), this involved the decriminalization of certain offences, the redefinition of minor criminal offences as regulatory offences (*Ordnungs-widrigkeiten*), and the elimination of 'moral crimes'.[60] A corollary view was that implementation and administration of criminal sanctions should be as restricted and proportionate as possible. Thirdly, the Social-Democrat welfare-oriented agenda included giving effect to the resocialization ideal through the determination and administration of criminal law sanctions.[61] This was to have an effect on the type and duration of sanctions included in the Penal Code and would necessitate a law regulating prisons with the primary aim of prisoner resocialization.

Against the background of German post-war rights consciousness,[62] this reformist climate was fertile ground for campaigners for a new Prison Act. Their case was made easier once the first two Penal Code Reform Laws,[63] which dealt with the classification and duration of criminal sanctions, had been completed.[64] Moves towards the enactment of a Prison Act could no longer be defeated by the argument that reform of sanctions within the Criminal Code had first to be completed. Thus, in the early 1970s, the debate turned to the content of legislation governing the administration of prisons. It was in this climate, that the proposals of the Prison Administration Reform Committee and the ideas of penologists committed to prisoners' rights and resocialization were adopted as the Government's legislative proposals. Likewise, it was in this context that the FCC made its

---

[55] Vogel (n 51) 1.   [56] Expressly guaranteed in Basic Law, art. 103(2) and (3).
[57] Schönke and Schröder (n 43) 1.   [58] Blau (n 45) 515.
[59] Vogel (n 51) 1.   [60] Blau (n 45) 516.
[61] Vogel (n 51) 1.   [62] See 2.1.
[63] 1 *Strafrechtsreformgesetz vom 25.6.1969* (BGBl I 645); 2 *Strafrechtsreformgesetz vom 4.7.1969* (BGBl I 717)
[64] Laubenthal (n 23) 46.

groundbreaking decisions in 1972 and 1973.[65] There was, to say the least, a clear relationship between the Court's interpretation of the Basic Law in these cases and the views presented in the legislative draft proposals at the time. Once the FCC had given these proposals constitutional authority and set a deadline for the completion and enactment of a Prison Act, all that remained was for the German legislature to agree upon the content of the Prison Administration Act. This final drafting process benefited from a broad consensus around the general aims of the Act but involved significant compromise as to their concrete application.

Before moving on it is helpful to highlight certain characteristics of the prison reform movement in Germany. Germany has experienced a strong impulse towards the codification of prison law for over a hundred years. Centred on defining the prisoner's legal status, codification was founded on interpretations of constitutional principles and the relationship between prison law and criminal law, which had itself been the object of intense codification activity since the late nineteenth century. The commitment to the codification of prisoners' rights in Germany was also shaped by the broader historical context. Crucial here were the imperatives of German unification in the 1870s, the reformist climate of the Weimar period, the resolute commitment to the 'rehumanization' of prison law after 1945, and the aggressive reformism of the Social-Liberal alliance in the 1970s.

Importantly, the codification impulse was inspired and dominated by the arguments of the legal and penal academy. This process began with the arguments of Hirzel, Mittermaier, and Von Holtzendorff in the 1860s, was continued by Freudenthal and Radbruch in the early 1900s and picked up by Müller-Dietz, Schüler-Springorum, and Würtenberger after 1945. Legislative reform proposals in the area of prison law were thus primarily 'professor-made'.[66] The extent of academic influence is characteristic of the rationalist and categorical style of the codification method,[67] and a signal of Germany's civilian legal culture which has been heavily influenced by 'learned jurists' since the sixteenth century.[68] It is also indicative of the high status of academics in the eyes of the German people who, as Craig tells us, 'have always had an inordinate respect for their professors'.[69] The substance of German prison law can thus be explained not only in terms of its particular constitutional and legal roots, but also as an indication of the

---

[65] See 2.2.

[66] R. van Caenegem, *Judges, Legislators and Professors: Chapters in European Legal History* (CUP, Cambridge, 1987) 67.

[67] V. Gessner *et al.*, 'Introduction: The Basic Settings of Modern Formal Law' in V. Gessner *et al.* (eds), *European Legal Cultures* (Dartmouth, Aldershot, 1996) 89.

[68] On historical basis see: Van Caenegem (n 66) ch. 2.

[69] While the student protests of 1968 challenged German's unquestioning faith in professors and resulted in some reform of university structures, Craig argues that in less radical parts of German society their status remained high and continues to do so. G. Craig, *The Germans* (Penguin, London, 1991) ch. 8.

close relationship between legal writings and legal form within German legal culture.

3.1.2 Resocialization and *Zeitgeist*[70]

Legislators, reformers, and policy-makers in the 1970s shared a noticeable commitment to resocialization as a substantive aim of imprisonment and as a guiding administrative principle around which prisoners' rights should be shaped. The strength of this commitment is peculiar from a comparative perspective in that belief in resocialization was at its strongest in Germany just when, in Anglo-American penal discourse, it had begun to decline.[71] This contrast is explored tentatively below: 'generalised and abrupt conclusions should be avoided when attempts are made to search for causal connections or even parallelisms between phenomena as complex and fluid as ideology in criminal justice and the prevailing spirit of the age'.[72] For an outsider the task is daunting, and would be even more so were it not that German penologists were themselves acutely conscious of this divergence.[73]

In the 1970s and 1980s, the 'rehabilitative model' faced a crisis of political legitimacy in Britain, the USA and, notably, Sweden.[74] This crisis of 'rehabilitation' was characterized inside Germany in the following way. First, German penologists noted that the treatment model had been severely contested by Martinson's empirical study in 1974.[75] This was understood to generate the attitude that 'nothing works' with respect to the treatment of offenders, explained in Germany as '*Behandlungsnihilismus*' (treatment nihilism).[76] Secondly, German penologists recognized that 'rehabilitation' was negatively associated with excessive restrictions of the offender's liberty. This was said to be due to the fact that 'rehabilitation' afforded judges, parole boards, and prison psychologists considerable discretion to determine the length and type of the prisoner's sentence based on their perception of the offender's 'improvement'.[77] While harmful in its own right, it had the additional consequence of effectively making rehabilitation compulsory.

---

[70] With apologies to G. Kaiser, 'Resozialisierung und Zeitgeist' in R. Herren *et al.* (eds), *Kultur-Kriminalität-Strafrecht: Festschrift für Thomas Würtenberger* (Duncker and Humblot, Berlin, 1977) 359.

[71] Kaiser (n 70) 362.

[72] L. Radzinowicz, *The Roots of the International Association of Criminal Law and their Significance* (MPI, Freiburg, 1991) 57.

[73] Kaiser (n 70); T. Weigend, 'Neoklassisismus—ein transatlantisches Mißverständnis' (1982) *ZStW* 801; Blau (n 29) 23.

[74] See, in general, D. Garland, *Culture of Control* (OUP, Oxford, 2001) ch. 3; B. Hudson, *Justice Through Punishment: a critique of the 'Justice' Model of Corrections* (Macmillan, London, 1987) ch. 1; A. Bottomley, *Criminology in Focus: Past Trends and Future Prospects* (Martin Robertson, Oxford, 1979) ch. 4.

[75] R. Martinson, 'What works?—questions and answers about prison reform' (1974) *The Public Interest* 22.

[76] Blau (n 29) 23.   [77] Kaiser (n 73) 805–8.

This, German penologists explained, had made a mockery of the treatment model which should, at the very least, be premised on the voluntary and active participation of the offender.[78] Finally, rehabilitation was understood in Germany as being inhumane and paternalistic in that it 'pathologized' criminal offenders, thereby eliminating their free will and moral agency. Yet despite full recognition of all the reasons for the crisis of the 'rehabilitative ideal' outside Germany, most German penologists viewed 'imprisonment *without* the offer of resocialization . . . as inhumane and retrograde'.[79]

German penologists defended 'resocialization' on a number of grounds. One line of defence consisted in distinguishing the German term 'resocialization' from the Anglo-American term 'rehabilitation'. It was argued that the differences in meaning rendered objections to 'rehabilitation', in the Anglo-American sense, irrelevant in Germany. Both the standard German criminological dictionaries maintain that while 'rehabilitation' refers to the treatment of a pathological offender, 'resocialization' merely signifies in neutral terms the process whereby the prisoner, who in offending violates the basic prerequisites of social co-existence, is reintegrated into society.[80] 'Resocialization' is said to be less about 'curing' offenders of their 'criminal illnesses' than to ensure that their relationship to society is sufficiently restored in order to prevent them from committing further criminal acts. This dissociation from offender 'pathology' was initially presented in Kaiser's 1977 defence of resocialization where he maintained: 'it is hardly ever seriously argued in this country that offenders are generally, or mostly, sick; rather it is usually contested'.[81] For Kaiser, 'treatment' was rarely meant in the strictly therapeutic sense, but rather referred to 'general care, social assistance and charitable endeavours'.[82] The terms 'resocialization' and 'treatment' in Germany denoted assistance towards social reintegration, argued Kaiser, not a clinical response to 'pathological' offenders.

Whether this dissociation from 'pathology' is entirely convincing is less clear. For one, the German definition can be criticized for overstating the 'pathological' implications of the Anglo-American concept of 'rehabilitation', which stems from a small number of highly publicized cases in US prisons.[83] Moreover, it is difficult to draw a clear distinction between the aims of seeking to 'treat an offender' and 'assisting an offender to reintegrate into society', when one considers the potential similarity between the means of achieving them. Neither was the view that 'resocialization' could be dissociated from offender pathology held by all German penologists alike.

---

[78] See 4.2.3.1.   [79] Kaiser (n 70) 371. Emphasis added.

[80] H. Schellhoss in G. Kaiser *et al.*, *Kleines Kriminologisches Wörterbuch* (Müller, Heidelberg, 1993) 429; H. Janssen in H. Kerner (ed.), *Kriminologie-Lexikon* (Kriminalistik, Heidelberg, 1990) 278.

[81] Kaiser (n 70) 367.   [82] Kaiser (n 70) 371.

[83] D. van Zyl Smit, 'Leave of Absence for West German Prisoners' (1988) 28 *PL* 1, 13.

Blau explicitly associated 'treatment' with 'sickness',[84] while Eser's 1974 article *'Resozialisierung in der Krise'* reflected a similar perspective.[85] Equally, overtones of pathology could be heard in Hassemer's later statement that 'resocialization' takes the 'odour of the gaoler from the punishing State and gives him the dignity of the doctor'.[86]

A more plausible defence of 'resocialization' in Germany, rests on the difference between the legal frameworks in which 'resocialization' and 'rehabilitation' are respectively applied. As explained in Chapter 1, resocialization in Germany refers to the purpose of prison administration, as distinct from the purpose of punishment in general.[87] Thus, Weigend argued that those supporting a shift in Germany towards Anglo-American neo-classical punishment models were labouring under a 'transatlantic misunderstanding'.[88] He pointed out that civil rights objections to 'rehabilitation' had no relevance in the German context where 'resocialisation (is) only applied in as far as the requirements of retribution . . . allow'.[89] Thus, discretion to determine sentence length afforded by 'rehabilitation' was not present within the German system where the aims of sentencing were distinct from those of imprisonment.[90] Furthermore, offenders' voluntary co-operation in their treatment was guaranteed in Germany by the constitutional protection of their free will.[91] As a result, Weigend maintained that it would be mistaken to associate 'resocialization' in Germany with the negative consequences of 'rehabilitation' deplored in Anglo-American discourse. Moreover, Weigend argued that the Germans, with their view of the 'constitutional State', did not display the distrust of government intervention found in the USA in the years following the Watergate scandal.[92] In short, the legal impact of 'resocialization' could only be accurately viewed in the context of Germany's legal and constitutional culture.

A final argument raised in defence of resocialization was that empirical objections raised by Martinson's research had done little to threaten academic belief in resocialization inside Germany.[93] This was because so-called *Behandlungsoptimismus* (treatment optimism), which had existed in Anglo-American discourse, had never taken hold in Germany. Rather, caution about the results of offender treatment had been present in German penology since the beginning of the 1960s. Given this attitude, German penology received Martinson's controversial study with circumspection.[94] Penologists

---

[84] G. Blau, 'Aufgaben und Grenzen der Kriminalpädagogik' in M. Busch and G. Edel (eds), *Erziehung zur Freiheit durch Freiheitsentzug* (Luchterhand, Neuwied, 1969) 383.

[85] A. Eser, 'Resozialisierung in der Krise' in J. Baumann and K. Tiedemann (eds), *Einheit und Vielfalt des Strafrechts: Festschrift für Karl Peters* (Mohr, Tübingen, 1974) 505.

[86] W. Hassemer, 'Resozialisierung und Rechtsstaat' (1982) *KrimJ* 161.

[87] See 2.2.2.1.   [88] Kaiser (n 73).   [89] Kaiser (n 73) 804.

[90] See 2.2.2.1.   [91] See 2.2.2.4 and 4.2.3.1.   [92] Kaiser (n 73) 804.

[93] Kaiser (n 70) 369; Blau (n 29) 23.

[94] e.g., G. Blau, 'Die Entwicklung des Strafvollzugs seit 1945—Tendenzen und Gegentendenzen' in H. Schwind and G. Blau (eds), *Strafvollzug in der Praxis* (Walter de Gruyter, Berlin, 1976) 30.

maintained that there were no grounds for abandoning a 'criminal political strategy' which had always been based on a 'realistic' understanding of the limitations of offender treatment.[95] Moreover, empirical evidence conducted in Germany did not justify a movement towards 'treatment nihilism'.[96] Instead it was argued that treatment techniques should be refined, in the belief that resocialization strategies could only be adequately measured if given the time and resources to prove themselves.

For comparative purposes, it is less important whether these arguments in defence of resocialization are persuasive. Rather, it is vital to note that the majority of German penologists, for various reasons, actively defended resocialization as a penal strategy. For, as already indicated, the approach taken by the academy was central in shaping the dominant language of penal reform. While academic support alone might have validated resocialization as a strategy, their arguments were made weightier through recourse to constitutional rights and principles. The relationship between the prisoner's legal status and the *Rechtsstaatsprinzip* had long been acknowledged, but it was Würtenberger's writings in the late 1960s which established the crucial connection between the Social State principle and resocialization. Würtenberger argued that a constitutionally acceptable prison administration must be 'suffused with the spirit of the Social State principle'.[97] As a result the prisoner's legal status should be framed not only as a negative rights status (*Abwehrstatus*) but in the positive sense of a 'social integration status' (*sozialer Integrationsstatus*). In this way, Würtenberger argued that the prisoner's status would reflect the conception of freedom as 'social freedom' under the German *Sozial- und Rechtsstaat.*[98]

Würtenberger's argument, after being picked up by Schüler-Springorum in 1969 and Müller-Dietz in 1970, quickly became the standard position of penologists.[99] The central idea that prisoners held both negative rights against state intervention and positive rights to state assistance in their social reintegration became commonplace in the penological parlance of the early 1970s. These ideas were adopted by the *Strafvollzugskommission* and gained the legal approval of the Federal Constitutional Court in the *Lebach* decision of 1973.[100] After this, the drafters of the Prison Act were compelled to give legislative expression to Würtenberger's arguments: illustrating the influence of legal writings on the shape of German law.

If academic and constitutional authority favoured resocialization in the 1970s, so did the broader political climate. The post-war prison reform movement had always been committed to the achievement of resocialization

---

[95] Kaiser (n 70) 369; Blau (n 29) 23.   [96] Blau (n 29) 23.

[97] T. Würtenberger, 'Reform des Strafvollzuges im sozialen Rechtsstaat' (1967) *JZ* 233.

[98] Würtenberger (n 35) 1748.

[99] Müller-Dietz (n 1) 93–100; Schüler-Springorum (n 49) 169; see, in general, K. Koepsel, *Strafvollzug im Sozialstaat* (Doctoral Dissertation, Hamburg, 1985) 2–10.

[100] See 2.2.2.2.

as an aim of prison administration. Set in opposition to National Socialist administrative aims of retribution and deterrence (*Vergeltung- und Abschreckungsvollzug*), resocialization came to embody the values of humanization and the aims of 'denazification'.[101] It signalled a 'restoration' of the ideals of the Weimar period, when correction-oriented prison legislation had been promoted. With the Social-Liberal coalition victory in 1969, resocialization was elevated from a reform ideal to a governmental policy.[102] On the one hand, Social-Liberals were committed to the *Rechtsstaat* tradition which had marked German political culture since 1945 and underlined the call for entrenched prisoners' rights. On the other hand, the coalition was distinct from its governmental predecessors in that it sought to bolster the impact of the constitutional Social State principle through legal reform, including support for resocialization.[103] In these ways the coalition aimed to fulfil both its liberal and welfare-oriented agendas.

Social-Liberal support reflected also a long-standing historical affinity between social democratic politics and the resocialization ideal. This close alliance was manifest in von Liszt's Modern Criminal Law School and International Association of Criminal Law which, in the 1880s, argued that criminal sanctions should follow the social purpose (*Zweck*) of 'special prevention',[104] in particular the correction (*Erziehung*) of the criminal offender.[105] Viewed as the father of the modern resocialization tradition in Germany,[106] von Liszt's view of crime as a 'social disease' and his belief that punishment should fulfil a 'social purpose' was permeated by an ideal of 'justice in the sense of social equalisation'.[107] Such a position, Radzinowicz argues, stemmed to a large extent from von Liszt's 'sincere and firm dedication' to Social Liberalism.[108] In the Weimar period, the relationship between Social Democratic ideals and the aim of resocialization was reinforced in the work of Gustav Radbruch, von Liszt's eminent disciple. Radbruch remains

---

[101] M. Walter, *Strafvollzug* (Boorberg, Stuttgart, 1991) 32; Blau (n 29) 19.

[102] Vogel (n 51).

[103] Vogel (n 51) 1.

[104] Radzinowicz (n 72) ch. 9.

[105] Von Liszt distinguished three offender types: occasional offenders (*Augenblickstäter*) who could be dealt with by individual deterrence, offenders capable of correction (*Besserungsfähige*) who should be corrected through punishment (*Besserungsstrafe*); and offenders who could not be corrected (*nicht Besserungsfähige*) who should be incapacitated (*Unschädlichmachung*). See H. Jescheck and T. Weigend, *Lehrbuch des Strafrechts: Allgemeiner Teil* (5th edn, Duncker and Humblot, Berlin 1996) 4–7.

[106] Kaiser (n 70) 359; Schönke and Schröder (n 43) 1; Jescheck and Weigend (n 105). While commonly viewed as the originator of the resocialization ideal, Von Liszt's ideas were not entirely original. Notions of prisoner correction had already been championed by Theodor Fliedner (1800–1864) and Johann-Heinrich Wichert (1808–1881) in Germany long before this. See Walter (n 101) 21–9.

[107] Radzinowicz (n 72) 48.

[108] Radzinowicz (n 72) 48. Radzinowicz goes on to argue that von Liszt was also influenced by the insights of social Darwinism and theories of social defence.

one of the major legal theorists of the Social Democratic tradition. His ideas, which founded the resocialization-oriented reforms of the Weimar period, continued to be invoked by Social Democrats after 1945.[109] This was the case despite a shift from the nineteenth-century concept of resocialization as 'correction' (*Erziehung*) to the post-1945 conception of 'treatment for social reintegration' (*Behandlung*).[110]

There can be little doubt that the strength of this post-war commitment to resocialization owed much to the historical affinity between the social democratic conception of justice and resocialization as an aim of punishment. On the one hand, the Social Democrats were keen to revive the ideals of the Weimar period, which represented a 'golden age' in the party's history. On the other hand, the social democratic picture of law as an instrument of 'social justice',[111] lent itself to the view that punishment must have a 'social purpose'. In the words of Radbruch, 'the improvement of the criminal law should manifest not in a better criminal law, but rather in a right to "correction", which would be better than the criminal law itself'.[112]

In conclusion, at the time when the Prison Act was being drafted, a complex web of academic, reformist, judicial, and political opinion favoured resocialization as an aim of prison administration just when the ideal of rehabilitation was being widely questioned in the outside world. The strength of support for resocialization was a signal of Germany's legal and political culture, contingent upon a particular historical context. If the general aim of resocialization enjoyed broad support, however, the specific meaning of its legal implementation remained to be settled. This was one of the central issues which had to be resolved in the legislative drafting of the Prison Act.

3.2 POLITICAL COMPROMISE

Whilst the foundations of the Prison Act and much of its content were shaped by the ideals of the prison reform movement, the Act was equally formed by political compromises made in the final stages of legislative drafting.

German legislators were centrally preoccupied with the legal implications of the resocialization ideal. The opacity of this concept invited diverse interpretations from reformers and legislators. No sooner had the Prison

[109] Vogel (n 51) 2–4.
[110] Blau (n 94) 29. While 'correction' connoted the 'moral improvement' of the prisoner in order to create an 'ideal type' or 'middle class' law-abiding citizen, *Behandlung* was concerned with assisting the offender in his social reintegration by remedying personality and socialization defects through social therapeutic methods.
[111] This ideal was enshrined explicitly in the Social Democratic 'Godesburg Program' in 1891. Vogel (n 51) 1.
[112] G. Radruch, *Rechtsphilosophie* (Koehler Verlag, Stuttgart, 1950) 269.

Administration Reform Committee and Government Legislative Drafts appeared, than the Alternative Draft of the Prison Act was published by the Working Group of German and Swiss Professors alongside various other contributions.[113] If the Government Draft represented a moderate and pragmatic view, the Alternative Draft represented the 'idealist' position.[114] The Government, in line with the Prison Administration Reform Committee, saw the Prison Act as achieving the liberalization, humanization, and legalization of prisons through a clear recognition of the prisoner's negative basic rights and positive rights to resocialization. The emphasis was on maintaining prisoners' relationships to the outside world and on reinforcing their capacity to live a crime-free life through rights to access to the outside world, to home leave, to regime relaxation, to open prisons, and to work.[115] But a concrete and comprehensive commitment to resocialization involved guarantees on state spending which the Federal Government was anxious to sidestep. Thus the Government toned down the Prison Administration Reform Committee's proposals to make compulsory state provision of professional education, remunerated work, social assistance, and unemployment insurance for prisoners. In order to pre-empt opposition from state administrations, the Government used transitional clauses (*Übergangsregelungen*) to defer the implementation of these more progressive and cost-intensive measures to a later date.[116]

The idealist view of the Alternative Draft was unconstrained by the imperatives of political viability. It proposed a social-therapeutic prison administration based on the ideal of a 'problem-solving community' where inmates were actively included in institutional decision-making.[117] While acknowledging that the humanization and liberalization of prisons were worthy aims, it maintained that the central purpose of the Prison Act should be to give prisoners the capacity to live in freedom and to avoid coming into conflict with the law. 'This necessitated a far more extensive offer of assistance which, shaped by the newest results of behavioural sciences, could influence the offender's proclivity towards criminal behaviour'.[118] Social and behavioural therapy and education were viewed as integral to the

---

[113] J. Baumann *et al.* (eds), *Alternativ-Entwurf eines Strafvollzugsgesetzes* (Arbeitskreis deutscher und schweizerischer Strafrechtslehrer, Tübingen, 1973); H. Müller-Dietz, *Probleme des modernen Strafvollzuges*, vol. 45 (Schriftenreihe der Juristischen Gesellschaft e.V., Berlin, 1974) 7ff.; G. Kaiser, *Begriff, Ortsbestimmung und Entwicklung des Strafvollzugs* in G. Kaiser *et al.* (eds), *Strafvollzug* (Müller, Karlsruhe, 1974) 1; H. Jung and H. Müller-Dietz (eds), *Vorschläge zum Entwurf eines Strafvollzugsgesetzes* (2nd edn, Fachausschuß I 'Strafrecht und Strafvollzug' des Bundeszusammenschlusses für Straffälligenhilfe, 1974); *Stellungnahme zum Entwurf eines Strafvollzugsgesetzes* (Bund der Strafvollzugsbediensteten Deutschlands e.V., 1974).

[114] H. Müller-Dietz, *Strafvollzugsrecht* (Walter De Gruyter, Berlin, 1977) 55.

[115] Müller-Dietz (n 114) 53ff.

[116] R. Calliess and H. Müller-Dietz, *Strafvollzugsgesetz* (9th edn, Beck, Munich, 2002) 5ff.

[117] Müller-Dietz (n 114) 54ff.

[118] Baumann *et al.* (n 113) 3.

organization of prison administration and at the heart of the idealist conception of resocialization.[119]

Both the idealist and the moderate visions of the Prison Act were challenged in the final stages of legislative drafting, however, as the imperatives of German federalism led to the delivery of a compromised Act (*Kompromißgesetz*).[120] Federalism has always been a central feature of modern Germany's political structure, being born of the constitutional settlement of German unification in 1871 and reinforced in the Weimar Constitution and Basic Law. Historically, the power of the states (*Länder*) had led to the defeat of a number of attempts to codify prison law.[121] Small wonder then, that in the mid-1970s, it gave rise to painstaking political compromise;[122] as Feest warns: 'to understand the German prison system, it is necessary to understand federalism—German style'.[123]

Under the Federal State principle (*Bundesstaatsprinzip*),[124] the Federal Parliament has competence to legislate on penal measures[125] while state executives have the responsibility for administering prisons.[126] The Prison Act, while legislated and enacted by the Federal Parliament (*Bundestag*), was subject to the consent of the Federal Council (*Bundesrat*), which consisted of representatives of each state government. It was therefore constitutionally classified as a consent Act (*Zustimmungsgesetz*). The final version of the Act was indelibly marked by the conflict between state and federal representatives: the Federal Council sought to protect state financial interests and administrative flexibility,[127] while the Federal Government promoted its reform ideals and the administrative and legal benefits of federally applicable legislation.[128] This contest was played out in the twenty-seven sittings of the Select Committee for Criminal Law Reform (*Sonderausschuß für Strafrechtsreform*),[129] and finally in the Mediation Committee (*Vermittlungsausschuß*) called by the Federal Council to settle the final draft of the Act.[130]

Administrators in the Federal Council, backed by the Christian Democratic Union and Christian Social Union minority in the Federal

---

[119] G. Kaiser and H. Schöch, *Strafvollzug* (5th edn, Müller, Heidelberg, 2002) 51.

[120] K. Rotthaus, 'Die Bedeutung des Strafvollzugsgesetzes für die Reform des Strafvollzugs' (1987) *NStZ* 1.

[121] See 3.1.2 above.   [122] Rotthaus (n 120) 1.

[123] J. Feest, *Imprisonment and the Criminal Justice System in the Federal Republic of Germany* (Arbeitspapiere des Forschungsschwerpunktes, Soziale Probleme: Kontrolle und Kompensation, Nr. 8, Bremen, 1982) 9.

[124] Basic Law, art. 20(1).   [125] Basic Law, art. 74, point 1.

[126] Basic Law, arts 30 and 83.

[127] See *Gesetzesvorschlag des Bundesrates* 1973 (BT-Dr. 7/918) 107ff.

[128] Rotthaus (n 120) 1.

[129] *Protokolle der Sitzungen des Bundestags-Sonderausschusses für die Strafrechtsreform* (Deutscher Bundestag 7. Wahlperiode, Stenographischer Dienst, 1975).

[130] BT-Dr. 7/4662.

Parliament,[131] were anxious that the entrenchment of a unitary purpose of resocialization in the Act would be too restrictive of prison administration. On the one hand, they wished to promote administrative flexibility by incorporating general aims of punishment in the statement of the purpose of prison administration.[132] This threatened a central aim of the prison reform movement which was to establish a unitary resocialization purpose,[133] and was met with strong resistance. On the other hand, opponents of the Act were concerned about the impact it would have on the maintenance of security in prisons. This was heightened by anxiety at the time about the threat posed by prisoners who belonged to the Red Army Faction.[134] Moreover, the economic climate during the mid-1970s meant that state budgets were heavily constrained.[135] In this frugal fiscal climate, state executives were keen to exploit the legislative leeway given in the *St. Pauli-Nachrichten* case that prison reform should be achieved 'within reason'.[136]

As a result, some of the most progressive provisions in the Act were weakened in last-minute negotiations.[137] Importantly, anxiety about security led to late insertions in the wording of the purpose of prison administration,[138] and a broadening of the extent of the possible infringements on prisoners' basic rights through a catch-all security clause.[139] Moreover, concern with administrative flexibility led to the inclusion of a high level of administrative discretion in the special provisions of the Prison Act.[140] Most damaging, however, was the insertion of a number of transitional provisions (*Übergangsregelungen*) at the end of the Act, which allowed for deferred implementation or indefinite suspension of cost-intensive measures within each state.[141] These were designed to give state administrations time to adapt their prison policies and administrations in line with the more radical elements of the Act. In practice, however, the implementation of some of the central reforms of the Act were significantly delayed or indefinitely shelved.[142] This included, *inter alia*, delaying provisions on the level of remuneration for prison work,[143] and the indefinite suspension of the inclusion of prisoners in medical insurance and pension schemes[144] and the presumption in favour of placing inmates in open prisons.[145] Walter therefore

---

[131] See statement of Eyrich in Select Committee for Criminal Law Reform, *Protokolle der Sitzungen des Bundestags-Sonderausschusses für die Strafrechtsreform* (n 129) 1733.
[132] *Gesetzesvorschlag des Bundesrates* (n 127) 108.　　　　　　　[133] See 2.2.2.1.
[134] F. Dünkel, 'Die Rechtsstellung von Strafgefangenen und Möglichkeiten der rechtlichen Kontrolle von Vollzugsentscheidungen in Deutschland' (1996) *GA* 518, 519.
[135] Rotthaus (n 120) 2.　　　　　　　　　　　[136] *BVerfGE* 40, 276. See 2.2.2.3.
[137] Feest (n 123) 9–11.　　　　　　　　　　　[138] See 4.2.1.1.
[139] See 4.2.3.2.
[140] J. Feest and W. Lesting, *Totale Institution und Rechtsschutz* (Westdeutscher Verlag, Opladen, 1997) 16.
[141] Prison Act, §§ 198 and 201.　　　　　　　[142] See 4.3.2.2.
[143] Prison Act, § 200.　　　　　　　　　　　[144] Prison Act, § 198.
[145] Prison Act, § 201.

states that 'in order to find out which provisions are valid one must read the Act from the back to the front'.[146]

To conclude, many of the aims expressed during the process of prison reform were undermined in the final stages of legislative drafting where the imperatives of German federalism and consensus politics prevailed. Note, however, that while opponents of the Act were able to strike a number of compromises on the wording of specific provisions in the Act, they could not destroy its spirit. The Act is underpinned by deep political and penological ideals and, more importantly, clearly enunciated constitutional principles. These underlying principles are central to the ongoing survival of the Prison Act and the continuing development of prisoners' rights under German law.

3.3 THE PRISON ACT IN A CHANGING CRIMINAL POLITICAL CLIMATE

The 1970s represented the high point of social liberal values within criminal justice politics in Germany. The congruence and weight of opinion found at this time around the foundations of criminal and prison law has since been eroded. Starting in the late 1980s, the general consensus around the ideal of minimum state intervention through criminal law (*ultima ratio Strafrecht*) and the ideal of resocializsation has been challenged. Signals of this can be seen in the shifting contours of the criminal law, namely the extension of powers of State intervention in the name of criminal prevention (*Risikostrafrecht*), the creation of new crimes and the sharpening of criminal sanctions for particular crimes. These challenges to the ideals of the 1970s reforms have been linked to increasing anxiety about the state of 'law and order' or 'internal security' (*Innere Sicherheit*) within Germany:[147] an anxiety based on fears about the rise of recorded crime generally and organized crime in particular as well as a decrease in clear-up rates.[148] The result, as Hassemer declares, is an increasing identification of 'criminal politics' with 'security politics', a weaker political commitment to the protection of prisoners' basic rights, and a shift from a coherent purpose-based conception of the criminal law to the use of criminal law as an 'instrument of crisis intervention'.[149]

---

[146] M. Walter, *Strafvollzug* (Boorberg, Stuttgart, 1991) 250.

[147] On the different meanings of 'law and order' and *Innere Sicherheit* see L. Zedner, 'In Pursuit of the Vernacular: Comparing Law and Order Discourse in Britain and Germany' (1995) *S&LS* 517.

[148] W. Hassemer, 'Aktuelle Perspektiven der Kriminalpolitik' (1994) *StV* 333, 334.

[149] Hassemer (n 148); W. Hassemer. ' "Zero tolerance"—Ein neues Strafkonzept?' in H. Albrecht (ed.), *Internationale Perspektiven in Kriminologie und Strafrecht: Festschrift für Günther Kaiser* (Duncker and Humblot, Berlin, 1998) 793, 796.

With respect to prison law, the careful coalition around resocialization has been challenged from various quarters. Political moves were made to achieve a plural purpose of prison administration to reinforce security and allow for retributive considerations in prison administration.[150] Moreover, dissension as to the desirability of a resocialization-based prison administration is evident within the academy. This has come from alternative criminologists in particular who, inspired by Mathiesen and Christie,[151] have criticized the oppressive potential of the resocialization purpose.[152]

This political and ideological climate is an ongoing challenge to the survival of the Act's foundational principles and the development of prisoners' rights thereunder. As Chapter 4 will show, however, the continuing survival of the Act is linked to its deep constitutional underpinnings, its continued reinforcement by the FCC and the active commitment to its ideals from those in political and academic forums who were responsible for its creation.

3.4 CONCLUSION

The Prison Act is the compromised realization of competing imperatives. Importantly, the Act fulfilled, after nearly a century of reform attempts, the goal of the codification of prison administration. This 'codification impulse' grew out of the desire to create 'unity' within the criminal law and to fulfil what reformists identified as the legal imperatives of the *Rechtsstaatsprinzip*. After 1945, codification became bound up with the humanization of the criminal justice system. This was the objective of reformists, whose claims were strengthened by recourse to constitutional principles, and finally the clear demand of the FCC. The timing of the Act was tied up with the dynamics of the broader reform of the criminal law, a process accelerated by an aggressively reformist Social Liberal Government, whose criminal justice politics were reflected in the content of the Prison Act. The codification impulse and the ideals of the Act were also inspired by an influential criminological academy, which actively supported resocialization as a guiding principle of prison administration just at the time when many outside Germany had abandoned it. The ideals expressed by the reform movement were entrenched by the FCC in the creation of the 'constitutional resocialization principle'. Ultimately, however, the Act was weakened by a Federal Council concerned to ensure administrative flexibility, fiscal restraint, and public security. In this sense, the ideals of the Act were undermined by the power of the federalist consensus built into the German Constitution. Moreover, the ideals now entrenched in the Act continue to face challenges

---

[150] See, in detail, 4.2.1.
[151] Discussion with Johannes Feest, 29 August 2002.
[152] R.-P. Callies, *Strafvollzugsrecht* (Beck, Munich, 1992) 25.

in a contemporary criminal political environment, characterized by concern with '*Innere Sicherheit*' and growing intolerance of the Act's welfare and humanist ideals.

4

The German Prison Act: Principles and Special Provisions

The German Prison Act is compromised legislation (*Kompromißgesetz*).[1] It was meant to regulate all aspects of prison administration and the prisoner's *administrative* status in line with the Federal Constitutional Court's (FCC's) interpretation of constitutional rights and principles. It was required to give life to society's general interest in, and the prisoner's substantive right to, resocialization, as well as clearly defining the negative limits of prisoners' basic rights.[2] But the Act was also shaped by state executives concerned with administrative flexibility, fiscal restraint, and the maintenance of security.[3] The Act thus reflects a compromise between the ideal of strengthening prisoners' rights and the political imperative of retaining administrative discretion in prisons. This compromise has weakened the statutory protection of the prisoner's legal status, making it vulnerable to attack in a criminal justice environment increasingly hostile to the reform ideals of the 1970s.[4]

As a result, the Prison Act has received mixed reviews from German penal observers.[5] Whilst it is accepted that the Act represents a significant advance on the past, critics argue that many of the Act's provisions and their judicial and administrative application have fallen short of the constitutional and reform ideals they were meant to fulfil.[6] Foreign onlookers point to these local criticisms as evidence that the Prison Act is a failure for prisoners' rights.[7] But local German criticisms should be viewed in their proper cultural context. The constitutional and reform ideals articulated in the 1970s continue to provide an ambitious benchmark against which prison law is measured and a platform for critical penal observers. Local criticism can thus be read both as a signal of the strength and ambitiousness of these ideals, as well as an indication of the shortcomings of prison law. One need only look at the mass of publications on the subject of prisoners' rights and

---

[1] K. Rotthaus, 'Die Bedeutung des Strafvollzugsgesetzes für die Reform des Strafvollzugs' (1987) *NStZ* 1.

[2] See 2.3.   [3] See 3.2.   [4] See 4.3.   [5] See 4.3.2 below.

[6] H. Müller-Dietz, '20 Jahre Strafvollzugsgesetz—Anspruch und Wirklichkeit' (1998) *ZfStrVo* 12; F. Dünkel and A. Kunkat, 'Zwischen Innovation und Restauration. 20 Jahre Strafvollzugsgesetz—eine Bestandsaufnahme' (1997) *NK* 24.

[7] J. Vagg, *Prison Systems* (OUP, Oxford, 1994) ch. 8; R. Prowse *et al.*, 'Rights in Prisons in Germany: Blueprint for Britain?' (1992) 20 *IJSL* 111.

prison law to establish the dynamism of this debate.[8] Neither should one underestimate the impact of critical debate on the shape and development of prison law and the close relationship between penal research, legal scholarship, and judicial action in Germany. Prison law and the prisoner's legal status is not static. It is developed by the courts in response to critical legal opinion and the deeper reform and constitutional principles upon which these criticisms are based.[9]

This chapter unravels the network of extra-legal, legal, and institutional factors that affect the way the Prison Act is interpreted and applied. It begins by exploring the broader interpretative environment surrounding the Act and the critical exchange shaping its development.

4.1 THE BROADER ENVIRONMENT OF THE PRISON ACT

The legal application and development of the Prison Act is shaped by general principles of constitutional, criminal, and administrative law,[10] and marked by the German legal community.

Constitutional law has a ubiquitous influence over prison law. Under article 1(3) of the Basic Law all public bodies must promote and protect the rights and principles enshrined in the Constitution. Courts at every level are duty bound to apply constitutional principles and respect basic rights, while administrators are obliged not only to respect the legal limits of their discretion but also properly to consider fundamental rights and principles in each decision-making process. As a legislative basis for limiting basic rights, the Prison Act is amended, interpreted, and applied in line with the constitutional development of these rights. Moreover, the principle of *verfassungskonforme Auslegung* (constitutional interpretation of law) obliges prison administrators and judges to interpret the law in line with its constitutional foundations.[11] This is not only crucial where legislation is drafted ambiguously, but also for defining and structuring decisions pursuant to the Act.

The FCC does not exercise exclusive control over the implementation and development of the Prison Act. It can only intervene where the issue has constitutional dimensions. Where the issue in question relates to the mere application or interpretation of the Prison Act, it falls under the competence

---

[8] A crude comparison of the length of bibliographies in the standard prison law textbooks in Germany and England reinforces this point. G. Kaiser and H. Schöch, *Strafvollzug* (5th edn, Müller, Heidelberg, 2002) has a bibliography of 68 pages. S. Livingstone, T. Owen and A. MacDonald, *Prison Law* (3rd edn, OUP, Oxford, 2003) has a bibliography of 9 pages.

[9] M. Walter, *Strafvollzug* (2nd edn, Boorberg, Stuttgart, 1999) 373.

[10] H. Müller-Dietz, *Strafvollzugsrecht* (Walter de Gruyter, Berlin, 1977) 25.

[11] *BVerfGE* 8, 28; B. Pieroth and B. Schlink, *Grundrechte—Staatsrecht II* (13th edn, Müller, Heidelberg, 1997) 20ff.

of non-constitutional courts.[12] Nevertheless, given the centrality of constitutional principles to the construction of the Prison Act and the definition of
the prisoner's legal status, the potential for the FCC to exercise corrective
power and influence is considerable.[13] The symbolic and institutional power
of this Court and its relative independence from public opinion has placed
it in a strong position to develop the basic principles of prison law. Since the
Prison Act took effect, the FCC has issued 102 decisions involving prison
law.[14] The jurisprudence of the FCC is discussed in detail at 4.4 below,
although its influence is evident throughout this chapter.

The relationship between prison law and criminal law was examined in
Chapter 2.[15] Strictly classified as criminal law, prison law falls outside the
jurisdiction of administrative courts. This is viewed as a mixed blessing. On
the one hand, the jurisdiction of criminal courts to oversee the administration of punishment is said to be a consequence of their competence to determine and impose punishment.[16] This reflects the 'internal relationship'
between criminal law and prison law.[17] Institutional and legal expertise
regarding criminal sanctions are said to be best concentrated in courts
charged both with determining questions surrounding the imposition and
execution of the custodial sentence as well as those regarding prison administration. On the other hand, substantive administrative law principles apply
to decision-making under the Prison Act, and determine the use of administrative guidelines drawn up by states.[18] Moreover, it is argued that provisions governing prisoners' access to legal redress are best regulated by
administrative procedural principles,[19] and the structural organization of
the prison administration service is said to reflect general principles of
'administration organisation law' (*Verwaltungsorganisationsrecht*).[20] Feest
thus argues that prison law should be classified as 'a special type of administrative law'.[21] Whilst, Müller-Dietz notes that prison law is under the jurisdiction of courts which, while well versed in criminal law and procedure,

[12] Walter (n 9) 374. Matters of non-constitutional law are termed ordinary law (*einfaches
Recht*). See C. Creifelds, *Rechtswörterbuch* (Beck, Munich, 2000) 1058.
[13] J. Feest (ed.), *Kommentar zum Strafvollzugsgesetz* (4th edn, Luchterhand, Neuwied,
2000) 8.
[14] At the time of writing, this is the number recorded in the German JURIS database. JURIS
records all legal decisions published in Germany.
[15] See 2.2.2.
[16] H. Müller-Dietz, 'Die Strafvollstreckungskammer als besonderes Verwaltungsgericht' in
Präsident des Landgerichts Saarbrücken (ed.), *150 Jahre Landgericht Saarbrücken* (Heymanns,
Cologne, 1985) 335, 338.
[17] See 3.1.1.
[18] Müller-Dietz 1985 (n 16) 340. See 4.3.2.1 below.
[19] K.G. Kösling, *Die Bedeutung verwaltungsprozessualer Normen und Grundsätze für das
gerichtliche Verfahren nach dem Strafvollzugsgesetz* (Centaurus, Pfaffenweiler, 1991).
[20] Müller-Dietz 1997 (n 10) 26.
[21] J. Feest (ed.), *Kommentar zum Strafvollzugsgesetz* (4th edn, Luchterhand, Neuwied,
2000) 1.

lack the requisite administrative law expertise.[22] Those seeking to enhance court control of prison administration thus continue to call for courts to integrate principles of administrative law in the interpretation and application of prison law more effectively.[23] This issue is examined in more detail at 4.3.2.2 below.

Germany diverges from England in that academic opinion has traditionally carried more weight within the legal community. This has a bearing not only on the shape of the Prison Act but also on its legal interpretation and development. Academic writings are admissible legal sources in German courts and are frequently cited in judgments on prison law. The most influential academic sources are legal commentaries on the Prison Act, which are used as standard reference texts by administrators, judges and lawyers. In these regularly updated commentaries,[24] the Act, judicial decisions, legislative amendments, changing legal arguments, and new empirical insights are summarized, interpreted, and explained.[25] The breadth of the sources examined in these commentaries is important. Trained in both law and penology, the authors aim to provide guidance on the application of the law within a broader penal context. In these texts, one is just as likely to find guidance on technical questions of administrative procedure as one is to find reference to the damaging effects of 'total institution' culture.

The status and influence of academic commentaries rests on a strong tradition in Germany of 'close co-operation between courts and legal writers in developing the law'.[26] This stands in contrast to England's 'strong tradition of judge created law' which displays far less influence of the writings of penal or legal academics.[27] Commentaries also influence administrative and judicial practice for practical reasons. The Prison Act foresees the creation of a criminological service in each state to conduct research aimed at enhancing the 'treatment methods' used by prison administrators.[28] Prison administrators are thus obliged by the Act to keep abreast of a significant

---

[22] Müller-Dietz 1985 (n 16) 340.

[23] U. Kamann, *Gerichtlicher Rechtsschutz im Strafvollzug* (Centaurus, Pfaffenweiler, 1991) 206 and 336; Kösling (n 19) 278ff.

[24] R.-P. Calliess and H. Müller-Dietz, *Strafvollzugsgesetz* (Beck, Munich, 2002) (henceforth Calliess/Müller-Dietz); H.-D. Schwind and A. Böhm, *Strafvollzugsgesetz* (3rd edn, Walter de Gruyter, Berlin, 1999) (henceforth Schwind/Böhm); J. Feest (ed.), *Kommentar zum Strafvollzugsgesetz* (4th edn, Luchterhand, Neuwied, 2000) (henceforth Feest).

[25] D. Frehsee, 'Neuere Tendenzen in der aktuellen Kommentar- und Lehrbuchliteratur zum Strafvollzug' (1993) *NStZ* 165.

[26] R. Zimmerman in W. Ebke and M. Finkin (eds), *Introduction to German Law* (Kluwer, The Hague, 1996) 22.

[27] J. Allison, *A Continental Distinction in the Common Law* (OUP, Oxford, 2000) 25–9; M. Forster, 'The Significance and Function of Legal Citations: Comparative-law efforts to Standardize Citation Practice' in V. Gessner *et al.* (eds), *European Legal Cultures* (Dartmouth, Aldershot, 1996) 128. This is shifting with the introduction of the HRA 1998. See 6.1.1 and 6.1.3.1.

[28] Prison Act, § 166.

amount of criminological research.[29] Moreover, the large number of judicial decisions makes it difficult for courts and administrators to maintain an overview.[30] In this context, commentaries that summarize the case law and empirical research are essential.

The focus and influence of academic commentaries is not uniform, however. The Calliess/Müller-Dietz commentary, written by one of the leading prison reformers of the 1970s, places the most emphasis on developing existing legal doctrine. It has significant influence on prison law jurisprudence, not least because it is published in the prestigious C.H. Beck commentary series.[31] The Schwind/Böhm commentary, comprising contributions from leading members of state justice and prison administrations, is oriented towards prison administrative practice. The Alternative Commentary is the most critical of the Prison Act, offering the most provocative interpretations and suggestions for change. It has less influence on the daily practice of judges and administrators but provides a useful forum for academic and political debate and is increasingly referred to in FCC judgments. Aside from legal commentaries, standard prison law textbooks also have influence,[32] while journal articles are usually only consulted by the highest courts and the academy. Both of these sources find their main exposure to the broader legal community through inclusion in relevant commentaries.

With no formal system of binding precedent in Germany, judicial decisions on the Prison Act are solely binding on the instant parties. The only formal authority which judges and administrators are bound to follow is the norm itself and certain decisions of the FCC.[33] Judicial decisions, like academic commentaries, are therefore formally viewed as persuasive material. The extent of the persuasiveness of each decision is dependent on its position within the court hierarchy. The Federal Supreme Court (*Bundesgerichtshof*—BGH) is of such a high status that its decisions amount to legal authority in practice. The Court's primary function is the achievement of legal uniformity across the states. It is thus called upon to make a final determination in non-constitutional questions of prison law, where a judgment of a Higher State Court deviates from previous decisions of other Higher Regional Courts or from that of the Federal Supreme Court. Given this position, the Federal Supreme Court also has significant influence on the meaning and application of the Prison Act and has made sixty-four decisions

---

[29] Calliess/Müller-Dietz, § 166.

[30] There are no official statistics relating to the number of first instance prisoner complaints. The number of appeals brought under the Prison Act ranges between 1,100 and 1,600 per annum and it is estimated that the number of first instance cases are probably about three times as high. J. Feest, W. Lesting, and P. Selling, *Totale Institution und Rechtsschutz* (Westdeutscher Verlag, Opladen, 1997) 38–9.

[31] A. Böhm, 'Zur "Verrechtlichung des Strafvollzugs" ' (1992) *ZfStrVo* 37.

[32] K. Laubenthal, *Strafvollzug* (2nd edn, Springer, Berlin, 1998); Kaiser/Schöch (n 8); Walter (n 9); R.P. Calliess, *Strafvollzugsrecht* (Beck, Munich, 1992).

[33] Constitutional Court Act, § 31.

on prison law since the Act came into force.[34] The remaining courts are divided into hierarchies within each state, with the Higher Regional Courts (*Oberlandesgericht*—OLG) at the peak and the regional courts (*Landgericht*—LG) below them. Higher Regional Court decisions form a significant part of the body of prison law.[35] All Higher Regional Court decisions have persuasiveness nationally but in practice they have greater legal weight in their home state. The first instance Prison Courts (*Strafvollstreckungskammer*) are chambers of the regional courts.[36] As courts of first instance, these decisions carry a low measure of legal persuasiveness. However, they deal with by far the highest number of prisoners' claims, and there remain a variety of legal questions which have only been addressed by these courts.[37]

Finally, it is worth noting that courts and academics can draw on published debates, committee reports, and other preparatory materials produced during the legislative drafting of the Prison Act. As a result, there is frequent recourse to arguments presented in the legislative reform process in the 1970s.[38] These are used to support interpretations of Prison Act provisions and invoked to reiterate its conceptual roots and ideals. Interpretations of the Prison Act are thus framed by the political and intellectual tone of its original drafters.

To sum up, the Prison Act stands against the background of a distinctively German interpretive community and broader principles of German constitutional, administrative, and criminal law. The influence of these factors on the development of the prisoner's legal status will become evident in the remainder of this chapter. Section 4.2 of this chapter addresses the substantive principles of the Act and the interpretative conflicts surrounding them. Section 4.3 deals with the special provisions of the Act and the concerns raised with respect to the enforcement of substantive prisoners' rights. Section 4.4 outlines recent jurisprudence of the FCC which has attempted to remedy many of the weaknesses of the Prison Act, and to address the concerns of the penal academy which have been raised over the last twenty-five years.

---

[34] This figure is from the JURIS database.

[35] At the time of writing, JURIS records 1,235 Higher Regional Court decisions on matters of prison law since 1976, although it is important to note that not all decisions are published.

[36] The small single-judge chambers are responsible for checking the exercise of prison administration on the basis of the Prison Act. The larger chambers, with three judges present, determine questions of sentence execution and parole on the basis of substantive and procedural criminal law.

[37] At the time of writing, JURIS records 217 Regional Court decisions since 1976, although this is only a small sample of the courts' work most of which remains unpublished.

[38] e.g., Dissenting opinion of Judge Mahrenholz in *BVerfGE*, 64, 261 at 285.

4.2 The Prison Act: Fundamental Principles

In a style characteristic of legal codes, the Prison Act's founding principles are set out in paragraphs 2–4. These regulate the statutory purpose of imprisonment, the basis of prison administration and the legal status of the prisoner. The remaining provisions of the Act are systematic and comprehensive concretizations of these fundamental principles and are meant to be interpreted purposively in line with them.[39] Given the centrality of the principles to the Prison Act and the prisoner's legal status, much hinges on their legal meaning. The following sections therefore examine these principles and the interpretative conflicts which have arisen around them.

4.2.1 The Statutory Purpose of Imprisonment

The resocialization purpose of the Prison Act, enshrined in paragraph 2, shapes the exercise of prison administration in a general and in a particular sense. Generally, it provides an overarching interpretative guide to the Prison Act and an ultimate criterion upon which administrative decisions are made. Under paragraph 155(1) of the Prison Act, the prison administration is bound to observe and safeguard the purpose set out in paragraph 2. Accordingly, under paragraph 154 of the Prison Act, prison administrative agents must work together towards the resocialization of offenders and prison officers should closely co-operate with, amongst others, parole officers, social workers, and employment agencies. Under paragraph 151(2) of the Prison Act, prison inspectors are advised to work with specialists when inspecting prison treatment and other measures. Furthermore, the Act requires each state justice administration (*Landesjustizverwaltung*) to establish a 'criminological service' which, together with penal research institutions, should develop and refine treatment methods to further resocialization.[40] Hence, in a general sense, 'the prison climate must be conducive to resocialization' (*resozialisierungsfreundlich*).[41]

In a particular sense, the resocialization purpose is established in provisions determining the rights of prisoners, the organization of the prisoner's sentence, and the structure and organization of the prison administration.[42] Provisions regulating the 'treatment examination' of the prisoner and the staged organization of the prisoner's sentence plan;[43] the prisoner's eligibility for open prison, regime relaxation measures, and prison leave;[44] prison work, education, and training;[45] access to the outside world;[46] and social

---

[39] Laubenthal (n 32) 123.   [40] Prison Act, § 166.
[41] Schwind/Böhm, §2, mn 10.
[42] Calliess/Müller-Dietz § 2, mn 3; Laubenthal (n 32) 52; Walter (n 9) 57, mn 53.
[43] Prison Act, §§ 6, 7.   [44] Prison Act, §§ 10, 11, 13.
[45] Prison Act, §§ 37–52.   [46] Prison Act, §§ 23–36.

assistance and therapeutic treatment[47] are all viewed as expressions of the statutory purpose of resocialization and are meant to be read in this light. The legal interpretation of paragraph 2 of the Prison Act is therefore fundamental to the exercise of prison administration and the prisoner's experience of imprisonment. It is also a primary indicator of the extent to which the Act fulfils the prisoner's constitutional right to resocialization.

4.2.1.1 A Unitary Resocialization Purpose?

As a result of the statutory and constitutional importance of resocialization, a central aim of reformers was that the Prison Act should entrench a unitary resocialization purpose of prison administration. However, the final wording of paragraph 2 of the Prison Act, which was amended to allay security fears,[48] was ambiguous on this issue. It states as follows:

In the administration of the prison sentence, the prisoner should become capable of leading a socially responsible life free of criminal activity (aim of imprisonment). The administration of the prison sentence also serves the protection of society from further criminal offences.

The wording raises two potentially conflicting purposes of prison administration: resocialization and the protection of the public from crime. With some exceptions,[49] however, the majority in the legal community argue that paragraph 2 enshrines resocialization as the primary aim of prison administration.[50] Given its form and context, it is generally argued that paragraph 2, sentence 2 does *not* represent an additional positive imprisonment aim which is equal to resocialization. The latter is viewed, not as a purpose, but as a reference to the intrinsic incapacitation (*Sicherung*) function of the prison.[51] When interpreting paragraph 2, commentators point to the words 'aim of imprisonment' in parentheses at the end of the first sentence, the word 'also' in the second sentence which is said to imply a hierarchy between the resocialization aim and the incapacitation function of imprisonment, governmental guidance and opinions expressed during legislative drafting, and the view of the FCC that the prisoner holds a constitutional right to resocialization. This categorical constitutional guidance,[52] which

---

[47] Prison Act, §§ 9 and 70–75.   [48] See 3.2.

[49] T. Grunau and E. Tiesler, *Strafvollzugsgesetz* (Heymanns, Cologne, 1977) § 2, mn 1.

[50] Kaiser/Schöch (n 8) 232; Walter (n 9) 271; Calliess/Müller-Dietz, § 2, mn 1ff.; Schwind/Böhm, § 2, mn 7 and 10ff.; Feest, § 2, mn 6; Laubenthal (n 32) 55; H. Schwind, 'Zum Sinn der Strafe und zum Ziel (Zweck) des (Straf-) Vollzugs' (1981) 23 *Bewährungshilfe* 351; G. Bemman, 'Im Vollzug der Freiheitsstrafe soll der Gefangene fähig werden, künftig in sozialer Verantwortung ein Leben ohne Straftaten zu führen' (1988) 12 *StV* 549; *BVerfGE* 35, 202; 40, 276; 45, 187; *BVerfG Beschl.* (1998) *NJW* 3337; (1998) *NStZ* 430; (1998) *StV* 434; *LG Frankfurt* (1987) *StV* 301ff.

[51] Calliess/Müller-Dietz, § 2, mn 1; Schwind/Böhm, § 2, mn 16.

[52] *BVerfGE* 35, 202; 40, 276.

has continued after the implementation of the Prison Act,[53] bolsters the general consensus that 'the earlier competition between the resocialisation aim and the aim of public security no longer exists'.[54]

What then is the relationship between resocialization and public security? The most influential view on this issue is presented in the Calliess/Müller-Dietz commentary:

While the aspect of imprisonment elucidated in sentence 2 is to be considered when pursuing the sole stated purpose of imprisonment in sentence 1, it does not present an independent aim of imprisonment. This is because the function [*Aufgabe*] of the protection of the public, while belonging to the nature [*Wesen*] of imprisonment, is neither its aim [*Ziel*] nor its purpose [*Zweck*].[55]

By this interpretation we are to understand that protection of the public, while inescapably part of imprisonment, is not its ultimate purpose. Rather, protection of the public is a necessary function of imprisonment which can temper the primary aim of resocialization. This intricate relationship is best explained by example. The Prison Act contains various regime relaxation[56] provisions aimed at enhancing prisoners' relationships with the outside world and thereby their chances of reintegrating into society after release. The realization of prisoners' rights under these provisions is, however, contingent upon establishing that there is no danger that prisoners would misuse their rights to commit further crimes (*Mißbrauchsgefahr*) outside the prison. Before placing prisoners in open prisons,[57] relaxing their sentence regime,[58] or granting leave from prison,[59] prison officials must be satisfied that there is no 'danger of misuse'. According to the Calliess/Müller-Dietz interpretation of paragraph 2, these special provisions should be construed in favour of resocialization. Thus, when exercising their discretion in these cases, prison officials must show clearly that a 'danger of misuse' and risk to public security exists and give reasons for their decision *not* to grant the prisoner leave. Deviation from achievement of the resocialization purpose on the grounds of protecting the public from further crimes therefore needs to be justified by prison officials, whereas achievement of the resocialization purpose does not.

Schwind/Böhm are less optimistic about the legislative balance between resocialization and public security. While agreeing that the wording of paragraph 2 implies a primacy of resocialization over public security, they argue

---

[53] *BVerfGE* 45, 187; *BVerfG Beschl.* (1993) *NJW* 3188; (1998) *NJW* 3337; (1998) *NStZ* 430; (1998) *StV* 434. See 4.4 below.

[54] Schwind (n 50).

[55] Calliess/Müller-Dietz, § 2, mn 1. Supported by: D. Haberstroh, 'Grundlagen des Strafvollzugsrechts' (1982) *Jura* 617, 619; Laubenthal (n 32) 66; Feest, § 2, mn 13.

[56] The term 'regime relaxation' refers here to transfer to open prison and various forms of leave, which is distinct from the term 'relaxations' (*Lockerung*) which strictly refers to leave measures under Prison Act, § 11.

[57] Prison Act, § 10.   [58] Prison Act, § 11.   [59] Prison Act, § 13.

that regime relaxation provisions give priority to security in that they allow for the 'danger of misuse' to disqualify a prisoner from being afforded their rights. On this basis, they argue that 'the legislator should have faced up to this unavoidable conflict of aims and been more courageous with respect to the balancing process between them in each individual case'.[60] Calliess/Müller-Dietz and others insist, however, that Schwind/Böhm fail to distinguish between the resocialization 'purpose' and the security 'function' of imprisonment and thus fail to appreciate the presumption in the Act's general and special provisions in favour of resocialization.[61] This presumption, which is consistent with the constitutional entrenchment of the prisoner's right to resocialization, has recently been reinforced in a number of FCC decisions dealing with regime relaxation.[62] The Calliess/Müller-Dietz perspective, therefore, now appears the more legally authoritative position.

There was also controversy in the 1980s regarding whether paragraph 2 of the Prison Act precluded prison administrators from following general aims of punishment, in particular, retribution. The controversy arose despite the clear wording of paragraph 2, which at no stage suggests the applicability of these aims. The problems began, shortly after the Act came into force, when Higher Regional Courts considered the legality of decisions declining applications for prison leave from life-sentenced prisoners convicted for 'inconceivably cruel' murders of Jews during the Third Reich.[63] These courts held that a decision not to grant leave under paragraph 13 of the Prison Act to particular categories of life-sentenced prisoners could be justified by reference to the seriousness of the original crime committed. Despite its ongoing support for the 'constitutional resocialization principle',[64] the FCC accepted, in 1983, that the gravity of the original offence could be considered where the crime committed was particularly 'heinous'.[65] Notwithstanding a strong dissenting opinion in this judgment[66] and widespread opprobrium from the legal academy,[67] Higher Regional Courts continued to apply the 'gravity of original offence' principle to an

---

[60] Schwind/Böhm, § 2, mn 8.

[61] Calliess/Müller-Dietz, § 2, mn 1; Laubenthal (n 32) 67; Kaiser/Schöch (n 8) 232.

[62] *BVerfG Beschl.* (1998) NStZ 430; (1998) StV 434; (1998) NJW 1133. See 4.4.1 below.

[63] *OLG Karlsruhe* (1978) JR 213; *OLG Frankfurt* (1979) NJW 1173; *OLG Nürnberg* (1980) ZfStrVo 122; *OLG Frankfurt* (1981) NStZ 157; *OLG Hamm* (1981) NStZ 495.

[64] The principle was explicitly endorsed immediately after the Prison Act came into force in *BVerfGE* 45, 187. Here the Court held that the 'right to resocialization' was held by *all* prisoners, including lifers who had to be given a realizable chance of regaining their freedom.

[65] *BVerfGE* 64, 261.

[66] Dissenting opinion from Judge Mahrenholz *BVerfGE* 64, 261, 285.

[67] P. Meier-Beck, 'Schuld und Generalprävention im Vollzug der Freiheitsstrafe' (1984) MDR 447; W. Hill, 'Tatschuld und Strafvollzug: Analyse eines Beschlusses des Bundesverfassungsgerichts' (1986) ZfStrVo 139; H. Müller-Dietz, 'Schuldschwere und Urlaub aus der Haft' (1984) JR 353; H. Müller-Dietz, 'Strafvollzug, Tatopfer und Strafzwecke' (1985) GA 147; H. Beckmann, 'Anmerkung zu BVerfGE 64, 261' (1984) StV 165.

even wider category of prisoners and dispositions under the Prison Act. It was accepted that all life-sentenced prisoners be judged on this basis,[68] as well as fixed-term prisoners who had committed heinous crimes.[69] Moreover, courts applied the gravity of offence principle to other provisions in the Act, such as further regime relaxation measures,[70] transfer provisions,[71] and rights to information under the Act.[72]

This controversial judicial trend was not uniform nationally. Certain Higher Regional Courts stated explicitly that the seriousness of the original offence was only relevant to leave applications from a narrow class of prisoners whose personal guilt was exceptionally high.[73] These decisions were in line with the class of offenders foreseen by the FCC in 1983.[74] Some courts noted that the gravity of offence was merely one element, amongst many, which could be taken into account in the exercise of discretion under the Act,[75] whilst other courts restated the resocialization purpose and opposed the application of the gravity of offence principle.[76] The more controversial judicial tendency, however, was picked up by state administrations, which began lobbying to amend the Prison Act in order to reinstate a plural prison administration purpose. Had such an amendment passed, the states would have succeeded in 'reshaping the law'.[77] After some debate, however, these proposals were dropped from the Bill for the Amendment of the Prison Act which was presented by the Federal Council in 1988.[78]

Needless to say, this controversial judicial activity and the threat of legislative amendment gave rise to extensive academic debate.[79] Most academics

---

[68] *OLG Nürnberg* (1984) *ZfStrVo* 114; *OLG Stuttgart* (1984) *NStZ* 525; *OLG Karlsruhe* (1989) *NStZ* 247.

[69] *OLG Frankfurt* (1983) *NStZ* 140; *OLG Nürnberg* (1984) *NStZ* 92.

[70] *OLG Nürnberg* (1980) *ZfStrVo* 1122; *OLG Stuttgart* (1984) *NStZ* 525; *OLG Stuttgart* (1986) *ZfStrVo* 117.

[71] *OLG Frankfurt* (1983) *NStZ* 140.

[72] *LG Hamburg* (1977) *ZfStrVo* SH 33; *OLG München* (1979) *ZfStrVo* SH 67.

[73] *OLG Celle* (1984) *ZfStrVo* 251.　　　[74] *BVerfGE* 64, 261.

[75] *OLG Stuttgart* (1984) *NStZ* 525.

[76] *OLG Stuttgart* (1985) *StV* 466; *LG Heilbronn* (1986) *StV* 259; *LG Heilbronn* (1986) *MDR* 697.

[77] Kaiser/Schöch (n 8) 241.

[78] *Konferenz der Justizminister und -senatoren, Beschlußprotokoll vom 4.6.1987* (BT 7/3218) 7.

[79] K. Peters, 'Beurlaubung von zu lebenslanger Freiheitsstrafe Verurteilten' (1978) *JR* 177; R. Scholz, '10 Jahre Strafvollzugsgesetz (1986) *Bewährungshilfe* 361; W. Bayer et al., 'Tatschuldausgleich und vollzugliche Entscheidungen' (1987) *MschrKrim* 167; H. Schüler-Springorum, 'Tatschuld im Strafvollzug' (1989) *StV* 262; F. Arloth, 'Strafzwecke im Strafvollzug' (1988) *GA* 403; F. Arloth, 'Aufgaben des Strafvollzugs' (1990) *ZfStrVo* 329; Bemmann (n 50); H. Schwind et al., *10 Jahre Strafvollzugsgesetz: Resozialisierung als alleiniges Vollzugsziel?* (Kriminalistik Verlag, Heidelberg, 1988); A. Böhm, 'Strafzwecke und Vollzugsziele' in M. Busch and E. Krämer (eds), *Strafvollzug und Schuldproblematik* (Centaurus, Pfaffenweiler, 1988) 129; A. Böhm, 'Vollzugslockerungen und offener Vollzug zwischen Strafzwecken und Vollzugszielen' (1986) *NStZ* 201; W. Vorndran, 'Zur kriminalpolitischen Situation des Strafvollzugs' in Gesellschaft für Rechtspolitik, Trier, *Bitburger Gespräche, Jahrbuch 1986/2* (Beck, Munich, 1986) 1; C. Mitsch, *Tatschuld im Strafvollzug*

argued that paragraph 2 of the Prison Act represented an exhaustive regulation of the purpose of prison administration and argued vehemently against
a return to a plural conception of this purpose. Their arguments drew on the
preparatory legislative materials to the Prison Act, the wording of paragraph
2, the continued recognition of the 'constitutional resocialisation principle'
by the FCC, and the three-pillar and dialectical unification theory.[80] It was
argued that there was a clear distinction between 'status' and 'administrative' decisions. 'Status' decisions are based on the retributive purpose of
punishment: a purpose met by the imposition of the custodial sentence and
taken into account in the determination of the date of release.
'Administrative' decisions are governed by the Prison Act, in which the
legislator had clearly entrenched a unitary resocialization purpose.[81]

The academy argued that the Federal Council's decision to withdraw their
proposed amendment in 1988 reconfirmed the legislator's original intention
that the Prison Act should entrench a unitary purpose. Given this clear
legislative intention, it was proposed that the controversial line of cases were
contra legem. In particular the FCC's 1983 decision was branded as undermining the doctrine of parliamentary sovereignty by reading into the Prison
Act that which the legislature had expressly intended to exclude. Moreover,
academics pointed to the dissenting opinion in this FCC judgment, thereby
arguing that it was too weak to undermine the clear and ongoing commitment of the FCC to the 'constitutional resocialization principle'.[82]

The outcome of this controversy was that a small category of offenders
sentenced to life for extremely heinous crimes had their right to resocialization weakened.[83] Nevertheless it remains the majority view in the legal
community that paragraph 2 entrenches a unitary resocialization purpose
for prison administration.[84] As Kaiser states:

... of 19 Higher Regional Courts only 5 have had the opportunity to make explicit
statements on this issue, while—as far as can be seen—State prison administrations
apply the relevant administrative guidelines in line with the overwhelming academic
opinion on this matter.[85]

Notwithstanding, the controversy is instructive for a number of reasons.
First, it revealed the fragility of the political consensus around the unitary
entrenchment of the resocialization purpose. Secondly, it highlighted the

---

(Doctoral Dissertation, Frankfurt am Main, 1990); H. Müller-Dietz, 'Die Aufgaben des
Strafvollzugs—kritisch gesehen' (1985) *ZfStrVo* 212; Müller-Dietz 1984 (n 67); Müller-Dietz
1985 (n 67); Meier-Beck (n 67); Hill (n 67).

[80] See 2.2.2.1.　　　　　　　　　　　　[81] See 2.2.2.1.

[82] Laubenthal (n 32) 72; Meier-Beck (n 67); Hill (n 67); Müller-Dietz 1984 (n 67); Müller-
Dietz 1985 (n 67); Beckmann (n 67).

[83] Walter (n 9) 58; Feest, § 11, mn 59; Schwind/Böhm, § 13, mn 43.

[84] Schwind/Böhm, § 2, mn 6; Calliess/Müller-Dietz, § 2, mn 1ff.; Feest, § 2, mn 6;
Laubenthal (n 32) 72; Walter (n 9) 89; Kaiser/Schöch (n 8) 242; Calliess (n 32) 28, 31.

[85] Kaiser/Schöch (n 8) 242.

important role of the academy in the ongoing development of prison law and policy and in the reinforcement of the 'constitutional resocialization principle'. Thirdly, it demonstrated how recourse to constitutional principles strengthened the academy's position and provided a normative compass in the turbulent world of penal politics.

4.2.2 The Guiding Principles of Prison Administration

Drafters of the Prison Act were particularly concerned to establish administrative guidelines aimed at countering the damaging institutional effects of imprisonment and the entrenched culture of prison administration. This reform aim is signalled in the three 'guiding principles of prison administration' (*Gestaltung des Vollzuges*) set out under paragraph 3 of the Prison Act, as follows:

(1) Life in prison should, as far as possible, reflect the general relationships of the outside world. (2) Administrators should work to limit the damaging effects of imprisonment. (3) The administration of prison is to be aimed at assisting the prisoner to adapt to life in freedom.

The first, the 'adjustment' principle (*Angleichungsgrundsatz*), obliges administrators to organize prisons so that the difference between the prison institution and the outside world is no greater than absolutely necessary. The second, the 'counter-measures' principle (*Gegensteuerungsgrundsatz*), places a duty on administrators to work against the negative effects of imprisonment. The third, the 'integration' principle (*Integrationsgrundsatz*), compels the administration to design the prison regime in order to reintegrate the prisoner into society.[86] It is argued that these principles do not give rise to directly enforceable prisoners' rights, but are broad guidelines on the general behaviour of prison administrators, basic minimum standards on the treatment of prisoners, and criteria for the interpretation and application of further provisions in the Act.[87]

While its broad drafting has led to varied interpretation,[88] the substantive aim of paragraph 3 of the Prison Act is generally argued to be two-fold: to promote a humane prison environment and to counter the negative effects of 'total institution'[89] culture.[90] With respect to the former aim, the standards reinforce the protection of the prisoner's human dignity (Basic

---

[86] Calliess/Müller-Dietz, § 3, mn 1ff.

[87] Feest, § 3, mn 1ff.; Laubenthal (n 32) 70; Calliess/Müller-Dietz, § 3, mn 2; Schwind/Böhm, § 3, mn 1.

[88] F. Arloth, 'Der Angleichungsgrundsatz des § 3 Abs. 1 StVollzG: Gestaltungsprinzip oder Leerformel?' (1987) *ZfStrVo* 328.

[89] E. Goffmann, 'On the Characteristics of Total Institutions: the Inmate World' in D. Cressey (ed.), *The Prison: Studies in Institutional Organisation and Change* (Holt, Rinehart and Winston, New York, 1961).

[90] Calliess/Müller-Dietz, § 3, mn 1; Laubenthal (n 32) 70ff.; Feest, § 3, mn 1ff.

Law article 1(1)) and intimate sphere (Basic Law article 2).[91] With respect to the latter aim, the obligations on the prison administration are viewed as limiting the prisoner's loss of personal autonomy and privacy; learnt helplessness; sensory, sensual, emotional, and material deprivation; loss of future perspective and prison acculturation or sub-acculturation.[92] In particular, paragraph 3 is viewed as a counter-balance to the security consciousness of the prison administration.[93] The courts have been influenced by the academic interpretations of paragraph 3, using it to impose duties on prison officers to knock before entering the prisoner's cell unless the security risk makes not doing so unavoidable,[94] avoid the general use of spy holes in prison cell doors,[95] and provide casual, non-institutional, clothing for use in the prisoner's free time.[96] The courts are yet to enforce the suggestion of commentators, however, that paragraph 3 places duties on prison guards to avoid using an authoritarian tone when addressing prisoners and to provide proper crockery instead of the commonly used tin and plastic variety.[97]

Where prisoners' rights enshrined in the Act are subject to the discretion of the prison administration, the guiding principles of paragraph 3 create a presumption in favour of granting these rights. The courts have relied heavily on paragraph 3 to reinforce the prisoner's discretionary right to furnish his cell with his own possessions[98] where the prison administration has maintained that these either involve undue administrative burdens or might present risks to security.[99] In addition, paragraph 3 is said to reinforce the Act's prison regime relaxation and 'outlet measures', rights to information, and general access to the outside world (media, telephone, correspondence).[100] Thus, courts have relied on paragraph 3 in emphasizing the importance of accommodating prisoners near to their homes.[101] However, they have rejected the suggestion that prisoners have a right, on the basis of paragraph 3, to cost-free telephone usage to enhance their contact with the

---

[91] Arloth (n 88); Calliess/Müller-Dietz, § 3 mn, 1ff.; Feest §3 mn 5; Laubenthal (n 32) 71.

[92] Calliess/Müller-Dietz, § 3, mn 1; Laubenthal (n 32) 70ff.; Feest, § 3, mn 3ff.

[93] Calliess/Müller-Dietz, § 3, mn 3; *LG Frankfurt* (1987) *StV* 301.

[94] *LG Bielefeld* (1986) *NStZ* 189; *OLG Celle* (1993) *StV* 488; *OLG Saarbrücken* (1993) *NStZ* 207; B. Schaaf, 'Anklopfen an Haftraumtür vor Betreten durch Vollzugsbedienstete' (1994) *ZfStrVo* 145.

[95] *BGH* (1991) *NStZ* 452ff.; *OLG Koblenz* (1991) *NStZ* 54; *OLG Hamm* Beschl. v. 11.6.1987–1 Vollz (Ws) 140/87; *KG* Beschl. v. 7.7.1989–5 Ws 83/88 Vollz.

[96] Prison Act, § 20, *OLG Celle* (1978) *ZfStrVo* 20.

[97] Calliess/Müller-Dietz, § 3, mn 1.   [98] Prison Act, § 19.

[99] CD Player and Radio: *OLG Celle Beschluß* v. 20.3.1981–3 Ws 498/80 [StrVollz]; *OLG Frankfurt* (1989) *ZfStrVo* 245; pets: *OLG Saarbrücken* (1994) *ZfStrVo* 1994, see also E. Vogelgesang, 'Kleintierhaltung im Strafvollzug' (1994) *ZfStrVo* 67; reading lamp: *OLG Celle* (1981) *NStZ* 238; day blanket: *OLG Koblenz* (1979) *ZfStrVo* 85; daily newspaper: *OLG Nürnberg* (1993) *ZfStrVo* 116.

[100] Prison Act, §§ 11, 13, 15, 23, 24, 32, 33, 36, 68, 69. See *OLG Celle* (1985) *StV* 333; *OLG Hamm* (1985) *NStZ* 189.

[101] *OLG Hamm* (1985) *NStZ* 573.

outside world.[102] Finally, paragraph 3 has been used to reinforce the prison administrator's duty to 'encourage' prisoners to make use of therapeutic counselling opportunities, alongside occupational therapy, vocational training, further education possibilities, and social assistance.[103] Nevertheless, courts have yet to accept that this establishes a prisoner right to social benefits which normally apply to persons at liberty.[104]

Despite the considerable number of court decisions drawing on paragraph 3, commentators continue to express dissatisfaction.[105] Lesting argues that, in practice, prison administration and Prison Court decisions reflect 'total institution' culture rather than any concerted attempt to minimize the difference between prisons and the outside world,[106] while Walter asserts that we are yet to see 'systematic interpretation' of prison administrative discretion 'in the light of these principles'.[107] The academy continues to urge courts to utilize these principles more frequently as a means of guiding prison administrative discretion.

4.2.3 The Legal Status of the Prisoner

The Prison Act was not only designed to fulfil the 'constitutional resocialization requirement' and to vindicate prisoners' rights to resocialization, but also to protect the negative aspect of prisoners' basic rights and the allied imperatives of the *Rechtsstaatsprinzip*. It was clear, however, that a central tension between prisoners' negative freedoms (*Abwehrrechte*) and the authorities' power to limit basic rights (*Eingriffsbefugnisse*) required resolution. While prison authorities were given a legitimate basis for basic rights infringements by the 'constitutional resocialization requirement', it remained moot to what extent such limitations could be made. Resocialization could theoretically involve highly invasive measures. How then, was this invasive potential to be limited in line with the protection of prisoners' basic rights and in accordance with the principles of the *Rechtsstaatsprinzip*?[108]

Equally, it was unclear to what extent prison authorities could limit basic rights on other institutional grounds such as security, discipline, and order. In short, it remained to be clarified where the line would be drawn between constitutionally justified state coercion and the constitutional protection of individual rights. These tensions are reflected in paragraph 4 of the Prison

---

[102] KG *ZfStrVo* 1998, 308.
[103] Calliess/Müller-Dietz, § 3, mn 3ff.; Feest, § 3, mn 4ff.; Laubenthal (n 32) 77; *LG Lüneburg* (1983) *StV* 24.
[104] *VGH* (2000) *ZfStrVo* 180.
[105] W. Lesting, 'Normalität im Gefängnis? Zum Umgang der Gerichte mit sozialwissenschaftlichen Erkenntnissen' (1988) *ZfRSoz* 259; W. Lesting, *Normalisierung im Strafvollzug: Potential und Grenzen des §3 Abs. 1 StVollzG* (Centaurus, Pfaffenweiler, 1988).
[106] Lesting, *Normalisierung* (n 105) 117.   [107] Walter (n 9) 375.
[108] See 2.2.2.4 and 2.3.

Act, which sets out both the 'social integration status' (paragraph 4(1)) and the 'negative rights status' (paragraph 4(2)) of the prisoner.[109] This provision sets the groundwork for the careful, if precarious, balance between the empowering and invasive elements of the Act. Commentators and courts continue to strive towards the achievement of this balance.

4.2.3.1 The Voluntary Co-operation Requirement

In paragraph 4(1), the Act attempts to limit the coercive potential of resocialization by stipulating that:

> The prisoner works with the authorities on the shaping of his treatment and on the achievement of the prison administration aim. His readiness to do so is to be stimulated and encouraged.

Commentators argue that the primary aim here is to entrench the prisoner's *active* participation in his treatment and in the achievement of the resocialization aim: what Calliess/Müller-Dietz refer to as a *Mitwirkungsnotwendigkeit* (voluntary co-operation necessity).[110] Alongside the practical benefits of the prisoner's active co-operation in the treatment process, the 'co-operation necessity' is viewed as upholding the constitutional protection of the prisoner's free will in that it makes him the subject, rather than the object, of his 'treatment'.[111]

The word 'treatment' is undefined in the Act, but in line with the Report of the Select Committee for Criminal Law Reform, is commonly taken to include:

> . . . particular therapeutic and general administration measures which, through education and training, advice on personal and financial problems and participation in the common purposes of the prison, draws the prisoner into social and economic life and serves the removal of criminal inclinations.[112]

From this definition it is fair to say that 'treatment' represents all measures aimed at the prisoner's resocializsation. 'Treatment' and 'resocialization' are therefore indistinguishable and equally broadly defined.[113]

Such broad definitions were seen by the Select Committee for Criminal Law Reform and most subsequent commentators as both realistic and desirable. They are meant to stimulate the scientific development of new treatment measures, while recognizing the dynamic nature of research and the need for broad professional discretion and personalized treatment. As Heike Jung points out, however, such imprecision precludes the characterization of

---

[109] See 2.3.   [110] Calliess/Müller-Dietz, § 4, mn 3.

[111] Calliess/Müller-Dietz, § 4, mn 3. See also 2.2.2.4.

[112] *Bericht und Antrag des Sonderausschusses für die Strafrechtsreform zu dem von der Bundesregierung eingebrachten Entwurf eines Gesetzes über den Vollzug der Freiheitsstrafe und der freiheitsentziehenden Maßregeln der Besserung und Sicherung—Strafvollzugsgesetz* (Bt-Dr. 7/3998) 45.

[113] H. Jung, 'Behandlung als Rechtsbegriff' (1987) *ZfStrVo* 38.

'treatment' or 'resocialization' as legally practicable concepts making them problematic for the purpose of defining the limitations of basic rights.[114] In particular, such terms are said to run counter to the constitutional 'clarity principle'.[115]

In the face of this legal imprecision and in the light of the potential force which can be inflicted in closed prison institutions in the name of resocialization or treatment, commentators insist that treatment be viewed as an 'offer' and not as an imposition.[116] Only then is the prisoner's free will respected in line with articles 1(1) and 2(1) and the 'essence guarantee' of article 19(1) of the Basic Law. Most commentators therefore promote the view of resocialization as *'Angebotsresozialisierung'* (offer-resocialization)[117] or *'Chancenvollzug'* (prison administration offering chances).[118] This is an approach best characterized by Ostendorf's maxim that 'we do not punish to resocialise, rather when we already have to punish then we try to resocialise'.[119] Central to *Angebotsresozialisierung* is the avoidance of coercing the prisoner to co-operate. For this reason academic commentary,[120] parliamentary reports,[121] and case law,[122] interpret paragraph 4(1) as deliberately *avoiding* a duty on the prisoner to work with the authorities on his treatment. Rather, paragraph 4(1) is said to place a duty on the prison authorities to 'stimulate and encourage', but not to force, the prisoner's readiness to co-operate.[123] In general, therefore, the prisoner's failure actively to co-operate cannot be punished by disciplinary sanctions or by indirect means such as loss of home leave. Moreover, the Act requires the prisoner's permission regarding regime relaxation measures, therapeutic treatment, further education or training, work in a private business, or carrying out a sentence in open prison.[124]

However, the prisoner does not have the right to be left alone.[125] This is reflected in provisions markedly discordant with the 'co-operation neces-

---

[114] Jung (n 113).   [115] See 2.2.2.4.
[116] Feest, § 4, mn 3; Calliess/Müller-Dietz, § 4, mn 6; Jung (n 113); B. Haffke, 'Gibt es ein verfassungsrechtliches Besserungsverbot' (1975) 4/5 *MschrKrim* 246, 251; H. Ostendorf, *Kommentar zum Jugendgerichtsgesetz* (Luchterhand, Neuwied, 1987) § 91, mn 11. See on the other hand Schwind/Böhm, § 4, mn 7, who argue that it is not enough merely to 'offer' re-socialization as many prisoners lack the motivation to make use of such a possibility.
[117] Feest, § 2, mn 10; Ostendorf (n 116) § 17, mn 11.
[118] Calliess (n 32) 25 ff.; Calliess/Müller-Dietz, § 4, mn 6.
[119] Ostendorf (n 116) § 91, mn 11.
[120] Calliess/Müller-Dietz, § 4, mn 3; Feest, § 4, mn 5; Kaiser/Schöch (n 8) 203ff.; Laubenthal (n 32) 83.
[121] *Bericht und Antrag des Sonderausschusses für die Strafrechtsreform* (n 112) 6; *Protokolle der Sitzungen des Sonderausschusses für die Strafrechtsreform* in *Gesetz über den Vollzug der Freiheitsstrafe und der freiheitsentziehenden Maßregeln der Besserung und Sicherung* (Deutscher Bundestag Abteilung Wissenschaftliche Dokumentation Parlamentsarchiv, Veröffentlichte Materialien, 1976) 1969.
[122] *OLG Nürnberg* (1980) *ZfStrVo* 250; *OLG Celle* (1980) *ZfStrVo* 184.
[123] Schwind/Böhm, § 4, mn 7.   [124] Prison Act, §§ 9(1), 10 (1), 11(2).
[125] Schwind/Böhm, § 4, mn 4.

sity'. For one, the prisoner is under a duty to work, a duty explicitly justified on resocialization grounds.[126] Expressly permitted under article 12(3) of the Basic Law,[127] the duty to work, and the use of disciplinary sanctions in response to a failure to fulfil it, has been upheld by the Constitutional Court and the lower courts.[128] Commentators are critical of the work duty, arguing that it contradicts the 'voluntary co-operation requirement' and that, given its humiliating and demotivating effects, it endangers the Act's commitment to resocialization. Equally, the work duty is said to undermine the constitutional protection of the prisoner's free will and the prohibition on making the prisoner the object of state action.[129] Calliess/Müller-Dietz attempt to ameliorate the coerciveness of the work duty, arguing that paragraph 4(1) obliges prison officers to strive to obtain prisoners' voluntary co-operation in their fulfilment of the work duty.[130] Such subtle interpretations, however, cannot resolve the essential tension between the Act's stated commitment to 'voluntary co-operation' and the prisoner's duty to work. Given the controversy surrounding the work duty, the Constitutional Court's recent intervention to improve prisoner pay, on the grounds that inadequate remuneration for prison work contradicts the 'constitutional resocialization principle', has been welcomed.[131]

Additional problems regarding the 'voluntary co-operation' requirement arise from the ambiguity of paragraph 101 of the Prison Act which carefully sidesteps a prisoner's right to refuse medical treatment or examination. Drafted at the time of the Baader-Meinhof hunger strikes, paragraph 101 strikes a compromise between recognizing the prisoner's rights to self-determination and political protest and the Social State duty to provide medical care for prisoners.[132] While the paragraph holds that the State's duty to forcibly treat a dying prisoner no longer exists where the prisoner can consciously resist, it avoids the prisoner's right against such treatment in general. Furthermore, the State must treat prisoners where they are unconscious or unable to express their position on the matter. The vagueness of the provision has been justified on the grounds that the treating physician must make the final decision according to her or his own professional, ethical position. Nevertheless, it remains evident that prisoners can be treated without their 'voluntary co-operation' or permission.[133] Given

---

[126] Prison Act, §§ 37(1), 41(1).

[127] Basic Law, article 12(3) states: 'Forced labour may only be imposed on people deprived of their liberty by court sentence'.

[128] Calliess/Müller-Dietz, § 41, mn 2; *BVerfG Beschl.* (1998) *NJW* 3337.

[129] Feest, § 41, mn 1–6.

[130] Calliess/Müller-Dietz, § 41, mn 2.

[131] *BVerfG Beschl.* (1998) *NJW* 3337; (2002) *NJW* 2023. See further 4.4.1. below.

[132] J. Wagner, 'Die Neuregelung der Zwangsernährung' (1976) *ZRP* 1; Calliess/Müller-Dietz, § 101, mn 2.

[133] Feest, § 101, mn 4.

this possibility, Bemmann argues that the provisions in paragraph 101 are 'incompatible with the prisoner's right to self-determination'.[134]

Finally, paragraph 4(1) does not help prisoners whose rights to resocialisation are limited by the resocialization requirement. Thus, prisoner consent is not required where, on the grounds of enhancing their resocialization, they are transferred to another prison,[135] their visiting and correspondence rights are limited,[136] or their access to newspapers and possessions is curtailed.[137] In these cases, the 'co-operation necessity' is said to be meaningless.[138] To sum up, while paragraph 4(1) of the Prison Act attempts to reconcile the invasive elements of resocialization with the fundamental protection of the prisoner's free will, the balance is undermined by paragraphs 43 and 101 of the Prison Act and the special rights restrictions afforded by resocialization under further provisions of the Act. Thus, commentators have argued that the Act's stated commitment to protecting the prisoner's free will might be better served if it contained no grounds for limitations of rights or creation of prisoner duties on the grounds of resocialization. Calls continue for courts to take a highly restrictive view of the powers of rights limitations afforded by resocialization under the special provisions of the Act. As 4.4.3 below shows, the FCC has been sensitive to these concerns.

4.2.3.2 *The Prisoner's Negative Rights Status*

In paragraph 4(2) of the Prison Act, the prisoner's negative rights status is regulated:

The prisoner is subject to the limitations of his freedom as outlined in this Act [sentence one]. To the extent that this Act does not include a particular regulation, the prisoner is only subject to further restrictions of his freedom where these restrictions are essential to the maintenance of security or the prevention of a serious disruption of the order of the prison institution [sentence two].[139]

Paragraph 4(2), sentence one clearly reflects the *Rechtsstaat* principles of the 'legal proviso' (*Gesetzesvorbehalt*) and 'respect for basic rights' (*Grundrechtsbindung*) by stipulating that prisoners bear all basic rights except where expressly limited by the Act.[140] Paragraph 4(2), sentence one therefore gives the prisoner the right to have administrative power executed within the limits of, and in line with, the general aims and specific provisions of the Act, and, importantly, with respect for his basic rights.[141] In this way

---

[134] G. Bemmann, 'Strafvollzug im sozialen Rechtsstaat' in G. Bemman and I. Manodelakis (eds), *Probleme des staatlichen Strafens unter besonderer Berücksichtigung des Strafvollzugs* (Nomos, Baden-Baden, 1989) 35.

[135] Prison Act, § 8(1)(1).   [136] Prison Act, §§ 25(2) and 28(2)(1).

[137] Prison Act, §§ 68(2) and 70(2)(1).   [138] Schwind/Böhm, § 4, mn 3.

[139] The sentence numbers inserted in parentheses are the author's own insertion.

[140] See 2.2.1.

[141] See 2.3, which shows how the administration is bound by the *Rechtsstaatsprinzip* to respect, apply, and obey primary statute law.

the provision explicitly rejects the 'special authority relationship' (*besonderes Gewaltverhältnis*) which had, for so long, negated the full basic rights status of prisoners.[142]

Paragraph 4(2), sentence two was inserted by the special committee of the Federal Council at the last moment. The committee was concerned that the clauses covering prison security in the Act were insufficient to cover all possible circumstances.[143] It therefore insisted on a residual power of rights intervention for extreme circumstances. Consequently, the clause has become known as the 'anxiety clause' (*Angstklausel*).[144] On its face the wording of sentence 2 raises serious problems regarding the extent of the infringements of prisoners' basic rights and the extent and nature of the security threat which could give rise thereto. Read broadly, it violates the constitutional 'clarity principle' and contradicts the FCC's stipulation to avoid 'general clauses' giving broad powers to infringe upon rights.[145]

Commentators all argue, therefore, for an extremely restrictive interpretation of sentence two. Invoking the principle of 'constitutional interpretation of statutory law,' and the *Rechtsstaat* ideal of *in dubio pro libertate*, they argue that the clause should only be invoked as an absolute last resort (*ultima ratio Klausel*). This means that basic rights restrictions are justified only where the restriction is 'essential' to 'security and order' and the 'threat to security and order' must be so grave as to threaten the 'very function of prison administration'. Moreover, it is argued that the clause cannot be used to extend administrative power where the issue at hand is regulated by a special provision in the Prison Act. It should only be used where a security threat was *not* foreseen by the Act. On this basis, commentators argue that the 'anxiety clause' is superfluous in an Act containing numerous provisions regulating security and order. In addition, they argue that the words 'security and order' here refer only to the 'internal security and order of the prison' and cannot be more broadly interpreted to mean 'protection of the public at large'. Finally, they argue that sentence two is to be viewed as secondary to sentence one and that the presumption, therefore, should be in favour of restricting administrative acts to those specified and regulated by the detailed provisions of the Prison Act.[146]

Prison administrators have attempted to use the 'anxiety clause' to legitimize rights restrictions not foreseen by the Act, but courts generally follow the restrictive line of commentators on this issue.[147] This is particularly the case where paragraph 4(2), sentence 2 is used to sidestep more detailed and restrictive regulations already contained in the Act. Courts have thus

---

[142] Schwind/Böhm, § 4, mn 12. See 2.2.1 on the 'special authority relationship'.
[143] BT-Dr. 7/918, 109. See 3.2.   [144] Schwind/Böhm, § 4, mn 19.
[145] *BVerfGE* 33, 1, 11. See 2.2.1 and 2.2.2.4.
[146] Calliess/Müller-Dietz, § 4, mn 18ff.; Feest, § 4, mn 9ff.; Schwind/Böhm, § 4, mn 21ff.; Kaiser/Schöch (n 8) 194ff.; Laubenthal (n 32) 94.
[147] Calliess/Müller-Dietz, § 4, mn 21.

stopped prison administrators from using the 'anxiety clause' to introduce glass screens for visits between prisoners, their lawyers, and other private visitors;[148] make prisoners wear visible identity cards during recreation time;[149] sanction a prisoner for work avoidance by exclusion from common recreational activities;[150] stop two prisoners from setting up a common bank account;[151] take obligatory urine samples for drug testing;[152] reject a life-sentenced prisoner's application for his wife to be artificially inseminated with his sperm;[153] impose blanket restrictions on correspondence between prisoners within a prison;[154] impose blanket restrictions on the transfer of low value goods between prisoners which are punishable with disciplinary sanctions;[155] impose a blanket requirement, in the absence of concrete evidence of a threat to security in the individual case, that spy holes on prison doors be left open or that prisoners be restrained from covering such spy holes from the inside of the cell;[156] and entering a prison cell without knocking and without regard for the prisoner's intimate sphere, the resocialization purpose (paragraph 2 of the Prison Act), and the 'adjustment' principle (*Angleichungsgrundsatz*) of paragraph 3 of the Prison Act.[157] Despite this substantial record, the courts' have not always been as restrictive of prison administrative practice as many commentators would like. They have accepted the prison administration's use of paragraph 4(2), sentence 2 to stop a violent prisoner from painting images glorifying violence,[158] stop the commercial delivery of goods to a prisoner to avoid a potential fraud being committed,[159] and stop mail connected with a prisoner's business enterprise being run from inside a closed prison.[160] All three of these judgments were criticized by the academy for sidestepping existing norms, both within the Prison Act itself and within general criminal law regulating the areas in question.[161]

Overall, however, the controversial insertion of the 'anxiety clause' in paragraph 4 may not have achieved the level of administrative flexibility that

---

[148] *BGH St* 30, 38; *OLG Saarbrücken* (1983) *NStZ* 94; *LG Augsburg* (1986) *ZfStrVo* 318; *OLG Hamm* (1993) *ZfStrVo* 309; *BVerfGE* 89, 315.

[149] *KG* (1981) *NStZ* 77; *OLG Koblenz* (1985) *ZfStrVo* 56.

[150] *OLG Nürnberg* (1980) *ZfStrVo* 250.

[151] *OLG Nürnberg* (1981) *ZfStrVo* 57.

[152] *OLG Koblenz* (1990) *ZfStrVo* 51; *LG Hamburg* (1997) *ZfStrVo* 108.

[153] *LG Bonn* (1989) *NStZ* 138. The application for this procedure was accepted in principle, but was subject to respect for any future child's human dignity, the absence of other regime relaxation measures available under the Prison Act which could be used for the purpose of having a child, the medical necessity of the procedure in question. The case gave detailed elaboration on the absence of a security threat in this instance.

[154] *LG Zweibrücken* quoted in *OLG Zweibrücken* (1984) *ZfStrVo* 178.

[155] *BVerfG Beschl.* (1996) *StV* 499.

[156] *BGHSt* 37, 380; *OLG Saarbrücken* (1985) *ZfStrVo* 374; *OLG Hamm* (1987) *ZfStrVo* 368; *LG Koblenz* (1982) *StV* 26.

[157] *BVerfG Beschl.* (1996) *NJW* 2643; *OLG Frankfurt* (1995) *StV* 428.

[158] *OLG Nürnberg* (1989) *ZfStrVo* 374.　　　　　[159] *OLG Hamm* (1988) *NStZ* 525.

[160] *LG Bonn* (1988) *NStZ* 245.　　　　　　　　　[161] Calliess/Müller-Dietz, § 4, mn 21.

the Federal Council would have liked. The academy have overwhelmingly argued, and the courts have predominantly shown, that mere invocation of 'security and order' cannot amount to administrative *carte blanche* in prisons. Paragraph 4(2), sentence two of the Prison Act cannot be understood, therefore, outside the broader legal and constitutional constraints on its interpretation.

4.2.4 Interim Conclusion

The principles contained in paragraphs 2–4 of the Prison Act flesh out the legal concept of the prisoner's rights status. They are marked by the legislative trade-off between prisoners' rights, administrative flexibility, and prison security. The legal impact of paragraphs 2–4, however, can only be measured in the broader context within which they are interpreted. Shaped by the German legal community, this context is dominated by constitutional principles and entrenched penological ideals. While the Prison Act continues to be stretched by those seeking greater administrative flexibility or more punitive treatment of prisoners, there can be little doubt that its constitutional foundations play a large part in the survival of the Act's principles. In short, the constitutional foundations of the prisoner's legal status have been a crucial element in the face of the legislative ambiguity or generality contained in the Prison Act. In addition, the academy's continued commitment and their strong interpretative influence greatly contributes to the Act's longevity and courts' continuing commitment to its penological and constitutional ideals.

The above elaboration of the principles underpinning the Prison Act is not intended solely to demonstrate the dynamics of German legal and criminal justice culture, however. The legal meaning of these principles is also central to the specific protections afforded to prisoners by the special provisions in the Act. This is particularly so where prisoners' rights are subject to administrative discretion. The following section examines the implementation and interpretation of the special provisions of the Prison Act.

4.3 THE SPECIAL PROVISIONS OF THE PRISON ACT

The Prison Act contains approximately 175 special provisions regulating prison administration. They are viewed as the comprehensive and systematic exposition of the substantive foundations laid out in paragraphs 2–4, and are meant to be read purposively in line with these general principles. The provisions regulate the organization, structure, and responsibilities of the different penal agencies;[162] the course of the prisoner's sentence, and the

---

[162] Prison Act, §§ 154–166. Including § 160, which obliges prison administrators to enable prisoners to participate in, and take co-responsibility for, the organization of the prison.

rights of prisoners in its administration;[163] the administration of women's prisons;[164] security, order and discipline in prisons;[165] the procedures and rights regarding the prisoner's legal redress and informal complaint rights;[166] various specialized forms of prison administration;[167] and the prisoner's rights to social welfare and unemployment insurance.[168]

Commentators generally acknowledge that the special provisions of the Prison Act represent a significant advance for the legalization (*Verrechtlichung*) of prison administration and the proper definition of the prisoner's legal status.[169] It is acknowledged that the last twenty-five years have seen the development of a rich and dynamic body of prison law jurisprudence in Germany. This jurisprudence is said to have strengthened the prisoner's legal status through the detailed clarification of the powers and duties of the prison administration under the Act.[170] Yet while the legalization of prison administration has been advanced by the Act, commentators also express concern that the courts' treatment of the Act's special provisions falls short of the broader reform and constitutional ideals underpinning the Act.[171] Similarly to debates regarding interpretations of the Act's fundamental principles, penal observers push for full realization of the ambitious ideals expressed in the 1970s. These calls have been heard by the FCC, whose interventions have been crucial in strengthening the prisoner's legal status. The following section examines problems identified with the implementation and interpretation of the special provisions of the Prison Act, while section 4.4 examines the response of the FCC to the calls of the penal community.

4.3.1 Access to Justice and Legal Complaints

The clearest signal of the 'legalization' of prison administration lies in the Act's strong protection of prisoners' complaint rights.

The prisoner has a right of informal complaint to a Prison Board (*Anstaltsbeirat*),[172] the prison governor,[173] a personal meeting with a representative of the State Prison Inspectorate (*Aufsichtsbehörde*) during their inspections,[174] and, additionally, the right to make a formal complaint

---

[163] Prison Act, §§ 5–75.   [164] Prison Act, §§ 76–80.
[165] Prison Act, §§ 81–107.   [166] Prison Act, §§ 108–121.
[167] Prison Act, §§ 122–153, 167–178.   [168] Prison Act, § 195.
[169] F. Dünkel, 'Die Rechtsstellung von Strafgefangenen und Möglichkeiten der rechtlichen Kontrolle von Vollzugsentscheidungen in Deutschland' (1996) *GA* 518, 520; Kaiser/Schöch (n 8) 55; Rotthaus 1987 (n 1) 1.
[170] G. Kaiser, H.-J. Kerner, and H. Schöch, *Strafvollzug* (Müller, Heidelberg, 1992) 40.
[171] See 4.3.2.2. and 4.3.3. below.
[172] Prison Act, §§ 108(2) and 164.
[173] Prison Act, § 108(1).
[174] Prison inspectorates are part of each state justice administration (*Landesjustiz-verwaltung*) and are regulated under Prison Act, § 151. Under para. 151(2) their inspection has to include professional assessment of the working practice, social work, further education and training, health, and other specialist treatment of the prisoner.

about the conduct of officials (*Dienstaufsichtsbeschwerde*) to the prison authorities.[175] A broad range of informal complaints can be brought. Prisoners' concerns need not be specifically related to a breach under the Prison Act, but can encompass suggestions, wishes, and complaints relating not only to administrative action in breach of the Act, but also to the general behaviour of prison officers. Prison governors, or their representatives, must ensure that regular office hours are kept for the purpose of receiving complaints.[176] Prison boards, comprising volunteer members of the public, are to work with the prison administration in support of the prisoner and may suggest ways of improving the prison regime.[177] In addition to receiving complaints, wishes, and suggestions from prisoners, they have the right to monitor their accommodation, work, training, food, medical treatment, and the layout of the prison as a whole.[178] They may visit prisoners in their cells which, along with correspondence, may not be monitored.[179] The exercise of prisoner's informal complaint rights have, generally, been viewed positively.[180] According to a survey done in North Rhine-Westphalia, up to one-third of informal complaints are successfully resolved.[181]

Moreover, the prisoner's constitutional right to petition[182] democratic bodies is acknowledged in the Act which protects such petitions, alongside all legal correspondence, from surveillance by prison authorities.[183] Prisoners can petition as individuals or as a group (*Sammelpetition*) about anything to do with prison life. The Federal and state parliaments are obliged by the Basic Law to set up committees to receive petitions from all citizens (*Petitionsausschuss*),[184] and some states (Rheinland-Pfalz, Mecklenburg-Vorpommern, Thuringen, and Schleswig Holstein) have permanent office holders for this purpose, known as citizen's representatives (*Bürgerbeauftragte*), a close equivalent of an Ombudsman. Prisoners' petitions are also often processed by state MPs elected by their parties to represent prisoners' interests (*Strafvollzugsbeauftragte*) in parliament and in the State justice departments.[185] A study conducted in 1981 showed that approximately 7 per cent of prisoners exercised their petition rights at least once during their sentence, with a success rate of 23 per cent.[186]

Informal complaint mechanisms and petition rights are supplemented by the right of individual complaint to a court and the right to a legal

---

[175] Prison Act, § 108(3).
[177] Prison Act, § 163.
[179] Prison Act, § 164(2).
[181] Dünkel 1996 (n 169) 524.

[176] Prison Act, § 108(1).
[178] Prison Act, § 164(1).
[180] Kaiser/Schöch (n 8) 363.
[182] Basic Law, art. 17.

[183] Prison Act, § 29. Prisoners can exercise this constitutional right both domestically and internationally (e.g. through the European Parliament).
[184] This flows from Basic Law, art. 17 and is enacted in art. Basic Law, 45c. See www.bundestag.de/gremiem15/a02/petitionsrecht_BRD.html.
[185] J. Oelmayer, *Strafvollzug und Parlamentarische Kontrolle: Bilanz 1 Jahr Strafvollzugsbeauftragter* (Bundnis 90/Die Grunen im Landtag von Baden-Wurttemberg 12.08.2002).
[186] K. Diepenbruck, *Rechtsmittel im Strafvollzug* (Doctoral Dissertation, Göttingen, 1981).

remedy.[187] Where prisoners' individual rights have been violated, they can ask the Prison Court for relief from a measure (*Anfechtungsantrag*);[188] to enforce a measure which has been refused (*Verpflichtungsantrag*);[189] to enforce an omitted measure (*Vornahmeantrag*);[190] to prevent the enforcement or repetition of a measure (*Unterlassungsantrag*); and to declare a measure illegal where it has already been enforced (*Feststellungsantrag*).[191] Moreover, the Act provides for interim legal protection where required.[192]

In the first instance, prisoners exercise their legal rights in Prison Courts (*Strafvollstreckungskammern*) set up to determine questions of prison administration under the Prison Act.[193] The Prison Court proceeding is conducted without an oral hearing,[194] although the court may call one where this would clarify the case at hand.[195] Prisoners can appeal the decisions of the Prison Courts in the Criminal Chamber of the Higher Regional Courts. These courts must grant leave to appeal where the decision would contribute to the general development of prison law or to national uniformity of prison law.[196] If a Higher Regional Court wishes to deviate from the decisions of other Higher Regional Courts or the Federal Supreme Court, it must refer the matter to the Federal Supreme Court for clarification.[197] Finally, prisoners have a subsidiary right of complaint to the FCC if they can show that their basic rights have been violated and that they have exhausted all other legal avenues.[198]

While it is clear that prisoners' access to legal redress is well developed in the Prison Act, observers identify a number of difficulties involved in the enforcement of their substantive rights in the courts. These problems can be classified into two mutually reinforcing categories: a) problems inherent to the legal construction of the Prison Act and its interpretation; b) institutional obstacles to substantive rights enforcement. The following sections deal with these issues in turn.

4.3.2 Substantive Rights Enforcement and Problems with the Prison Act

The problem of legal protection in prisons lies less with any deficit in access to courts of law than in the definition of the prisoner's legal rights.[199]

---

[187] Prison Act, § 109(2).
[188] Prison Act, §§ 109(1), sentence 1 and 115(2), sentence 2.
[189] Prison Act, § 109(1), sentence 2.   [190] Prison Act, §§ 109(1), sentence 2 and 113.
[191] Prison Act, §§ 115 (3); see, in general, Laubenthal (n 32) 309.
[192] Prison Act, § 114.   [193] Müller-Dietz 1985 (n 16) 335.
[194] Prison Act, § 115(1).
[195] Feest, § 115, mn 9; Calliess/Müller-Dietz, § 115, mn 4.
[196] Prison Act, § 116   [197] Constitution of Courts Act, § 121(2).
[198] Basic Law, art. 93 No. 4a in connection with Federal Constitutional Court Act, § 90(1).
[199] Dünkel 1996 (n 169) 524.

The largest part of the Prison Act regulates the relationship between prisoners and the prison administration and specifies all aspects of the prisoner's sentence and daily routine.[200] The prisoner's legal position is set out in detailed regulations concerning the planning of the prison sentence and sentence relaxation measures;[201] accommodation and diet;[202] contact with the outside world;[203] work, education, and training;[204] religious practices;[205] health services;[206] recreation;[207] social services;[208] security and order;[209] circumstances where direct force may be used on prisoners;[210] and disciplinary offences and sanctions.[211]

Each of these sections begins with a statement of principle (*Grundsatz*) asserting prisoners' general rights and obligations and/or referring to the founding principles of the Act or other constitutional principles. For example, paragraph 23 of the Prison Act states that 'the prisoner has the right to communicate and relate with persons outside the prison within the framework of this law. Such communication with persons outside the prison is to be encouraged'. Whilst paragraph 37 of the Act states that 'work, occupational therapy, education and training serve in particular the purpose of promoting the prisoner's capacity to undertake gainful employment after release'. The statement of principle with respect to security and order is a clear example of an attempt to balance the maintenance of security with the protection of the prisoner's basic rights. It states:

(1) The prisoner's sense of responsibility for good order and co-existence within the prison is to be instilled and promoted. (2) The duties and limitations placed on the prisoner in pursuit of security and order in the prison should be proportional to their purpose and should not encroach upon the prisoner for longer than is absolutely necessary.[212]

These statements of broader principles are followed in each section by provisions setting out a) the specific duties of the prison administration and the administration's powers of rights intervention (*Eingriffsbefugnisse*) and b) prisoners' individual duties and rights.

Prison administration duties give rise to correlative rights for prisoners. For example, paragraph 5(2) of the Prison Act provides that 'the prisoner is to be informed about his rights and duties'. Equally, under paragraph 6 of the Act prison authorities must undertake a 'treatment examination' of the prisoner and discuss with the prisoner the content of his 'sentence plan' (*Vollzugsplan*). Many of these duties, however, are subject to administrative discretion resulting in a correlative discretionary prisoner right. Thus, paragraph 11(1) of the Act states: 'In order to relax the regime of the prisoner

---

[200] Prison Act, §§ 5–107.   [201] Prison Act, §§ 5–16.   [202] Prison Act, §§ 17–22.
[203] Prison Act, §§ 23–36.   [204] Prison Act, §§ 37–52.   [205] Prison Act, §§ 53–55.
[206] Prison Act, §§ 56–66.   [207] Prison Act, §§ 67–70.   [208] Prison Act, §§ 70–75.
[209] Prison Act, §§ 81–93.   [210] Prison Act, §§ 94–101.
[211] Prison Act, §§ 102–107.   [212] Prison Act, § 81.

the following provisions *may* be ordered' (emphasis added). Moreover, the exercise of these discretionary duties is often subject to conditions which vest the prisoner with what we might call a correlative conditional discretionary right. Hence, paragraph 11(2) states that 'regime relaxation measures may be arranged with the permission of the prisoner when it is not feared that the prisoner will use such measures to escape from prison or misuse such measures in order to commit further crimes'.

'Powers of rights intervention' (*Eingriffsbefugnisse*) set out what prison officials may do to prisoners, thereby stipulating the conditions under which prisoners must forbear limitations of basic rights. For example, paragraph 84(1), sentence one of the Prison Act states that 'the prisoner's possessions and cell may be searched'. These 'powers of rights intervention' are usually subject to qualifications which vest prisoners with correlative rights. Thus, in paragraph 84(1), sentences two and three state that: 'the search of male prisoner cells is to be conducted by men, the search of female prisoner cells to be conducted by women. A sense of shame is to be spared'. Other 'powers of rights intervention' are subject to conditions which also vest prisoners with correlative rights. Hence, paragraph 84(2), sentence one states: 'only where there is a danger arising out of delay, or on the order of the prison governor in the individual case, is it permissible to undertake a full body search of the prisoner'.

Prisoners' duties are typically expressed in unambiguous terms. For example, paragraph 41, sentence one of the Prison Act states that 'the prisoner is under an obligation to undertake work, occupational therapy or other occupations that he is physically capable of undertaking'. There are exemptions to some of these duties which prisoners can try to claim. Thus, paragraph 42 sets out the conditions whereby a prisoner can claim exemption from the duty to work.[213] However, there is no exemption to most of the duties, particularly those concerning security and order.[214] If, after an oral hearing and full clarification of the facts of the case,[215] it is established that a prisoner 'knowingly' breached a duty, the prison governor can order disciplinary sanctions against him.[216] The Act states that governors must discuss their disciplinary decisions with persons responsible for the prisoner's treatment,[217] and that such sanctions cannot be awarded where a warning would suffice.[218] Prison governors have a number of sanctions at their disposal, the harshest of which is 'arrest', which consists of segregation within the prison of up to four weeks, which the Act stipulates can only be imposed in the most severe cases or where disciplinary offences have repeatedly been committed.[219] Arrest is executed in solitary confinement, although the prison

---

[213] W. Pfister, 'Freistellung des Gefangenen von der Arbeitspflicht (§ 42 StVollzG)' (1988) *NStZ* 117.

[214] Prison Act, § 82. [215] Prison Act, § 106(1). [216] Prison Act, § 102(1).
[217] Prison Act, § 106(2). [218] Prison Act, § 102(2). [219] Prison Act, § 103(2).

governor has the discretion to allow prisoners to remain in their cells.[220] All disciplinary sanctions may also be imposed as a whole or in part as suspended sanctions of up to six months.[221] Not included in the list of disciplinary sanctions, however, is any power to extend the length of the prisoner's sentence (e.g. by not allowing days spent in arrest to count towards the total sentence length).[222] Such a power, which until very recently was afforded to prison governors in England,[223] would amount to a transgression of the German distinction between rights limitations pursuant to judicial 'status' decisions and rights limitations arising from the 'administrative decisions' of prison officials.[224]

Finally, several provisions are expressed as prisoners' rights and not as administrative duties giving rise to correlative prisoner rights. These are expressed in a number of ways. Prisoners may be vested with clear rights (*Rechtsansprüche*). For example, paragraph 28(1) of the Prison Act states that 'a prisoner has the right to receive and send an unlimited amount of correspondence'. Such rights are often subject to qualifications which afford prison authorities additional 'powers of rights encroachment'. Thus, paragraph 28(2) states that 'the prison governor can forbid correspondence with particular persons where (1) the security and order of the prison is endangered, (2) with persons not included in the family where the correspondence would have a damaging influence on the prisoner's resocialisation'. Prisoners also bear discretionary rights. For example, paragraph 32 states that 'a prisoner may receive telephone calls and telegrams'. Again, such discretionary rights can be qualified where the prison authorities can show a threat to security and order, or resocialization. Many other provisions vest prisoners with conditional discretionary rights. Thus, whilst paragraph 13 states that 'a prisoner may receive leave from prison of up to 21 days a year' this is conditional on the absence of a 'danger of misuse' on the part of the prisoner. Prisoners' rights might also be qualified by words which give rise to discretion or evaluative leeway.[225] This can be found in paragraph 19(1), which states that the prisoner may furnish his cell 'to an appropriate extent'.

Some prisoners' rights are subject to 'transitional provisions' (*Übergangsregelungen*).[226] This is the case with paragraph 10(1) of the Prison Act, which creates a 'conditional discretionary right' in favour of placing prisoners in open prisons and then makes this subject to the broad discretion of the administration in a transitional provision. Thus, while paragraph 10(1) states that the prisoner 'should be placed in an open prison where he gives his consent, fulfils the requirements of open prisons and is therefore not

---

[220] Prison Act, § 104(5), Calliess/Müller-Dietz, § 104, mn 3.
[221] Prison Act, § 104(2). [222] Calliess/Müller-Dietz, § 103, mn 4.
[223] See ch. 5, n 132. [224] See 2.2.2.1.
[225] See 4.3.2.1 below on 'evaluative leeway'.
[226] See 3.2 on 'transitional provisions'.

likely to flee from or misuse his environment to commit further crimes', this is subject to transitional provision paragraph 201 No. 1 of the Prison Act, under which the prisoner can be placed in a closed prison on 'accommodation, personnel or organisation grounds'.

The special provisions of the Prison Act are implemented in administrative regulations (*Verwaltungsvorschriften*). These detailed criteria guide prison administrators in exercising discretion under the Act.[227] The states have agreed on federally applicable administrative regulations such as the Administrative Guidelines on the Prison Act (*Verwaltungsvorschriften zum Strafvollzugsgesetz*), the Service and Security Guidelines for Prison Administration (*Dienst- und Sicherheitsvorschriften für den Strafvollzug*), and the Prison Standing Rules (*Vollzugsgeschäftsordnung*). In addition, individual states have developed their own detailed internal regulations. A number of these administrative regulations have been criticized for taking a restrictive view of the rights afforded to prisoners under the special provisions of the Act.[228]

To sum up, individual provisions under the Prison Act provide prisoners with differing degrees of legal protection. They provide clear rights, qualified rights, qualified discretionary rights, or conditional discretionary rights. Moreover, some of these rights are subject to transitional provisions which afford further layers of administrative discretion and thus weaken the prisoner's legal position. In addition, administrative guidelines which supply detailed guidance on the special provisions in question might also take a restrictive view of the prisoner's right in question. In the absence of a clear right, the prisoner's legal position depends on the extent to which the courts will check the discretion of the prison administration. In order to assess court control, however, it is necessary to briefly outline the legal principles involved in judicial control of administrative discretion in Germany.

4.3.2.1 *Judicial Control of Discretion and 'Evaluative Leeway'*

Under German law discretion can arise in two forms: either as discretion (*Ermessen*) or as what Germans call 'evaluative leeway' (*Beurteilungsspielraum*).[229] The distinction flows from the German conception of the structure of a statutory norm. Under this conception, a norm is divided between the statutory conditions for administrative action (*Tatbestand*) and the legal consequences of these statutory conditions (*Rechtsfolgen*). Where a legal term is included in the legal consequences of the statutory conditions,

---

[227] There are two types: interpretive guidelines (*Auslegungsrichtlinien*) and discretion guidelines (*Ermessensrichtlinien*). H. Müller-Dietz, 'Die Rechtssprechung der Strafvollstreckungskammern zur Rechtsgültigkeit der VVStVollzG' (1981) *NStZ* 409, 417.

[228] K. Koepsel, 'Das Vollzugskonzept des Strafvollzugsgesetzes und seine Veränderung durch Verwaltungsvorschriften und Erlasse der Landesjustizverwaltungen' (1992) *ZfStrVo* 46.

[229] This distinction is less clear in the area of planning law, see H. Maurer, *Allgemeines Verwaltungsrecht* (11th edn, Beck, Munich, 1997) 146ff.

and where this term gives rise to the possibility of an administrative decision being made (e.g. 'can' or 'may'), a measure of administrative discretion arises.[230] Where an indeterminate legal term (*unbestimmter Rechtsbegriff*) is included in the statutory conditions for administrative action, the court can either claim full judicial control over the interpretation of this term and the substance of the decisions made pursuant to it or it might decide that a measure of 'evaluative leeway' has arisen on the part of the administrator over which the court has more restricted control.[231]

A significant number of Prison Act provisions contain indeterminate legal terms which form part of the conditions for administrative action. These either qualify prisoners' rights or make their enforcement conditional. Many of these terms and the decisions made pursuant to them have been subjected to the full control of the courts. This includes all of the indeterminate legal terms included in 'powers of rights restriction' as well as many provisions affording qualified or conditional prisoners' rights.[232] But the Federal Supreme Court has decided that 'evaluative leeway' arises in the prison context where an indeterminate legal term requires an administrative prognosis or predictive evaluation of facts which could give rise to a number of different but, from a legal point of view, equally valid decisions.[233] This is particularly the case where the decision requires a prognostic evaluation of the likelihood of the prisoner attempting to escape or abusing his freedom to commit further crimes (*Mißbrauchsgefahr*). Courts have thus held that 'evaluative leeway' arises in decisions to place a prisoner in an open prison,[234] grant a regime relaxation measure,[235] grant a prisoner leave from prison,[236] or to place a prisoner under exceptional security measures.[237] Furthermore, 'evaluative leeway' is said to arise in deciding whether to segregate a prisoner during work hours,[238] in determining the 'appropriate extent' to which a prisoner can spend his own money[239] and in determining whether a prisoner is suitable for further education or training.[240]

The principles governing judicial control of discretion and 'evaluative leeway' differ slightly. Both forms of discretion restrict judicial scrutiny, although it would be unduly pessimistic to suggest that the prisoner is

---

[230] See Maurer (n 229) 119–29. [231] Maurer (n 229) 129–39.

[232] Feest, § 115, mn 33; Schwind/Böhm, § 115, mn 21; Calliess/Müller-Dietz, § 115, mn 22; D. Justen, *Unbestimmte Rechtsbegriffe mit 'Beurteilungsspielraum' im Strafvollzugsgesetz* (Doctoral Dissertation, Mainz, 1995) 70–1.

[233] *BGHSt* 30, 320.

[234] Prison Act, § 10; *OLG Karlsruhe* (1985) *ZfStrVo* 245; *OLG Frankfurt* (1983) *ZfStrVo* 379.

[235] Prison Act, § 11; *BGHSt* 30, 320.

[236] Prison Act, § 13; *BGHSt* 30, 320.

[237] Prison Act, § 88; *OLG Saarbrücken* (1985) *ZfStrVo* 58.

[238] Prison Act, § 17(3); *OLG Nürnberg* (1981) *NStZ* 78.

[239] Prison Act, § 22(3); *BGHSt* 35, 101.

[240] Prison Act, § 37(3); *OLG Celle* (1988) *INFO* 27.

without legal safeguards in both instances.[241] Where discretion arises, the prisoner has a right to the faultless exercise of discretion (*Recht auf fehler-freien Ermessensgebrauch*) under paragraph 115(5) of the Prison Act. This provision states that the court can control whether the decision-maker has stayed within the bounds of their legal discretion (*Ermessensüberschreitung*) or whether the decision-maker has made a decision which goes outside the 'statutory purpose' of the discretion given (*Ermessensfehlgebrauch*). The latter will arise where the decision-maker has failed to use their discretion; considered irrelevant factual or legal matters; accounted for criteria which do not reflect the statutory purposes of the norm in question; failed to take into account relevant criteria; and/or incorrectly weighed up relevant criteria.[242] The concept of 'purpose' is a broad one, in that it refers both to the purpose of the individual provision and the general purposes of the Prison Act. Thus courts can insist upon the proper consideration of paragraphs 2 and 3 of the Prison Act in each decision-making process.[243] In addition, a fault in the exercise of discretion arises where the decision vio-lates basic rights and general principles of administrative law, in particular the principles of proportionality (*Verhältnismäßigkeitsgrundsatz*) and the constitutional prohibition on arbitrary decision-making (*Willkürverbot*).[244]

In the case of 'evaluative leeway' under the Prison Act, the Federal Supreme Court has stipulated that the principles regarding control of dis-cretion under paragraph 115(5) of the Act apply. In addition, it has stated that 'Prison Courts should consider whether the prison official has decided on the basis of a relevant and complete factual base, if the decision-maker has applied appropriate standards and if the decision-maker has stayed within the bounds of their "evaluative leeway"'. Moreover, it stated that where the court finds that the decision-maker has failed to fulfil any of these conditions it must specify the facts to be taken into account, the standards to be adopted, and the legal boundaries of the 'indeterminate legal term' and ask the decision-maker to make a new decision on the basis of its instruc-tions. The Federal Supreme Court emphasized that the court must not replace the official decision with its own. It took the view that courts were not in a position to make prognostic decisions involving both 'objective standards as well as subjective evaluations'.[245] Nevertheless, the decision is said to establish the principle that where 'evaluative leeway' arises, judicial scrutiny should be more exacting, and the onus on decision-makers to jus-tify their decisions will be greater, than when discretion arises.[246]

When controlling both discretion and 'evaluative leeway', courts often address the administrative guidelines relevant to the provision. Under German law all administrative regulations are classified as internal law

---

[241] Schwind/Böhm, § 115, mn 22.   [242] Maurer (n 229) 124–8.
[243] Feest, § 115, mn 50.   [244] Maurer (n 229) 128; Feest, § 115, mn 50.
[245] *BGHSt* 30, 320, 325 and 327.
[246] B. Volckart, 'Anmerkung zu BGHSt 30, 320' (1982) *NStZ* 174.

(*Innenrecht*) which, while binding on the administration, is not binding on the courts.[247] Thus, strictly speaking, administrative guidelines are classified as 'orientation and decision assistance' only.[248] As a matter of law these guidelines are not meant to be applied generally at the expense of concrete consideration of each individual case (*Einzelfallprüfung*),[249] or in such a way that limits basic rights further than provided by the Act.[250] Prisoners cannot directly challenge administrative guidelines, however, as court consideration of their conformity with the Prison Act is incidental to their control of administrative decisions under the Act. Nevertheless, in the process of this incidental check, courts can strike down guidelines which contradict the spirit of the provision or the Act.[251] Finally, the courts' scrutinizing function is reinforced by the duty on prison officials to give a full account of their decision-making process.[252]

On the basis of these standards of review, there is substantial scope for the judicial scrutiny of administrative discretion and for the strengthening of the prisoner's legal position. But commentators have criticized judicial reluctance to fully scrutinize official discretion and 'evaluative leeway' or to set out standards clarifying the prisoner's legal position.

4.3.2.2 Criticisms of the Control of Administrative Discretion under the Prison Act

In the late 1980s, the penal academy shifted its focus from the protection of the foundational principles of the Prison Act to the problem of legal enforcement of individual prisoners' rights. Despite acceptance that the courts had significantly advanced the prisoner's legal status under the Prison Act,[253] concerns remain about the courts' recognition of 'evaluative leeway' in prison administration. Although courts have held most 'indeterminate legal terms' in the Act to be subject to full judicial control,[254] controversy has arisen regarding those provisions where courts recognized 'evaluative leeway' on the part of the prison administration. While some commentators argue that it is necessary to allow prison administrators a measure of evaluative freedom in certain areas,[255] many critics argue that the continued recognition of 'evaluative leeway' by the Higher Regional Courts and Federal Supreme Court threatens the 'de-legalization' (*Ver-un-rechtlichung*) of prison administration and thus undermines the reform aims of the Prison

---

[247] Laubenthal (n 32) 12; Maurer (n 229) 596. On '*Innenrecht*' see 2.2.1.
[248] *OLG Zweibrücken* (1977) *ZfStrVo SH* 13; *OLG Saarbrücken* (1978) *ZfStrVo* 182; *OLG München* (1979) *ZfStrVo SH* 25.
[249] *OLG Frankfurt* (1981) *ZfStrVo* 122; Calliess/Müller-Dietz, § 2, mn 27.
[250] Schwind/Böhm, § 4, mn 14.
[251] Müller-Dietz, (n 227) 409.
[252] Feest, § 115, mn 47.   [253] Walter (n 9) 373.
[254] Justen (n 232) 70–1.   [255] Laubenthal (n 32) 324; Schwind/Böhm, § 115, mn 22.

Act.[256] The concern is particularly strong where courts recognize 'evaluative leeway' in provisions central to the achievement of the resocialization aim, such as prison leave, regime relaxation, and access to open prison.[257] It is argued that despite the exacting standards stipulated by the Federal Supreme Court, Prison Courts and Higher Regional Courts define 'evaluative leeway' too generously and are not sufficiently rigorous in their scrutiny of the factual basis upon which decisions are made.[258] Consequently, prison administrators are given scope to undermine prisoners' positive rights to resocialization and to conceal their reasons for doing so.[259] The resultant unpredictability which prisoners experience in the vindication of these positive rights is said to exacerbate prisoners' alienation from the prison administration and to undermine their general readiness to co-operate in their resocialization.[260]

Critics argue for the full judicial supervision of many of the indeterminate legal terms under the Prison Act.[261] In particular, they point to the inconsistency that Prison Courts are required by law to make a prognosis on the offender's likelihood of committing further crimes when considering their eligibility for parole under paragraph 57(1) of the Penal Code, but are not viewed by the higher courts as being capable of making the same prognostic decision regarding prison leave or regime relaxation measures.[262] Moreover, there is concern that Prison Courts are out of line with the growing tendency of administrative courts to assume full judicial control of indeterminate legal terms and to recognize 'evaluative leeway' only in exceptional circumstances.[263] This trend has been echoed by the FCC, which argues that the density of control over indeterminate legal terms should be higher where basic rights are at stake and that 'evaluative leeway' should only be recognized where the decision is so 'specialized' or 'complex' that its control by a court would not be possible.[264] There are therefore ongoing calls for the Prison Courts and Higher Regional Courts to follow general administrative law trends on this issue.

Moreover, Higher Regional Courts have been criticized for failing to take more active control of discretion and 'evaluative leeway' through asserting the founding principles of the Act. As previously indicated, commentators are particularly concerned that courts have not fully utilized the administra-

---

[256] U. Kamann, 'Der Beurteilungsspielraum und sein Einfluß auf die Ver-un-rechtlichung des Strafvollzuges' (1994) *ZRP* 474.

[257] U. Dopslaff, 'Abschied von den Entscheidungsfreiräumen bei Ermessen und unbestimmten Rechtsbegriffen mit Beurteilungsspielraum im Strafvollzugsgesetz' (1988) *ZStW* 567, 567–9.

[258] Kamann (n 256) 477; Justen (n 232) 73–138.

[259] H. Preusker, 'Erfahrungen der Praxis mit dem Strafvollzugsgesetz' (1987) *ZfStrVo* 11, 14; Kamann (n 256) 476–7.

[260] Dopslaff (n 257) 569.   [261] Dopslaff (n 257) 585.

[262] Böhm (n 31) 37.

[263] Maurer (n 229) 133–134; Kamann (n 256); Kaiser/Schöch (n 8) 254.

[264] *BVerfGE* 84, 34 and 59.

tive guidelines afforded under paragraph 3 of the Prison Act.[265] On the other hand, the academy has congratulated the Higher Regional Courts and Federal Supreme Court for their readiness to strike down restrictive administrative guidelines, for downplaying the application of these guidelines in the decision-making process, and for emphasizing the importance of full consideration of each individual case (*Einzelfallgerechtigkeit*).[266]

Finally, there is continued alarm at the ongoing application of 'transitional provisions' in the Act. Many of these provisions continue to apply despite the fact that the dates stipulated therein have long since passed. It is argued that the realization of the resocialization aims of the Act through the vindication of positive rights of prisoners, such as their rights to inclusion in medical insurance and pension schemes and placement in open prisons, have been significantly undermined by the continued reliance on transitional provisions by states.[267] Müller-Dietz has thus warned that the prison reform ideals of the 1970s could be 'ruined'.[268]

As already indicated,[269] however, the shortcomings of judicial scrutiny under the Prison Act are not the only hindrance for prisoners hoping to uphold their rights; equally problematic are the institutional dynamics which hinder their vindication in practice.

4.3.3 Institutional Obstacles to the Enforcement of Prisoners' Rights

4.3.3.1 *Failings of the Prison Courts* (Strafvollstreckungskammern)

Introduced in 1975 after the success of the specialized juvenile courts, the Prison Courts (*Strafvollstreckungskammern*) were touted as a 'fundamental element of prison reform'.[270] They were intended to work in close, yet impartial, co-operation with all elements of the prison institution, display criminological and penological expertise, and provide a constructive conflict resolution forum for prisoners and prison administration.[271] The courts, however, have failed to fulfil reformers' high expectations.[272] Judges view their work as low status and they are too overloaded to deal with many of the cases adequately.[273] A study conducted in 1985 showed that

---

[265] See 4.2.2 above.   [266] Walter (n 9) 376.
[267] See 3.2 and 3.3.   [268] Calliess/Müller-Dietz, § 198, mn 1.
[269] See 4.3.1. above.   [270] Müller-Dietz 1985 (n 16) 335.
[271] G. Blau, 'Die Strafvollstreckungskammer' in H. Schwind and G. Blau (eds), *Strafvollzug in der Praxis* (Walter de Gruyter, Berlin, 1988) 339; K. Rotthaus, 'Die Zusammenarbeit zwischen Justizvollzugsanstalt und Strafvollstreckungskammer' in H. Schwind (ed.), *Festschrift für Günter Blau* (Walter de Gruyter, Berlin, 1985) 327.
[272] Rotthaus 1985 (n 271); R. Northoff, 'Strafvollstreckungskammer: Anspruch und Wirklichkeit' (1987) *ZfStrVo* 207; H. Dünkel, 'Die Strafvollstreckungskammer—weiterhin ein unbeliebter Torso?' (1992) *Bewährungshilfe* 196; U. Kamann, 'Der Richter als Mediator im Gefängnis: Idee, Wirklichkeit und Möglichkeit' (1993) *KrimJ* 13; D. Eschke, *Mängel im Rechtsschutz gegen Strafvollstreckungs- und Strafvollzugsmaßnahmen* (R. v. Decker's Verlag, Heidelberg, 1993) 120ff.
[273] Northoff (n 272).

approximately 57 per cent of all prisoners exercise their legal rights at first instance, resulting in the case quota of the smaller Prison Courts being 26 times that of a normal first instance criminal court.[274] Judicial specialization is also undermined by the organization of the court system in which there is a high turnover of Prison Court judges, who are allocated to courts on the basis of need rather than interest. Judges with an interest in prison law are often not allocated to Prison Courts, whereas those who are allocated are often less interested in their role.[275]

The result is that Prison Court judges tend to process prisoners' applications on formal grounds, because they do not have the time, expertise, or inclination to act as informal prison mediators or to check carefully the substance of each case.[276] This tendency is exacerbated by the fact that the judges make decisions on the papers in the first instance, as no oral hearing is required under the Prison Act.[277] Moreover, the restrictive interpretation by the higher courts regarding the possibility of substantive control of 'evaluative leeway' provides a useful excuse for overloaded first instance Prison Courts to take a more hands-off approach where possible.[278]

Alarm is also fuelled by the fact that prisoners are successful in their applications to Prison Courts in only 5 per cent of cases, with nearly half of these applications failing at the outset for purely formal reasons.[279] In addition, while nine out of ten appeals to the Higher Regional Courts are permitted, only 8 per cent of these applications are successful. As a result, Feest and Selling argue that the overall success rate of prisoners' legal applications is as low as 1 per cent.[280] There is some controversy, however, as to how these statistics should be interpreted. Certain commentators argue that the low success rate is due to the shortcomings of the Prison Courts and the permissive approach to 'evaluative leeway' in the Higher Regional Courts.[281] Others argue that the statistics display the extent to which the prison administration is acting in accordance with the Prison Act and the guidance of the courts.[282] Another difficulty in assessing these statistics is that they do not account for the problem of querulous and litigious prisoners who make repeat applications.[283] Nevertheless, the figures have prompted continuing

---

[274] Northoff (n 272).   [275] Walter (n 9) 385.

[276] Dünkel 1992 (n 272).

[277] K. Rotthaus, 'Der Schutz der Grundrechte im Gefängnis' (1996) *ZfStrVo* 1, 9.

[278] U. Kamann, 'Die Blindheit der Justitia oder: die reaktionäre Entwicklung im Strafvollzug' (1996) *NK* 14.

[279] U. Kamann, *Gerichtlicher Rechtsschutz im Strafvollzug: Grenzen und Möglichkeiten der Kontrollen vollzuglicher Maßnahmen am Beispiel der Strafvollstreckungskammer beim Landgericht Arnsberg* (Centaurus, Pfaffenweiler, 1991) 180ff.

[280] J. Feest and P. Selling, 'Rechtstatsachen über Rechtsbeschwerden—Eine Untersuchung zur Praxis der Oberlandesgerichte in Strafvollzugssachen' in G. Kaiser *et al.*, *Kriminologische Forschung in den 80er Jahren* (MPI, Freiburg, 1988) 259.

[281] Kamann (n 279) 180ff.; Feest/Selling (n 280); Dünkel 1996 (n 169) 526.

[282] Kaiser/Kerner/Schöch (n 170) 40.

[283] Böhm (n 31) 38.

calls for better protection of prisoners' rights in first instance Prison Courts and Higher Regional Courts.[284]

4.3.3.2 Prison Administration

Prison administrators, under the auspices of each state administration, are fully bound by the Prison Act. This is a direct outcome of the *Rechtsstaat* principle of 'legality of administration' (*Gesetzmäßigkeit der Verwaltung*).[285] Despite this, administrative culture in German prisons remains characterized by widespread institutional resistance to legal regulation.[286] Delayed implementation or non-implementation of judgments as well as the hindrance of prisoners' access to legal redress, in particular interim legal protection, is common. This is complicated by the fact that the Prison Act does not include administrative law regulations on the enforcement of judgments, but rather refers to criminal law procedure. As a result, prison officials cannot be fined for failure to execute Prison Court judgments in good time.[287] The problem of 'refractory prison officials' (*renitente Strafvollzugsbehörde*) is highlighted by penal observers, who call for increased court vigilance and institutional reforms regarding their behaviour.

4.3.3.3 Legal Assistance and Legal Aid

In addition to the problems created by overloaded Prison Courts and 'refractory prison officials', observers have identified weaknesses regarding prisoners' access to legal information and legal aid. Under the Prison Act, prison officials must inform prisoners of their rights and duties.[288] The Higher Regional Court of Celle has held that officials must at the very least give a spoken explanation and hand a copy of the Prison Act to the prisoner.[289] Nevertheless, it has been shown that prison officials often fail to fulfil this minimum standard and that prisoners are frequently ill-informed.[290] These problems are exacerbated for prisoners who cannot speak German, as there are no translated texts of the Prison Act available and often no translators present at interviews.[291] While prisoners have the right to receive visits from their lawyers at any time,[292] their access to legal aid is dependant on the likely success of their case.[293] This often works to the prisoner's

---

[284] For summaries of these criticisms see Walter (n 9) 385; Laubenthal (n 32) 332–3.

[285] Explained in more detail at 1.5.

[286] See, in general, W. Lesting and J. Feest, 'Renitente Strafvollzugsbehörden. Eine rechtstatsächliche Untersuchung in rechtspolitischer Absicht' (1987) ZRP 390; Feest *et al.* (n 30); U. Kamann, 'Die Erweiterung des Renitenzbegriffs im Strafvollzug (1993) ZfStrVo 206; T. Ullenbruch, 'Vollzugsbehörde contra Strafvollstreckungskammer' (1993) NStZ 517.

[287] Dünkel 1996 (n 169) 527.   [288] Prison Act, § 5(2).

[289] *OLG Celle* (1987) NStZ 44.   [290] Feest, § 5, mn 10.

[291] Feest Exkurs II before § 5, mn 7.   [292] Prison Act, § 26.

[293] Civil Procedure Code, §§ 114 ff.; Prison Act, § 120(2).

disadvantage in placing a legal claim. In addition, it is commonly acknowledged that German lawyers are uninterested in prison law work due to the low fees involved.[294] Given the inequality between the level of legal advice available to prisoners relative to that of the prison administration, critics argue all the more for Prison Courts to assist prisoners in their applications, and if need be, to call an oral hearing for clarification of the claim.[295] Needless to say, the tendency for Prison Courts to decline prisoners' applications on the basis of formal legal errors is viewed as highly problematic in this context.

4.4 THE FEDERAL CONSTITUTIONAL COURT AND THE SURVIVAL OF THE PRISON ACT

The concerns regarding the protection of prisoners' substantive rights have not escaped the attention of the FCC. In contrast to its more tentative line in the 1980s,[296] the FCC has taken an activist stance since the early 1990s and has attempted to resolve many of the challenges identified by the penal academy. Of the 102 FCC decisions on the question of prison law since the Prison Act came into force, approximately 76 were made during the last ten years. Unlike the broad-based foundational decisions of the 1970s, these recent decisions are attempts to root prisoners' individual rights protections in the broader constitutional foundations of the Prison Act. The specificity of these decisions and the activist approach of the FCC have not gone unnoticed. Commentators universally agree that the FCC has made the single most important contribution to the development of prisoners' rights since the Act came into force.[297]

The FCC has made contributions in a number of different areas that will be dealt with in turn.

4.4.1 Positive Rights and the 'Constitutional Resocialization Principle'

The FCC has advanced prisoners' positive rights in a number of cases in which it has invoked the 'constitutional resocialization principle'. The most well known is the 1998 decision on pay for prison work.[298] This was a weighty decision in which empirical data was presented, the opinions of

---

[294] Dünkel 1996 (n 169) 531.   [295] Feest, § 115, mn 10.

[296] E. Niebler, 'Die Rechtsprechung des Bundesverfassungsgerichts zum Strafvollzug' in W. Fürst, R. Herzog, and D. Umbach (eds), *Festschrift für Wolfgang Ziedler* (Walter de Gruyter, Berlin, 1987) 1567.

[297] Rotthaus 1996 (n 277) 3; K. Kruis and G. Cassardt, 'Verfassungsrechtliche Leitsätze zum Vollzug von Straf- und Untersuchungshaft' (1995) *NStZ* 521; K. Kruis and G. Cassardt, 'Fortschreibung der verfassungsrechtlichen Leitsätze zum Vollzug von Straf- und Untersuchungshaft' (1998) *NStZ* 593; Walter (n 9) 373; Dünkel 1996 (n 169) 527.

[298] *BVerfGE* 98, 169.

leading penologists were heard and the concepts of resocialization and work were discussed in detail.[299] The FCC stated that the 'duty to work' under paragraph 41 of the Prison Act could only be viewed as an effective means of resocialization if the work was remunerated appropriately. While such remuneration need not be financial, it must provide sufficient acknowledgement of the work done so as to reinforce the value of work to the prisoner as a means of forming an independent and crime-free life in the future. As a result, the FCC held that paragraph 200(1) of the Prison Act, a transitional provision that delayed planned reforms of prison work remuneration, was incompatible with the 'constitutional resocialization principle'. It gave the legislature until 31 December 2000 to implement a new law regulating prisoners' pay in line with the guidelines provided by the Court. While this decision was praised for sending a clear signal in favour of the 'constitutional resocialization principle' in a time of increasing punitivism,[300] it was not without critics. The latter seek more radical solutions such as the abolition of the 'duty to work' as well as the elimination of other transitional provisions which prevent full inclusion of prisoners in medical insurance and pension schemes.[301] Notwithstanding, the decision has been hailed as the single most important constitutional decision on prison law since the *Lebach* decision in 1973.[302] Moreover, it sent a signal to the states (*Länder*) that continuing reliance on 'transitional provisions' in the Act may not be tolerated by the FCC.

In response to this decision, the Federal Parliament passed the Fifth Amendment of the Prison Act, which took effect in January 2001.[303] Subsequently, the FCC was called upon to assess whether this legislation was compatible with the principles set out in their 1998 decision.[304] The legislation raised prisoner's pay in real terms by 80 per cent,[305] and permitted the use of non-monetary benefits, such as reduction in the sentence term and relaxation of the prison regime, as payment for prison work. The Court recognized a wide margin of discretion on the part of the legislator in fulfilling the 'constitutional resocialization requirement', and noted that the low productivity of prison work, in combination with high levels of unemployment

---

[299] F. Dünkel, 'Germany' in F. Dünkel and D. van Zyl Smit (eds), *Prison Labour: Salvation or Slavery? International Perspectives* (Dartmouth, Aldershot, 1999) 77, 81–4.

[300] G. Britz, 'Leistungsgerechtes Arbeitsentgelt für Strafgefangene?' (1999) *ZfStrVo* 195, 197–8.

[301] U. Kamann, 'Das Urteil des Bundesverfassungsgerichts vom 1.7.1998 (StV 98, 438) zur Gefangenenentlohnung, ein nicht kategorischer Imperativ für den Resozialisierungsvollzug' (1999) *StV* 438.

[302] Dünkel 1999 (n 299) 84. On the *Lebach* decision, see 2.2.2.2.

[303] *5. Gesetz zur Änderung des Strafvollzugsgesetzes* vom 27. Dezember 2000 (BGBl I 2000, 2043).

[304] *BVerfG Beschl.* (2002) *NJW* 2023.

[305] The rate was raised from 5% to 9% of the reference wage (a wage level, set by social security law, at which employees are eligible for employee contributions to social security benefits). This was said by the FCC to be an increase in real terms of 80%.

and state debt in the open market, restricted the range of options available. It argued that that the new legislation fulfilled 'minimum constitutional requirements', but urged the legislator to assess the level of remuneration at regular intervals in the future. The test for the FCC was whether the level of remuneration, in combination with other non-financial benefits, reinforced the value of work to the prisoner as a means of forming an independent and crime-free life in the future. Satisfied that this test was fulfilled, it held the new legislation to be consistent with the 'constitutional resocialization requirement' and thereby with the prisoner's basic rights under articles 1(1) and 2(1) of the Basic Law.

Aside from the question of remuneration for work, the FCC has made a number of decisions fortifying prisoners' positive rights to resocialization. The first of these was made in 1993 regarding prisoners' sentence plans.[306] The Prison Act stipulates that prisoners should have, from the beginning to the end of their sentence, a staged 'sentence administration plan' (*Vollzugsplan*) for their resocialization.[307] This plan should be drafted after a 'treatment examination' (*Behandlungsuntersuchung*). Prisoners have a right to this examination,[308] and a right to discuss their treatment with the administration during this examination.[309] The plan must, at the very least, include concrete statements capable of being implemented[310] on the placement of the prisoner in an open, closed, or social therapeutic prison or social and therapeutic group, the proposed relaxation of the prison regime, measures to address the prisoner's special therapeutic needs, to promote the prisoner's vocational and further education, and to prepare for his release.[311]

A life-sentenced prisoner challenged his 'sentence administration plan' in its entirety, arguing that the plan did not fulfil the minimum requirements of the Prison Act and that he had not been given the opportunity to discuss his treatment before the plan was concluded. The Prison Courts rejected his claim arguing that, as a matter of procedure,[312] the prisoner was only allowed to challenge individual measures in the plan, but not the plan in its entirety. The FCC held that the Prison Court's narrow and formalistic interpretation of the prisoner's rights in this respect violated the basic right to effective legal protection under article 19(4) of the Basic Law. It stated that the plan enjoys significant legal protection and that the plan was the 'individual concretization' of the 'constitutionally protected resocialization purpose' that serves as an 'orientation framework' for the prisoner and prison administration. The FCC argued that the Act placed a duty on the prison administration to work together both with prisoners and social workers to

---

[306] *B VerfG Beschl.* (1993) NStZ 301.   [307] Prison Act, § 6(2) and (3).
[308] Prison Act, § 6(1).
[309] Prison Act, § 6(3). Calliess/Müller-Dietz (1998), § 6, mn 1 and 7.
[310] *B VerfG Beschl.* (1993) NJW 3188.   [311] Prison Act, § 7(2).
[312] Prison Act, § 109.

create plans reflecting the minimum standards of the Prison Act and furthering the prisoner's resocialization. It therefore held that the plan in its entirety, as well as the procedure by which it was executed, could be challenged in court. In addition, the FCC reinforced the general view of the academy that while prisoners do not have a clear right to the inclusion of a specific measure in the plan, they do have a right to the exercise of faultless discretion in the composition of the sentence plan.[313]

In various additional decisions, the FCC strengthened the prisoner's positive rights to regime relaxation and prison leave.[314] It has done this by increasing the density of court control over 'evaluative leeway' in determining the conditions for refusal of such applications, namely whether a 'danger of misuse' exists.[315] While the FCC has accepted that it is constitutional to tolerate a measure of 'evaluative leeway' on the part of the prison administration, it nevertheless imposed high standards of justification on decision-makers and indicated that Prison Courts must improve the density of judicial scrutiny of such decisions. The FCC has repeatedly stated that refusal of prison leave and regime relaxation, and thereby the possibility of hindering the damaging effects of long-term imprisonment and the chances of enhancing social reintegration, is a restriction of the constitutionally protected right to resocialization.[316] As a result, in evaluating the prisoner's application for either of these measures, prison administrators must demonstrate that they have fulfilled the constitutional principle of proportionality and properly weighed the prisoner's right to resocialization in their deliberation process. Moreover, prison administrators should set out 'concrete facts' which justify a fear of a 'danger of misuse' in the individual case. It is not sufficient for the decision-maker to refer in an 'abstract' manner (*abstrakte Hinweise*) to 'danger of misuse', or to justify the decision to decline prison leave or regime relaxation on the basis of 'mere generalised statements and undifferentiated evaluations' (*bloße, pauschale Wertungen*). In addition, the FCC linked regime relaxation and prison leave to parole eligibility.[317] Because courts are likely to view failure to obtain prison leave or regime relaxation as a negative indicator in their consideration of parole, the FCC views decisions to decline applications for leave and regime relaxation as impinging upon prisoners' basic right to personal freedom as guaranteed under article 104 of the Basic Law. This, along with the constitutionally protected right to resocialization, underpins the general presumption in favour of granting prisoners' applications in these cases. These recent decisions

---

[313] *BVerfG Beschl.* (1993) *NStZ* 301.

[314] *BVerfG Beschl.* (1997) *NJW* 1133; (1998) *NStZ* 430; (1998) *ZfStrVo* 180; M. Heghmanns, 'Die neuere Rechtsprechung des Bundesverfassungsgerichts zur gerichtlichen Überprüfung der Versagung von Vollzugslockerungen—eine Trendwende?' (1999) *ZStW* 647; T. Müller, 'Offener Vollzug und Vollzugslockerungen (Ausgang, Freigang)' (1999) *ZfStrVo* 3.

[315] See 4.3.2.1 above.

[316] *BVerfG Beschl.* (1997) *NJW* 1133; (1998) *NStZ* 430; (1998) *ZfStrVo* 180.

[317] *BVerfG Beschl.* (1998) *NJW* 1133.

reinforced the standards of the Federal Supreme Court in the determination of 'evaluative leeway' under the Prison Act[318] and sent a clear message to Prison Courts and Higher Regional Courts that lack of vigilance in the scrutiny of 'evaluative leeway' is no longer constitutionally acceptable. This represents a welcome response to the problems raised by the academy in this respect.[319]

Finally, the FCC has vindicated a life-sentenced prisoner's claim to psychiatric treatment outside the prison.[320] This case concerned a Prison Court's interpretation of paragraph 65(2) of the Prison Act, which affords prisoners the right to be treated outside a prison or prison hospital where the required treatment cannot be provided inside the institution. The prison administration and lower Prison Court held that the provision could not be used by the prisoner to receive psychiatric treatment that was designed to enhance the prisoner's suitability for life outside the prison. This interpretation was struck down by the FCC, which held that restricting the prisoner's access to such psychiatric treatment interfered with the prisoner's basic right to resocialization. Moreover, because such psychiatric treatment was likely to improve his chances for parole, the court held that the decision interfered with his right to personal freedom under article 104 of the Basic Law.

4.4.2 Prison Conditions and Accommodation

4.4.2.1 Prison Conditions

In 1993, the FCC stated that the temporary accommodation of a prisoner in a cell flooded by effluent from an overflowing toilet was a grave violation of the prisoners' right to human dignity.[321] The FCC held that, as to prison administration, protection of human dignity requires maintenance of the basic preconditions of individual and social existence. Where these basic conditions are not met, the State cannot rely on a prison allocation order to defeat the prisoner's right to an immediate transfer to another cell or prison, or to the immediate improvement of the conditions in the cell. The case has additional procedural implications, which are discussed at 4.4.3.1 below.

4.4.2.2 Prison Accommodation

Paragraph 146(1) of the Prison Act expressly forbids the use of single cells for double accommodation; however, paragraph 146(2) of the Act allows for temporary exceptions upon authorization of the prison supervisory authority (*Aufsichtsbehörde*). The problem of prison overcrowding has been highlighted by critics who argue that the exception permitted under paragraph 146(2) is too frequently relied upon and too broadly interpreted by

---

[318] *BGHSt* 30, 320. See 4.3.2.1 above.   [319] See 4.3.2.2 above.
[320] *B VerfG Beschl.* (1996) NStZ 614.
[321] *B VerfG Beschl.* (1993) StV 487. See further 4.4.3.1 below.

states' administrative guidelines.[322] This concern was addressed by the Higher Regional Court of Celle in 1999, which warned that paragraph 146(2) was not to be used to cure chronic overcrowding.[323] In two recent cases the FCC ordered that temporary accommodation of more than one prisoner in a single cell violated the prisoner's right to human dignity under article 1(1) of the Basic Law.[324] In the first case, the prisoners, who were due for transportation to another prison, were placed for five days in a cell 7.6 metres square without a partition between the cell and toilet area. They were only allowed to leave the cell for one hour a day.[325] In the second case, two prisoners were held for three months in a cell 8 metres square due to temporary, and unavoidable, overcrowding of the prison.[326] Again, the cell had no partition between the cell and toilet area. In both cases the prison administration and lower courts argued that because their accommodations were now significantly improved and the prison agreed to place the prisoners in appropriate accommodation in the future, the prisoners had no right to *ex post facto* declarations of illegality regarding the temporary conditions in which they had been held. The FCC rejected this argument, asserting that 'the right to human dignity has the highest weight under the Constitution and is to be understood as the fundamental constitutive principle of the system of basic rights'.[327] Where grave infringements of the right to human dignity arise, the FCC argued, prisoners have a legal interest in an *ex post facto* declaration of illegality and courts must fully consider the circumstances of the case in this context. These decisions have recently been associated with political moves to decrease the prison population in order to avoid prison overcrowding.[328]

4.4.3 The Right to Effective Legal Protection

4.4.3.1 *Simplifying the Enforcement of Prisoners' Rights*

The FCC has made a concerted effort to shift the formalist approach of the Prison Courts and the refractory behaviour of prison officials. This has been done primarily by developing prisoners' rights to effective legal protection under article 19(4) of the Basic Law. In this context, it is particularly conscious of the fact that many legal applications are written by the prisoners themselves in non-legal language and in a manner that falls short of the strict procedural requirements of the Prison Courts and that 50 per cent of prisoners' legal applications were failing at the outset on purely formal grounds.[329]

---

[322] Schwind/Böhm, § 146, mn 8; Feest, § 146, mn 7; Rotthaus, 1987 (n 1) 3.
[323] *OLG Celle* (1999) *ZfStrVo* 57.
[324] *BVerfG Beschl.* (2002) *NJW* 2699; (2002) *NJW* 2700.
[325] *BVerfG Beschl.* (2002) *NJW* 2699. [326] *BVerfG Beschl.* (2002) *NJW* 2700.
[327] *BVerfG Beschl.* (2002) *NJW* 2700.
[328] C. Schmidt, 'Schwitzen statt sitzen', *Der Spiegel*, 21 July 2003.
[329] See 4.3.3.1 above.

Thus, a cluster of FCC decisions has established safeguards concerning prisoners' applications for emergency interim legal protection against the execution of disciplinary sanctions.[330] It is a violation of the right to effective legal protection for prison officials immediately to execute a disciplinary sanction that the prisoner wished to challenge, without giving courts a chance to evaluate the prisoner's application for emergency interim legal protection. The FCC requires that prison officials ensure that the prisoner's application reach the court for a timely decision to be made. It suggested that the administration fax the application to the court when required for purposes of 'effective legal protection'. Moreover, Prison Courts have been told to decide prisoners' applications as quickly as possible and to not allow lack of clarity, technical mistakes or formal errors in an application to prevent granting such protection. Thus, Prison Courts should clarify any confusion in the prisoner's application or seek to remedy any formal errors as quickly as possible. This may include telephoning the prisoner or prison officials for clarification. In a recent FCC decision, a delay of one week by the Prison Court, which resulted in the sanction being executed, was heavily criticized. The FCC argued that emergency interim legal protection should have been awarded to stop execution of the sanction before the Court could properly consider the application.[331]

The FCC does not view interim legal protection only as a prohibition to act. It has also held that an HIV-infected prisoner who was dependent on his work income to subsidize his medication should have been granted effective legal protection to reinstate him temporarily to the workplace after his dismissal on disciplinary grounds.[332] Likewise, as discussed at 4.4.2.1 above, a Prison Court was censured for taking a narrow and formalist view of a prisoner's application to be immediately moved from a cell that was flooded with toilet effluent.[333] The decision held that the Prison Court's formalistic interpretation of the prisoner's application for interim relief violated the prisoner's right to effective legal protection as well as his right to human dignity.

Beyond interim legal protection, Prison Courts have been criticized by the FCC for taking a formalist or obtuse approach to applications challenging administrative decisions, requesting legal aid, and the reinstatement of a claim after the statutory time limit had expired.[334] These decisions have established the principle that misinterpreting the plain meaning of an application to the prisoner's procedural disadvantage violates the right to equal and effective legal protection and the constitutional prohibition on arbitrary

---

[330] *BVerfG Beschl.* (1993) *StV* 482; (1995) *ZfStrVo* 372; (1994) 3 *BlStVKunde* 6–7; (1994) *ZfStrVo* 245; (1994) *NJW* 3089; (2001) *NJW* 3770.

[331] *BVerfG Beschl.* (2001) *NJW* 3770.

[332] *BVerfG Beschl.* (1994) *NStZ* 101.   [333] *BVerfG Beschl.* (1993) *StV* 487.

[334] *BVerfG Beschl.* 2 BvR 2989/95; (1990) *NStZ* 557; (1993) *NJW* 1380; (1993) *StV* 451; (1994) *StV* 201; (1996) *StV* 445.

decision-making (*Willkürverbot*). Rather the FCC takes the view that Prison Courts should interpret the Prison Act's procedural provisions generously, and seek to remedy the prisoner's procedural mistakes so as to fulfil the prisoner's right to effective legal protection.

4.4.3.2 Insults and the Right to Effective Legal Protection

In two decisions, the FCC set standards regarding the courts' approach to legal applications containing insults (*Beleidigung*).[335] In the first case,[336] the Regional Court of Heidelberg had rejected five applications from a detainee in a psychiatric hospital because they contained serious insults which the prisoner would not retract. The prisoner's constitutional application, based upon article 19(4) of the Basic Law, failed on the grounds that he had not exhausted the legal process before applying to the FCC. The Court noted, however, that, in the light of the right to effective legal protection, rejection of applications containing insults is permitted only in exceptional circumstances, namely where the application consists almost entirely of insults and the substance of the application cannot be established. The FCC noted that this standard applies especially when the applicant is detained in a psychiatric hospital. It concluded that the appropriate means of sanctioning insults is through criminal law, not through limitation of legal protections under procedural laws.

In the second decision,[337] a prisoner's application to the court was rejected because he had written numerous letters to MPs containing death threats and serious insults against the prison administration and the regional judiciary. The legal application itself contained no insults, but the Higher Regional Court of Karlsruhe read the application in the light of these letters. The FCC was highly critical of this decision. Whilst it accepted that the Higher Regional Court could consider the letters, it argued that a general forfeiture of legal protection against public administrative measures based upon threatening letters not only irrelevant to the application, but without further consideration of it, violated article 19(4) of the Basic Law. The FCC stated that the test for abuse of process is not whether the applicant made the procedure difficult. Rather, the test must be whether the applicant used his procedural rights for unforeseen or impermissible purposes, to damage his legal opponent or to burden the Court. The Court was therefore under a duty to consider the application properly to establish whether the applicant asserted a factually justified and legally protected procedural right. Otherwise, the Court's refusal to consider the application fully constituted a sanction for the applicant's improper behaviour, which is properly regulated under criminal law, and thereby constituted a violation of article 19(4).

---

[335] Under Penal Code, § 185 it is a criminal offence to 'insult' another person.
[336] *BVerfG Beschl.* (2001) *NJW* 3615.   [337] *BVerfG Beschl.* 2 BvR 282/00.

4.4.4 Restricting Discretion and Powers of Rights Intervention

The majority of FCC decisions over the last ten years deal with provisions granting powers of rights restrictions (*Eingriffsbefugnisse*) to the prison administration. The FCC has sought to restrict these powers and set exacting standards for the scrutiny of discretion exercised in this context. It has attempted to draw a balance between the purposes of the powers given and the protections of constitutional rights and principles.

4.4.4.1 Correspondence

The FCC has been particularly vigilant in the protection of prisoners' correspondence. While the Prison Act expressly protects prisoners' legal correspondence from any surveillance,[338] prisoners' non-legal correspondence does not enjoy such immunity and the Act allows the interception of letters for various reasons. Thus, prisoners' correspondence can be stopped where it endangers the aim of resocialization and security and order; the prison officer would commit a crime by delivering it; the letter includes 'gross misrepresentations' of relations within the prison or 'gross insults' against others; the letter might endanger the integration of other prisoners; or the correspondence is written in code or illegibly.[339] The FCC has been confronted by a number of challenges from prisoners regarding the interception of their non-legal correspondence. These prisoners argue that, in deciding to intercept their correspondence on any one of the above grounds, prison officials failed to account properly for their basic rights to freedom of expression and protection of correspondence under article 5(1) of the Basic Law and their right to freedom of the personality under articles 2(1) and 1(1) of that Law. In addition, it is argued that, in scrutinizing official decisions to intercept correspondence, the Prison Courts and the Higher Regional Courts have not sufficiently weighed prisoners' basic rights.

While less inclined to accept these arguments during the 1980s,[340] the FCC has been more proactive since the early 1990s. In particular, the FCC has addressed restrictions on intercepting correspondence that includes 'gross insults' to others.[341] In a number of cases the FCC has insisted that the interception of correspondence on this ground should not be used to censor the prisoner. Arguing that the provisions regarding correspondence must be construed in accordance with the resocialization aim of imprisonment and prisoners' basic rights to freedom of the personality and freedom of expression, the FCC stressed the importance of unhindered correspondence with the outside world as a necessary outlet for offenders in confinement.

---

[338] Prison Act, § 29.　　　　　　　　　　[339] Prison Act, § 31(1).
[340] *BVerfG Beschl.* 2 BvR 250/81; 2 BvR 330/85.
[341] *BVerfG Beschl.* (1993) *StV* 600; (1994) *NJW* 244; (1994) *NStZ* 403; (1995) *NJW* 1477; (1996) *NStZ* 55.

Given this context, the FCC has sought to ensure that the interception of correspondence should only occur in severe cases of 'gross insults' and not where the prisoner expresses frustration with prison officials or judges.[342] As a result, the FCC argues that the standard for finding a 'gross insult' should be higher for prisoners' correspondence than that applied under the Penal Code to persons at liberty.[343] The FCC has also pointed out that 'statements of frustration' only surface upon surveillance of the correspondence in question. As a result, the FCC has stated that interception of correspondence should only occur where the insult was sufficiently grave or where it was clear that the prisoner had purposefully aimed to insult persons involved in the surveillance of correspondence.[344] The FCC has thus rejected the suggestion that accusing Higher Regional Court judges of being Nazis[345] or prison officials of being 'well-known misanthropes',[346] 'cretins', power hungry 'perverts' or 'concentration camp officials' amounts to a 'gross insult' for the purpose of intercepting prisoners' correspondence with the outside world.[347]

The FCC has, however, accepted that a highly exaggerated and critical representation of a prison institution in a prisoner's letter published in a right-wing magazine amounted to a 'gross misrepresentation' as well as a 'gross insult' under paragraph 31 of the Prison Act and general criminal law. In this circumstance the FCC accepted that interception was additionally justified to show the prisoner the consequences of his criminal actions and further his resocialization.[348]

Finally, the FCC has accepted that interception of correspondence between two convicted prisoners involved in the same crime could be justified where statements in the correspondence potentially threatened the chances of either prisoner's social reintegration.[349]

4.4.4.2 Right to Information

In addition to protecting prisoners' rights to correspondence, the FCC has set standards on restrictions of prisoners' access to written information. Paragraph 68 of the Prison Act allows the restriction of newspapers or magazines if they threaten the resocialization aim or security and order within the prison. The FCC has set standards regarding the application of this provision in the light of the right to freedom of information under article 5(1) of the Basic Law.[350] It stated that magazines and newspapers could only be restricted where there is a 'real and concrete danger to the prisoner's

---

[342] These principles are set out in *BVerfG Beschl.* (1994) *NStZ* 403 and in all of the decisions in n 341.

[343] Penal Code, § 185 criminalizes 'gross insults'.

[344] *BVerfG Beschl.* (1995) *NJW* 1477. [345] *BVerfG Beschl.* (1993) *StV* 600.

[346] *BVerfG Beschl.* (1996) *NStZ* 55. [347] *BVerfG Beschl.* (1994) *NStZ* 403.

[348] *BVerfG Beschl.* (1994) *NJW* 244. [349] *BVerfG Beschl.* (1996) *NStZ* 55.

[350] *BVerfG Beschl.* (1996) *ZfStrVo* 244; (1996) *ZfStrVo* 176.

resocialisation or to security and order in the individual case' and where such restrictions are 'suitable and necessary for the avoidance of this danger'.[351] In the first of two cases on this issue, the FCC accepted that the prison had fulfilled these constitutional standards when stopping an offender from reading a right-wing magazine. The FCC accepted that this decision had been made on legitimate resocialization grounds, as the offender in question had committed his original offence due to his right-wing beliefs.[352] In the second case, the FCC condoned the interception of an article for security reasons on the grounds that it contained highly exaggerated criticisms of the prison institution. However, the FCC indicated that it would not accept restrictions of 'readily available media sources in which normal criticisms of the prison institutions were contained'. The FCC believes such restrictions would 'patronize' the prisoner.[353]

4.4.4.3 Discipline

In a number of cases, the FCC specified rigorous standards for imposing disciplinary sanctions.[354] Thus, all disciplinary sanctions, like criminal sanctions, are subject to the principle of proportionality (*Schuldangemessenheit, Verhältnismäßigkeitsgrundsatz*), which is said to derive its constitutional importance from the *Rechtsstaatsprinzip* and the right to equality before the law under article 3 of the Basic Law. As the FCC stipulated in these cases, this broad principle has procedural and substantive dimensions. The procedural dimension requires full and proper consideration of the individual facts of each case to establish the level of the offender's culpability. The substantive dimension requires that the sanction imposed be commensurate with the offender's culpability and the harm caused. Equally, the sanction imposed must be the least possible invasion of prisoners' basic rights that can achieve the disciplinary purpose. In addition, the FCC argues that the decision whether to impose a disciplinary sanction or the choice of disciplinary sanction must be made in the light of the resocialization purpose set out in paragraph 2 of the Prison Act, the guiding principles of prison administration in paragraph 3 of that Act and broader preventative goals.[355] In this light, the added institutional pressures of imprisonment must be considered when weighing the culpability of the offender.[356]

On the basis of these principles, the FCC has struck down decisions to impose disciplinary sanctions on a prisoner whose breath smelt of alcohol but who had not undergone a breathalyser test and had no previous record of alcohol abuse;[357] a prisoner who had lost his temper and insulted a prison

---

[351] *BVerfG Beschl.* (1996) *ZfStrVo* 244.   [352] *BVerfG Beschl.* (1996) *ZfStrVo* 176.
[353] *BVerfG Beschl.* (1996) *ZfStrVo* 244.
[354] *BVerfG Beschl.* (1993) *NStZ* 605; (1994) *StV* 473; (1995) *NJW* 1016; (1995) *ZfStrVo* 53; (1995) *StV* 651.
[355] *BVerfG Beschl.* (1994) *StV* 473; (1995) *NJW* 1016.
[356] *BVerfG Beschl.* (1995) *NJW* 1016.   [357] *BVerfG Beschl.* (1993) *NStZ* 605.

officer in breach of duties regarding prison behaviour under the Act;[358] a prisoner who insulted prison officials in his complaint to the prison authorities (*Dienstaufsichtsbeschwerde*);[359] and two prisoners who refused to work on health grounds even though a cursory doctor's examination declared them fit to work.[360]

In all of these judgments the decisions of the Prison Courts were criticized alongside those of the prison officials for failing to consider fully the rights and principles detailed above.

4.4.4.4 Personal Possessions

The FCC has also provided guidelines on decisions on the prisoner's right to retain personal possessions. This is regulated under paragraph 70 of the Prison Act, which states in section 1 that, 'the prisoner can retain an appropriate number of books and other personal articles for use in his free time'. Sections 2 and 3 provide that permission to retain personal articles can be 'refused' or 'withdrawn' when such possession is subject to criminal sanction or presents a danger to the aim of prison administration or the security and order of the prison.

The FCC has set out standards regarding the refusal and withdrawal of permission to retain personal possessions. It has stated that, although it is constitutionally acceptable to decline permission to retain 'objectively dangerous objects' without consideration of the prisoner's individual circumstances, discretion as regards other objects remains subject to the constitutional principles of proportionality and equality before the law.[361] Thus, the FCC struck down a decision refusing an electronic keyboard to a prisoner on the grounds that the decision-maker failed to balance its importance for the prisoner's further education and potential resocialization against the 'relatively limited danger of the object' to the security and order of the prison.[362] Further, the FCC rejected a decision refusing a prisoner's application to replace his broken watch with one of similar value and restricting him to a watch of much lower value. It held this decision to be arbitrary, despite the justification offered by the prison administration that ownership of expensive watches threatened the resocialization purpose through its potential to create sub-cultural trade and bartering systems.[363]

The FCC has also stipulated that where a personal possession was already granted, the subsequent decision to withdraw it is subject to the principle of legitimate expectation (*Vertrauensschutz*).[364] In Germany, this principle is

---

[358] *BVerfG Beschl.* (1995) *NJW* 1016.   [359] *BVerfG Beschl.* (1994) *StV* 473.
[360] *BVerfG Beschl.* (1995) *ZfStrVo* 53 ; (1995) *StV* 651.
[361] *BVerfG Beschl.* (1994) *NStZ* 453; (1994) *ZfStrVo* 376; (1996) *StV* 683; (2000) *EuGrZ* 552.
[362] *BVerfG Beschl.* (1996) *StV* 683.   [363] *BVerfG Beschl.* (2000) *EuGrZ* 552.
[364] *BVerfG Beschl.* (1994) *StV* 432; (1994) *NStZ* 100; (1996) *StV* 48; (1997) *ZfStrVo* 367.

derived from the *Rechtsstaatsprinzip* and article 2(1) of the Basic Law (free-dom of the personality). It stipulates that where the citizen has been placed in a legal position by a decision-maker and relies thereupon, they have a legitimate expectation which must receive full consideration in the author-ity's subsequent decisions.[365] In such cases, the official decision-maker must balance the citizen's right to have their legitimate expectations protected and the general interests of the public to have this position changed. According to the FCC, prisoners' legitimate expectations are also underpinned by the resocialization principle. It has stated:

> The withdrawal of an object already granted to the prisoner, without clear evidence that the prisoner has himself created the reasons for such a course of action, is regularly experienced by prisoners as highly invasive and unjust and runs counter to the aim of prison administration namely the resocialisation or socialisation of the prisoner.[366]

As a result, the FCC holds that where the prison administration wishes to withdraw objects for which prisoners have already obtained permission, there must be 'clear and concrete factors' or 'changes in the circumstances in the individual case' justifying the decision and outweighing prisoners' legitimate expectations in this regard.[367] Accordingly, the FCC has struck down decisions to withdraw permission for prisoners to retain a stereo set,[368] stereo loudspeakers,[369] and a special day blanket.[370] The FCC was, however, satisfied that the confiscation of an electric typewriter with a lim-ited memory capacity was justified on security grounds, because the prisoner could use this memory capacity to exchange information with other prison-ers and the outside world which the prison administration could not properly control.[371]

4.4.4.5 Prison Visits

The FCC has considered whether the placement of a glass screen between prisoners and their visitors was constitutionally permissible.[372] The Act per-mits surveillance of prisoners' visits for security and order but does not stip-ulate explicitly whether this includes the use of glass screens.[373] The FCC accepted that glass screens could be used for 'surveillance' under paragraph 27 of the Prison Act,[374] but argued strongly that this would only be permis-sible in 'individual cases' where there was 'concrete evidence of a real threat to security and order' in the prison. Such decisions would be subject to a

---

[365] See *BVerfGE* 59, 128, 164.   [366] *BVerfG Beschl.* (1996) *StV* 48.
[367] *BVerfG Beschl.* (1994) *NStZ* 100, (1996) *StV* 48, (1994) *StV* 432, (1997) *ZfStrVo* 367.
[368] *BVerfG Beschl.* (1994) *NStZ* 100.   [369] *BVerfG Beschl.* (1996) *StV* 48.
[370] *BVerfG Beschl.* (1994) *StV* 432.   [371] *BVerfG Beschl.* (1997) *ZfStrVo* 367.
[372] *BVerfGE* 89, 315.   [373] Prison Act, § 27.
[374] The FCC rejected the use of Prison Act, § 4(2), sentence 2 as a legal foundation for the use of glass screens. See 4.2.3.2 above.

strict test of proportionality. The prison therefore must demonstrate that it properly balanced the protections of the prisoner's basic right to the free exercise of the personality against the threat to security and order involved. Moreover, where the prison wishes to use glass screens during visits with family, the prison must also consider the protections of article 6 of the Basic Law (state protection of the family) and the prisoner's right to resocialization, which includes retaining family bonds.

4.4.4.6 Prison Cell

The FCC has ruled on whether entering a prisoner's cell without knocking is a violation of article 13 of the Basic Law (privacy of the home), article 1(1) of the Basic Law (human dignity), and article 2(1) of the Basic Law (freedom of the personality).[375] The FCC held that such action does not violate article 13 as the prison cell does not qualify as the prisoner's home. Nevertheless, the manner of entry into a prisoner's cell could amount to a violation of the prisoner's rights under articles 1(1) and 2(1). It argued that these rights, the doctrine of proportionality, and the constitutional prohibition on arbitrary decision-making (*Willkürverbot*) obliged prison officials to enter the cell with sensitivity. When considering whether any of these rights or principles had been violated, courts should consider surrounding circumstances, including the necessity of entering a prison cell without notice. In addition, the FCC noted that in many cases the noise of the keys in the door amounts to sufficient forewarning to the prisoner to protect his human dignity and intimate sphere. This particular FCC decision relates to the protections of prisoners' basic rights and does not negate various decisions by non-constitutional courts that paragraph 3 of the Prison Act gives rise to a general duty on prison officers to knock before entering the cell.[376] In a closely related decision, the FCC also considered whether placing the names of prisoners on cell doors was constitutionally problematic.[377] The FCC held that where such action was necessary for the organization of the prison, no constitutional objections could be made on the basis of the right to informational self-determination.[378]

4.4.4.7 Allocation and Use of Prisoners' Income

The Prison Act has a number of detailed regulations regarding allocation and use of a prisoner's income. A prisoner's income is made up of remuneration for work, pocket money, or educational grants. The Prison Act stipulates that a prisoner's income should be divided into three broad categories: a) personal income (*Hausgeld*); b) bridging money after release

---

[375] *BVerfG Beschl.* (1996) *NJW* 2643.   [376] See 4.2.2. above.
[377] *BVerfG Beschl.* (1997) *ZfStrVo* 111.
[378] This right is developed from Basic Law, art. 2(1) in connection with Basic Law, art. 1(1).

(*Überbrückungsgeld*); and c) personal savings (*Eigengeld*), if applicable. [379] The FCC has dealt with many complaints in this area.

The FCC rejected a decision to set costs awarded against the prisoner in a number of Prison Court proceedings against the prisoner's savings and future pocket money allowance.[380] The prison administration's decision went beyond the clear and detailed wording of the Prison Act, which stipulated that costs of legal proceedings could only be set against the prisoner's 'personal income' (*Hausgeld*) provided that at least 30DM of it was reserved for the prisoner.[381] The FCC held that the decision and subsequent approval thereof by the Prison Court and Higher Regional Court of Frankfurt, was a legally unfounded and serious violation of the prisoner's basic right to freedom of the personality under article 2(1) of the Basic Law. As a result, the decision also violated the 'legal proviso' and the principle of the legality of administration (*Gesetzmäßigkeit der Verwaltung*).[382]

Another complaint concerned a prison administration's decision refusing a prisoner permission to have his clothes laundered by a private company and sent by parcel to the prison on the grounds that a person outside the prison was paying for this service. The prisoner was not able to work on health grounds, received minimal 'personal income' from the prison authorities, and had limited personal financial resources. The prison administration argued that it could not permit an outsider to pay for a service which the prisoner should pay for himself. The prison felt that permitting outsiders to pay for prisoners in this way would create a hierarchy within the prison between those with wealthy relatives and those without and this would lead to dependency relationships between poorer and richer prisoners. In any event, the prison argued, if the prisoner could not afford to have his own clothes laundered he could wear the clothes provided by the institution. The FCC held that this decision was arbitrary and violated the prisoner's basic right to equality under article 3 of the Basic Law. It held that the administration's reasons for the decision were unsustainable given that the prisoner could not afford the service through no fault of his own. Furthermore, the FCC suggested that the aim of avoiding wealth hierarchies within prisons might not be commensurate with the 'adaptation' principle (*Angleichungsgrundsatz*) under paragraph 3(1) of the Prison Act, which stipulated that the prison environment should reflect the outside world as far as possible.[383]

Finally, the FCC has held that consideration of the prisoner's own private income in the determination of his monthly 'personal income' allowance was not a question of constitutional law.[384] The FCC also held that deducting unemployment insurance from a prisoner's work income, when the prisoner would be deported to a country where he could not benefit from this

---

[379] Prison Act, §§ 47–52.
[380] *BVerfG Beschl.* (1996) *NJW* 3146.
[381] Prison Act, § 121(5).
[382] See 2.3.
[383] *BVerfG Beschl.* (1996) *StV* 681.
[384] *BVerfG Beschl.* (1996) 315.

insurance, did not violate his right to equality under article 3 of the Basic Law.[385]

4.4.4.8 Placement of Prisoners

In an unusual case, the FCC held that a prisoner had a legitimate expectation to remain in the prison in which he had been placed for over two years, although the original placement decision was not legally sound. The FCC argued that the prisoner's legitimate expectation was underpinned by his right to resocialization, which would be undermined by moving him and breaking the social bonds established within the prison.[386]

4.4.4.9 Security Measures

Paragraph 85 of the Prison Act allows measures to secure containment of a prisoner where there is a 'heightened danger of escape or threat to security and order'. In a case challenging the constitutionality of an order to chain a prisoner under this provision, but which had been resolved before the matter could be decided, the FCC indicated that decisions to chain prisoners for security reasons would be subject to a rigorous proportionality test and to the heightened scrutiny of the courts in the future.[387]

4.4.4.10 Prisoner Clothing

Paragraph 20(1) of the Prison Act stipulates that prisoners are normally required to wear prison institution clothing. Under paragraph 20(2) of the Prison Act, however, the prison administration has the discretion to permit prisoners to wear their own clothing where it is expected that the prisoner will not attempt to escape. These provisions do not specify whether the prisoner should be allowed to wear personal clothing before a court, but the FCC has indicated that a prisoner's basic rights to freedom of the personality under articles 2(1) and 1(1) of the Basic Law could be violated where prisoners are not permitted to wear their own clothes during court proceedings. The FCC has stipulated that in making a decision in this respect, prison authorities must fully consider the prisoner's personality rights and balance these against the risk of escape.[388]

4.5 CONCLUSION

This chapter concludes our account of the method and manner of conceiving of the prisoners' legal status in Germany. This was an account, written for an audience foreign to Germany, which has sought to illuminate the broader cultural and legal context within which German prisoners' rights

---

[385] B VerfG Beschl. (1995) 1 BlStVKunde 8.
[387] B Verf Beschl. (1997) 3 BlStVKunde 6.
[386] B VerfG Beschl. (1993) NStZ 300.
[388] B Verf Beschl. (2000) NStZ 166.

are conceived, interpreted, and applied. Chapter 1 highlighted the symbolic importance of constitutional rights within German legal and constitutional culture and the distinctive way in which these rights are viewed. It explained how the prisoner's fundamental rights status and the constitutional resocialization principle were shaped within the German constitutional environment. Chapter 2 examined the dynamics of the prison reform process. It highlighted the strength of the German impulse towards the codification of prison law and the entrenchment of prisoners' rights, while examining the congruence of political and academic opinion around the aim of resocialization in Germany in the 1970s. Equally, however, it showed how the prisoner's legal status under the Prison Act was weakened by political compromises between a reformist Federal Government and resistant state administrations and how it continues to be threatened by the contemporary political climate.

To conclude this account, this chapter examined the substantive principles of prison administration and the prisoner's individual rights under the Prison Act, and suggested that the early promise of the Prison Act is yet to be fully realized. Prisoners' legal rights have been weakened by compromises made during the drafting of the Prison Act; the continued resistance of state administrations to the ideals of the Act; the initial restraint of the Higher Regional Courts in structuring and checking prison administrative discretion; the failure of Prison Courts to fulfil the expectation of reformers; the refractory culture of prison administrators; and the lack of prisoners' access to legal support. Yet while these difficulties exist, another story can also be told about the progress of prisoners' rights under the Act. Despite the many obstacles in the way of their development, prisoners' rights continue to be strengthened by deeper constitutional and reform ideals. These ideals provide a normative compass to those facing the many obstacles in the way of the advancement of prisoners' rights. An influential academy committed to the deeper ideals of the Act and a powerful and activist Constitutional Court receptive to the views of the academy, has bolstered the development of both the principles and special provisions of the Prison Act. In short, the prisoner's legal status in Germany continues to be shaped by the tension between the pursuit of constitutional and penological principle and the institutional and political obstacles placed in the way of their realization.

PART II

ENGLAND AND WALES

5
Penal Politics and Prison Law

This chapter and the following two chapters embark on an explicitly comparative exercise.[1] The leading question they seek to answer is why, and in what way, the English conception of the prisoner's legal status is like or unlike that found in Germany? To begin this examination, this chapter examines the shape, nature, and criminal justice context of prison law in England in light of German prison law. Chapter 6 examines comparatively the place of fundamental rights in English constitutional culture and the judicial conception of the prisoner's legal status, while Chapter 7 looks closely at the judicial development of prisoners' rights in England.

One caveat must be made before moving on. Part II of this book mirrors Part I in focusing on what Germans refer to as the prisoner's administrative legal status. Accordingly, the development of rights as regards sentencing and parole, what Germans define as 'status' rights, will not be examined in depth.[2]

5.1 Prison Law and Prisoners' Rights

It is characteristic of the English genius for practical affairs that we are suspicious of system . . . Thus our law is not disposed to arrange itself in consistent, comprehensive, and logical codes: certainly neither our prison system nor the penal system of which it forms part derives from such a code.[3]

The German Prison Act sought legally to define prisoners' basic rights and constitutionally permissible limitations thereof whilst at the same time to fulfil a substantive purpose of prison administration in line with both the broader conception of the criminal code and deeper constitutional principles. As Part I demonstrated, these aspirations are the product of the German criminal justice and constitutional context. The German Prison Act can be viewed as an indicator of the strength of rights rhetoric in the process of prison legislative reform and as an expression of the institutional power and interpretative bravery of the Federal Constitutional Court (FCC).[4] This

---

[1] See 1.5.   [2] See 2.2.2.1 on 'status' and 'administrative' rights.
[3] L.W. Fox, *The English Prison and Borstal Systems* (Routledge & Kegan Paul, London, 1952) 3.
[4] See chs 2 and 3.

can in turn be linked to the strength and legitimacy of the Basic Law and the deep faith in fundamental rights in Germany.[5] Equally, the Act is a product of a powerful codification impulse centred on the definition of the prisoner's legal status, present in Germany for over a century.[6] The mentality and style of codification was inherently non-incrementalist—seeking the wholesale replacement of a multiplicity of prison regulations with a comprehensive statutory prison code. Those behind codification sought an overarching design of prison administration by enacting fundamental principles in line with both the general purposes of the criminal law and the objectives of the Basic Law from which detailed provisions were carved. Whatever the pitfalls and disappointments involved in the drafting and implementation of the German Prison Act, there is little doubt that the criminal justice and consti-tutional ideals which shaped this legislation and the conception of the prisoner's legal status continue to operate as a benchmark against which German prison law is measured, interpreted, and developed.[7]

The fundamental principles shaping German prison law are not reflected in the legal regime governing prisons in England. With no compelling codi-fication impulse, no dominant rights rhetoric within prison policy-making, nor a Constitutional Court with the institutional and symbolic power to force a legislature to define prisoners' rights, England is without a statutory code of prisoners' rights and an overarching systemic conception of prison administration. Before examining the broader reasons for, and full nature of, this difference, a brief sketch of the statutory arrangement governing prisons in England is necessary.[8]

The English Prison Act 1952 is the primary source of legislative authority governing prisons. The 1952 Act differs little in its aims or content from its predecessors the Prison Act 1877 and the Prison Act 1898.[9] Both of these Acts, in particular the Prison Act 1877, placed local prisons under central government supervision and nationalized prison administration.[10] This was the culmination of almost one hundred years of reformist efforts in England during the eighteenth and nineteenth centuries;[11] it was part of their quest

---

[5] See ch. 2.   [6] See 3.1.   [7] See ch. 4.

[8] A more detailed examination of the Prison Rules is conducted at 5.4.3 below.

[9] S. Livingstone, T. Owen, and A. MacDonald, *Prison Law* (3rd edn, OUP, Oxford 2003) 1–5.

[10] S. McConville, *A History of English Prison Administration* (Routledge, London, 1981) 468–82.

[11] The beginning of this movement in England is most commonly associated with John Howard's famously critical report *The State of Prisons* in 1777. Central control of local pris-ons started with the Gaol Act of 1823 implemented under Home Secretary, Sir Robert Peel. The prison reform process was later advanced by the work of Sir Edmund Du Cane, Chairman of the Prison Commission, and culminated in the Report of the Gladstone Committee in 1895. In the early 20th century the movement received further impetus in Margery Fry's founding of the Howard League for Penal Reform and the appointment of Alexander Paterson as Prison Commissioner after the First World War. Paterson's reformism was to dominate the penal landscape for the next 20 years. See, in general, L. Radzinowicz, *A history of English criminal law and its administration from 1750, Volume 1, The Movement for Reform* (Stevens, London,

to make prisons humane and decent institutions which could provide constructive regimes for the correction of the offender.[12] Unlike German prison reformers, whose aspiration to codify the prisoner's legal status was unfulfilled in the nineteenth century, English reformers succeeded in nationalizing and centralizing prison administration. In order to achieve these progressive aims, prison legislation placed the Home Secretary in a pivotal role in the administration of prisons and extended the monitoring arm of central government over prison administrators and officials.

In the benign spirit of its historical antecedents, the Prison Act 1952 'calls upon the Home Secretary to create and police an internal regime for prisons'.[13] Vesting a high level of policy and administrative control in the Home Secretary, it is a skeletal statute aimed primarily at defining the responsibilities of different agencies in the administration of prisons and lines of accountability to the Minister. The Act also provides mechanisms of political accountability by requiring the Home Secretary to report annually to Parliament,[14] and establishing an Inspectorate of Prisons, and Boards of Visitors to monitor prisons and report to the Home Secretary and Parliament.[15] Moreover, the possibilities of political scrutiny and grievance resolution have more recently been extended by the creation of a non-statutory Prisons Ombudsman who receives prisoners' complaints, and reports to the Home Secretary and Parliament.[16]

Whilst the Act provides these mechanisms of political oversight,[17] the extent of policy-making and administrative discretion vested in the Home Secretary is significant. The Act is described as 'little more than a series of enabling provisions designed to give the Home Secretary maximum discretion in the organisation of the prison system'.[18] A central enabling provision of this Act affords the Home Secretary the power to make and amend detailed rules regulating prisons.[19] These Rules are considerably more detailed than the Prison Act and provide the primary legal guidance on the administration of prisons. However, they were initially intended as regulatory directions only and were not designed to be legally enforceable.[20] Thus, neither the general statutory framework governing prisons, nor the rules

---

1948); L. Radzinowicz and R. Hood, *A history of English criminal law and its administration from 1750, Volume 5, The Emergence of Penal Policy* (Stevens, London, 1986).

[12] Livingstone *et al.* (n 9) 3–5.   [13] Livingstone *et al.* (n 9) 6.

[14] Prison Act 1952, s. 5. G. Richardson, *Law, Process and Custody: Prisoners and Patients* (Weidenfeld & Nicolson, London, 1993) 8.

[15] Prison Act 1952, ss. 5A and 6.

[16] The Prisons Ombudsman remains non-statutory at the time of writing, but proposals have been made to place this office on a statutory footing. See further 5.3 and 5.4.2.4 below.

[17] Richardson (n 14) 9–11, 50–4.   [18] Livingstone *et al.* (n 9) 5.

[19] Prison Act 1952, s. 47.

[20] N. Loucks, *Prison Rules: A Working Guide* (Prison Reform Trust, London, 2000) 7.

governing the day-to-day administration of prisons, 'purport to provide a code of directly legally enforceable rights in prisoners'.[21]

In contrast to Germany, there is no legislative invitation to the courts to engage with prison administration. As Lord Justice Shaw stated in 1979, 'in the scheme envisaged by the Act and shaped by those Rules, the courts have no defined place and no direct or immediate function'.[22] Rather, English courts have carved out their own role through the assertion and development of their inherent jurisdiction under public law. Conscious of their intruder status, they have gingerly encroached on the executive terrain of prison administration. This has been a painstaking process in which the courts, over the last few decades, have developed prisoners' legal rights under common law and given the Prison Rules some legal force. Encouraged by the decisions of the European Commission and Court of Human Rights, English courts have chipped away at executive discretion and only relatively recently settled the extent of their own jurisdiction over prison administration and the legal status of the Prison Rules. Although the extent of this jurisdiction is now settled, the courts remain hesitant in their role as the guardians of prisoners' 'administrative' rights and inconsistent as to the level of judicial scrutiny which applies to large areas of prison administration.

A more detailed examination of the rules governing prison administration is conducted at 5.4 below, whilst a detailed account of the judicial treatment of prisoners' rights is included in Chapter 7. Enough has been said at this stage, however, to demonstrate that the foundations of German prison law are starkly different from those of England. German prison law aims to define the prisoner's constitutional and legal rights and establish deeper constitutional and penal principles regarding prison administration. Whilst establishing foundations for political accountability, the predominant aim of this law is to ensure high levels of *legal* accountability in line with the *Rechtstaatsprinzip*. Whilst concern with administrative flexibility has significantly affected the content of the German Prison Act, courts are nevertheless charged with striking a principled balance between administrative freedom and the protections of constitutional rights and principles under a detailed statutory code. Thus, as shown in Chapters 2 and 4, the constitutional and legislative framework governing prisons in Germany centres on the definition of the prisoner's legal status and places courts in a central position in the process of prison administration.

The English statutory regime reflects primarily a concern to clarify lines of *political* control and accountability. In addition to the traditional responsibility of the Home Secretary to Parliament, the political accountability of

---

[21] G. Richardson, 'Prisoners and the Law: Beyond Rights' in C. McCrudden and G. Chambers (eds), *Individual Rights and the Law in the UK* (Clarendon Press, Oxford, 1993) 179, 183.

[22] *R v Board of Visitors of Hull Prison, ex p St Germain and others* [1978] 1 QB (CA) 425, 454.

prison administration is enhanced through the use of monitoring and complaints bodies such as the Prisons Inspectorate, the Boards of Visitors, and the Prisons Ombudsman. But these aims of political accountability are coupled with a powerful pragmatic concern to ensure an effective, flexible, and politically responsive prison administrative structure by vesting high levels of policy-making discretion and administrative control in the Home Secretary and the prison administration. In this context, the English courts are uninvited guests, carefully sketching out individual prisoners' rights in the interstices of a system aimed at ensuring political accountability and control.

5.2 The Prisoners' Rights Lobby

There has been no shortage of calls for the reform and modernization of the statutory regime governing prisons, for the better definition and extension of prisoners' rights, and for the provision of an independent adjudicative forum in which these can be properly enforced. Beginning in earnest with PROP's activism and their early success in the *St Germain* case,[23] a broad alliance of penal pressure groups,[24] activists and academics,[25] prison administrators and inspectors,[26] and judges acting extra-curially,[27] have called for the introduction of a set of specific and enforceable prison standards and prisoner entitlements. The proposals for reform vary in tone. Pressure groups, such as the Prison Reform Trust and NACRO, and academics, such as Richardson, Morgan and Casale, call for a more 'specific' and 'more prescriptive statutory framework' creating prisoner entitlements and regime

[23] *R v Board of Visitors of Hull Prison, ex p St Germain* [1978] 1 QB (CA) 425. See further ch. 7. PROP ('The Union for the Preservation of the Rights of Prisoners') was made up of prisoners and ex-prisoners. They were closely supported in the 1970s by Radical Alternatives to Prison (RAP) and the National Deviancy Conference (NDC). See in more detail M. Ryan, *Penal Policy and Political Culture in England and Wales* (Waterside, Winchester, 2003) Part II.

[24] These vary from special interest pressure groups to more general civil liberty pressure groups. In the area of prisoners' rights the primary organizations are: The Howard League, The National Association for the Care and Resettlement of Offenders (NACRO), The Prison Reform Trust (PRT), Liberty, and Justice. R. Light, 'Pressure Groups, Penal Policy and the Gaols' (1995) 100 *Prison Service Journal* 27.

[25] Richardson 1993 (n 21) 203; Louks (n 20) 14–17; R. Morgan, 'Imprisonment' in M. Maguire, R. Morgan, and R. Reiner (eds), *Oxford Handbook of Criminology* (3rd edn, OUP, Oxford, 2002) 1113, 1126–28; R. Morgan, 'Prison Accountability Revisited' (1993) *PL* 314; S. Casale ,'Conditions and Standards' in E. Player and M. Jenkins (eds), *Prisons After Woolf: Reform through Riot* (Routledge, London, 1993) 66; S. Casale and J. Plotnikoff, *Minimum Standards for Prisons: A Programme of Change* (NACRO, London, 1989).

[26] *Prison Disturbances April 1990: Report of an Inquiry by the Rt. Hon. Lord Justice Woolf (part I and II) and His Honour Judge Stephen Tumin (Part II)* (Cm. 1456); Morgan 1993 (n 25) n 21.

[27] Lord Justice Woolf 'We still fail our prisoners' *The Times* 2, 1 February 2001; Woolf Report (n 26).

standards enforceable at law.[28] The Woolf Report, co-authored by Lord Justice Woolf and the then Chief Inspector of Prisons, Sir Stephen Tumin, identified 'justice' as a central area in need of enhancement in prisons.[29] Although the report avoided the language of prisoners' rights *per se*,[30] it did propose, *inter alia*, giving prisoners reasons for decisions, a system of prison compacts which give rise to 'legitimate expectations' vested in prisoners enforceable by judicial review, a national system of accredited standards which would be made legally enforceable over time, and the provision of a properly independent complaint body with adequate powers of enforcement.[31]

Whilst England's tradition of prison reform activism dates back to the eighteenth century,[32] the contemporary prisoners' rights movement is interlocked with the rise of an international prisoners' rights movement post-1945, resulting in an international prison law.[33] In particular, the highly publicized visits and criticisms of the European Committee for the Prevention of Torture and Inhuman and Degrading Punishment or Treatment (CPT) provide a useful impetus for domestic reformers. As Stephen Shaw argued: 'the publicity—which to the CPT's displeasure, attached to its visit—added to the public view of Britain's prisons as antiquated and in need of thoroughgoing reform'.[34]

Proponents of reform are decidedly more wary of court intervention in prison management than their German counterparts. Most envision a system of 'extra-judicial' routine enforcement where the courts' role is limited to providing a mechanism of 'last-resort enforcement'.[35] Nevertheless, while differing in emphasis, these proponents argue for the introduction of a set of prison standards and prisoner entitlements which will provide complaints and inspection bodies with clear frameworks in their work, and the introduction of a truly independent complaints body with proper powers of enforcement.[36] It certainly cannot be said that England is without a prisoners' 'rights rhetoric' within contemporary penal culture.

[28] Morgan 1993 (n 25) 332; Plotnikoff (n 27); Richardson (n 21) 203 and 207.

[29] The Woolf Report (n 26) makes repeated reference to 'justice', see in particular para. 14.19. See further 5.3 below.

[30] G. Richardson, 'From Rights to Expectations' in E. Player and M. Jenkins (eds), *Prisons After Woolf: Reform through Riot* (Routledge, London, 1994) 92.

[31] Woolf Report (n 27) para. 1.167.   [32] See n 11.

[33] N. Rodley, *The Treatment of Prisoners under International Law* (2nd edn, Clarendon Press, Oxford, 1999) ch. 1; M. Evans and R. Morgan, 'The CPT: An Introduction' in R. Morgan and M. Evans (eds), *Protecting Prisoners: The Standards of the European Committee for the Prevention of Torture in Context* (OUP, Oxford, 1999) 3; V. Stern, *A Sin Against the Future* (Penguin, London, 1998) chs 10–12. See also ch. 1, n 4.

[34] S. Shaw, 'The CPT's Visits to the United Kingdom' in Morgan and Evans (n 33) 265, 271.

[35] Morgan 1993 (n 25) 331–332; Richardson 1993 (n 21) 203–4.

[36] This call echoes a core principle of international prisoners' rights law. See, e.g., *Body of Principles for the Protection of All Persons under Any Form of Detention or Imprisonment* (UN General Assembly Res. 43/173, 9 December 1988) which calls for the protection of prisoners' rights by a 'judicial body' or 'other authority under the law whose status and tenure affords the strongest possible guarantees of competence, impartiality and independence'.

Many advances in prison regimes and individual prisoner entitlements in England have been won by this movement,[37] but fundamental reform of the prison legislative regime and a clear set of enforceable prisoners' rights are yet to fully materialize. This absence might be explained as a simple matter of political fact:

Prisons may be news when prisoners sit on roofs, burn them down, or dramatically escape from them. For the majority of the voting public, however, they are marginal and . . . the government has priorities more pressing than prisoners' rights. Real change it seems will only occur when it is no longer politically acceptable to delay reform.[38]

Given the low political capital to be gained from providing prisoners with legally enforceable rights, we might conclude at this point by arguing that resistance to prisoners' entitlements is a direct outcome of England's constitutional arrangements. Put simply, in England's political constitution, governments which dominate the legislature gain nothing politically in promoting prisoners' rights and jealously guard the discretion afforded them by current legislative arrangements, courts do not have the power to force the legislature to entrench a code of prisoners' rights, and the legislature is neither willing nor has the teeth to shape or resist governmental prison policies. But the absence of legislative reform of prisoners' rights in England can also be explained in a deeper sense by reference to the dynamics of contemporary English penal politics.

5.3 PENAL POLITICS IN ENGLAND

Before embarking on our analysis of English penal politics, we must revisit the comparative example of Germany. Germany experienced a particular constellation of factors which contributed to the ascendance of the prisoners' rights movement. Important amongst these was a powerful 'codification impulse' which grew from the desire to create unity within the criminal law and, after 1945, the general project of rehumanization of the criminal law, the views and arguments of a highly influential academy, and the politics of an aggressively reformist Social-Liberal Government during the 1970s.[39] Equally important, was that this reform movement took place in a legal culture dominated by faith in constitutional rights and by hegemonic rights rhetoric.[40] It was impossible to talk of legal reform in Germany without showing strong fidelity to constitutional rights and principles. Consequently 'rights rhetoric' had a powerful defining influence over the language of prison law reform and the shape of prison law. The use of 'rights rhetoric' was underpinned by the explicit relationship set out by the FCC between

[37] See 5.3 below.　　[38] Richardson (n 21) 206.　　[39] See 3.1.1 and 3.1.2.
[40] See 2.1.

constitutional rights, the *Rechtsstaatsprinzip*, and the prisoner' legal sta-tus.[41] Of course, Germany has experienced alternative penal discourses which militate against prisoners' rights rhetoric.[42] This was evident both in the process of legislative drafting and since the German Prison Act 1976 came into force. But these competing penal discourses are mediated by the powerful FCC and an influential academy committed to the achievement of constitutional rights and principles. In short, it has been shown that 'rights rhetoric' continues to enjoy a strong currency relative to other discourses in the definition of penal policy in Germany.

Unlike Germany, 'rights rhetoric' in the English penal political environ-ment has struggled for influence in the face of powerful competing discourses.[43] Since the 1970s, the politicization of crime and penal policy has increased,[44] and the pursuit of 'law and order' has come to occupy a central place in English political culture. Alongside sentencing, prison policy is especially vulnerable to the political motivations of ministers and their governments, who both incite and exploit the public's concern with crime and justice.[45] This politicization of criminal justice feeds off, and into, the statutory reinforcement of successive Home Secretaries' control of penal policy. These statutory powers, originally created for benign and progressive purposes, now militate indirectly against the extension of prisoner entitle-ments. Moreover, the politicization of criminal justice has weakened the policy influence of the moderate penal 'professional elite', who up to the 1970s had enjoyed greater respect from policy-makers within criminal jus-tice and relative immunity from political pressure.[46] It is against these forces that the prisoners' rights lobby has battled. It cannot claim the backing of an activist judiciary or a decisively influential academy, nor, in its use of 'rights rhetoric' can it claim to have a 'higher' constitutional purchase over the definition of penal policy. Notwithstanding the introduction of the Human Rights Act 1998, 'rights rhetoric' in England continues to be under-mined by the traditionally ambivalent English relationship to rights gener-

---

[41] See 2.2.1.   [42] See 3.3.

[43] A. Bottoms, 'The Philosophy and Politics of Punishment and Sentencing' in C. Clarkson and R. Morgan (eds), *The Politics of Sentencing Reform* (Clarendon Press, Oxford, 1995) 17.

[44] D. Downes and R. Morgan, 'The skeletons in the cupboard: the politics of law and order at the turn of the millennium' in M. Maguire, R. Morgan, and R. Reiner, *The Oxford Handbook of Criminology* (OUP, Oxford, 2002) 286.

[45] Bottoms (n 43) 40.

[46] D. Garland, *The Culture of Control* (OUP, Oxford, 2001) 36–7; R. Hood, 'Penal Policy and Criminological Challenges in the New Millennium' (2001) 34 *The Australian and New Zealand Journal of Criminology* 1. The extent and nature of criminology's influence over penal policy is controversial. Whilst the political influence of academia declined in England after the 1970s, less visible and reconstituted networks of policy influence remain. Moreover, the con-cepts produced by theoretical criminology feature regularly in penal rhetoric. See L. Zedner and A. Ashworth, *The Criminological Foundations of Penal Policy* (OUP, Oxford, 2003); D. Faulkner, *Crime, State and Citizen: A Field Full of Folk* (Waterside Press, Winchester, 2001); Ryan (n 23) chs 1 and 4.

ally.[47] Moreover, the relative weakness of 'rights rhetoric' in defining penal policy has been compounded by the ascendancy of the discourses of 'instrumental managerialism', 'populist punitivism', and more recently 'public protection'.[48] All of these competing discourses grow out of and are constructive of the particular circumstances of the post-war English penal system which require further examination.

Since 1945, the English penal system has operated under considerable strain. Dogged by rising prison numbers, overcrowding, understaffing and staff unrest, prisoner escapes and riots, deteriorating conditions, increased security risks and decreasing control, prisons have presented successive governments with high costs and political risks.[49] The practical challenges of the penal system have been accompanied by changes in the penal environment which have intensified since the 1970s. It was then that the prevailing consensus around the rehabilitative ideal was undermined, and penal thinking and criminal justice strategies shifted and fragmented.[50] This weakening of the 'penal-welfare strategy'[51] in England was interlocked with the decline of the welfare state consensus, brought on by economic and fiscal crisis, and the rise of the new right with its peculiar mix of 'free market economics, anti-welfare social policy and cultural conservatism'.[52] Crime control became represented as central to the maintenance of social order, and exploitation of fear of crime and promises of public protection a core feature of political strategy. Without the ideological lighthouse of

---

[47] See 6.1.

[48] 'Instrumental managerialism' refers to managerial strategies aimed at enhancing the actuarial values of economy, efficiency, and effectiveness for their own sake. 'Populist punitivism' refers to the strategy of politicians 'tapping into and using for their own purposes, what they believe to be the public's generally punitive stance'. Bottoms (n 43) 33 and 40. 'Public protection' manifests itself in 'the need for security, the containment of danger, the identification and management of any kind of risk'. D. Garland, *The Culture of Control* (OUP, Oxford, 2001) 12.

[49] M. Cavadino and J. Dignan, *The Penal System* (2nd edn, Sage, London, 1997) ch. 5; R. King and K. McDermott, 'British Prisons 1970–1987: The Ever Deepening Crisis' (1989) 29 *BJC* 107; Morgan 2002 (n 25) 1137–41.

[50] See 3.1.2. B. Hudson, *Justice Through Punishment: a critique of the 'Justice' Model of Corrections* (Macmillan, London, 1987) ch. 1; A. Bottomley, *Criminology in Focus: Past Trends and Future Prospects* (Martin Robertson, Oxford, 1979) ch. 4; R, Ericson and K, Carriere, 'The Fragmentation of Criminology' in D. Nelken (ed.), *The Futures of Criminology* (Sage, London, 1994) 89; Garland 1996 (n 44) 447–8, 450–66.

[51] This term is developed and used repeatedly in D. Garland, *Punishment and Welfare* (Gower, Aldershot, 1985). On its breakdown, see D. Garland, *The Culture of Control* (OUP, Oxford, 2001) ch. 3. The consensus around welfarism and its subsequent collapse in penal practice and criminological thought in England should not be overstated, however, just as its incipient political and intellectual revival around the millennium should not be ignored. L. Zedner, 'Dangers of Dystopia' (2002) 22(2) *OJLS* 341, 344–6. See also 3.1.2 on Germany's rather different response in the 1970s.

[52] A. Gamble, 'Privatisation, Thatcherism, and the British State' (1989) 16 *JLS* 1; D. Garland and R. Sparks, 'Criminology, Social Theory and the Challenge of Our Times' (2000) 40 *BJC* 189, 197.

rehabilitation the penal system began to drift in a 'policy' and 'moral vacuum'.[53] Prison policy-makers became reactive, responding to particular crises at particular times within a broader climate of fiscal restraint, declining social sympathy, and increased anxiety about crime.

The strategy of the New Right to exploit anxieties about the state of 'law and order' in England had varying implications for prison policy. In the 1980s, Conservative policy was characterized by the search to reconcile the twin aims of bolstering 'law and order' whilst remaining committed to fiscal restraint.[54] This led to the adoption of a 'twin-track approach', and 'bifurcation' between harsh treatment of serious offenders and liberal treatment for less serious offenders. Conservative Home Secretaries were able, on fiscal grounds, to justify a relatively liberal approach to sentencing and penal policy in the 1980s, in particular restraint in the use of custodial sentencing, in an attempt to reduce the escalating cost of the prison population.[55] Accompanying sentencing reform initiatives, the Conservative Government implemented managerial reform within the prison system aimed primarily at enhancing financial accountability to the centre.[56] Initiated by the May Inquiry,[57] and taken up later in the programme of Fresh Start in 1987, policies were aimed at increasing the 'efficiency', 'economy', and 'effectiveness' of the prison administration and at reforming a highly unionized and supposedly intransigent Prison Service.[58] At the same time government began enquiring into the possibility of contracting-out prisons,[59] a policy later adopted in 1991 followed by the private financing of prison building.[60] Although 'enhancing prison regimes' was a central legitimating aim of these managerial reforms, early studies showed that substantive goals were mostly

[53] D. Downes and R. Morgan, 'Dumping Hostages to Fortune' in M. Maguire, R Morgan and R. Reiner, *The Oxford Handbook of Criminology* (2nd edn, OUP, Oxford 1997) 123–5; V. Stern, *Bricks of Shame* (Penguin, Harmondsworth, 1987) 229.

[54] N. Lacey, 'Government as Manager, Citizen as Consumer' (1994) 57 *MLR* 534, 536–42.

[55] The Criminal Justice Act 1991, promoted heavily inside the Home Office by David Faulkner, was the culmination of this movement. Bottoms (n 43) 40–1; T. Newburn, 'Youth, Crime, and Justice' in M. Maguire, R. Morgan and R. Reiner (eds), *The Oxford Handbook of Criminology* (2nd edn, OUP, Oxford, 1997) 613, 643–5; A. Ashworth, *Sentencing and Criminal Justice* (3rd edn, Butterworths, London, 2000) 78–84; Lacey (n 54) 536–42.

[56] A. Fowles, 'Monitoring Expenditure on the Criminal Justice System: The Search for Control' (1990) 29 *Howard Journal* 82.

[57] *Report of the Committee of Inquiry into the United Kingdom Prison Services* (Cmnd. 7673); C. Train, 'Management Accountability in the Prison Service' in M. Maguire, J. Vagg and R. Morgan (eds), *Accountability in Prisons: Opening Up a Closed World* (Tavistock, London, 1985) 177.

[58] K. McDermott and R. King, 'A Fresh Start: The Enhancement of Prison Regimes' (1989) 28 *Howard Journal* 161.

[59] *Private Sector Involvement in the Remand System* (Cm. 434).

[60] Criminal Justice Act 1991, s. 84; Criminal Justice Act 1991 (Contracted Out Prisons) Order 1992, SI 1992 No. 1656.

impoverished by the priority given to the pursuit of the instrumental goals of 'economy' and 'efficiency'.[61]

In line with the rest of the public sector, these managerial reforms marked the beginning of a fundamental cultural change in prison administration and policy-making.[62] They ushered in an important shift from traditional public law values of political and legal accountability to those associated with market discipline and financial accountability.[63] The focus moved to strategies of New Public Management. This involved a redefinition of the traditional notion of citizenship in consumerist terms, a fragmentation of the 'monolithic' State through the hiving-off of executive functions to semi-autonomous agencies and the private sector, an organizational shift from vertical structures of accountability and control to horizontal 'control through contract', the injection of competition into the public sector through the use of quality and performance indicators, the separation of the purchaser and provider role within the State, and an emphasis on financial accountability mechanisms such as value-for-money audit and other regulatory strategies.[64] Cumulatively, these strategies set out to alter the 'landscape' of political 'control' within the penal system.[65]

To the extent that managerial reforms promised transparency, consistency and the enhancement of regime standards, they had significant potential to advance prisoners' interests. Nevertheless, at root managerialism is 'driven and fashioned almost entirely by a political economic impetus . . . with virtually no legal or constitutional consciousness'.[66] With its focus on aggregate targets and output measurement, it is not intrinsically inclined towards the protection of individual and specific interests.[67] The central challenge facing supporters of prisoners' rights was to harness a managerial discourse with a predilection towards instrumental goals such as 'economy' and 'efficiency' to further substantive aims such as individual dignity, humanity, and justice.[68] In this fiscally conscious climate, talk of prison reform or prisoners' rights without some recourse to managerial rhetoric was likely to fail.[69]

In 1990, the large-scale riots at Strangeways Prison shocked penal policy makers, for a brief moment, into recognizing that partial managerial reform

---

[61] C. Jones, 'Auditing Criminal Justice' (1993) 33 *BJC* 187, 198. It is also questionable whether managerial initiatives made significant advances in respect of either 'economy' or 'efficiency' (McDermott and King (n 58) 161).

[62] Jones (n 61) 199–200.

[63] C. Scott and A. Barron, 'The Citizen's Charter Programme' (1992) 55 *MLR* 526.

[64] Scott and Barron (n 63); J. Stewart and K. Walsh, 'Change in the Management of Public Services' (1992) 70 *Public Administration* 499; C. Scott, 'Accountability in the Regulatory State' (2000) 79 *JLS* 38, 39–48; M. Power, *The Audit Society* (OUP, Oxford, 1999).

[65] I. Loader and R. Sparks, 'Contemporary Landscapes of Crime' in M. Maguire, R. Morgan and R. Reiner (eds), *Oxford Handbook of Criminology* (OUP, Oxford, 2002) 83, 88.

[66] M. Loughlin, *Public Law and Political Theory* (OUP, Oxford, 1992) 260.

[67] Livingstone *et al.* (n 9) 565–6.   [68] Bottoms (n 43) 33.

[69] This is the strong message in the concluding paragraphs of Livingstone *et al.* (n 9) 565–6.

and prioritisation of efficiency was an inadequate response to the deeper structural problems of the prison system. The resultant scale of the inquiry by Lord Justice Woolf and Stephen Tumin reflected the seriousness of the riots and the widespread concern with their root causes.[70] The Woolf Report emphasized the crucial link between security, control, and justice in prisons, attempting to use this turning point to advance prisoners' interests whilst also employing prevailing managerial rhetoric.[71] Prisoner 'contracts' or 'compacts' were one example of Woolf's attempt to harness a language of, what might be termed, 'liberal managerialism' to the prisoner's advantage. These mechanisms were to 'underline both the prisoners' and the establishment's responsibilities' in order to 'substantially improve the position of the inmate since it would make clear . . . his legitimate expectations'.[72]

But, while many of Woolf's proposals were accepted by the Government in the immediate aftermath of the report,[73] the tentative advancement of prisoners' entitlements was to prove short lived. Government reforms tended to advance more instrumental managerial goals over substantive values such as enhanced legal or political accountability. Woolf's proposal for a 'code of mimimum standards' was absorbed into managerial dialect and became 'operating standards' under the Prison Service's *Corporate Plan*.[74] While these stated that 'prisoners will be treated with fairness, justice and respect', they were 'not intended to be legally enforceable' nor give rise to 'prisoner entitlements'.[75] Moreover, Key Performance Indicators (KPIs) were criticized for prioritizing quantitative, internally measurable, 'outputs' over qualitative 'outcomes'.[76] As the Chief Inspector of Prisons stated in 1998:

KPIs are exactly what they imply; indicators of quantitative measures of performance against laid down targets, nothing more than that. The current list of KPIs do not inform Ministers or the public on the details of treatment and conditions of individual types of prisoners, and the evidence they give is not wholly relevant as a result. The danger about using them for anything more, such as management determinants, is that they tend to encourage a quantitative 'tick-in-the-box' response, while doing nothing to indicate the quality of the performance.[77]

Neither was the promise of transparency and accountability through contracting out immediately realized. Illustratively, a year after the creation of the Prison Service Executive Agency, one of the most conspicuous failures of

---

[70] Woolf Report (n 27).
[71] M. Cavadino, I. Crow and J. Dignan, *Criminal Justice 2000: Strategies for a New Century* (Waterside Press, Winchester, 1999) 134.
[72] Woolf Report (n 27) para. 12.129.   [73] *Custody, Care and Justice* (Cm. 1647).
[74] *HM Corporate Plan 1994–1997* (HMSO, London, 1994) 16. On current managerial frameworks see 5.4.1 below.
[75] Prison Service, *Operating Standards* (HMSO, London, 1994) Introduction.
[76] Loucks (n 20) 16; Loader and Sparks (n 65) 88; Morgan (n 25) 1125.
[77] *Annual Report 1997–98 of HM Chief Inspector of Prisons* (HMSO, London, 1998) 23.

political accountability of the 1990s took place between the Home Secretary and the Director General of the Prison Service over the escapes at Whitemoor and Parkhurst prisons.[78] Far from strengthening accountability, the crisis exposed the potential for managerial reform to leave the Prison Service in political limbo. Moreover, at the first sign of conflict between the newly established Prisons Ombudsman and Home Secretary, the terms of reference were changed to increase the control of the Home Secretary.[79] The result fell far short of the Woolf Report's vision of an Independent Complaints Adjudicator. On the face of it, Woolf and Tumin had been defeated in their attempt to capture managerial discourse for a progressive cause.

One major factor stalled Woolf's liberal managerial agenda. It was signalled in the announcement to the Conservative Party Conference in 1993 by Home Secretary, Michael Howard, that 'prison works' and that prison regimes should be 'austere'. This proclamation marked a break with the 'twin track' tone of the 1980s, where 'law and order' rhetoric was mixed in with liberal policy initiatives, and ushered in a period of intense 'populist punitivism' and 'penal austerity'.[80] The cause of this marked shift in Tory policy can, on one level, be attributed to the different personal agendas of the Home Secretaries in power. Douglas Hurd and Kenneth Clarke had been moderate Conservatives, whilst Michael Howard was part of the increasingly powerful Tory Right. Moreover, Hurd and Clarke had governed in a time when Conservatives enjoyed a relatively comfortable majority, whilst Howard was operating during Tory decline and facing a confident New Labour opposition. Further, the British recession between 1989 and 1992 had marked an increase in unemployment and a rise in the crime rate by almost 50 per cent and consequently 'for the first time in over 30 years, the Conservative lead over Labour as the party best able to guarantee law and order vanished'.[81] The punitive policies adopted by Howard in prisons, which were made possible by the extent of his statutory powers under the Prison Act 1952, were thus tools of political survival.

While political opportunism explains Howard's approach, the political capital to be gained from a strategy of 'populist punitivism' has also been placed in a larger historical context. Bottoms views it as a consequence of the 'disembedding processes of modernity' which in combination with rising crime rates 'have led to a fairly widespread sense of insecurity, . . . as former social certainties are eroded, and the abstract systems upon which people are

---

[78] Michael Howard refused to accept ministerial responsibility, arguing that failures in security were 'operational' matters, and then fired Derek Lewis, Director General of the Prison Service.

[79] See 5.4.2.4 below.

[80] Bottoms (n 43) 17; R. Sparks, 'Penal "Austerity": The Doctrine of Less Eligibility Reborn?' in R. Matthews and P. Francis (eds), *Prisons 2000* (Macmillan, Basingstoke, 1996) 74, 75.

[81] D. Downes, 'The *macho* penal economy' (2001) 3(1) *P&S* 61, 69.

expected to rely sometimes seem inadequately reassuring'.[82] A cultural formation has arisen, at least in the USA and the United Kingdom over the last thirty years, which Garland terms the 'crime complex of late modernity'. In this culture, acceptance of high crime rates as a normal social fact is widespread, popular anxiety about crime and feelings of 'fear, anger and resentment' are commonplace, crime issues are politicized and represented in emotive terms, concerns about victims and public safety dominate at the expense of rights and civil liberties, and crime consciousness is institutionalized by the media and popular culture.[83] It is a culture which has produced the preconditions in which punitiveness and the pursuit of public protection flourish,[84] a climate in which politicians can easily exploit the insecurities of the electorate by promising to be tough on crime. Without strong alternative discourses within criminal justice politics, or robust constitutional constraints on those wielding power, these political strategies of punitivism and crime control gain currency.

While rooted in this broader context, the rise of populist punitivism and penal austerity in England was reinforced by crisis within the penal system. This was the escape of high security prisoners from Whitemoor and Parkhurst prisons in 1994, both of which were publicly linked to generous provision related to prisoners' possessions and privilege entitlements.[85] The publicity surrounding these escapes and the proposals of the resultant Learmont and Woodcock Reports hardened the Government's position, led to an emphasis on security and public protection as the central purpose of prison administration, and legitimated restrictive and punitive practices within prisons.[86] The ambitions of the prisoners' rights lobby and the liberal agenda of the Woolf Report, with its attempt to balance security, control, and justice found less political currency in such an environment. Rather, the dominant language of penal administration shifted to one of punitive managerialism with a central focus on public protection and security.[87] This shift was epitomized by the use of Woolf's prisoner compact. Instead of vehicles for prisoner empowerment, compacts were used as a medium of prisoner control. Government followed Woodcock's recommendation that 'the underlying premise should be that all allowances are "privileges", to be earned by good behaviour and work performance, with sanctions for bad

---

[82] Bottoms (n 43) 47.   [83] Garland (n 44) chs 1 and 7.

[84] Garland (n 44) 367–9.

[85] A. Bottoms, 'Theoretical Reflections on a Penal Policy Initiative' in L. Zedner and A. Ashworth (eds), *The Criminological Foundations of Penal Policy* (OUP, Oxford, 2003) 107, 116.

[86] Sir John Woodcock, *Report of the Enquiry into the Escape of Six Prisoners from the Special Security Unit at Whitemoor Prison, Cambridgeshire, on Friday 9th September 1994* (Cm. 2741); General Sir John Learmont, *Review of Prison Service Security in England and Wales and the Escape from Parkhurst Prison on Tuesday 3rd of January 1995* (Cm. 3020); R. Morgan, 'Learmont: Dangerously Unbalanced' (1996) 35 *Howard Journal* 346.

[87] Cavadino *et al.* (n 71) 144.

behaviour'.[88] As Michael Howard argued, they should be designed to eliminate the public image of 'prisoners living with luxuries and free from control'.[89] This twist to the scheme was testimony to the fragility of Woolf's liberal intentions in an increasingly punitive political culture.

Labour's return to power did little to quell the populist punitive tone of criminal justice rhetoric. From the late 1980s Labour had sought in opposition to outdo Tory punitivism, and crucially to disassociate from its 'soft on crime' image.[90] With Blair's politically acute exploitation of the mantra 'Tough on Crime, Tough on the Causes of Crime' in 1993,[91] Labour sealed the 'new consensus on Law and Order', while sweetening the punitive pill with a dose of welfarism.[92] Since coming to power in 1997, Labour's criminal justice rhetoric has sought legitimation in both of these manifesto aims: 'tackling crime' as a 'social justice priority'.[93] But it is widely argued that the subtext, 'tough on criminals', has characterized much of Labour's penal practice.[94] A breathtaking array of policies now exists to further New Labour's mission to increase public protection through the criminal justice system. Some examples include[95] cracking down on anti-social behaviour;[96] imposing local child and home detention curfews for juveniles;[97] extension of electronic monitoring;[98] the abolition of *doli incapax* thereby reducing the age of criminal responsibility to ten;[99] the removal of the automatic right to trial by jury;[100] relaxation of the double jeopardy rule;[101] relaxation of

---

[88] Woodcock Report (n 86) recommendation 50; Bottoms (n 85) 107.

[89] Quoted in Bottoms (n 88) 117.

[90] Downes and Morgan 2002 (n 44) 299.

[91] The phrase was Gordon Brown's but was first used publicly by Blair as Shadow Home Secretary in 1993. Ryan (n 23) 123

[92] Downes and Morgan 2002 (n 44) 295.

[93] *Justice for All* (Cm. 5536) para. 1.2; J. Young, 'Crime and Social Exclusion' in M. Maguire, R. Morgan and R. Reiner (eds), *Oxford Handbook of Criminology* (3rd edn, OUP, Oxford, 2002) 459, 460.

[94] Downes and Morgan 2002 (n 44) 297–8; Downes (n 81) 69; A. Ashworth, 'Sentencing' in M. Maguire, R. Morgan and R. Reiner (eds), *Oxford Handbook of Criminology* (OUP, Oxford, 2002) 1077; N. Lacey, 'Principles, Politics and Criminal Justice' in Zedner and Ashworth (n 46) 79.

[95] Many of these reforms follow recommendations of the Halliday Report (John Halliday, *Making Punishment Work: Report of a Review of the Sentencing Framework for England and Wales July 2001* (Home Office, London, 2001)) and the Auld Report (Lord Justice Auld, *A Review of the Criminal Courts of England and Wales* (The Stationery Office, London, 2001)).

[96] Anti-Social Behaviour Bill 2003; Police Reform Bill 2002, cl. 44; Crime and Disorder Act 1998, s. 1

[97] Crime and Disorder Act 1998, ss. 14–15, 99–100.

[98] Criminal Justice Act (CJA) 2003, s. 215. Electronic monitoring is used for suspects on bail (CJA 2003, s. 16(3)(e)); offenders on community sentences (CJA 2003, s. 177(3) and (4)); offenders on custody plus (CJA 2003, s. 182(3) and (4)); on suspended sentences (CJA 2003, s. 190(3) and (4)); on release on licence (CJA 2003, s. 253(1)(b)); on default orders (CJA 2003, s. 300(4)); and is used for juvenile offenders on home curfews (Crime and Disorder Act 1998, ss. 99–100).

[99] Crime and Disorder Act 1998, s. 34.   [100] CJA 2003, ss. 43–50.

[101] CJA 2003, s. 76.

hearsay evidence rules;[102] the use of indeterminate sentences for dangerous offenders;[103] increasing magistrates' sentencing powers;[104] permitting evidence of offenders' bad character and past offences in trial and sentencing proceedings;[105] minimum mandatory sentences;[106] a new 'custody plus' sentence extending short terms of imprisonment to include further periods of 'enforced programme in the community' with breach of the community element leading to automatic return to prison;[107] and the abandonment of 'desert' as the primary sentencing rationale and the endorsement of rationale plurality, including 'crime reduction', 'public protection' and 'punishment'.[108] Over and above these initiatives, the rising prison population is itself illustrative of the 'abiding strain of severity' within Labour's criminal justice politics.[109]

Seeking to ensure cost-efficient and effective pursuit of public protection, Labour has embraced the managerialist programme of its governmental predecessors with zeal, entailing a notable U-turn on pre-election promises as regards privatization and private financing of prisons.[110] Far from diluting New Public Management techniques in the criminal justice sector, New Labour has added layers of performance assessment to a system already surfeited with targets and objectives.[111] There is now widespread evidence-based assessment of the effectiveness of criminal justice policies and agents in the pursuit of 'crime reduction',[112] with strong promotion of inter-agency and local partnerships ('joined up justice') to deal with crime and criminals pivotal to Labour's strategy.

Prisons are no exception to this trend. They have been targeted, in partnership with the sentencing courts and probation service, as a key delivery service for the effective treatment of offenders to 'reduce re-offending and protect the public'.[113] In January 2000, the Home Secretary, Jack Straw, announced the establishment of a working group on 'Targeted Performance Improvement', to 'develop proposals for enhancing management arrangements' in prisons. The resultant Laming report produced a number of recommendations focused on enhancing line management, integrating

---

[102] CJA 2003, s. 114.
[103] CJA 2003, ss. 225(4) and 226(4).
[104] CJA 2003, ss. 154 and 155.   [105] CJA 2003, ss. 98–99.
[106] CJA 2003, ss. 287 and 269. See also Sch. 21.
[107] CJA 2003, ss. 181–182.   [108] CJA 2003, s. 142.
[109] A. Travis, 'Jail Numbers to top 80,000' *The Guardian*, 16 July 2003. Ashworth 2002 (n 94) 1077.
[110] Ryan (n 23) 94.
[111] For current Performance Management Framework see 5.4.1 below.
[112] The Government's 'Crime Reduction Task Force' set out its strategy in 1999. A programme of 'concerted action . . . to drive crime down' was announced including: raising the performance of the police and the Crime and Disorder Reduction Partnerships; reducing burglary and property crime; tackling vehicle crime; dealing with disorder and anti-social behaviour; dealing effectively with young offenders; dealing effectively with adult offenders; helping victims and witnesses. See www.crimereduction.gov.uk.
[113] *Home Office Public Service Agreement*, Aim 4.

standards for performance evaluation, and enhancing contacts with outside agencies and communities.[114] In September 2000, the 'What Works in Prison? Strategy Board' was set up to develop a strategy for continuous assessment of offender risk, offender needs and intervention effectiveness, in the pursuit of a 5 per cent reduction in reoffending by 2004.[115] A new era of prison managerial policy has arisen; involving a redefined legitimation of rehabilitation centering less on individual welfare than on crime control.[116] As Jack Straw announced in 1997:

The government came into office with a commitment to tackle crime. An intrinsic part of that commitment is the constructive regimes we promise for prisons. Common humanity alone demands this. But this is not some disinterested, philanthropic venture. We believe prisons can be made to work as one element in a radical and coherent strategy to protect the public by reducing crime.[117]

Where does this leave prisoners? To the extent that public protection and the pursuit of rehabilitation leads to positive custody regimes and fulfils the aspiration towards 'common humanity', Labour's approach is a clear shift from the Tory emphasis on 'austerity'. Indeed, the Labour Government has publicized significant investment in education, offender behaviour programmes, drug rehabilitation, healthcare and custody-to-work programmes.[118] Moreover, Labour's commitment to refining prison policy on the basis of evidence-based practice has resulted in the fairer administration of the 'Incentive and Earned Privileges' policy.[119] Likewise, the Prison Service under Labour has aggressively pursued the improvement of prison regimes through 'market testing' and the publication of previously unseen prison league tables to 'name and shame' failing prisons and promote better performance.[120]

---

[114] *Modernising the Management of the Prison Service: An Independent Report by the Targeted Performance Initiative Working Group* (Chaired by Lord Laming of Tewin CBE) (London Home Office Communications Directorate 2000). Crucially, this included a proposal to conduct a review of the performance of Boards of Visitors (rec. 16) and urged the Inspectorate to work together with the Prison Service on an agreed set of standards against which performance would be evaluated (rec. 12).

[115] HM Prison Service *What Works in Prison Strategy* (HMSO, London, 2002).

[116] Garland (n 44) 176.

[117] Rt. Hon Jack Straw, PRT speech 22 July 1998—quoted in *Annual Report 1997–98* (n 77) 19.

[118] *Justice for All* (Cm. 5536) ch. 6.

[119] *Incentive and Earned Privileges; Earned Community Visits and Compacts*, Prison Service Order 4000, 2000. Bottoms (n 85) 187–8. The change is said to have come about in response to criticisms in A. Liebling, G. Muir, G. Rose and A. Bottoms, 'Incentives and Earned Privileges for Prisoners: An Evaluation', *Home Office Research Findings No. 87* (Home Office, London, 1999) and Prison Reform Trust, *Prison Incentives Schemes: Briefing Paper* (Prison Reform Trust, London, 1999), as well as feedback from HM Inspectorate of Prisons and from local Boards of Visitors.

[120] BBC News 'League Tables Shame Worst Prisons', 24 July 2003 http://news.bbc.co.uk/2/hi/uk_news/3091949.stm.

On the other hand, Labour's criminalization and sentencing policies have exacerbated prison overcrowding and significantly undermined the achievement of positive regimes.[121] Equally problematic, is that the political aspiration towards positive regimes remains rooted in the instrumental goal of effective crime and recidivism reduction. While this may be a clever rhetorical device, and another example of Labour's tendency to 'talk tough' while acting progressively,[122] it has within it some potential for its own downfall. It remains to be seen, in a managerial culture aimed at effective and efficient targeting and a political culture dominated by public protection, what will happen if recidivism is not reduced or if these prison programmes come into conflict with security (as in the 1990s). It is not inconceivable that, in the face of negative evidence on re-offending and security, the financial commitment to positive regimes might wane. Moreover, the pursuit of the aggregate targets of crime reduction need not always support individual prisoner interests, and the risk remains that 'one-to-one and non-accredited work important for the development of some individuals or for staff-prisoner relationships generally will be driven out'.[123] Despite the 'what works' programme's professed commitment to 'equality of opportunity', it is unclear what would constitute 'unfair or irrelevant' discrimination or how it would be squared with the commitment to 'value for money'.[124] An implicit tension remains between effectiveness as a basis for targeting interventions and universal 'equality of access' to constructive regimes.

What then of Labour's commitment to human rights, loudly trumpeted with the introduction of the Human Rights Act 1998? What of their early manifesto commitments to the 'justice' of the Woolf Report? How has this been translated in their approach to prison administration in practice? There is, of course, a strong appeal to the language of fairness and justice in Home Office and Prison Service documents.[125] But there is also growing, if less publicized, evidence that this commitment is being met. The appointment of Stephen Shaw (former Director of the Prison Reform Trust) as Prisons Ombudsman, Anne Owers (former Director of Justice) as Chief Inspector of Prisons, and Rod Morgan (well known campaigner for prisoners' rights) as Chief Inspector of Probation, is some indication of Labour's practical commitment here. There is also encouragement to be found in Labour's retraction of most of the fetters placed on the Prisons Ombudsman by Michael Howard,[126] the relocating with the Home Secretary of the responsibility for

---

[121] *Annual Report of HM Chief Inspector of Prisons for England and Wales 2001–2002* (HMSO, London, 2002). See also: BBC News 'Numbers pressure causing prison suicides', 17 August 2003, http://news.bbc.co.uk/2/hi/uk_news/3157873.stm.

[122] S. Savage and M. Nash, 'Law and Order under Blair' in S. Savage and R. Atkinson (eds), *Public Policy Under Blair* (Palgrave, Basingstoke, 2001).

[123] Morgan (n 25) 1126.

[124] *What Works in Prisons Strategy* (n 115) para. 9.11.   [125] See 5.4.2.1 below.

[126] See 5.4.2.4 below.

answering parliamentary questions on operational matters of prison admin-istration,[127] the overhaul of the internal prison grievance mechanism,[128] and the recent creation of a National Council designed to enhance the 'independence' of Boards of Visitors.[129] Furthermore, Labour's plans to place the Prisons Ombudsman office on a statutory footing, announced in the fine print of *Justice for All*, is a potential advance for prisoners' rights.

Whilst these are all welcome and important developments, governmental commitment to prisoners' legal entitlements remains elusive. Labour revised the Prison Rules in their entirety in 1999, but failed to use the opportunity to make any fundamental changes to their substance or legal status.[130] In 2000, a number of references to 'proportionality' were inserted in the Rules with a view to ensuring Convention compliance, but without active judicial scrutiny these do not in and of themselves further prisoner entitlements.[131] More recently, disciplinary rules have been revised in the light of *Ezeh and Connors v UK*.[132] As with many important amendments in the history of the Prison Rules, these were forced by the activism of the European Court of Human Rights. But in general the call of the prisoners' rights lobby for a radical overhaul remains unfulfilled:

The new Rules endorse the operational reality and legal position *status quo ante*, they remain ungenerous in their provision, are seldom specific, and even when specific, generally grant prison managers extensive discretion as to whether facilities will be provided.[133]

To summarize, Labour's political record on the question of prisoners' rights is mixed. The Labour Government displays a stronger commitment to constructive regimes than its immediate predecessors, and a dedication to evidence-based practice and performance management to this end. However, the aspiration towards positive regimes is undermined by broader criminal justice strategies leading to prison overcrowding and is rooted, pre-cariously, in the instrumental goal of crime reduction. Positive regimes remain matters of political will rather than prisoner entitlement. Reforms of

[127] Cavadino *et al*, (n 71) 145; Scott (n 64) 47. See 5.4.2.3 below.

[128] Prison Service Order 2510. Amongst a number of changes, the new scheme is unam-biguous about giving prisoners reasons for administrative decisions.

[129] See 5.4.2.3 below.

[130] Loucks (n 20) 1; Livingstone *et al*. (n 9) 16. The main changes were: elimination of the disciplinary offence of 'in any way offending against good order and discipline' (previous r. 47(21); four new disciplinary offences directed at protecting prisoners from racist abuse (amended r. 51); changes to the use of Closed Supervision Centres (r. 46); the deletion of ref-erences to prisoners under a sentence of death (previously rr. 72–76); permission for uncon-victed prisoners to pay for specially fitted accommodation (r. 25); revision of the rule on education to allow for the possibility of distance learning (r. 32).

[131] See 6.1.3.1 and 7.4.2 on the judicial approach to proportionality.

[132] *Ezeh and Connors v UK* (2002) 35 EHRR 28. The Prison (Amendment) Rules 2002 introduce a new r. 53A which takes away the governor's power to award 'additional days' and passes this to an independent adjudicator.

[133] Morgan (n 25) 1124.

the Ombudsman's powers, grievance mechanisms, the accountability of the Home Secretary regarding prison administration, the appointments of Anne Owers, Stephen Shaw, and Rod Morgan, changes to the Board of Visitors system, and the publication of prison league tables with a view to improving prison performance, are evidence of a concrete commitment to improving prison accountability mechanisms. But Labour has yet to overhaul fundamentally the legislative provision of prisoners' rights, and critics continue to argue that 'the case for having legally enforceable, detailed living standards remains as strong as ever'.[134]

5.4 THE STATUTORY REGIME GOVERNING PRISONS

England does not have a code of prisoners' rights or a statutory acceptance of the courts' role in the process of prison administration. This chapter sought to explain this absence in the context of England's penal and political culture. The significance of this absence for the prisoner's legal status has not yet been fully discussed, however. As indicated, the Prison Act 1952 vests the Home Secretary with the constitutional responsibility for administering prisons in England and Wales. It vests him with the power to make, and duty to enforce, rules for 'the regulation and management of prisons, remand centres . . . and for the classification, treatment, employment, discipline, and control of persons required to be detained therein'.[135] These rules are particularly relevant to the prisoners' legal status and are examined at 5.4.3 below, but first they must be placed in the broader context of the managerial and accountability structure governing prisons in England.

5.4.1 Managerial Accountability Framework

Since the Prison Service Agency was set up in 1993, the management and accountability structure for the Service has been set out in the Prison Service *Framework Document,* as revised in 1998. This document restates the pivotal role of the Home Secretary under the Prison Act 1952, specifying that he is: 'accountable to Parliament for the Prison Service in England and Wales',[136] 'sets the strategic direction of the Prison Service', 'specifies outputs and targets' for, and 'allocates resources to', the Prison Service.[137] The Home Secretary determines the 'strategic direction in the context of wider Ministerial planning for the criminal justice system as a whole',[138] agrees the annual corporate plan submitted to him by the Director General of the

---

[134] Morgan (n 28) 1128.   [135] Prison Act 1952, ss. 1, 4 and 47.
[136] HM Prison Service *Framework Document* (HMSO, London, 1998) para. 3.1.
[137] Para. 3.2.
[138] Para. 3.3.

Prison Service, and must present to Parliament an annual Prison Service report.[139] Finally, the Home Secretary may 'approve amendments to the Framework Document at any time in the light of experience or changed circumstances, having taken advice from the Permanent Secretary and the Director General and having consulted the Cabinet Office and The Treasury'.[140]

The Director General of the Prison Service Agency, who is appointed by the Home Secretary,[141] is 'delegated authority for the day to day management of the Service' and is 'responsible to the Home Secretary for the Prison Service and . . . for its performance against the corporate plans and targets'.[142] The document further notes that the Director General is 'accountable to the Home Secretary for the performance of contracted out prisons'.[143] The performance of contracted-out prisons, which are meant to promote competition and innovation in the prison system as a whole, contributes to the development of Key Performance Indicators.[144]

The *Framework Document* clarifies the 'role', 'task', 'aim', 'objectives', 'principles', 'purpose', and 'key performance indicators' of the Prison Service. These are intended as managerial and operational objectives and have no legal standing. The Prison Service is part of the criminal justice system which works to 'reduce crime and fear of crime, and their social and economic costs' and 'to dispense justice fairly and efficiently and promote the rule of law'.[145] The purpose of the Prison Service identified by the Home Office Public Service Agreement is the 'effective execution of the sentences of the courts so as to reduce re-offending and protect the public'.[146] Its objective is therefore 'to protect the public by holding in custody those committed by the Courts in a safe, decent, and healthy environment' and 'to reduce crime by providing constructive regimes which address offending behaviour, improve educational and work skills and promote law abiding behaviour in custody and after release'.[147] This is encapsulated and reiterated in the Prison Service Statement of Purpose:

Her Majesty's Prison Service serves the public by keeping in custody those committed by the courts. Our duty is to look after them with humanity and help them lead law-abiding and useful lives in custody and after release.[148]

In support of these aims and objectives, the Service has to follow in its work principles which ensure that it will:

. . . deal fairly, openly, and humanely with prisoners and all others who come into contact with us; encourage prisoners to address offending behaviour and respect others; value and support each other's contribution; promote equality of opportunity for all and combat discrimination wherever it occurs; work constructively with

---

[139] Para. 3.5.   [140] Para. 6.1.   [141] Para. 3.11.   [142] Para. 3.9.
[143] Para. 3.18.   [144] Para. 3.18.   [145] Para. 2.1.   [146] Para. 2.2.
[147] Para. 2.3.   [148] Para. 2.5.

criminal justice agencies and other organisations; obtain best value from resources available.[149]

Moreover, the document notes that Prison Service performance is 'monitored against a wide range of measures and indicators' which change to 'reflect new priorities' and are developed to 'measure the success of the Prison Service in achieving high quality outputs within a framework of efficiency and economy consistent with the Home Office Public Service Agreement'.[150]

The current performance management framework is set out and applied in the Prison Service Annual Report.[151] Targets set under the Spending Review 2000 and published in the Home Office Public Service Agreement (PSA) are contained in the Prison Service Delivery Agreement (SDA). The annual Key Performance indicators correspond to PSA and SDA targets and translate into Key Performance Targets (KPTs) against which Prison Service outputs are measured. In addition, Prison Service Performance Standards deal with the qualitative aspect of the Service's work.[152] These are relevant to all areas of prison life, ranging from education to mother and baby units. They are, like most of the managerial framework, intended to promote consistency of service and do not have any legal force authorizing rights limitations or giving rise to entitlements.[153] Rather, all Performance Standards are subject to an ongoing programme of self-audit and periodic audit by the Standards Audit Unit (SAU) to check compliance and service delivery. Performance targets and audit results are part of bilateral reviews and the Weighted Scorecard (WSC) which measures individual prison performance. Work on performance rating systems for establishments is ongoing. Recently the 'decency' agenda of former Prison Director and recently appointed Corrections Commissioner, Martin Narey, became an SAU project which is now conducting 'Measuring Quality of Prison Life' (MQPL) surveys.[154]

Over and above this panoply of managerial targets and principles, the framework document notes that the Prison Service's 'main statutory duties are set out in the Prison Act 1952 and rules made under that Act'.[155] As their weighting and low-visibility in this document indicates, the Prison Rules form only one element of the Prison Service's operations, alongside an extensive network of managerial accountability and control. Perhaps it is testimony to their symbolic status in this environment that the Rules no longer feature in the Director General's annual reports.[156]

---

[149] Para. 2.4.   [150] Para. 2.6.
[151] HM Prison Service *Annual Report and Accounts April 2002–March 2003* (HC 885, HMSO, London, 2003) 16.
[152] Contained in HM Prison Service, *Standards Manual 2002* (HMSO, London, 2002).
[153] Livingstone *et al.* (n 9) 23.
[154] *Annual Report 2002–2003* (n 151) 29.   [155] Para. 1.3.
[156] See, e.g., *Annual Report 2002–2003* (n 151).

5.4.2 Monitoring and Grievance Mechanisms

Supporting the operations of the Home Secretary and Director General of the Prison Service are HM Inspectorate of Prisons, Boards of Visitors (Independent Monitoring Boards), a Home Office Controller of contracted-out prisons, and the Prisons Ombudsman. These form a network of scrutiny and complaint resolution vital to, and complementary of, the Home Secretary's control and management of the prison system.

5.4.2.1 HM Inspectorate of Prisons

The Prison Act 1952 provides for a Chief Inspector of Prisons who reports to the Home Secretary and submits an annual report to Parliament 'on the treatment of prisoners and conditions in prisons'.[157] The *Framework Document* notes in addition that the 'Director General will act in accordance with the protocol about the handling of the Chief Inspector's reports agreed between the Prison Service and the Chief Inspector and endorsed by Ministers'.[158] The Prisons Inspectorate was recommended by the May Committee in 1979 and instituted in 1981.[159] It submits annual reports, reports on individual prison institutions and publishes thematic reviews.[160] Its remit does not extend to investigating individual complaints, which are left to the Prisons Ombudsman.

Although the Prisons Inspectorate is part of the Home Office, there can be little doubt that the holders of the office of Chief Inspector of Prisons have demonstrated conspicuous independence from the Home Secretary and Prison Service. Chief Inspectors are highly critical of prison conditions and government policy and are often publicly in conflict with the Home Secretary of the day. Sir Stephen Tumin's term of office was prematurely terminated by Michael Howard who sought to silence criticism of his 'Prison Works' policy. Howard's hope that Tumin's successor, Sir David Ramsbottom, would be more subservient to his views was subsequently dashed. Anne Owers continues this tradition of independence and is critical, along with Rod Morgan (Chief Inspector of Probation) of the 'output' orientation and 'paper exercises' of the Prison Service as well as the current conditions provoked by prison overcrowding.[161] While Inspectorate reports and criticisms form a crucial part of the accountability landscape, their recommendations are not binding on prison service agents or the Home Secretary and have no formal legal standing.[162] Their public reports have variable impact, depending on the level of co-operation among the Home

---

[157] Prison Act 1952, s. 5a.   [158] *Framework Document* (n 136) 3.22.
[159] May Report (n 57) 92–6.
[160] www.homeoffice.gov.uk/justice/prisons/inspprisons/index.html.
[161] *Through the Prison Gate: A Joint Thematic Review by HM Inspectorates and Probation* (HMSO, London, 2001) Foreword. *Annual Report* 2001–2002 (n 121) 11.
[162] S. Creighton and V. King, *Prisoners and the Law* (2nd edn, Butterworths, London) 8.

Office, the Prison Service and the Inspectorate, the specific issues involved, and the level of public sympathy these invoke.

As an annex to his final report,[163] Sir David Ramsbottom published the *Expectations: Criteria for Assessing the Treatment of and Conditions for Prisoners*. Influenced by 'domestic rules' and 'international standards', these were designed to 'concentrate on the quality and effectiveness of what happens to prisoners in line with the Prison Service's published Statement of Purpose' and produced to 'provide detailed guidance to inspectors, and others' to 'assist them in making accurate and consistent judgements'.[164] The incoming Chief Inspector, Anne Owers, has promised to publish a revised set of *Expectations*, to expose where Prison Service commitments and practice diverge from them, and to assist in revising the Service's own standards.[165] The impact of these *Expectations* on the prisoner's legal status remains to be seen.

5.4.2.2 Boards of Visitors (Independent Monitoring Boards)

The Prison Act 1952 provides for Boards of Visitors who monitor individual prisons and hear prisoner complaints.[166] The Boards have a right of free access to any part of the prison or to see any prisoner at any time.[167] Prison Rules 74–80 provide more detailed regulations regarding the Board's conduct and composition. In addition, the Prison Service *Framework Document* notes that the 'Home Secretary receives an annual report from Boards of Visitors. The Designated Minister will respond to such reports after taking advice from the Prison Service'.[168] The Boards have been described as the 'eyes and ears' of Ministers and the public,[169] but do not have any statutory powers to change the decisions of prison staff or to alter policy decisions at a higher level.

The Boards' reputation for independence is somewhat less scintillating than that of the Prisons Inspectorate. Matters were improved by the removal of the Boards' dual function as both disciplinary and complaint bodies, in line with the recommendations of the Woolf Report, in the early 1990s. However, the Boards have maintained a cosy relationship with prison management and have failed to develop a reputation as 'independent, fearless, public critics' or to gain any greater legitimacy with prisoners.[170] Rather, their performance fulfilled Richardson's initial doubts that the Boards could

---

[163] *Annual Report of HM Chief Inspector of Prisons for England and Wales 1999–2000* (HMSO, London, 2001) Annexe 7.

[164] See Introduction to Annex 7.

[165] *Annual Report 2001–2002* (n 121) 11. The Laming Report (n 114) had proposed that the Inspectorate and Prison Service work together in this respect (rec. 12).

[166] Prison Act 1952, ss. 6–9.   [167] Prison Act 1952, s. 6(3).

[168] *Framework Document* (n 136) para 3.24.

[169] Home Office Minister, Hilary Benn, speaking at the launch of the 'Independent Monitoring Boards' see www.homeoffice.gov.uk/docs/imbprlaunch.pdf.

[170] Livingstone *et al.* (n 9) 11.

ever 'possess sufficient status and independence to provide on their own, an adequate external safeguard of the rights and interests of prisoners'.[171] After the recent Lloyd Review, which confirmed the Boards' limited impact on prison administration,[172] they were rebranded as 'Independent Monitoring Boards' and a new National Council was set up to 'lead, support and guide Boards towards greater effectiveness'.[173] Whether these changes will greatly enhance their reputation as 'independent watchdogs' remains to be seen.

5.4.2.3 Home Office Controller

Section 84 of the Criminal Justice and Public Order Act 1994 provides for the Secretary of State 'to contract with another person for the provision or running (or the provision and running by him), or (if the contract so provides) for the running by subcontractors of his, of any prison or any part of a prison'. Private prisons are thus governed by an agreed contract between the government and the prison company. Prisoners are not party to this contract and cannot enforce its terms, although Livingstone et al argue they might be able to base a claim of legitimate expectation upon it.[174]

A Home Office Controller is placed in each private prison to monitor performance under the contract and enforce compliance with the Prison Rules, adjudicate on disciplinary charges and investigate allegations against staff.[175] While it is argued that private prisons are thus more accountable than public prisons, [176] and deliver better and cheaper regimes through contractual incentives,[177] scepticism remains. Critics are concerned that the Controller's role could lead to a conflict of interests in 'judging how the contractor succeeds in keeping good order and also to be personally responsible for maintaining good order'.[178] There is also unease about the lack of public visibility of prison contracts which are not published by the Home Office on the grounds of commercial confidentiality.[179]

5.4.2.4 Prisons Ombudsman

There is an extensive internal complaints procedure which prisoners can and do use. The prisoner can pursue a request or complaint to the governor and

[171] Richardson (n 30) 94.

[172] Sir Peter Lloyd, *Review of the Boards of Visitors: A Report of the Working Group* (HMSO, London, 2001). This review followed on from the Laming Report (n 114) rec. 16.

[173] www.homeoffice.gov.uk/justice/prisons/imb/index.html; and www.homeoffice.gov.uk/docs/imbprlaunch.pdf.

[174] Livingstone *et al.* (n 9) 35–6.

[175] CJA 1991 s. 85(1)(b); CJPOA 1994, s. 85; *Framework Document*, para. 3.18.

[176] R. Harding, *Private Prisons and Public Accountability* (Open University Press, 1997).

[177] I. Park, *Review of Comparative Costs and Performance of Privately and Publicly Operated Prisons 1998–99*, Statistical Bulletin 6/00 (Home Office, London, 2000).

[178] Livingstone *et al.* (n 9) 33.

[179] D. McDonald, 'Public Imprisonment by Private means' (1994) 34 *BJC* 29; Livingstone *et al.* (n 9) 34.

the Board of Visitors.[180] Having exhausted this procedure, prisoners can complain to the Prisons Ombudsman who sits at the apex of the internal complaints system. On the basis of his findings, he can recommend changes in practice or resolutions of the individual case to the Director of the Prison Service. The Prisons Ombudsman also publishes annual reports for the Home Secretary and Parliament.[181]

At the time of writing, the office of Prisons Ombudsman is non-statutory, created in the exercise of the Home Secretary's powers, and reports to the Home Secretary. The 1996 terms of reference were highly restrictive of the Ombudsman's remit, by giving the Home Secretary the final say on the eligibility of a complaint or the interpretation of the terms of reference, but this was remedied in 2001 when the Ombudsman obtained greater powers to determine complaint eligibility. More recently the Ombudsman's remit has been extended to include the Probation Service.[182] Currently, the Ombudsman may consider the merits of any decision relating to prison administration, discipline, and medical treatment. The current terms of reference restrict the jurisdiction of the Ombudsman by expressly excluding, *inter alia*, ministerial policy decisions, official ministerial advice, and the merits of ministerial decisions without prior ministerial consent.[183] The Prisons Ombudsman does not have the power to overturn a decision, but can make recommendations to the Director General of the Prison Service who has discretion to accept or reject such recommendations.[184]

Like the Chief Inspectors of Prisons, the former and present holders of the Prisons Ombudsman office have been highly active in defending their independence, extending their remit, and promoting accessibility to prisoners. There has been a significant increase in complaints to the Ombudsman as a result of these efforts,[185] and impressive progress continues in promoting the office.[186] Prisoners' rights campaigners note the limitations of the Ombudsman as a vehicle for challenging policy decisions of ministers, however.[187] It remains to be seen whether the proposal to place the Prisons Ombudsman on a statutory footing will also result in extending the Ombudsman's jurisdiction to the Home Secretary's policy decisions.

---

[180] Prison Rule 11. Livingstone *et al.* (n 9) 38–52.

[181] *Framework Document* (n 136) para. 3.23.

[182] M. Seneviratne, 'The Prisons Ombudsman' (2001) 23(1) *Journal of Social Welfare and Family Law* 93.

[183] Terms of reference as published in *Towards Resettlement: Prisons and Probation Ombudsman for England and Wales Annual Report 2002–2003* (HMSO, London, 2003).

[184] *Framework Document* 1998 (n 136) para. 3.23.

[185] Prisoner complaints to the Ombudsman rose by 62% between 2000 and 2003. In 2003 the Ombudsman upheld or resolved 33% of these complaints. See *Towards Resettlement* (n 183) 14ff.

[186] *Towards Resettlement* (n 183) 7; A. Travis, 'A look inside' *The Guardian*, 12 July 2003.

[187] Livingstone *et al.* (n 9) 50.

5.4.2.5 Interim Conclusions

Monitoring and informal grievance mechanisms are a successful and crucially important part of the accountability landscape in England. The
Prisons Inspectorate and Ombudsman have bravely and creatively utilized
their role to advance standards and fairness in prisons. The recent reforms
of Boards of Visitors and the proposals to place the Ombudsman's office on
a statutory footing are particularly encouraging. However, the competence
and remit of these bodies remain complementary to the pivotal policy role
of the Home Secretary. Courts remain the only bodies at present with the
power to overturn the decisions of the Home Secretary as well as the prison
administration. Given the power of the Home Secretary and Home Office
ministers in shaping prisoners' entitlements, the development of prison
policy, and the Prison Rules, it is small wonder that prisoners in England
continually turn to courts of law to further their interests.

5.4.3 The Prison Rules

If individual prisoners wish to argue specific legal entitlements, their primary
legislative material, alongside the Human Rights Act 1998, are the Prison
Rules. These are drawn up and amended by the Home Secretary and are, as
statutory instruments, approved by Parliament through a negative resolution
procedure.[188] Until 1999, the Prison Rules in force were based on those
enacted in 1964, although these rules were frequently amended. These have
now been replaced by the Prison Rules 1999 which came into force on
1 April 1999.[189] The Rules were subsequently amended in 2000 and 2002.[190]
    The new rules contain some individual amendments but in general retain
the structure and style of the Prison Rules 1964.[191] The Prison Rules are
augmented by a plethora of Standing Orders (SOs) and Circular Instructions
(CIs) which provide formal statements of a prisoner's privileges and obligations, and internal guidance on administrative issues and procedures respectively. SOs and CIs have no legal standing and cannot be relied on by prison
administration to increase their powers beyond those permitted under the
Rules. They do not vest prisoners with rights,[192] but the Prison Service
might be constrained in deviating from these if the court accepts that they
comprise an 'independent administrative practice' which gives rise to legitimate expectations in prisoners.[193] Success in such a claim is subject to the
nature of the practice in question and is discussed more fully in Chapter 7.

---

[188] G. Zellick, 'The Prison Rules and the Courts' (1981) *CLR* 602, 612.
[189] SI 1999 No. 728.   [190] See 5.3 above.
[191] Loucks (n 20) 1. See n 130.
[192] *Raymond v Honey* [1983] 1 AC 1; Livingstone *et al.* (n 9) 23–5.
[193] Creighton and King (n 162) 15.

There is also a separate statutory framework for the administration of private prisons.[194] However, the Prison Rules apply to both sectors.[195]

The legal status of the Prison Rules is complex. The Rules place duties on the prison administration in the sense that it is obliged to act as the Home Secretary stipulates under the Prison Act 1952. These duties can be monitored by the Home Secretary who is under a duty in the Act to ensure compliance with the Rules.[196] But the extent to which the Prison Rules give rise to legally enforceable entitlements vested in prisoners is a matter of judicial interpretation. The judicial approach to the Rules has changed over time and the current position was only settled in 1992. Whilst Chapter 7 examines this in more detail, some guidance can be provided at this point. Originally, all Prison Rules were held to be 'regulatory directions only, giving rise to no cause of action'.[197] This position has shifted somewhat. Individual rules are now justiciable in the sense that breaches of the Rules are subject to judicial review and may give rise to a public law remedy which the court has the discretion to award.[198] The Rules do not create rights in prisoners directly enforceable at private law and a prisoner cannot bring any claim for breach of statutory duty in respect of the Rules.[199] Breach of the Rules may nevertheless serve as evidence in support of ordinary negligence actions,[200] but such a breach by the administration does not give rise to an action for the tort of false imprisonment.[201]

Judicial review actions therefore form the main body of prisoners' rights cases. The prisoner may challenge a decision, if granted leave to do so,[202] if it is *ultra vires* the empowering legislation. This means a potential challenge arises if the decision-maker has: a) gone outside the discretion afforded to them; b) exercised their discretion illegally (for improper purposes, on the basis of irrelevant considerations or in bad faith); c) made an unreasonable decision; and d) violated the rules of procedural justice (including fairness in general, and the doctrine of legitimate expectation in particular).[203] An additional head of illegality exists where a Prison Rule, administrative guidance, or decision is found to violate a fundamental right at common law.[204] This has now been strengthened by the Human Rights Act (HRA) 1998, which requires public authorities, such as the Prison Service, to respect Convention rights.[205] If a prisoner is successful in any of these claims, the

---

[194] CJA 1991, s. 84 as amended by the CJPOA 1994, s. 96.

[195] CJPOA 1994, s. 84(2); Livingstone *et al.* (n 9) 31–6 raise some concerns about the appropriate respondent in such cases.

[196] Prison Act, s. 4(2).

[197] *Becker v Home Office* [1972] 2 QB 407, 418.

[198] *Hague v Deputy Governor of Parkhurst Prison* [1991] 3 All ER 733, 737 and 752 h–j.

[199] [1991] 3 All ER 733.   [200] [1991] 3 All ER 733, 752a.

[201] [1991] 3 All ER 733, 756.

[202] In this regard, see, P. Craig, *Administrative Law* (4th edn, Sweet & Maxwell, London, 1999) chs 21–23.

[203] Craig (n 202) chs 13–19.

[204] *R v Home Secretary, ex p Leech (No. 2)* [1994] QB 198.   [205] HRA 1998, s. 6(1).

court can compel the administrator to make a particular decision or have the administrative decision quashed, reversed, prohibited, returned for revision, and stopped, or obtain a statement of illegality.[206] If a breach of a Convention right is established, the court, under section 8(1) of the HRA 1998, may grant such remedies as it considers appropriate, including an award of damages if on the facts this would amount to 'just satisfaction' (under section 8(2)) of the injured party. Courts therefore have a potentially significant corrective function in their assessment of the Prison Rules, which has now been increased by the HRA 1998. But the realization of this potential very much depends on the extent of judicial activism and the judicial conception of the protections afforded by fundamental rights in prisons. These are matters which are taken up further in Chapters 6 and 7.[207]

Although, in theory, all Prison Rules are now justiciable under public law, as Chapter 7 shows, the extent to which prisoners can claim protection under the Prison Rules in a court of law has been dependent on the nature of the rule in question and the subject matter involved. The Prison Rules, which are considerably more detailed than the Act, contain a mixture of provisions ranging from statements of broad prison administration policy to more specific obligations and duties on the Prison Service. Zellick, whose classic analysis of the Prison Rules 1964 remains relevant to the Prison Rules 1999, analysed the Rules as falling into five categories.[208] These are statements of 'general policy objectives', such as the purpose of prison administration set out in Prison Rule 3; 'rules of a discretionary nature', which govern matters such as temporary release and communications with persons outside; 'rules of general protection', which prescribe certain minimum standards in matters of health and welfare; 'rules of institutional structure and administrative functions', which cast duties on the prison administration as regards their dealings with prisoners; and 'rules of specific individual protection', which chiefly cover areas of discipline and order, stipulating disciplinary offences and penalties.[209]

Zellick argued that differing degrees of justiciability applied to his five categories of rules.[210] Although judicial attitudes have changed significantly since Zellick wrote, many of his ideas on justiciability are reflected in the manner in which English courts have chosen to intervene in prisons. Of particular significance, from a comparative perspective, was his argument that rules of 'general policy objectives' were too broad to be justiciable. He argued that 'it is inconceivable that a departure from them, even if it were capable of demonstration, would be amenable to judicial supervision'.[211]

---

[206] Craig (n 202) ch. 22.
[208] Zellick (n 188) 602.
[210] Zellick (n 188) 612–15.

[207] See 6.2 and ch. 7.
[209] Zellick (n 188) 612–15.
[211] Zellick (n 188) 613.

There is indeed very little judicial attention to 'rules of general policy objectives', in particular to Prison Rule 3 which states that 'the purpose of the training and treatment of convicted prisoners shall be to encourage and assist them to lead a good and useful life'. Ralph Gibson LJ mentioned 'rules of general policy objectives' in the course of his reasoning in *Weldon*, noting that 'the Prison Rules may be regarded as the detailed provisions designed to achieve the purpose stated in Rule 1 and 2(1)'.[212] This could be read as an indication that the purpose of imprisonment as set out in these rules might be regarded as an interpretative guide or provide principles in evaluating the exercise of discretion under the Prison Rules. But this potentially purposive argument did not have any real significance in the case in question which turned on whether 'intolerable conditions' could form a basis for an action for false imprisonment.[213] There has not, to my knowledge, been any further judicial mention of the potential use of rules of 'general policy objectives' for the establishment of a legal claim. Equally, there is no mention in Prison Rule 2, which provides guidance on the interpretation of the Rules, that any purposive approach might be adopted in the interpretation of the Rules or that 'rules of general policy objectives' might form the basis of such an approach.

Lack of judicial attention is not the only evidence that 'rules of general policy objectives' under the Prison Rules are not considered to provide any deeper legal principles guiding prison administration. In practice, those employed in prison administration and in its regulation no longer view the Rules as offering authoritative guidance on the purpose of prison administration. As 5.4.1 showed, the 'purposes', 'objectives', and 'principles' governing prison administration are now governed by managerial documents such as the *Framework Document*, the Home Office Public Service Agreement, and the Prison Service Delivery Agreements and are promoted through audit mechanisms. The Prisons Inspectorate does not focus on Prison Rule 3 as a standard in the analysis of prison regime quality, having developed their own *Expectations*, which embrace a broader spectrum of managerial objectives, domestic and international rules, and standards.[214] The Prison Service Director General's annual reports do not mention the Prison Rules generally or Rule 3 in particular, and the Prisons Ombudsman recently admitted: 'I do not know what prison is for. I have been trying to find out for twenty years'.[215]

A lack of permanency and consensus on the purpose of prison administration has been characteristic of official policy on prisons since the decline of the rehabilitative ideal in England in the mid-1970s. Ever since the first

---

[212] *Weldon v Home Office* [1992] 1 AC 128. Reference was made here to the Prison Rules 1964. Under the Prison Rules 1999, the purpose of imprisonment is now stated in Prison Rule 3 and has the same wording as r. 1 of the Prison Rules 1964.

[213] See further 7.2.　　　　　　　[214] Loucks (n 20) 24.

[215] S. Shaw, 'The Right to Liberty and Humanity' (2001) 136 *Prison Service Journal* 39, 42.

challenge to the official purposes of the Prison Rules was heard from King and Morgan and the May Committee in 1979, the purpose of imprisonment and prison administration has been changing with the tides of penal politics, attitudes, and debate.[216] In this context the search for an overarching unitary legal purpose of prison administration, such as that found in Germany, is pointless. This multiplicity of purpose in prison administration is reflective, and constructive, of the absence of a purposive judicial approach to prison law in England. Whether articulated as 'humane containment',[217] 'positive custody',[218] 'security, control and justice',[219] or the 'protection of the public', statements of prison purpose in England certainly do not amount to statements of legal or constitutional principle. They are policy statements and ultimately matters of executive fiat. They do not provide the background substantive and principled basis upon which prisoners can establish more specific legal claims. In such an environment it is hardly surprising that Zellick viewed 'rules of general policy objectives', under the Prison Rules, as non-justiciable.

The absence of any deep legal principles guiding the interpretation of the Prison Rules and the evaluation of the discretion exercised thereunder is in marked contrast to the German purposive approach to prison law. As Part I showed, the conception and development of prisoners' rights in Germany centres on legal principles defining the purpose of imprisonment and prison administration. Paragraph 2 and the guiding principles of prison administration under paragraph 3 of the German Prison Act have thus formed the basis of judicial interpretation of individual provisions and provide substantive legal guidance as to the exercise of discretion.[220] Equally, the German 'constitutional resocialization principle' guides the courts' interpretation of the protections and limitations of the prisoner's basic rights within prisons and underpins the general provisions in the Act. This shows a stark contrast between the German and English approach to prison law and it is repeated in the conception of the prisoner's legal status discussed in Chapter 6.[221]

The absence of fundamental legal principles to structure administrative discretion has a profound impact on the prisoner's legal status in England, as most of the Rules dealing with prisoners' basic needs and day-to-day existence fall under Zellick's second category: 'rules of a discretionary nature'. A strong discretionary element can be found, for example, in rules governing classification, temporary release, physical activity, time out of cell, work, education, correspondence and communications, and earned

---

[216] Morgan 1997 (n 27) 1146–8.
[217] R. King and R. Morgan, *The Future of the Prison System* (Gower, Aldershot, 1980) ch. 1.
[218] May Report (n 57) para. 4.26.
[219] Woolf Report (n 27).
[220] See 4.2.
[221] See 6.2.

incentives and privileges.[222] Many of these rules are characterized by words
such as 'may', 'so far as reasonably practicable', 'where possible', 'subject to
any directions of the Secretary of State', or 'where the Secretary of State
permits'. In addition, Prison Rule 8 makes explicit that 'nothing in this rule
shall be taken to confer on a prisoner any entitlement to any privilege'. The
broad discretion in these rules is filled in by detailed prison administrative
guidance contained in the Prison Service Orders and Instructions, supplemented by the Prison Service Standards. As indicated above, these do not
have any legal status: neither legitimating infringements of prisoners' human
rights, empowering prison administrators beyond the Statutory Rules, nor,
in the absence of a legitimate expectation which courts recognize, giving rise
to specific legal entitlements in prisoners.

Zellick recognized that establishing a breach under discretionary rules
would be difficult, although he accepted that judicial intervention would
be possible in principle where the exercise of discretion was not properly
exercised.[223] Judicial intervention in the exercise of prison administrative
powers can thus occur where it is held that a legal standard or right has been
breached in the exercise of such discretion. With no general legal standards
of prison administration to call upon, prisoners must rely on general principles of judicial review and/or fundamental rights in that particular case.
They have to mould these broader legal propositions to the specific questions of prison administration. As Chapter 7 demonstrates, the extent to
which the courts will recognize the existence of a prisoner's right and the
weight accorded to that right in considering the exercise of discretion is variable, depending on the court's view of the subject matter involved. Whilst
courts are quicker to uphold rights where the decision involved directly or
indirectly affects the length of the prisoner's sentence or the prisoner's access
to justice, they are reluctant to interfere in the exercise of 'operational' or
'managerial' discretion within prisons, in particular where matters of security are involved.

Similarly, reticence characterizes the judicial approach to Zellick's rules of
'general protection' which he saw as too 'generally formulated' and 'impre-
cise' to have been intended to be justiciable.[224] These rules provide minimum standards of nutrition, accommodation, health, and cleanliness. The
argument for non-justiciability in this instance was based on an objection to
judicial intervention in the 'minutiae of day-to-day prison administration'.[225] This, by and large, accords with the attitudes of the courts who,
short of clear evidence of 'intolerable conditions' or 'gross neglect', have
refrained from meddling with decisions regarding welfare and conditions
and are reluctant to impose positive obligations on the prison administration.[226] Moreover, courts have been known to qualify the duty of care owed

---

[222] See Prison Rules 1999, rr. 7, 8, 9, 19, 29, 30, 31, 34 and 35.
[223] Zellick (n 188) 13.   [224] Zellick (n 188) 612–13.
[225] Zellick (n 188) 614.   [226] See ch. 7.

to prisoners by healthcare workers, on the basis that 'resources available for the public service are limited and that the allocation of resources is a matter for parliament'.[227]

The rules which Zellick identified as most amenable to judicial supervision were 'rules of institutional structure and administrative function' and 'rules of specific individual protection'. Rules in the first category cast duties on prison administrators from which prisoners can claim correlative entitlements. Such rules require, for example, a Board of Visitors to hear a prisoner's application,[228] a chaplain to make a specified number of visits to a prisoner,[229] a prison governor to hear a prisoner complaint, or a prison doctor to take care of a prisoner's health.[230] 'Rules of specific individual entitlement' are rare and usually only found in rules setting out disciplinary offences, behaviour classified as a threat to good order or discipline, and the procedures to be followed in determining whether a prisoner has committed an offence and the penalties awarded. Zellick argued that rules of specific entitlement were 'so concrete and precise in nature that it is inconceivable that any latitude should be left to the prison authorities in their implementation' and argued that 'strict compliance goes hand in hand with judicial oversight'.[231] Indeed, as Chapter 7 shows, the courts, urged on by the decisions of the European Court of Human Rights, have been most rigorous with respect to the procedural rights of prisoners charged with disciplinary offences, in particular where the penalties awarded have an impact on the length of the prisoner's sentence. This intervention has primarily been corrective in that judges have upheld rules of natural justice or the right of access to the courts, thereby prompting amendments of the Rules. Domestic judicial intervention is less forthcoming, however, where the penalties awarded are less serious or with respect to rules protecting good order and discipline which are classified as having a 'managerial' or 'operational' character.[232]

To sum up, the rules governing the day-to-day administration of prisons in England do not amount to a code of prisoners' rights. Drafted and amended by the Home Secretary, the Prison Rules are 'regulatory' and do not give rise to actionable rights in private law. Although the Rules have been justiciable under public law since 1991, the judicial record in upholding public law entitlements has been variable and dependent on the rule in question and the subject matter involved. This is exacerbated by the absence of any judicially recognized principles of prison administration which bind the Rules together, or assist in the interpretation and enforcement of the Rules and in the scrutiny of the many discretionary powers granted thereunder.

---

[227] *Knight v Home Office* [1990] 3 All ER 237, 243. This decision remains authoritative, but has not been followed by *Brooks v Home Office* [1999] 2 FLR 33.
[228] Prison Rules 1999, r. 78. [229] Prison Rules 1999, r. 14.
[230] Prison Rules 1999, rr. 11 and 20. [231] Zellick (n 188) 614. [232] See ch. 7.

5.5 CONCLUSION

The legislative regimes governing prisons in England and Germany reflect the different political, penal, and constitutional landscapes of each country. England places its greatest emphasis on mechanisms of political control, accountability, and oversight, the courts have no historically defined place within prison administration and the statutory regime places the Home Secretary in a pivotal position in the determination of prison policy and prisoners' rights. Germany's Prison Act, while setting out clear lines of political accountability, rests ultimately on the definition of the prisoner's legal status. It lays out special prisoners' rights and provides leading principles in paragraphs 2–4 which act as strong interpretative guidance in the exercise and supervision of discretion afforded under the Act. Consequently, there is a significant difference between England and Germany in terms of the body of special rights which prisoners can seek to claim and the principles upon which these rights might be founded.

The statutory regimes in England and Germany are not wholly conclusive of the prisoners' legal status, however. To differing degrees, both statutory regimes vest discretion in prison administrators. It would be myopic, therefore, to locate the difference between the prisoner's legal status in Germany and England in statutory law alone. Centrally significant to the prisoner's legal status in both countries is the broader constitutional context within which judges are operating, their approaches to the scrutiny of administrative discretion, and interpretation of fundamental rights protections within prisons. The following chapter discusses these elements in turn.

6

Prisoners and the Parliamentary Constitution

Corresponding to the physical security of an engineer's design and the intellectual security of a philosophical system is the political security of Germany's *Rechtsstaat*: every possible contingency seems covered by some law. Law, courts and constitution regulate everything. In Britain, much depends not on law, but on custom and tradition. Law itself is the by-product of custom built up by habit. Precedent is more important than purpose. The German state was designed—and rather well designed. The British state grew—although it is none the worse for that. Each country is very different both for the way the state works and what people think about it.[1]

Germany displays a strong belief and support for fundamental rights.[2] The German Basic Law entrenches fundamental rights unequivocally, starting out with a clear positive duty on the State to protect human dignity and by making rights under the Constitution unamendable. As an 'expression of a deep revulsion against a distasteful past',[3] it sought to safeguard against the vagaries of democratic political processes both by guarding against strong government in the political provisions of the Constitution[4] and by vesting guardianship of basic rights in the hands of a judiciary with considerable powers of legislative review.[5] In German 'rhetoric about rights' we saw considerable judicial, academic and political faith in fundamental rights, expressed in widespread advocacy of a natural rights philosophy that views fundamental rights as pre-state and the State's very existence as justified and legitimized by its ability to safeguard and protect these rights. Just like the provisions of the Basic Law, this strong faith in fundamental rights displayed in 'rhetoric about rights' is also rooted in Germany's recent political history. At its simplest, it expresses the strong resolve to guarantee against the abuses of the past. At its most fundamental, 'rhetoric about rights' in Germany expresses a political project of relegitimizing a State that had forfeited any claim to legitimacy. While rights scepticism is present in Germany, and has increased in recent years, the primary consensus remains that of faith in fundamental rights. This faith is determinative of legal and political

---

[1] M. Uchida, 'Chalk and Cheese' (Feb 1998) *Prospect* 24, 28. [2] See 2.1.
[3] P. Merkl, *The Origin of the West German Republic* (OUP, New York, 1963) 176.
[4] Basic Law, art. 20(1). C. Degenhart, *Staatsrecht I* (13th edn, Müller, Heidelberg, 1997) 1–138.
[5] Basic Law, art. 93.

relations generally and in turn has led to the dominance of 'rights rhetoric' when invoking arguments concerning social, legal, and political change, not least those regarding prison policy and reform.

The English do not share with the Germans the political history that has made constitutional rights so fundamental to them. Constitutionally entrenched rights in England have far fewer immediate symbolic connotations. Rather, when shadowed by German faith in fundamental rights, the English display a marked ambivalence towards the role and place of fundamental rights in political and legal culture. English constitutionalism contains a variety of conflicting and conflicted approaches to fundamental rights, ranging from overt scepticism to mere acceptance and, more recently, glimmers of rights optimism with the introduction of the Human Rights Act (HRA) 1998. This ambivalence about rights is equally rooted in England's distinctive history. If German faith in rights expresses a determined rejection of the past and an admission of the failure of local political processes to safeguard against this past, English ambivalence about constitutionally entrenched rights springs from the relative continuity of its local democratic traditions,[6] conventions, and institutions. This continuity generates faith in the legitimacy of local political institutions and a belief that England is blessed with a 'general culture of tolerance and forbearance'.[7] While the discontinuity of Germany's history explains the need constitutionally to design most aspects of society, the historical continuity of England's democratic past explains faith in the flexibility and evolutionary nature of her constitutional arrangements and belief in Parliament, rather than the judiciary, as the ultimate protector of individual liberty. Grounded in the confidence gained from the longevity of its political and legal institutions and so-called culture of liberty, English constitutionalism has attributed the historical success of its constitution to its organic and unwritten nature:

The phrase 'an unwritten constitution' is something of a confidence trick. In the context of the United Kingdom it suggests that we manage without the need of a real constitution: we know how to govern ourselves and do not have to write it down;

---

[6] The English constitution has not evolved without interruption, but can nevertheless be thought of as continuous, relative to Germany. The question whether the Parliamentary Rebellion of 1652 and the Cromwell Republic represented a complete break in constitutional history is a matter of debate. See on the one hand, C. Munro, *Studies in Constitutional Law* (Butterworths, London, 1999) 5; S. De Smith and R. Brazier, *Constitutional and Administrative Law* (Penguin, London, 1998) 8–9 who argue that the return to the old order was sufficient to restore the continuity of the constitution. In opposition, see P. Craig, 'Public Law, Political Theory and Legal Theory' (2000) *PL* 211, 215.

[7] P. Norton, *The Constitution in Flux* (Blackwell, Oxford, 1986) 22; K. Ewing and C. Gearty, *Freedom under Thatcher: Civil Liberties in Modern Britain* (Clarendon Press, Oxford, 1990) 2. This 'culture of tolerance' has been shown to be more evident in the political elite of Britain than amongst the population at large. See D. Barnum, L. Sullivan and M. Sunkin, 'Constitutional and Cultural Underpinnings of Political Freedom in Britain and the United States' (1992) 12(3) *OJLS* 362, 370.

common sense and tradition tell us what to do; written constitutions are for nations which have to work out how they should be governed.[8]

Thus, until the enactment of the HRA 1998, England lacked the most observable trapping of a rights culture, namely a clearly defined, unified, and authoritative declaration as to what individual fundamental rights citizens held. Rather, England exhibited a 'liberty-consciousness'. This meant, first, that 'residual' freedom was always protected where it was not prohibited by law,[9] and secondly, that included in the Diceyan conception of the rule of law, were general constitutional principles that expressed the rights and liberties of private persons.[10] These rights and liberties, which were subject to the express limitation of Parliament, were determined by the decisions of common law judges and did not derive from any general principles of a written constitution.[11] Rather, individual rights and liberties were tacitly accepted as part of the common law. They were the creation of judicial pronouncements over time: 'the incidental consequence of ordinary litigation'.[12]

The introduction of the HRA 1998 represents a break with this incidental and organic approach to rights and liberties. It is the culmination of deeper cultural shifts within English constitutionalism which themselves require elaboration.

6.1 Fundamental Rights and English Constitutionalism

6.1.1 The Tradition of Rights Scepticism

German constitutionalism is idealist and rationalist and aspires to the comprehensive and systematic protection of entrenched constitutional rights in line with overarching interpretative guidelines and constitutional purposes.[13] These aspirations are not part of English constitutional orthodoxy

---

[8] S. Sedley, 'Governments, Constitutions, and Judges' in G. Richardson and H. Genn (eds), *Administrative Law and Government Action* (Clarendon Press, Oxford, 1994) 35.

[9] A.V. Dicey, *Law of the Constitution* (10th edn, Macmillan, London, 1959) 270–2; D. Feldman, *Civil Liberties and Human Rights in England and Wales* (Clarendon Press, Oxford, 1993) 60–1; De Smith and Brazier (n 6) 388.

[10] Dicey (n 9) 189–91; J. Jowell, 'The Rule of Law Today' in J. Jowell and D. Oliver (eds), *The Changing Constitution* (3rd edn, OUP, Oxford, 1994) 58–9; P. Craig, 'Formal and Substantive Conceptions of the Rule of Law: An Analytical Framework' (1997) *PL* 467, 470–4; I. Harden and N. Lewis, *The Noble Lie—The British Constitution and the Rule of Law* (Hutchinson, London, 1986) ch. 1 and 194–6.

[11] A.V. Dicey, *The Law of the Constitution* (8th edn, Macmillan, London, 1927) 191.

[12] T. Allan, 'Pragmatism and Theory in Public Law' (1988) 104 *LQR* 422.

[13] D. Kommers, *The Constitutional Jurisprudence of the Federal Republic of Germany* (Duke University Press, Durham, 1997) 40. This is also due to the civil law culture in which it exists. On rationalism in civilian legal culture, see H. Glenn, *Legal Traditions of the World* (OUP, Oxford, 2000) 132–5.

which is pragmatic, empiricist, positivist, and highly sceptical of idealist notions of natural rights or 'comprehensive ideology of any kind'.[14] Instead, English constitutional orthodoxy, commonly expressed in Diceyan terms,[15] is 'anti-rationalist' and rooted in tradition and practical experience.[16] These values were expressed in a vision of an organic constitution governed by the political conventions and traditions of a sovereign Parliament and articulated by pragmatic common law judges subordinate to Parliament.

Thus, the first fundamental principle of English constitutional orthodoxy is expressed in the doctrine of parliamentary sovereignty, as articulated in the judgments of the common law and in the views of, *inter alia*, Blackstone, Coke, Dicey and Wade.[17] Parliament, it was argued, had proved over time a better safeguard of rights and freedoms in practice than any legal safeguard entrenched in a Bill of Rights. The English were the proud recipients of liberty under a Parliament that, as a matter of 'clearly accepted conven-

[14] This scepticism has been traced, beyond Dicey, to a variety of sources within English political culture and philosophy. Credit has been given to the authoritarianism of Hobbes, the constitutionalism of Mill and Bagehot, the legal positivism of Bentham and Austin, the radical scepticism of Bentham and Mill, the conservative scepticism and common law traditionalism of Burke, and even Hume's jurisprudence. See J. Gray, *Enlightenment's Wake: Politics and Culture at the Close of the Modern Age* (Routledge, London, 1995) 172–3; A. Ryan, 'The British, the Americans, and Rights' in M. Lacey and K. Haakonssen (eds), *A Culture of Rights* (CUP, Cambridge, 1991) 375–95; P. Atiyah, *Pragmatism and Theory in English Law* (Stevens and Sons, London, 1987) 18–26; K. Minogue, 'What is wrong with rights' in C. Harlow (ed.), *Public Law and Politics* (Sweet & Maxwell, London, 1986) 209, 209–12; A. Lester, 'Human Rights and the British Constitution' in J. Jowell and D. Oliver (eds), *The Changing Constitution* (4th edn, OUP, Oxford, 2000) 89, 90–2 and M. Loughlin, *Public Law and Political Theory* (Clarendon Press, Oxford, 1992) where Oakeshott's conservatism is viewed as an exemplar of the political philosophy underlying this peculiar form of English constitutionalism.

[15] Diceyan orthodoxy is the dominant interpretation of Dicey's views. (Loughlin 1992 (n 14) 184; C. Harlow and R. Rawlings, *Law and Administration* (2nd edn, Butterworths, London, 1997) 37). This form of Diceyan constitutionalism has been consistently challenged in England both in direct opposition to Dicey's theory (e.g. W.A. Robson, *Justice and Administrative Law* (Macmillan, London, 1928); I. Jennings, *Law and the Constitution* (University of London Press, London, 1938)) and in an ongoing dispute as to the correct interpretation of Dicey's views (e.g. Craig (nn 6, 10); T. Allan, *Law, Liberty and Justice* (Clarendon Press, Oxford, 1993)). Notwithstanding, Dicey continues to form the starting point of constitutional analysis in England. As C. Harlow stated in 'Changing the Mindset: The Place of English Administrative Law' (1994) 14(3) *OJLS* 419, 426: 'Whether or not Dicey "got it wrong", his work has become, to the chagrin of many, the orthodox background theory of the twentieth century constitution'. See also J. Goldsworthy, *The Sovereignty of Parliament: History and Philosophy* (Clarendon Press, Oxford, 1999) ch. 10.

[16] Loughlin calls this constitutionalism 'conservative normativism' (Loughlin 1992 (n 14)), Harlow and Rawlings refer to it as 'red light theory'(Harlow and Rawlings (n 15) ch. 2), Harden and Lewis as 'whig constitutionalism' (Harden and Lewis (n 10) 1). I do not seek to identify the background political theory here, but rather to describe a cultural attitude to the entrenchment of fundamental rights. In this sense I am closer to McCrudden's characterization of the orthodox English attitude to rights as 'pragmatic empiricism'. See C. McCrudden and G. Chambers, *Individual Rights and the Law in Britain* (Clarendon Press, Oxford, 1994) 585.

[17] W. Wade, 'The Basis of Legal Sovereignty' (1955) *CLJ* 172; De Smith and Brazier (n 6) ch. 1; A. Bradley, 'The Sovereignty of Parliament—in Perpetuity' in J. Jowell and D. Oliver (eds), *The Changing Constitution* (3rd edn, OUP, Oxford, 1994) 79, 85–9; Goldsworthy (n 15) chs 3–9.

tion', would 'not use its unlimited sovereign power . . . in an oppressive or tyrannical way'.[18] Belief in Parliament as a guarantor of freedom runs very deep within English political and legal culture.[19] Even when the practices of governments, party politics and developments in European law were eroding its very foundations, the rhetoric of parliamentary sovereignty was sufficiently compelling to resist persistent calls for the inclusion of a Bill of Rights over the last thirty years.[20]

The strength of the appeal to parliamentary sovereignty is grounded in continuing faith in the ideals of majoritarian and unitarian democracy.[21] Equally, parliamentary optimism in England rests on a belief in a benign political culture where the proper limits of governmental power are taken for granted and where the political elite all share an intrinsic sense of proper government.[22] As Sajó notes, 'the exercise of power' in England 'is *built on trust*, contagious trust'.[23] For 'whig constitutionalists', trust in the benignity of English political culture was bolstered by anachronistic and chauvinist views of continental Europe as the home of absolutism and despotism, against which Britain's culture of liberty shone out. As Dicey hinted, what came effortlessly to the English had to be written in legal documents elsewhere.[24]

Parliamentary sovereignty and the relationship of the courts to Parliament and the executive were never defined in positive law. This was left to a pragmatic common law judiciary committed to upholding the ideals of the 'balanced constitution'. As guardians of the common law constitutional tradition, courts understood best how to respect the sovereignty of Parliament whilst articulating the traditional freedoms inherent in the 'spirit of the common law'.[25] Protection of freedom in this way was held up against the pretensions of an idealist, rationalist, and metaphysical approach to fundamental rights.[26] Rather, under orthodox English constitutionalism, questions of individual freedoms were to be settled not by an appeal to ideals of natural rights but through a common law rooted in custom and common

---

[18] G. Marshall, *Constitutional Conventions* (Clarendon Press, Oxford, 1984) 9.

[19] Goldsworthy (n 15) chs 3–9; Ryan (n 14) 395–406.

[20] A. Bradley, 'The Sovereignty of Parliament—Form or Substance?' and A. Lester, 'Human Rights and the British Constitution' in J. Jowell and D. Oliver (eds), *The Changing Constitution* (4th edn, OUP, Oxford, 2000) 23, 51–2 and 89, 90–2, 97–100.

[21] P. Craig, *Administrative Law* (4th edn, Sweet & Maxwell, London, 1999) 4–7. For in-depth analysis see Goldsworthy (n 15) ch. 10.

[22] Ryan (n 14) 405; K. Ewing and C. Gearty, *Freedom Under Thatcher* (OUP, Oxford, 1990) 1–2; Barnum *et al.* (n 7) 370. This was assisted after the Second World War by a sustained period of political consensus on matters of governmental policy (McCrudden and Chambers (n 16) 5).

[23] A. Sajó, *Limiting Government: An Introduction to Constitutionalism* (CEU Press, Budapest, 1999) 10.

[24] Dicey (n 9) 192.

[25] K. Ewing and C. Gearty, *The Struggle for Civil Liberties* (OUP, Oxford, 2000) 25–9.

[26] Ryan (n 14) 378; Minogue (n 14) 209–11.

sense.[27] There is 'a profoundly English belief that an independent judiciary, and a judiciary with the power to issue practical orders, was more important than any number of grand theoretical declarations about the Rights of Man'.[28]

This common sense or pragmatism was cherished and protected by a legal profession insulated from, and distrustful of, academic opinion or theoretical argument.[29] A profession which saw itself as the guardian of the 'artificial reason' that grew from the experience, traditions, and uses of the common law. Legal knowledge in this tradition was not founded on rational and logical reasoning but rather 'historically evidenced custom'.[30] Thus, in the development of freedoms, the common law would aspire not to construct a comprehensive system of principles and rights but to find the best practical resolution of each individual case. As Wilberforce famously pronounced, 'English Law fastens not on principles but on remedies'.[31]

Belief in the sensible and balanced approach of the judiciary was implicit in England's 'inchoate' principle of the separation of powers:

In modern Britain the concept of the separation of powers is cloudy and the notion of the independence of the judiciary remains primarily a term of constitutional rhetoric. Certainly its penumbra, and perhaps even its core, are vague. No general theory exists, although practically the English have developed surprisingly effective informal systems for the separation of powers.[32]

What this orthodox 'political culture' produced was a tacit consensus that the judicial role should be conceived in apolitical terms. In the vision of a unitarian democracy, unelected judges lacking the mandate of elected politicians, were not viewed as a legitimate part of the political process.[33] A broad division between 'the judicial control of legality and the parliamentary control of the political' was thus established.[34] The common law judge was to safeguard the limits of executive action by policing the laws of the sovereign Parliament whilst marrying this with the traditions of the common law.[35] Judicial review, in particular, was confined to checking the legality (as opposed to the merits) of executive action, in the narrow sense of its

---

[27] On the anti-categorical, anti-rationalist, anti-theoretical, and pragmatic approach of the common law see J. Allison, *A Continental Distinction in the Common Law* (OUP, Oxford, 2000) 122–8; Atiyah (n 14) ch. 1; Harlow (n 15); G. Postema, *Bentham and the Common Law Tradition* (Clarendon Press, Oxford, 1986) ch. 1. On the historical conditions which led to the anti-rationalistic bent within the common law, see R. Van Caenegem, *Judges, Legislators and Professors: Chapters in European Legal History* (CUP, Cambridge, 1987).
[28] Atiyah (n 14) 22. As Atiyah notes, however, judges also act on 'implicit theories' of their role and of the English constitution (ch. 4).
[29] Allison (n 27) 74.   [30] Postema (n 27) ch. 1.
[31] *Davy v Spelthorne BC* [1983] 3 All ER 278 at 285.
[32] R. Stevens, 'A Loss of Innocence? Judicial Independence and the Separation of Powers' (1999) 19(3) *OJLS* 365, 367.
[33] Craig (n 21) 5–7; Goldsworthy (n 15) 233.   [34] Allison (n 27) 158.
[35] W. Wade and C. Forsyth, *Administrative Law* (7th edn, Clarendon Press, Oxford, 1994) 5–7; Craig (n 21) 7; Harlow and Rawlings (n 15) 578–9.

conformity to empowering legislation and to the common law rules of procedure and process. Judges, imbued with this orthodox view, conceived of their role in particularly formalist terms.[36] Vesting in judges the *explicit* power to check parliamentary and executive action on the grounds of their own interpretation of constitutionally entrenched rights, challenged this cultural view of the apolitical judge. A Bill of Rights threatened to politicize the judiciary and to break the tacit balance between the legislative and judicial functions.[37] Gradual incremental judicial development of residual civil liberties, process standards, and procedural safeguards could only be accommodated within the careful balance of the organic English constitution as an extension of parliamentary will and thus as a less explicitly political enterprise.[38]

If constitutional orthodoxy was sceptical of entrenched fundamental rights, placing faith in tradition, radical constitutionalism was sceptical of fundamental rights on opposite grounds. Those concerned with political and social change focused their energies not on the entrenchment of a Bill of Rights or the pursuit of a rights consciousness, but on changing the make-up of government and forcing legislative reform.[39] Protection of liberty was a matter for Parliament, because it was as elected MPs that reformists could define the scope of such liberty. In contrast to Germany's influential social-democratic vision of the *soziale Rechtsstaat* and historical promotion of social constitutional rights,[40] English socialists tended to view a Bill of Rights as an idealist facade for the entrenchment of liberal values of egoistic individualism and the vision of a limited State.[41] Rather than trust a conservative and insulated judiciary with a bias towards private individualistic freedoms, left-wing constitutionalists placed faith in the increased political power of the legislature.[42] Far from supporting fundamental rights, they

---

[36] M. Hunt, 'The Human Rights Act and Legal Culture: The Judiciary and the Legal Profession' (1999) 26(1) *JLS* 86, 93.

[37] J. Young, 'The Politics of the Human Rights Act' (1999) 26(1) *JLS* 27, 30; Barnum *et al.* (n 7) 370 and 373; Stevens (n 32) 395.

[38] C. Forsyth, 'Of Fig Leaves and Fairy Tales: The Ultra Vires Doctrine, the Sovereignty of Parliament and Judicial Review' (1996) 55(1) *CLJ* 122, 136–7.

[39] Goldsworthy (n 15) 233, 215–20, 228.   [40] See 2.1.

[41] F. Klug, *Values for a Godless Age* (Penguin, London, 2000) 154; Minogue (n 14) 211. Loughlin also attributes left-wing rights scepticism to the pragmatic/realist and empiricist strains of functionalist thought (Loughlin 1992 (n 14) ch. 6, 165–76, 190–205). Functionalism, also termed 'green light theory' by Harlow and Rawlings ((n 15) ch. 3) is a view of law as an instrument of politics and government. It rejects the notion of judicial interpretation of basic rights as a normative exercise, but rather one soaked in political preferences. It also views the adjudicative model and rights as a deficient means of resolving polycentric disputes within the public sector.

[42] See, e.g., J. Griffiths, *The Politics of the Judiciary* (4th edn, Fontana, London, 1991) and 'The Political Constitution' (1979) 42 *MLR* 1; K. Ewing and C. Gearty, *Freedom under Thatcher: Civil Liberties in Modern Britain* (Clarendon Press, Oxford, 1990) ch. 8; K. Ewing and C. Gearty, *The Struggle for Civil Liberties* (OUP, Oxford, 2000) ch. 8.

viewed the prospect of increased judicial power with deep-felt suspicion.[43] For Labour, common law judges threatened the necessary extension of the State for the attainment of socialist goals.[44] Entrenched fundamental rights, which the Left (in line with orthodox constitutionalism) viewed as primarily negatively conceived, only gave judges more political power to stem the tide of welfarist reform. Rather, a strong government was required with the power to implement, under statute, positive rights to state resources.[45] Equally, these rights should be defined and implemented in a modern administrative system that was free of the formalist, restrictive view of the common law and understood the need to effect a dynamic and workable administrative State.[46] Thus, for very different reasons, both conservative constitutional orthodoxy and a particularly English brand of radical socialist constitutionalism rejected the notion of a Bill of Rights.[47] Both placed their faith in Parliament to realize their competing aims. As Ryan states, 'political radicals have always looked to Parliament to legislate in their desired direction, just as conservatives have looked to Parliament to hold off the changes they feared'.[48]

Despite this rights sceptical consensus between conservatives and radicals, there can be little doubt that an incipient 'rights consciousness' has slowly been building over the last thirty years, in particular within the legal profession.[49] With the introduction of the Human Rights Act (HRA) 1998 this process was explicitly acknowledged.[50] The shift to a Bill of Rights represents a departure from both orthodox and radical constitutional traditions, and is bound up with a reinvention of English constitutionalism as expressing a systematic, rationalist, principled, and rights-based consciousness.[51] For Loughlin and Ryan, incorporation of a Bill of Rights is far from the inevitable outcome of a process of constitutional evolution, rather it is tantamount to an 'exercise in political reform'.[52] Given this apparent volte-face, we might ask why and how such a cultural shift has come about?

6.1.2 The Shift to a Rights Consciousness

Recourse to arguments for a Bill of Rights came initially in the form of liberal political objections to the immigration policies of Labour in the 1960s and 1970s.[53] Later, the phrase 'elective dictatorship' was exploited by

---

[43] K. Ewing, 'The Human Rights Act and Parliamentary Democracy' (1999) 62 *MLR* 79, 80.
[44] Ewing (n 43) 80.
[45] Ryan (n 14) 409–10; Loughlin 1992 (n 14) 197–201; Harlow and Rawlings (n 15) 602–4.
[46] Harlow and Rawlings (n 15) ch. 3.
[47] Young (n 37) 30.   [48] Ryan (n 14) 413.
[49] M. Hunt, *Using Human Rights Law in English Courts* (Hart, Oxford, 1998) ch. 5.
[50] Ewing (n 43) 79.   [51] Loughlin 1992 (n 14) 210.
[52] Loughlin 1992 (n 14) 210; Ryan (n 14) 419.
[53] Klug (n 41) 153.

Conservatives to stem the tide of state expansion.[54] But it was not until the 1980s that a broader consensus developed in support of entrenching a Bill of Rights. The Thatcher Governments' erosions of parliamentary scrutiny, civil and political freedoms, and local governmental power, undoubtedly inspired those on the left and centre of British politics, as well as the moderate Right,[55] to review their assumption that English liberty consciousness was immutable.[56] England's effortless culture of liberty so internalized by the political elite had been fundamentally challenged by the authoritarian and centralist style of three consecutive Thatcher Governments. Concerns arose that the organic development of the constitution by the common law judiciary could not keep up with the threats to civil liberties posed by modern British government.[57] The threat of Thatcherism was coupled with the challenge to government legitimacy presented by the political events of Northern Ireland.[58] Moreover, New Right ideology and its associated brand of New Public Management led to a redefinition of the State which threatened traditional political accountability mechanisms.[59] This heightened the disjuncture between constitutional orthodoxy and political reality, and increased the perception that parliamentary controls over executive power were becoming more symbolic than effective.

As a result, during the 1980s in Britain, political activism towards the entrenchment of a Bill of Rights sharply increased. A new liberal democratic party intensified its calls for constitutional reform and a Bill of Rights and civil liberties groups, such as Liberty and Charter 88, proliferated.[60] This was accompanied by the intensification of domestic human rights scholarship signalled in the first two textbooks on human rights law (as opposed to civil liberties) in Britain in 1993 and 1994 respectively.[61] Following on from this political and scholastic activism were changes in the internal attitudes of

[54] Lord Hailsham, *The Dilemma of Democracy: Diagnosis and Prescription* (Collins, London, 1978).

[55] S. Jenkins, *Accountable to None: The Tory Nationalization of Britain* (Penguin, London, 1995).

[56] Ryan (n 14) 429.

[57] Ewing and Gearty (n 42) 257; A. Lester, 'European Human Rights and the British Constitution' in J. Jowell and D. Oliver (eds), *The Changing Constitution* (3rd edn, OUP, Oxford, 1994) 32, 41.

[58] C. McCrudden, 'Northern Ireland and the British Constitution' in J. Jowell and D. Oliver (eds), *The Changing Constitution* (3rd edn, OUP, Oxford, 1994) 323.

[59] G. Drewry, 'Revolution in Whitehall: The Next Steps and Beyond' in J. Jowell and D. Oliver (eds), *The Changing Constitution* (3rd edn, OUP, Oxford, 1994) 155; I. Harden, *The Contracting State* (Open University Press, Buckingham, 1992); R. Baldwin, 'The Next Steps: Ministerial Responsibility and Government by Agency' (1998) *MLR* 622; J. Stewart and K. Walsh, 'Changes in the Management of Public Services' (1992) *PA* 504.

[60] Ryan (n 14) 428. For a full list of the pressure groups in the UK see Appendix C in McCrudden and Chambers (n 16). On the make-up of the movement for constitutional reform see Loughlin 1992 (n 14) 220–4.

[61] McCrudden and Chambers (n 16); D. Feldman, *Civil Liberties and Human Rights in England and Wales* (Clarendon Press, Oxford, 1993). See also A. Tomkins, 'Inventing Human Rights Law and Scholarship' (1996) 16 *OJLS* 153.

the Labour Party as regards the need for a Bill of Rights. Crucially, in 1992, New Labour placed on its agenda its intention to incorporate the European Convention on Human Rights (ECHR). Once the rights-sceptical alliance between Left and Right had been broken, the course to the HRA 1998 was set down.[62]

It cannot be denied, however, that constitutional reform might also have occurred without shifting the basic premises of the English constitutional consensus against the entrenchment of a Bill of Rights. Ewing and Gearty saw the solution not in resort to a Bill of Rights, but in the reinvigoration of England's liberty consciousness by strengthening the doctrine of separation of powers and bolstering parliamentary power over state activity.[63] The move away from a pragmatic, organic, and political constitutionalism sceptical of constitutionally entrenched rights can be attributed also to additional cultural shifts.

The most obvious of these comes in the globalization of human rights discourse and the growing influence of foreign legal cultures on Britain's local tradition. Consciousness of constitutional rights was heightened by shifts in other common law jurisdictions.[64] Senior judges, who were increasingly internationally mobile, became more receptive to the development of an international common law of human rights.[65] This human rights internationalism was also fostered in part by the activities of the judiciary on the Privy Council which had been called upon to decide on matters of human rights in Commonwealth jurisdictions.[66] Further, within the academy the dominant legal positivist tradition in England had been fundamentally challenged by the import of US legal scholarship, in particular Ronald Dworkin, and therewith liberal theories of law as a system of rights and principles.[67]

The most significant element of this process of globalization was undoubtedly the influence of European law and the ECHR on the consciousness of politicians and, importantly, the judiciary.[68] Under European law, English courts were *de facto* being called upon to review the constitutionality of parliamentary legislation, a role which drew them closer to the political stage.[69] It also brought common law judges and academics closer to continental style rationalist principles.[70] Moreover, the provision of direct access to the European Commission and the European Court of Human Rights (ECtHR)

---

[62] Young (n 37) 33; Ewing (n 43) 80–2.
[63] Ewing and Gearty (n 42 above) 262–75; C. Gearty in A. Cygan, *Constitutional Civil Liberties in Germany and the United Kingdom* (Civil Liberties Research Unit Kings College and Goethe-Institut, 1998) s. 2.1.
[64] e.g., Canada and New Zealand.
[65] M. Hunt, *Using Human Rights Law in English Courts* (Hart, Oxford, 1998) 24–5.
[66] Stevens (n 32) 395.
[67] Loughlin 1992 (n 14) 206. A primary disciple of Dworkin in public law theory is Trevor Allan, see T. Allan, 'Dworkin and Dicey: the Rule of Law as Integrity' (1988) 8(2) *OJLS* 266.
[68] Young (n 37) 34–37; Hunt (n 65) ch. 5; Lester (n 57) 34.
[69] Stevens (n 32) 402.   [70] Harlow (n 15) 429.

in 1965 raised the rights consciousness of individuals, interest groups, the broader legal profession, public administration, and the legal academy.[71] The common law had to adapt to the existence of the Convention and was steered towards the recognition of fundamental rights.[72] Traditional English constitutionalism, sustained by institutional and historic continuity, was challenged by changes in the international environment. Britain was no longer an island, and the organic constitution was evolving from the protector of England's national identity to an expression of global principles.

In part because of the changes in the local political and constitutional environment and in part because of the impact of globalization, 'the role, power and self perception' of the higher English judiciary began to change as did their view on the function of the common law.[73] One of the most telling signals of this changing self-perception of the judiciary lies in the expansion of common law doctrines of judicial review over the last thirty years.[74] Concerned about the weakness of Parliament, the judiciary sought to limit growing executive powers by actively developing public law doctrine.[75] Within this process the courts showed more willingness to articulate their supervisory jurisdiction in the language of rights rather than parliamentary intention and to develop fundamental rights at common law.[76] This was coupled by the increased propensity of the higher judiciary to enter into public debates in order to advance a 'rights consciousness'.[77] These shifts in judicial attitude tested the orthodox view of the judiciary as pragmatic apolitical servants of parliamentary will and in turn generated re-evaluation of England's constitutional tradition.[78]

Signals of this re-evaluation could be found in the debate amongst senior members of the English judiciary and public law academics as to the constitutional foundation of judicial review.[79] In this debate two broad propositions were formulated. First, there were those who remained within the

---

[71] Lester (n 57) 35–6.

[72] In *Brind v Secretary of State for the Home Department* [1991] 1 All ER 720, HL it was accepted that the ECHR had an impact on domestic law through the presumption in the interpretation of statutes that Parliament did not intend to legislate against it and that the courts could pay attention to it in the development of the common law. Furthermore, the Convention has been used as a basis for the interpretation of Community law in domestic courts. Feldman (n 61) 66ff.; Hunt (n 65) chs 4–7.

[73] Stevens (n 32) 393.

[74] G. Richardson and H. Genn, *Administrative Law and Government Action* (Clarendon Press, Oxford, 1994) Introduction, chs 2 and 3; Craig (n 21) Part II.

[75] Sedley (n 8) 38–43.

[76] J. Jowell, 'Of Vires and Vacuums: The Constitutional Context of Judicial Review' (1999) *PL* 448; P. Craig, 'Competing Models of Judicial Review' (1999) *PL* 428.

[77] Hunt (n 65) 164–74; Stevens (n 32) 395; M. Loughlin, 'Rights Discourse and Public Law Thought in the United Kingdom' in G. Anderson (ed.), *Rights and Democracy: Essays in UK-Canadian Constitutionalism* (Blackstone, London, 1999) 193.

[78] Loughlin 1999 (n 77) 193; M. Loughlin, 'Courts and Governance' in P. Birks (ed.), *Frontiers of Liability* (OUP, Oxford, 1994) 91, 111; Harlow and Rawlings (n 15) ch. 3, ch. 17 particularly 602–4.

[79] Loughlin 1994 (n 78) 201–11.

terms of constitutional orthodoxy and continued to root judicial review in parliamentary intention.[80] The second position, broadly defined, rooted the foundation of judicial review on a view of the common law as anchored in ideas of justice, the rule of law, and individual rights. Challenging constitutional orthodoxy, proponents of this position sought to restore a common law rights consciousness and a principled constitutionalism which, it was argued, had been dormant since the nineteenth century.[81] They questioned, both normatively and empirically, the notion of English constitutional heritage as necessarily pragmatic and empiricist. There are a variety of views within this second approach and not all of those who belong in this category necessarily viewed the incorporation of a Bill of Rights as desirable or inevitable,[82] nor did they all embrace rights activism.[83] Nevertheless, many argued for the incorporation of a Bill of Rights as the necessary extension and clarification of what was fast becoming the self-perceived role of the judiciary.[84]

To sum up, the legal cultural foundations of rights scepticism were called into question both by judicial activism in the courts and by extra-judicial and academic re-evaluation of the nature of English constitutionalism.[85]

6.1.3 The Human Rights Act

English constitutional culture displays a continuing tension between a tradition of rights scepticism, rooted in sovereignty and pragmatism, and an emergent rights consciousness, founded on a view of the law as a body of

[80] Forsyth (n 38); W. Wade and C. Forsyth, *Administrative Law* (7th edn, Clarendon Press, Oxford, 1994) 342; M. Elliot, 'The Demise of Parliamentary Sovereignty? The Implications for Justifying Judicial Review' (1999) 115 *LQR* 119; M. Elliot, 'The Ultra Vires Doctrine in a Constitutional Setting: Still the Central Principle of Administrative Law' (1999) *CLJ* 129.

[81] Allan (nn 12, 15, 67); T. Allan, 'Legislative Supremacy and the Rule of Law: Democracy and Constitutionalism' (1985) *CLJ* 111; Craig (nn 6, 10); P. Craig, 'Ultra Vires and the Foundations of Judicial Review' (1998) *CLJ* 63; P. Craig, *Public Law and Democracy in the United Kingdom and the United States* (OUP, Oxford, 1990); J. Jowell and A. Lester, 'Beyond Wednesbury: substantive principles of administrative law' (1987) *PL* 368 and 'Courts and Administration in Britain: Standards, Principles and Rights' (1988) *Israel Law Review* 409; D. Oliver, 'Is the Ultra Vires Rule the Basis of Judicial Review' (1987) *PL* 543; Lord Woolf, 'Droit Publique—English Style' (1995) *PL* 57; Lord Browne Wilkinson, 'The Infiltration of a Bill of Rights' (1992) *PL* 397; Sir John Laws 'Is the High Court the Guardian of Fundamental Constitutional Rights?' (1993) *PL* 59; Sir John Laws, 'Law and Democracy' (1995) *PL* 72; Sir John Laws, 'The Constitution: Moral and Rights' (1996) *PL* 622; S. Sedley, 'Human Rights—A Twenty First Century Agenda' (1995) *PL* 386.

[82] T. Allan, 'Constitutional Rights and Common Law' (1991) 11(4) *OJLS* 454; Lord Browne Wilkinson (n 81); Sedley (n 81).

[83] Laws 1995 (n 81).

[84] e.g., Sir Thomas Bingham MR, 'The European Convention on Human Rights: Time to Incorporate?' (1993) 109 *LQR* 390; Lord Taylor, 'The Judiciary in the 1990s' 1992 Dimbleby Lecture (30 November 1992).

[85] Loughlin 1999 (n 77).

rights and principles.[86] The HRA 1998 is the product of this tension. It is animated by the attempt to balance a rights approach with the profound constitutional attachment to parliamentary sovereignty.[87] This much is evident in the provisions of the HRA 1998,[88] the political rhetoric surrounding the Act,[89] as well as academic and extra-curial analysis.[90] To say that the reconciliation of these dual, and 'apparently opposite positions',[91] lies at the centre of the HRA 1998 is uncontroversial. Far more controversial is how the balance between these two aims should be achieved in England.

Consequently, there are a range of positions within the English legal community about the extent to which the human rights project should be taken and the extent to which the HRA 1998 legitimizes such a project. A rights optimist vision (expressed by human rights pressure groups, activist lawyers, and some members of the judiciary) seeks to embrace the Act to develop a 'transformative constitutionalism', a 'culture of justification', and a 'constitutional State' in England.[92] Their view is that it offers the unique opportunity to engage the legislature, judiciary, and executive in a reflective

---

[86] M. Loughlin, 'The Underside of Law: Judicial Review and the Prison Disciplinary System' (1993) 23 *CLP* 40.

[87] Ewing (n 43) 98; Craig (n 21) 553; C. Gearty, 'Reconciling Parliamentary Democracy and Human Rights' (2002) 118 *LQR* 248.

[88] The HRA 1998 requires that, as far as it is possible to do so, judges should read and give effect to primary and secondary legislation in a way which is compatible with Convention rights (HRA 1998, s. 3). Where it is not possible to read such legislation compatibly with the Convention, judges should declare that legislation incompatible with the ECHR. But, pointedly, the Act does not give judges power to strike down such legislation. The incompatible legislative provision remains valid unless Parliament amends this legislation and the Act gives Parliament the discretion whether to remove the incompatibility (HRA 1998, s. 4).

[89] J. Straw and P. Boateng, *Bringing Rights Home: Labour Plans to incorporate the ECHR into UK law*, December 1996 (published in (1997) 1 *EHRLR* 71); *Rights Brought Home: The Human Rights Bill* (Cm. 3782). For analysis of parliamentary debate relevant to all sections of the HRA 1998, see, Lord Lester and D. Pannick, *Human Rights Law and Practice* (Butterworths, London, 1999) ch. 2.

[90] e.g., Ewing (n 43); Gearty (n 87); D. Feldman, 'The Human Rights Act 1998 and constitutional principles' (1998) *LS* 165; J. Jowell, 'Beyond the Rule of Law: Towards Constitutional Judicial Review (2000) *PL* 671; Lord Irvine, 'Constitutional Reform and a Bill of Rights' (1997) 5 *EHRLR* 483; Lord Irvine, 'The Development of Human Rights in Britain under an Incorporated Convention on Human Rights' (1998) *PL* 221, 225; Lord Irvine, 'The Impact of the Human Rights Act: Parliament, the Courts and the Executive' (2003) *PL* 308; Lord Hoffmann, 'The Separation of Powers' (2002) 7(3) *JR* 137; Lord Steyn, 'Human Rights: The Legacy of Mrs Roosevelt' (2002) *PL* 473.

[91] Gearty (n 87) 248.

[92] Variations on this position can be found in M. Hunt, 'The Human Rights Act and Legal Culture' (1999) *JLS* 86; M. Hunt, 'Sovereignty's Blight: Why Contemporary Public Law Needs the Concept of 'Due Deference'' in N. Bamforth and P. Leyland (eds), *Public Law in a Multi-Layered Constitution* (Hart, Oxford, 2003) 337; F. Klug, *Values for a Godless Age* (Penguin, London, 2000); F. Klug and K. Starmer, 'It's all about cultural change' *The Times*, 1 August 2000; Lord Steyn, 'Democracy through Law' (2002) 6 *EHRLR* 723; Lord Steyn, 'The New Legal Landscape' (2000) 6 *EHRLR* 549; J. Jowell, 'Beyond the Rule of Law: Towards Constitutional Judicial Review' (2000) *PL* 672; R. Edwards, 'Judicial Deference under the Human Rights Act' (2002) 65 *MLR* 859; Editorial, 'Human Rights Need Bite' *The Guardian*, 16 May 2003.

'dialogue' about the proper balance between rights and the public interest. Rights moderates within the legal community view the 1998 Act through the prism of the orthodox constitutional relationship between the parliament, executive and judiciary. They seek the incremental development of fundamental rights coupled with strong judicial deference to Parliament and other political processes;[93] to see the judiciary steer a course between the 'Scylla of excessive activism and the Charybdis of a failure to protect guaranteed rights'.[94] Others remain highly sceptical of the human rights project,[95] even if some have grudgingly accepted that it is here to stay.[96] Despite their assertion that they represent a marginal voice in the clamour of 'liberal self-congratulation' around the HRA 1998,[97] rights sceptics' claims continue to have considerable resonance within the contemporary English constitutional environment. Sceptics underestimate the depth and continuity of the anti-categorical, pragmatic, and democratic traditions of English constitutional and legal culture. At the very least, the strength of rights scepticism underpins the ongoing popular and political suspicion of the HRA 1998,[98] as well as the growing defensiveness of many of the Act's supporters.[99]

[93] See variations on this position in W. Wade, 'The United Kingdom's Bill of Rights' in J. Beatson (ed.), *Constitutional Reform in the United Kingdom: Practice and Principles* (Hart, Oxford, 1998) 61, 66; G Marshall 'Interpreting Interpretation in the Human Rights Bill (1988) *PL* 167; G. Marshall, 'Two kinds of compatibility: more about section 3 of the Human Rights Act 1998' (1999) *PL* 377; J. Laws, 'The Limitations of Human Rights' (1998) *PL* 254; Craig (n 21) 559–63; Lord Irvine 2003 (n 90) 316; Lord Hoffmann (n 90); Lord Hoffmann in *ProLife Alliance v BBC* [2003] 2 WLR 1403, paras 75 and 76; Laws LJ in *Secretary of State for the Home Department v International Transport Roth GmbH and others* [2002] 1 CMLR 52, paras 69–87.

[94] Laws 1998 (n 93) 261.

[95] J. Redwood, 'Freedom to confuse' *The Independent*, 7 October 2000, 9; J. Griffiths, 'The Political Constitution' (2001) 117 *LQR* 42; J. Griffiths, 'Brave new world of Sir John Laws' (2000) 63 (2) *MLR* 159; T. Campbell, K. Ewing and A. Tomkins (eds), *Sceptical Essays on Human Rights* (OUP, Oxford, 2001).

[96] K. Ewing, 'Social Rights and Constitutional Law' (1999) *PL* 104.

[97] A. Tomkins, 'Introduction' in Campbell *et al.* (n 95) 2.

[98] See amongst many others, Redwood (n 95); Editorial, 'Judges as Politicians' *Daily Telegraph*, 13 December 2000; Editorial, 'Bringing Rights Home' *The Economist*, 26 August 2000; M. Shrimpton, 'Legal Status of Human Rights Act' *The Times*, 7 September 2000; G. Argent, 'I don't want this human rights waffle—and I'm a lawyer' *Mail on Sunday*, 1 October 2000; J. Pascoe-Watson, 'The human rights laws that could bring chaos to every area of our lives' *The Sun*, 2 August 2000; J. Laughland, 'British Law Should not be undermined by these Euro outsiders; Human Rights Ruling Destroys our Freedom' *Express*, 7 May 2001; R. Bennett, 'Britain may opt out of human rights convention' *The Times*, 20 February 2003; P. Johnston and G. Jones, 'Blair to take on judges over asylum' *Daily Telegraph*, 20 February 2003; P. Gilbride, 'More Killers are being released under Euro law' *Express*, 4 June 2003.

[99] It is interesting how many supporters of the HRA 1998 seek to emphasize how little has changed as a result of the Act. See Lord Irvine 2003 (n 90); J. Straw, 'Parliament Decides' *The Daily Telegraph*, 15 December 2000; F. Klug, 'A Law Fit for a Prince' *The Guardian*, 3 October 2002; N. Tait, 'Judges Exercise Human Rights Powers "Conservatively"' *Financial Times*, 7 March 2003; G. Phillips, 'Still waiting for the outrageous and bizarre' *The Times*, 1 October 2002; R. Verkaik, 'Civil Liberties: Shortage of new cases confounds critics of the nutters' charter' *The Independent*, 27 May 2003; K. Starmer, 'Two years of the Human Rights Act' (2003) 1 *EHRLR* 14.

Whilst the controversy surrounding the extent of the English rights project underpins almost every area affected by the HRA 1998,[100] there can be no better illustration of this than the emerging discourse of judicial deference. A discourse which, as Chapter 7 shows, is intricately connected to the recent and future development of prisoners' rights in England. A closer look at the ongoing judicial development of notions of deference reveals just how stable and prevalent the culture of sovereignty remains in England.[101] It reveals, too, the distinctive challenge of developing a human rights jurisprudence when 'operating in a schizophrenic world oscillating between a legal culture rooted in sovereignty and one constructed on the foundation of individual rights'.[102]

6.1.3.1 *Judicial Deference and Constitutional Culture*

Our judgment as to the deference owed to the democratic powers will reflect the culture and conditions of the British State.[103]

Since the introduction of the HRA 1998, judicial deference claims, while normally not wholly determinative of the decisions in question,[104] have manifested with respect to applications testing the Convention-compatibility of primary legislation,[105] and those regarding acts of public authorities.[106] They have arisen when assessing the legitimacy of rights restrictions expressly permitted under the Convention;[107] as well as the scope of rights which do not expressly allow for limitations.[108] In the three years after the 1998 Act entered into force, recourse to the language of deference, while varying considerably in expressions of its scope, has been ubiquitous in

---

[100] Note the debates on the true meaning of the interpretive obligation under HRA 1998, s. 3 (F. Bennion, 'What interpretation is possible under section 3 of the HRA?' (2000) *PL* 77; Marshall 1998 and 1999 (n 93)); the horizontal impact of Convention rights under the HRA 1998 (N. Bamforth, 'The True "Horizontal Effect" of the Human Rights Act 1998' (2001) 117 *LQR* 35; M. Hunt, 'The Horizontal Effect of the Human Rights Act' (1998) *Public Law* 423; W. Wade, 'Horizons of Horizontality' (2000) 116 *LQR* 48); the meaning of 'public authority' under HRA 1998, s. 6; (D. Oliver, 'The Frontiers of the State: Public Authorities and Public Functions under the HRA' (2000) *PL* 476; M. McDermont, 'The Elusive Nature of the "Public Function": Poplar Housing and Regeneration Community Association Ltd v Donoghue' (2003) 66 *MLR* 113) and the development of social and economic rights (Ewing 1999 (n 96); G. Van Bueren, 'Including the Excluded: the Case for an Economic, Social and Cultural Human Rights Act' (2002) *Public Law* 456).

[101] Hunt 2003 (n 92).   [102] Loughlin 1994 (n 78) 94.

[103] Laws LJ in *Secretary of State for the Home Department v International Transport Roth Gmbh* [2002] 1 CMLR 52, 81.

[104] Edwards (n 92) 861.   [105] HRA 1998, ss. 3 and 4.

[106] HRA 1998, s. 6.

[107] Primary examples being Arts 8(2), 9(2), 10(2), 11(2) and 12(2) ECHR.

[108] e.g., Arts. 2, 3, 5 and 6 ECHR. In the context of Art. 6 in particular, the domestic courts are strongly diverging from the prevailing Strasbourg approach in taking the view that the scope of the rights connected to the right to a fair trial may be broadly balanced against public interest considerations. See, e.g., *Brown v Stott* [2001] HRLR 9. On this point, see A. Ashworth, *Human Rights, Serious Crime and Criminal Procedure* (53rd Hamlyn Lecture, Sweet & Maxwell, London, 2002) ch. 2.

judicial analysis of Convention rights.[109] This language of deference can be traced to the debate prior to the Act's entry into force.

A two-year preparation period for judges, lawyers, and government was provided between the passing of the Act and its entry into force. In this environment, where the accumulated experience of the common law could no longer be relied upon, published arguments concerning the impact of the Act and Convention law became unusually influential.[110] Having been required by the HRA to have regard to an entirely new body of law, judges, administrators and lawyers fell upon the words of Convention law specialists. This opportunity was not lost by those seeking to anticipate and influence the likely impact of the HRA 1998.[111] Among the many questions which these specialists sought to answer, in their quest to reconcile a system of human rights protection with constitutional fidelity to Parliament, were those relevant to judicial deference. What would be the impact of the ECtHR doctrine of proportionality on the intensity of judicial review of both parliamentary and public authority decisions?[112] Would it replace the *Wednesbury* standard of review, which had been modified to an 'anxious scrutiny' test with regard to fundamental rights under common law?[113] Should the domestic courts develop their own variant of the 'margin of appreciation' doctrine, developed by the ECtHR as a means of recognizing the limits of its own competence (as a supra-national court) to judge fully the domestic issues at hand when examining the legitimacy of rights restrictions permitted under the Convention?[114] How could judges stay true to Convention rights while

---

[109] Edwards (n 92); Hunt 2003 (n 92); F. Klug, 'Judicial Deference Under the Human Rights Act 1998' (2003) 2 *EHRLR* 125; I. Leigh, 'Taking Rights Proportionately: Judicial Review, the Human Rights Act and Strasbourg' (2002) *PL* 265; P. Craig, 'The Courts, The Human Rights Act and Judicial Review' (2001) 117 *LQR* 589.

[110] The increase in academic influence on judicial decisions under the HRA 1998 may well be one of the most fundamental cultural changes to accompany the Act. Contrast 4.1.

[111] K. Starmer (ed.), *European Human Rights Law* (Legal Action Group, London 1999); Lester and Pannick (n 89); R. Clayton and H. Tomlinson, *The Law of Human Rights* (OUP, Oxford, 2000); S. Grosz, J. Beatson and P. Duffy, *Human Rights: The 1998 Act and the European Convention* (Sweet & Maxwell, London, 2000). See also nn 89, 90, 92, 93, 100.

[112] This doctrine specifies that rights restrictions are 'necessary in a democratic society' which in turn requires that restrictions correspond to a 'pressing social need' and is 'proportionate to the legitimate aim pursued' (*Golder v UK* (1975) 1 EHRR 524).

[113] The 'anxious scrutiny' test is expressed as follows: (1) In conducting a review of a decision affecting human rights, the Court would subject the decision to the most 'anxious scrutiny'. Where the decision interfered with human rights, the Court would require substantial justification for the interference in order to be satisfied that the response fell within the range of responses open to a reasonable decision-maker. The more substantial the interference, the more is required to justify it (*Ex p Smith* [1996] QB 517, 554). This test was rejected in *Smith and Grady v UK* (1999) 29 EHRR 493, para. 138 because the threshold of review had been placed so high in *Smith* that it effectively excluded any consideration by the domestic courts of the question whether the interference with the applicant's rights answered a pressing social need or was proportionate to a legitimate aim.

[114] On the 'margin of appreciation doctrine' see *Handyside v UK* (1976) 1 EHRR 737 at 754: 'By reason of their direct and continuous contact with the vital forces of their countries, state authorities are in principle in a better position than the international judge to give an

scrutinizing public authority action without undermining the traditional common law distinction between review and appeal (the former being a test of legality, the latter being a test of the merits of a decision) and thereby the orthodox constitutional vision of parliamentary sovereignty and the separation of powers? The centrality of these questions to the debate surrounding the HRA 1998 was a strong indicator of the dilemmas courts were soon to face.

Responses to these questions varied according to the position of the contributors. Those hoping to advance the protections of the Convention under domestic law were concerned that the submissive *Wednesbury* approach would be resurrected behind the language of deference. While accepting that degrees of deference to decision-makers would apply, depending on the facts and rights in question, they rejected the broad brush language of the margin of appreciation doctrine.[115] Those seeking to stress continuity with the foundations of constitutional orthodoxy warned that courts would afford 'a very considerable margin of appreciation' to democratic decision-makers.[116] Ultimately, the view of Lester and Pannick's *Human Rights Law and Practice* had the most weight. Co-edited by the most senior and active proponent of the Act and including contributions from a number of leading specialists in the field, the book quickly achieved a status approximating that of a German style commentary.[117] It is to this text that the notion of the 'discretionary area of judgment' is most commonly attributed. It accepted that the proportionality doctrine should be applied to Convention cases and that domestic courts should reach their 'own judgment' on whether the Convention had been breached. But, while the ECtHR margin of appreciation doctrine was not part of domestic law, an 'analogous doctrine' should be recognized whereby courts could defer in specified circumstances to the 'opinion of the legislature, executive or other relevant person or body' when assessing whether a breach had occurred.[118]

As soon as the courts began addressing these questions, even before the HRA 1998 came into force, it was clear that they intended to develop their

opinion on the exact requirements as well as on the 'necessity' of a "restriction" or "penalty" intended to meet them . . . Nevertheless [the Convention] does not give the contracting states an unlimited power of appreciation. The Court, which . . . is responsible for ensuring the observance of those states' engagements is empowered to give the final ruling on whether a "restriction" or "penalty" is reconcilable with [the Convention]. The domestic margin of appreciation thus goes hand in hand with a European supervision'.

[115] R. Singh, M. Hunt and M. Demetriou, 'Is there a Role for the "Margin of Appreciation" in National Law under the Human Rights Act?' (1999) 1 *EHRLR* 15; M. Hunt, 'Judicial Review after the Human Rights Act' (1999) 2 *QMWLJ* 14, 15–16; J. Wadham and H. Mountfield, *Human Rights Act 1998* (Blackstone, London, 1999) 13–18.

[116] Lord Bingham, 'Incorporation of the ECHR: The Opportunity and the Challenge' (1998) 2 *Jersey Law Review* 257, 269–70.

[117] Cf. 4.1.

[118] Lester and Pannick (n 89) 71–6. See also D. Pannick, 'Principles of interpretation of Convention rights under the Human Rights Act and the discretionary area of judgement' (1998) *PL* 545.

own 'autonomous concept of deference'.[119] In *Kebeline*, Lord Hope, quoting Lester and Pannick, argued that although the 'margin of appreciation' doctrine did not apply in domestic law, the courts would recognize an analogous 'area of judgment within which the judiciary will defer, on democratic grounds, to the considered opinion of the elected body or person whose act or decision is said to be incompatible with the Convention'. Lord Hope noted that while deference to decision-makers was more likely to arise where the Convention already specified limitations of rights, it could also arise where the courts were not 'well placed to assess the need for protection' such as in the case of social or economic policy.[120] Here was an early attempt to stake out the boundaries of judicial intervention. In his use of the spatial metaphor of 'areas of judgment' in which the courts would defer, he established the legal roots of what has come to be characterized as the 'spatial approach' to deference.[121]

Others joined the chorus of deference, although differences in tone were evident from the start. In *Lambert*, Lord Woolf argued that 'as a matter of constitutional principle, courts should pay *a degree of deference* to the view of Parliament as to what is in the interest of the public generally when upholding the rights of the individual'.[122] Similarly, in *Brown v Stott*, Lord Steyn explained that while 'under the Convention system the primary duty is placed on domestic courts to secure and protect Convention rights', 'national courts may accord to the decisions of national legislatures *some deference where the context justifies*'.[123] Moreover, Lord Bingham felt compelled to remind us that:

Judicial recognition and assertion of the human rights defined in the Convention is not a substitute for the processes of democratic government but a complement to them. While a national court does not accord the margin of appreciation recognised by the European Court as a supra-national court, it *will give weight to the decisions of a representative legislature and a democratic government within the discretionary area of judgment accorded to those bodies.* . . . The Convention is concerned with rights and freedoms which are of real importance in a modern democracy governed by the rule of law. It does not, as is sometimes mistakenly thought, offer relief from 'The heart-ache and the thousand natural shocks that flesh is heir to'.[124]

Importantly, while there was confirmation in these cases of the possibility of deference and, in Lord Bingham's case, the existence of a discretionary area of judgment, these arguments accepted the possibility of the courts scrutinizing justifications within those specified areas. Lord Woolf spoke of paying a 'degree of deference', Lord Steyn of 'some deference' where 'the

[119] Craig (n 109) 590.   [120] *R (Kebeline) v DPP* [1998] 4 All ER 801, 844.
[121] Hunt 2003 (n 92).
[122] *R v Lambert* [2001] HRLR 4, para. 16. Emphasis added.
[123] *Brown v Stott* [2001] HRLR 9, para. 58. Emphasis added.
[124] Para. 39. Emphasis added.

context justifies' and Lord Bingham spoke of according 'weight' to decisions 'within' the 'discretionary area of judgment'.[125]

After the HRA 1998 entered into force, members of the higher judiciary sought early on both to reinforce the importance of deference to Parliament and to outline their view of its ambit when assessing human rights claims. In *R v A*, Lord Hope reaffirmed his 'spatial approach' in *Kebilene*, taking as his 'starting point . . . the proposition that there are areas of law which lie within the discretionary area of judgment which the court ought to accord to the legislature', and arguing that 'it is appropriate in some circumstances for the judiciary to defer, on democratic grounds, to the considered opinion of the elected body as to where the balance is to be struck between the rights of the individual and the needs of society'.[126] Adopting a rather more submissive tone than in *Lambert*, Lord Woolf argued in *Poplar Housing*, that in the social and economic context 'the courts must treat the decisions of Parliament as to what is in the public interest with particular deference . . . when deciding whether there has been a breach of the Convention'.[127] His assertion of deference in this instance precluded any proper deliberation on the limitations of the right in question.[128]

Similarly, in *Alconbury*, the House of Lords overturned a declaration that the planning scheme which allowed the Secretary of State to determine both planning policy and to decide individual applications, was incompatible with the right to a fair trial under Article 6 ECHR.[129] Lord Hoffmann noted that 'in a democratic country, decisions as to what the general interest requires are made by democratically elected bodies or persons accountable to them'. In seeking to show that there was 'no conflict between human rights and the democratic principle' Hoffmann distinguished rights which are justiciable by the courts from matters over which 'the only fair method of decision is by some person or body accountable to the electorate'. The former category of rights should be 'overridden only in very restricted circumstances' because they 'belong to individuals simply by virtue of their humanity, independently of any utilitarian calculation', whilst the latter category concerned 'decisions which have to be made every day (for example, about the allocation of resources)'.[130] Here deference was justified by explicit reference to the orthodox constitutional separation between the judicial control of legality and parliamentary control of the political.

In *Wilson v First County Trust*, however, the Court of Appeal took a rather different view of the possibilities for judicial scrutiny in the economic and social arena:

---

[125] Hunt 2003 (n 92) fn 29.   [126] *R v A (No. 2)* [2001] HRLR 48, para. 58.
[127] *Poplar Housing and Regeneration Community Association v Donoghue* [2002] QB 48, para 71.
[128] Edwards (n 92) 868.
[129] *R (Holding & Barnes Plc and Alconbury Developments Ltd) v Secretary of State for the Environment, Transport and the Regions* [2001] 2 WLR 1389.
[130] Paras 69 and 70.

. . . unless deference is to be equated with unquestioning acceptance, the argument that an issue of social policy falls within a discretionary area of judgment which the courts must respect recognises, as it seems to us, the need for the court to identify the particular issue of social policy which the legislature or the executive thought it necessary to address, and the thinking which led to that issue being dealt with in the way that it was. It is one thing to accept the need to defer to an opinion which can be seen to be the product of reasoned consideration based on policy; it is quite another thing to be required to accept, without question, an opinion for which no reason of policy is advanced.[131]

In Sir Andrew Morritt's language we find a clear rejection of the notion that rights might be non-justiciable within designated areas and the assertion of the all-important distinction between 'deference' and 'unquestioning acceptance'. Instead of invoking orthodox constitutional justifications to limit scrutiny, Sir Andrew Morritt emphasized the court's role in advancing a 'culture of justification' by scrutinizing the reasons provided for the rights infringement in question. It comes as no surprise, perhaps, that the Court found section 127 of the Consumer Credit Act 1974 to be incompatible with the right to a fair trial under Article 6(1) of the ECHR.

Alongside these early articulations of deference to Parliament, were cases addressing the impact of section 6 of the HRA 1998 on the intensity of judicial review of public authorities.[132] In *B*, Sedley LJ made it clear that the test for substantive review, where a Convention right was engaged, was no longer that of *Wednesbury*-style rationality. While conceding that this meant judges had to take a 'closer look' at the merits of the decision than they were 'previously accustomed' to do, he argued that:

. . . our public law . . . now has to accommodate and give effect to the requirements of the . . . European Convention. It means making up our own minds about the proportionality of the public law measure—not simply deciding whether the Home Secretary's or the Tribunal's view of it was lawful and rational.

On the basis that the assessment of proportionality was a legal question, Sedley LJ rejected the call for deference to the view of the decision-maker on this question.[133] Simon Brown LJ confirmed this approach, arguing that, as assessment of proportionality is a question of law, the 'the court is required to form its own view on whether the test is satisfied'. The deference to the decision-maker in question would be limited to their appreciation of the facts of the case. Nevertheless, he argued, 'it would not be proper for us to say that we disagree with the Tribunal's decision on proportionality but that, since there is clearly room for two views and their view can not be stigmatised as irrational, we can not interfere'.[134]

---

[131] *Wilson v First County Trust* [2001] HRLR 44, para. 33.
[132] HRA 1998, s. 6 places an obligation on 'public authorities' to respect Convention rights.
[133] *B v Secretary of State for the Home Department* [2000] Imm. AR 478, paras 18, 23–7, 36.
[134] Para. 40.

In *Mahmood*,[135] Laws LJ and Lord Phillips MR took a different view. Both were concerned that judges should not look 'too closely' at the decision-making process. Laws LJ argued vehemently that the 'Human Rights Act 1998 does not authorise the judges to stand in the shoes of Parliament's delegates, who are decision-makers given their responsibilities by the democratic arm of the state'. Were judges to think differently they would 'usurp those functions of government which are controlled and distributed by powers whose authority is derived from the ballot-box'. He thus called for a 'principled distance' between judges and decision-makers which he referred to as the 'margin of discretion'.[136] Lord Phillips MR confirmed *Kebeline* and adopted Lester and Pannick's doctrine of the 'discretionary area of judgment'.[137] While admitting that rights restrictions should be subject to the most 'anxious scrutiny', he asserted that the test for establishing the legitimacy of rights restrictions, was 'whether the decision maker could reasonably have concluded that the interference was necessary to achieve one or more of the legitimate aims recognised by the Convention' (not whether the restriction was legitimate *per se*).[138] The approach taken by *Mahmood* was quickly sanctioned by Schiemann LJ in *Isiko*, which both stressed the deference which judges should accord to public decision-makers and restated the reasonableness requirement when assessing the legitimacy of rights restrictions.[139]

Such was the potential force of the *Mahmood* approach, that Lord Steyn devoted his entire speech in *Daly* to addressing, and rejecting in part, the implications of its reasoning.[140] Lord Steyn considered the *Mahmood* test to be formulated in language reminiscent of the *Wednesbury* test. He stressed that while there was an overlap between the proportionality approach and the traditional grounds of judicial review at common law, the intensity of review is somewhat greater under the proportionality approach. He went on to argue for the adoption of the ECtHR's proportionality approach when dealing with Convention rights, but nevertheless was concerned to show that this did not mean a shift to 'merits review'. In doing this, he accepted the general point of *Mahmood* that the 'intensity of review would depend on the subject matter in hand' and acknowledged that 'in law context is everything'. His failure to elaborate on this final tantalizing point left the door open to a variety of interpretations; not least those consistent with a 'spatial approach' to deference.

After *Daly*, the courts turned to the scope and application of the doctrines of proportionality and deference in different legal contexts. In *Samaroo*,[141]

---

[135] *R (Mahmood) v Secretary of State for the Home Department* [2001] 1 WLR 840.
[136] Para. 33.   [137] Para. 38.   [138] Para. 40.
[139] *R (Isiko) v Secretary of State for the Home Department* [2001] 1 FLR 930, paras 30–1.
[140] *R (Daly) v Secretary of State for the Home Department* [2001] 2 AC 532, paras 24–8.
[141] *Samaroo v Secretary of State for the Home Department* [2001] UKHRR 1150, paras 13–37.

the Court of Appeal read *Daly* as making 'no other criticisms' of the decision in *Mahmood* other than the 'clarification' of Lord Phillips statement.[142] It was argued that *Daly* referred to blanket policy decisions where consideration of 'less invasive measures' was an issue. However, where no 'less invasive measures' were open to the decision-maker, a 'fair balance' test should be applied which 'left a significant margin of discretion to the decision maker'.[143] In trying to find a line between merits review and *Wednesbury* review, Dyson LJ read Lord Steyn's comments on 'context' as legitimating the broad margin of appreciation doctrine recognized in *Mahmood*.

In *Rehmann*, members of the House of Lords varied in their view of the deference to be accorded to the executive when assessing rights infringements of those suspected of threatening national security. Lord Steyn argued that while deference should be accorded to the executive in this context, 'it is well established in the case law that issues of national security do not fall beyond the competence of the courts'. Thus, when assessing rights infringements the courts can nevertheless 'address the questions: Does the interference serve a legitimate objective? Is it necessary in a democratic society?'[144] Lord Hoffmann, devoted more energy to outlining the constraints on judicial competence in this context. Whilst acknowledging the courts' jurisdiction to assess matters of national security, he argued that it was imperative that courts recognize the 'constitutional boundaries between judicial, executive and legislative power'.[145] This entailed recognizing that 'under the constitution of the United Kingdom and most other countries, decisions as to whether something is or is not in the interests of national security are not a matter for judicial decision. They are entrusted to the executive'.[146] Whilst courts could assess the factual basis of the Home Secretary's evaluation as to the risk to national security, they must afford a 'considerable margin to the primary decision-maker' in their evaluation of those facts.[147] The court's restraint here flowed from 'a common-sense recognition of the nature of the issue and the differences in the decision-making processes and responsibilities' of the executive and the judiciary.[148]

Lord Hoffmann reinforced his argument in favour of deference in his postscript written one month after the attacks of 11 September 2000 in the USA. There can be few *dicta* more grounded in the orthodox vision of the English constitution and more designed to incite future judges to act in deference to democratic decision-makers:

I wrote this speech some three months before the recent events in New York and Washington. They are a reminder that in matters of national security, the cost of failure can be high. This seems to me to underline the need for the judicial arm of

---

[142] Para. 33.   [143] Para. 36.
[144] *Secretary of State for the Home Department v Rehman* [2003] 1 AC 153, para. 31.
[145] Para. 49.   [146] Para. 50.   [147] Para. 57.   [148] Para. 59.

government to respect the decisions of ministers of the Crown on the question of whether support for terrorist activities in a foreign country constitutes a threat to national security. It is not only that the executive has access to special information and expertise in these matters. It is also that such decisions, with serious potential results for the community, require a legitimacy which can be conferred only by entrusting them to persons responsible to the community through the democratic process. If the people are to accept the consequences of such decisions, they must be made by persons whom the people have elected and whom they can remove.[149]

The next major judicial contribution to the development of a doctrine of deference after *Rehman*, came from the Court of Appeal in *Roth*.[150] This case dealt with the Convention compatibility of the regulatory scheme under the Immigration and Asylum Act 1999 with Article 6 ECHR.[151] All three judges felt compelled at the outset to engage with the principle of judicial deference. But, as in *Rehman*, the conception and weight accorded to deference varied. Simon Brown LJ recognized the 'high degree of deference due by the Court to Parliament when it comes to determining legality' and 'acknowledged that our law is now replete with dicta at the very highest level commending the courts to show such deference'. He argued however, that 'the court's role under the 1998 Act is as the guardian of human rights. It cannot abdicate this responsibility. If ultimately it judges the scheme to be quite simply unfair, then the features that make it so must inevitably breach the Convention'.[152] Jonathan Parker LJ argued that 'parliament's discretionary area of judgment in the instant case should, in my judgment, be regarded as being as wide as possible'. But nevertheless maintained that 'if the courts are properly to discharge the duty which Parliament has placed upon them by enacting the Human Rights Act', intervention becomes 'unavoidable' where the 'bedrock' of the right 'begins to be eroded'.[153] Both these judgments suggested that where the rights argument was clear it necessarily trumped the high degree of deference accorded to democratic decision makers. On the facts, the majority of the court was satisfied that this was one of those moments.

In his dissenting opinion, Laws LJ placed more weight on the question of deference. He set out by noting that, because the British constitution is at an intermediate stage between parliamentary supremacy and constitutional supremacy, a tension exists between 'the maintenance of legislative sovereignty and the vindication of fundamental, constitutional rights'.[154] Hence, argued Laws LJ, 'the court has to strike a balance between the claims of the

---

[149] Para. 62.

[150] *Secretary of State for the Home Department v International Transport Roth GmbH and others* [2002] 1 CMLR 52.

[151] A particular issue here was whether the scheme in question could be categorized as 'criminal' or 'civil' for the purposes of Art. 6 ECHR.

[152] *Secretary of State for the Home Department v International Transport Roth GmbH and others* [2002] 1 CMLR 52, para 26.

[153] Para. 139.   [154] Paras 71–2.

democratic legislature and the claims of the constitutional right'. Critical to the court's search for this balance is the 'degree or margin of deference it pays to the democratic decision-maker'. The development of principles of deference, he proposed, was the 'one of the most important challenges which the common law must meet'.

Laws LJ set out four principles of judicial deference, on the basis of recent case law. First, that greater deference would be paid to an Act of Parliament than to an executive or subordinate measure; secondly, that there was more scope for deference where the Convention expressly allowed for restrictions of rights, but that deference could arise in terms of the interpretation given to the meaning of unqualified rights where there 'may be scope for reasonable differences of view as to the conditions which have to be met' in order to fulfill the right; thirdly, that deference would be greater where the subject matter fell peculiarly within the constitutional responsibility of the decision-maker and 'less when it lies more particularly within the constitutional responsibility of the courts'; and fourthly, that greater deference would be accorded where the subject matter fell within the expertise of the decision-maker. [155]

Laws LJ's six-page analysis of judicial deference in *Roth* was the most extensive yet delivered. Of particular interest, was his allusion to the separate 'constitutional responsibilities' and 'expertise' of decision-makers and the courts, which was very close to Lord Hoffmann's language in *Alconbury* and *Rehmann*. Here was a justification for deference grounded in the orthodox Diceyan vision of the English constitution, where clear lines are drawn between the competing constitutional 'supremacies' of the judiciary, executive and Parliament.[156] Over and above his language, the *Roth* judgment demonstrated just how well established the principle of deference had become in English law. It was striking that eighteen months after the HRA 1998 entered into force, all judges in *Roth* engaged with the principle of deference at the beginning of their reasoning, even if their conclusions and their view of the balance between deference and rights protection differed. Rights arguments in England were now being made in the shadow of deference.

After *Roth*, the House of Lords returned to the question of proportionality and the margin of appreciation doctrine in the national security context in *Shayler*.[157] The case held the scheme under the Official Secrets Act 1989, regulating the disclosure of classified information, to be compatible with the right to freedom of expression under Article 10 ECHR, despite the absence of a public interest defence for those seeking to release information. This was because judicial review of decisions restricting such disclosure applied

---

[155] Paras 81–7.   [156] Hunt 2003 (n 92) 339
[157] *R v Shayler* [2002] 2 WLR 754.

the test of proportionality. All three Law Lords confirmed the proportionality approach in line with *Daly*, with Lords Bingham and Hope delivering extensive accounts of how the courts should apply the doctrine when assessing administrative restrictions on disclosure of classified information. Given that the Convention compatibility of the procedures in question depended on the level of judicial scrutiny available, the Lords stressed that proportionality allowed courts to 'conduct a much more rigorous and intrusive review than was once thought to be permissible'.[158] Consequently, as regards future scrutiny of disclosure decisions (under section 6 of the HRA 1998), the Lords remained silent on the question of judicial deference or the margin of appreciation doctrine.

Shayler went further than *Daly* by detailing the extent of the scrutiny of public authority decisions now possible under the proportionality doctrine. Nevertheless, Lord Hope explicitly endorsed a wide margin of appreciation to the legislature when assessing the Convention compatibility of national security legislation. For him, the question was 'whether the scheme of the Act, safeguarded by a system of judicial review which applies the test of proportionality, falls within the wide margin of discretion which is accorded to the legislature in matters relating to national security'.[159] Thus, in *Shayler*, we see a bifurcation between exacting scrutiny of public authority decisions and deference to legislative decisions.

Given how central this bifurcation was to the reasoning and outcome of the *Shayler* decision, it is striking that one month later the Court of Appeal highlighted the importance of the margin of appreciation doctrine when scrutinizing public authority decisions in *Farrakhan*.[160] Here, again, the courts were called on to resolve the tension between public security and freedom of expression. Lord Phillips MR took the view that the Home Secretary's exclusion of the leader of the Nation of Islam from the United Kingdom, on the grounds that his presence would threaten relations between the Muslim and Jewish communities, could be justified under Article 10(2) ECHR (restrictions on freedom of expression). Lord Phillips approached the proportionality doctrine through the prism of deference. He rejected the *Wednesbury* approach because it left a margin of discretion which is 'far too wide to accommodate the demands of the Convention'. The difference between the tests, he argued, lay in the fact that proportionality allowed for a variable margin of appreciation depending on the right in question and facts of the case, whereas the *Wednesbury* test had not allowed for this flexibility.[161]

Importantly, Lord Phillips MR stressed that, 'when applying a test of proportionality, the margin of appreciation or discretion accorded to the

[158] Para. 33.   [159] Para. 80.
[160] *Farrakhan v Secretary of State for the Home Department* [2002] 3 WLR 481.
[161] Para. 64.

decision maker is all important, for it is only by recognising the margin of discretion that the court avoids substituting its own decision for that of the decision maker'.[162] Thus, for Lord Phillips, the margin of appreciation allowed courts to walk the tightrope between testing the legality and the merits of a decision. Just as Laws LJ in *Roth* had turned to deference to resolve the tension between parliamentary and constitutional sovereignty, so Lord Phillips pointed to deference as the means by which to preserve the orthodox constitutional foundations of judicial review.

The tension between public security and individual rights was also at the centre of the *SIAC* case where Lord Woolf responded to Hoffmann's call in *Rehman*.[163] Here the Court of Appeal was asked to evaluate the Convention compatibility of the Government's derogation from Article 5 ECHR (right to liberty) on the grounds that international terrorism now constituted a 'public emergency threatening the life of the nation'.[164] The challenge, brought by eleven foreign nationals suspected of terrorist activities, rested on the argument that the derogation was discriminatory in permitting only suspected terrorists who were non-nationals to be detained without trial. It also challenged the validity of the derogation on the basis that it had not been established that it was 'strictly required given the exigencies of the situation'.[165] Lord Woolf, echoed by Brooke LJ, argued that 'decisions as to what is required in the interest of national security are self-evidently within the category of decisions in relation to which the court is required to show considerable deference'.[166] This was a significant factor influencing his dismissal of the challenge in question.

In *Mendoza*, however, the Court of Appeal struck a different tone on the question of deference as regards discrimination.[167] The case dealt with the Convention compatibility of the Rent Act 1977 which treated the surviving partners of heterosexual and homosexual relationships differently. Buxton LJ started out by acknowledging that 'it is not in issue that courts will exercise "deference" in relation to decisions of Parliament, even where Convention rights are potentially engaged'.[168] Where discrimination had been established, however, he argued, it was 'simply not enough to claim that what had been done falls within the permissible ambit of Parliament's discretion'. If the discriminator was to discharge the burden of establishing a 'reasonable and objective justification' for discrimination a 'much more positive argument is required'.[169] The presence of 'complex questions of social or economic policy that the courts should only enter with trepidation' in this case, did not negate the fact that 'courts should not shrink from' issues of 'high constitutional importance'.

---

[162] Para. 67.
[163] *A, X, Y v Secretary of State for the Home Department* [2002] EWCA Civ 1502.
[164] Art. 15 ECHR.   [165] Art. 15 ECHR.
[166] [2002] EWCA Civ 1502, para. 40.   [167] *Mendoza v Ghaidan* [2003] 2 WLR 478.
[168] Para. 16.   [169] Para. 18.

Despite conceding that *Kebilene* and *Poplar* had encouraged deference in the economic and social context, it was Buxton LJ's view that 'deference has only a minor role to play' when assessing the justification for discrimination.[170] Rather, 'once it is accepted that we are not simply bound by whatever Parliament has decided . . . then we need to see whether the steps taken in implementation of the supposed policy are, not merely reasonable and proportionate, but also logically explicable as forwarding that policy'.[171] Here, in Buxton LJ's words, was a clear rejection of the notion that a 'category' of decisions leading to rights infringements could be beyond the consideration of the courts. By asserting the justificatory requirement of the proportionality doctrine, he rooted himself in England's incipient culture of rights.

A similarly robust approach to deference was articulated by Laws LJ in *Prolife* in a notably different tone to that adopted in *Roth*. Here the question was whether the BBC and other terrestrial broadcasters had been justified in refusing to transmit a party election broadcast by Prolife, a registered political party, during the general election in 2001. The broadcast included depictions of aborted foetuses and described various abortion techniques; and the broadcasters took the view that they would be in breach of their legal obligations as regards taste and decency if they were to transmit these images. Laws LJ argued that the question was one of 'justified censorship'. In assessing this question, he reminded us that common law authority showed that the 'courts owe a special responsibility to the public as the constitutional guardian of the freedom of political debate' and are the ultimate 'trustees of our democracy's framework'.[172]

Arguing that the English courts are not 'Strasbourg surrogates', Laws LJ stressed the difference between the international margin of appreciation and the municipal 'margin of discretion'. He declared that

. . . our duty is to develop, by the common law's incremental method, a coherent and principled domestic law of human rights. In doing it, we are directed by the HRA (s. 6) to insist on compliance by public authorities with the standards of the Convention, and to comply with them ourselves. We are given new powers and duties (HRA ss. 3 and 4) to see that that is done.[173]

All these considerations, in his view, gave the lie to the plea for deference to decision-makers.[174]

The shift in Laws LJ's tone from *Roth* was striking. This was not because he took a different view of the weight and importance of the rights in question. Rather, the contrast between these two cases lay in his differing perspective on the role of the courts under the HRA 1998. No doubt Laws LJ would square his two positions by arguing that the issues of free speech

---

[170] Para. 19.   [171] Para. 20.
[172] *ProLife Alliance v BBC* [2002] 2 All ER 756, para. 36.
[173] Para. 33.   [174] Para. 37.

fall within the 'constitutional responsibility' of the courts (as defined in *Roth*) as the 'guardians of democracy'. Or that, as he explained in *Roth*, less deference should be paid to public authorities. But the contrast between his broad and ambitious assertion of the courts role as the guardian of human rights in *Prolife* and his focus on deference in *Roth* is conspicuous. It is one thing to weigh rights differently or to take contrasting views on the balance between rights and the public interest, it is another thing to slip between divergent views of the courts' competence to embark on such an exercise. That the same judge could slip between these two views of the courts role, is testimony to the controversy surrounding fundamental rights at the heart of English constitutionalism.

Equally compelling evidence of this constitutional controversy is the extent to which Lord Hoffmann disagreed with Laws LJ when the House of Lords overturned the *Prolife* decision. Hoffmann's distinct view of the territories into which courts may venture was articulated not in terms of deference, but rather as a matter of legal principle. He rejected the idea that the court's decision as to the appropriate decision-making powers could be captured by the term 'deference' with 'its overtones of servility, or perhaps gracious concession'. Instead he argued:

The principles upon which decision-making powers are allocated are principles of law. The courts are the independent branch of government and the legislature and executive are, directly and indirectly respectively, the elected branches of government. Independence makes the courts more suited to deciding some kinds of questions and being elected makes the legislature or executive more suited to deciding others. The allocation of these decision-making responsibilities is based upon recognised principles. The principle that the independence of the courts is necessary for a proper decision of disputed legal rights or claims of violation of human rights is a legal principle. It is reflected in article 6 of the Convention. On the other hand, the principle that majority approval is necessary for a proper decision on policy or allocation of resources is also a legal principle. Likewise, when a court decides that a decision is within the proper competence of the legislature or executive, it is not showing deference. It is deciding the law.[175]

In replacing the opaque notion of deference with a bright line vision of the separation of powers, Lord Hoffmann sought to entrench the limits of judicial competence in the foundations of constitutional orthodoxy.

It is interesting, however, to note Laws LJ's recent reading of Hoffmann's speech in *Carson*,[176] which dealt with the differential treatment of pensioner's resident outside the United Kingdom and job seekers below the age of 25. Having accepted the line in *Mendoza* that it wasn't enough simply to claim that the decision in question fell within Parliament's discretion', Laws LJ went on to soften Lord Hoffmann's words. While arguing that different

---

[175] *ProLife Alliance v BBC* [2003] 2 WLR 1403, paras 75 and 76.
[176] *Carson and Reynolds v Secretary of State for Work and Pensions* [2003] EWCA Civ 797, paras 72 and 73.

branches of government had distinct roles, Laws LJ noted that they may also 'operate in the same field'. Consequently, 'they are not marked off by walls without windows; they are in constellation with each other, so that what government may settle as policy may be qualified by the constraint of law, settled by the judges'. For Laws LJ, Lord Hoffmann's speech could be taken to ground the idea that the 'decision-making power of this or that branch of government may be greater or smaller' depending on the areas in question. Consequently, 'where the power is possessed by the legislature or executive, the role of the courts to constrain its exercise may correspondingly be smaller or greater'.

Laws LJ in *Carson* shifted noticeably from his vision in *Roth* that the court's competence to decide on rights arguments could be resolved by reference to 'subject matter' or 'constitutional responsibilities'. In this way, he conceded that rights arguments cut across the orthodox vision of the separation of powers. In *Carson* we see an attempt not only to reconcile the difference between himself and Hoffmann in *Prolife*, and perhaps the divergence between his own two positions in *Roth* and *Prolife*. More importantly, we see a refashioned attempt to resolve the tension at the centre of English constitutionalism between a culture of sovereignty and an emergent culture of rights.

To conclude, the language of judicial deference has become commonplace in the three years and a half since the HRA 1998 entered into force. Two visions are emerging as to what the notion entails. The first view is grounded in the orthodox vision of the English constitution. In the language of deference articulated by Lord Hope in *Kebilene*, Lord Woolf in *Poplar* and *SIAC*, Laws in *Mahmood* and *Roth*, Hoffman in *Alconbury*, *Rehmann* and *Prolife*, and Lord Phillips in *Mahmood* and *Farrakhan*, is an attempt to absorb rights arguments within the established template of Diceyan constitutionalism. Deference, here, becomes the means by which the tension between the orthodox vision of parliamentary sovereignty and the separation of powers on the one hand, and the protection of individual rights on the other, is resolved. Thus, in *Farrakhan* deference was central to retaining the line between a review of legality and a review of the merits of a decision. In *Roth* it was identified as the method by which to resolve the tension between constitutional and parliamentary supremacy.

A second vision has also emerged, however. Whilst acknowledging parliamentary sovereignty, it nevertheless seeks to reconcile a doctrine of deference with a 'culture of justification'. Here the judicial protection of human rights cuts across the traditional constitutional territories of the judicial and the political. The focus shifts to the quality of the justification in question, regardless of the constitutional territory in which it falls. It is interesting that Lord Steyn has seldom sought to draw boundaries around the territories in which rights arguments may fall, but rather has spoken in more open-ended terms about the 'context' in which decisions are justified (*Daly* and *Brown v Stott*). Even where he has conceded that 'deference' should be shown, he has rejected the notion that these territories fall outside the court's competence (*Rehman*). Similarly, Lord Bingham talked of degrees of deference 'within' certain designated areas (*Brown v Stott*). Whilst, Brown LJ and Parker LJ did not fall back on the territorial argument in *Roth*, preferring instead to talk of degrees of rights infringements. Even Laws LJ now speaks in *Carson* of 'walls' with 'windows' between the constitutional territories which he identified in *Roth*. But perhaps the strongest exposition of this view of deference comes from Buxton LJ in *Mendoza*, Sir Andrew Morrit in *Wilson*, and Sedley LJ in *B*. Here, the mere assertion of deference as a means by which to exclude judicial consideration of justifications for rights infringements was explicitly rejected. Rather it was openly accepted that the ultimate decision as to the proportionality or legitimacy of the rights infringement in question lies with the judiciary. While deference plays its part in consideration of the justifications provided for the decision in question, it does not limit the court's competence to consider these reasons at the outset.

From a comparative perspective, the relative merits or demerits of these competing conceptions of deference are not our concern. Rather, their existence suggests a deep controversy in England as to the extent to which the human rights project should be embraced. They are also a reflection of the difficulty of establishing a consensus as to the constitutional foundations of judicial competence under the HRA 1998. The point of this discussion is to demonstrate the conditions under which human rights in general, and prisoners' rights in particular, are conceived, interpreted, and executed in England. To that extent, recent discourse around judicial deference is an instructive indicator of the contemporary cultural conditions of the English constitution. It is the language in which members of the English legal community seek to reconcile their conflicting constitutional visions. As regards the judiciary in particular, deference discourse is the expression of the intrinsic ambiguity of the judicial position in a constitution dedicated to preserving the two ideals of parliamentary sovereignty and the protection of human rights. This is a very different constitutional context to that of Germany. If Germany views democracy through the lens of fundamental rights, England views fundamental rights through the lens of parliamentary democracy. If German constitutional judges are confident and assertive in their role as guardians of the constitutional State, English judges are charged with the complex task of protecting human rights 'without trespassing on Parliamentary sovereignty'.[177]

---

[177] HL Debs, vol. 582, col. 1229.

6.1.4 Prisoners and Rights Ambivalence

The development of prisoners' rights in England over the last thirty years must be viewed against the backdrop of the controversy within English constitutional culture as regards the judicial protection of human rights in general. As Chapter 7 shows, judicial development of prisoners' rights in England has been marked by a struggle between the competing discourses of pragmatism and sovereignty on the one hand and individual rights on the other. This struggle underpinning judicial treatment of prisoners' rights in England is a point of substantial comparative significance with Germany. The ambivalence at the heart of English constitutional culture about the ideal of fundamental rights protection is not present within Germany, nor has it marked German judicial treatment of prisoners' rights. Once the anomaly of the prisoners' constitutional position was removed in Germany by the rejection of the doctrine of *besonderes Gewaltverhältnis* in 1972,[178] prisoners' rights development has been rooted in the broader aspiration within the German legal community towards the systematic protection of fundamental rights and principles. Crucially, this common objective frames the quest in Germany to balance administrative flexibility, public security, and prisoners' humanity. As Chapter 7 shows, however, the judicial development of prisoners' rights in England has been characterized by continuing ambivalence as to the very project of prisoners' rights protection. English judges have vacillated between parallel discourses, on the one hand using rights discourse to advance the cause of prisoners' rights and on the other hand hindering their development through recourse to the language of sovereignty and pragmatism. Consequently, there is little common language with which to define prisoners' rights or to balance the competing demands of administrative flexibility and the maintenance of prison security against them. The very foundation upon which prisoners' rights protection depends is a matter of judicial controversy. In short, as Chapter 7 shows, the story of prisoners' rights protection in England is testimony to the broader ambivalence about rights at the centre of English constitutional culture.

Whilst prisoners' rights in England are shaped by the constitutional environment in which they were developed, a further, but related, factor distinguishes treatment of prisoners' rights in England from that of Germany. This is the contrasting judicial conception of the prisoner's fundamental rights status in both countries.

---

[178] See 2.2.1.

6.2 The English Conception of the Prisoner's Fundamental Rights Status

This section sets out the contrast between the German conception of the prisoners' fundamental rights status and that applicable in England. Chapter 7 examines the implications of this contrast in detail. At this stage, however, it is important to highlight, in abstract terms, what these contrasts are.

The German conception of the prisoner's basic rights status is made up of two basic elements. First, the prisoner's legal status is divided between those rights which are relevant to the length, type and duration of his sentence—known as status rights—and those rights which are relevant to the actual administration of the prison sentence—known as administrative rights. This division stems from the systemic conception of German criminal law which strictly distinguishes between decisions taken with regard to the criminal sentence (*Strafzumessung* and *Strafvollstreckung*) and decisions taken during the administration of the prison sentence (*Strafvollzug*). This conception is equally reflected in constitutional law which clearly distinguishes between the limitations and protections of fundamental rights which arise as a result of the imposition of a custodial sentence and those which occur during the process of prison administration. Thus the German Basic Law expressly regulates the legality of status decisions by giving the State competence to imprison criminal offenders,[179] and laying out criteria by which a person may be punished,[180] detained or sentenced to imprisonment.[181] In addition, a separate constitutional justification for the restriction of rights at the administrative level has been founded by the Federal Constitutional Court (FCC) in the 'constitutional resocialization principle', which itself is derived from the rights and principles of the Constitution.[182]

The recognition of administrative rights as distinct from status rights in Germany, provides a legal and constitutional expression of Paterson's *dictum* that prisoners are sent to prison as punishment not for punishment.[183] This accepts that, while the imposition of a custodial sentence might restrict certain rights, rights protections will remain in the course of administering the custodial sentence. Similarly, this distinction is premised on recognition of the institutional threats to liberty which imprisonment represents. Goffmann argues that the total regulation of the prisoner's life by the prison regime constitutes a 'mortification' of his 'civilian self'.[184] Protection of administrative rights can thus be viewed as an attempt to preserve the

---

[179] Basic Law, art. 74, point 1.   [180] Basic Law, art. 103(2).
[181] Basic Law, art. 104.   [182] See 2.2.
[183] D. Van Zyl Smit, 'Leave of Absence for West German Prisoners' (1988) 28 *BJC* 1.
[184] E. Goffmann, 'On the Characteristics of Total Institutions: the Inmate World' in D. Cressey, *The Prison: Studies in Institutional Organisation and Change* (Holt, Rinehart & Winston, New York, 1961) 16, 23.

essence of this 'civilian self' for prisoners in the course of their imprisonment.

Having identified a distinct administrative rights status for the prisoner in Germany, the FCC has constructed this administrative status in the following way. The prisoner is viewed as a bearer of both negative fundamental rights against state infringement (*Abwehrstatus*) and positive rights to state action (*sozialer Integrationsstatus*). The prisoner's negative rights status ensures that, while prison administrators can limit fundamental rights, core fundamental rights protections remain within prisons. In addition, the prisoner bears a general positive right to a particular form of prison regime and particular kind of imprisonment. The prisoner's positive rights status is rooted in his basic constitutional 'right to resocialization' and the 'constitutional resocialization principle'. This principle is drawn from articles 1(1) and 2(1) of the Basic Law combined with the Social State principle enshrined in article 20 of the Basic Law.[185] The 'constitutional resocialization principle' determines the nature and purpose of the prison regime and the ways in which permissible limits on the prisoner's negative rights can occur. It also acts as a counter to the potential limitations of rights which might occur in the course of the attainment of internal security or public protection. While these are recognized as inherent functions of imprisonment, they have to be balanced against the constitutional purpose of prison administration.[186] Moreover, the prisoner's right to resocialization gives courts a substantive basis upon which to scrutinize the nature of the prison regime and the FCC in particular the power to force the State to implement policies within prison.[187] In short, prisoners can be said to hold an economic and social right to the direction of State resources towards the realization of their resocialization.

Although challenged in the mid-1980s, the German definition of the prisoner's legal status based on a *divisible* conception of the prisoner's administrative and status rights and on a *dual* conception of the prisoner's positive and negative rights has survived. The definition has served both as a guideline for the interpretation of the Prison Act 1976 and as the basis of the corrective function which the FCC continues to perform over the development and amendments of the Act. The prisoner's constitutional status has provided a framework within which German penal politics must operate and German judges are called upon at all levels of the legal hierarchy to decide on the legality and constitutionality of a significant number of questions which arise in the day-to-day administration of the prison.

To say that a consistently applied conception of the prisoner's legal status exists in England would be to iron out conflicts within the common law. As

---

[185] See 2.2.2.2.   [186] See 4.2.1.   [187] See 4.4.

Chapter 7 shows, this conception remains unsettled. It is possible nevertheless to point to what we might call the 'best' conception of the prisoner's
fundamental rights status in England. This 'best' conception is an amalgam
of the principles set out in *Raymond v Honey* and *Leech (No. 2)*. In
Raymond v Honey Lord Wilberforce, summarizing the words of Lord
Justice Shaw in *St Germain*,[188] stated that 'under English law, a convicted
prisoner, in spite of his imprisonment, retains all the civil rights which are
not taken away expressly or by necessary implication'.[189] This *dictum* was
extended by Lord Steyn in *Leech (No. 2)* where he stated that 'the more
fundamental the right interfered with and the more drastic the interference,
the more difficult becomes the implication'.[190] Moreover, that even where
restrictions of rights were permitted by necessary implication 'the authorised
intrusion must . . . be the minimum necessary to ensure' the 'statutory objective'.[191] When taken together the principles in *Raymond v Honey* and *Leech
(No. 2)* amount to much more than a mere statement of residual rights.
Rather they amount to the stronger statement that, in the absence of
Parliament's express words to the contrary, the negative aspect of prisoners'
fundamental rights would be protected as far as possible and in line with a
principle of proportionality designed to ensure minimum interference with
those rights.

    With the introduction of the HRA 1998 the prisoner's rights status takes
on a new dimension in that prisoners' Convention rights are now positively
enacted in domestic law. Under the HRA 1998 courts are required to 'take
into account' European Convention jurisprudence on the issue at hand.[192]
It is noteworthy therefore that the 'best' conception of prisoners' rights in
England is not far removed from that of the ECtHR which was originally
developed in *Golder*.[193] In this case, the ECtHR departed from its prior
doctrine that certain forms of rights restrictions were an 'inherent feature' of
imprisonment.[194] Instead it argued that rights restrictions were to be
assessed 'having regard to the ordinary and reasonable requirements of
imprisonment'. Moreover, it argued that these restrictions had to be 'stipulated by law' and in accordance with the proportionality test developed in
general ECtHR jurisprudence, namely that the restrictions be 'necessary in
a democratic society' and for the attainment of a 'legitimate aim' stipulated
in the Convention. The court accepted that the 'legitimate aim' of the 'prevention of disorder and crime may justify wider measures of interference in
the case of . . . a prisoner than in that of a person at liberty'. But, in line with

---

[188] *R v Board of Visitors of Hull Prison, ex p St Germain and others* [1978] 1 QB (CA) 425,
455.
[189] *Raymond v Honey* [1982] 1 All ER 756, 759; [1983] 1 AC 1, 10.
[190] *R v Home Secretary, ex p Leech (No. 2)* [1994] QB 198, 209.
[191] [1994] QB 198, 217.   [192] Human Rights Act 1998, s. 2.
[193] *Golder v UK* (1979–80) 1 EHRR 524.
[194] F. Jacobs and R. White, *The European Convention on Human Rights* (2nd edn,
Clarendon Press, Oxford, 1996) 198–9 and 297–301.

the proportionality principle, the ECtHR required that any such restrictions were no greater than was necessary to address a 'pressing social need'.[195] To summarize, the *Golder* test starts out from the position of the prisoner as the bearer of Convention rights and then requires that restrictions of these rights, be they express parliamentary words or delegated legislation, be assessed in the context of 'the ordinary requirements of imprisonment' and against the doctrine of proportionality.

The English and European conception of prisoners' rights whilst, roughly speaking, in accord with the German view of the prisoner's negative rights status, differs from the German view in two important respects. First, there is no explicit division in this conception between the definition of rights at the 'status' level and those which apply at the 'administrative' level. Once a criminal offender has been convicted under the criminal law and sentenced to a term of imprisonment there is no additional constitutional or legal rationale found for the limitation or protection of his or her rights at the 'administrative' level. From the court's perspective, imprisonment might or might not involve restrictions of the prisoner's civil and political liberties and rights, but there is no articulated legal distinction between the limitation of rights as a result of the imposition of the criminal sentence and limitation of rights during the day-to-day administration of prisons.

Nevertheless, the maxim in *Raymond v Honey* is grounded in an implicit distinction between 'status' liberty and 'administrative' rights. To say that 'a convicted prisoner, in spite of his imprisonment, retains all the civil rights which are not taken away expressly or by necessary implication' involves an acceptance that while a prisoner's liberty is lawfully restricted by the imposition of the prison sentence (i.e. the restriction of liberty at the status level), residual liberty continues to apply within the prison context (i.e. at the administrative level). Equally the rejection in *Golder* of the 'inherent limitations doctrine' and the acceptance that rights must be protected whilst the offender is in prison would suggest a tacit acceptance of administrative rights. That this distinction constitutes an implicit underpinning to judicial reasoning on prisoners' rights, is more than evident in the English case law, as Chapter 7 seeks to show. However, it will be shown that the German legal and judicial focus on the definition and protection of prisoners' administrative rights is not nearly as pronounced in the English courts.

The second marked difference between the English/European conception and the German conception of prisoners' rights is the absence of a positive rights status attributed to the prisoner at the administrative level. There is no explicit relationship between fundamental rights and the purpose or purposes of prison administration. As with the English Prison Rules, no clear overarching principles operate as benchmarks against which to evaluate what prison is for, what it should achieve, and how it should be

---

[195] *Golder v UK* (1979–80) 1 EHRR 524, in particular para. 45.

administered. The English courts and the ECtHR have not developed substantive or principled guidance for determining what the acceptable limitations of negative rights should be in the process of imprisonment, nor is there a substantive foundation for the development of special positive rights of prisoners which apply at the administrative level. Instead either the courts evaluate decisions by casting them in terms of the narrow objects of each separate administrative measure,[196] or references to purposes of imprisonment or prison administration are too general to provide any purposive guidance. For example, whilst the *Golder* test asserts that permissible limitations of Convention rights must be proportionate to their specific aim, there is no attempt to define what the 'ordinary and reasonable requirements of imprisonment' may entail other than in the individual case. Similarly, there is no positive rights conception which could act as a counter against other potential functions of imprisonment such as security and protection of the public. This contrasts with Germany where the Prison Act 1976 and the courts attempt to balance the imperatives of the German 'constitutional resocialization principle' with the security function of imprisonment.[197]

Under the English and European formulas individual positive rights or correlative positive duties can be developed by asserting the protections of negative Convention or common law rights in line with the principle of proportionality. This is clearly the case in a number of the cases discussed in Chapter 7. But in the absence of any overarching principles or standards this approach remains piecemeal, as the ECtHR explicitly argued in *Golder*:

It is not the function of the Court to elaborate a general theory of the limitations admissible in the case of convicted prisoners, nor even to rule in abstracto on the compatibility of . . . the Prison Rules 1964 with the Convention. Seised of a case which has its origins in a petition presented by an individual, the Court is called upon

---

[196] e.g., *R v Home Secretary, ex p Leech (No. 2)* [1994] QB 198, 212–13 where the assessment of whether there was a 'self-evident and pressing need' for the measure in question was not measured against any general principle of imprisonment, but rather against the purposes of the specific powers in question.

[197] The absence of a positive rights conception which gives rise to overarching principles of prison administration in both the European and English test has been acknowledged by commentators. Livingstone concluded that while 'the Strasbourg institutions . . . have encouraged an emphasis on judicial supervision of imprisonment . . . they have left it open as to whether compliance with human rights standards requires a particular view of the purposes of imprisonment . . . there is little indication as to whether the authorities are under an obligation to provide positive programmes for those who are detained other than simply for retribution' (S. Livingstone 'Prisoners' rights in the context of the European Convention on Human Rights' (2000) 2(3) *P&S* 309, 321). Equally Livingstone, Owen, and MacDonald have concluded in their study of the English courts' attitude to prisons that 'the impression the courts give is primarily of a desire to ensure that the bureaucracy functions correctly according to its defined goals. There is less concern with shaping what these goals might be, something which goes some way towards explaining the greater degree of caution courts have displayed when it comes to ruling on the content of the prison authorities' powers'. (S. Livingstone, T. Owen, and A. MacDonald, *Prison Law* (OUP, Oxford, 2003) 552).

to pronounce itself only on the point whether or not the application of those Rules in the present case violated the Convention to the prejudice of Golder.[198]

Whilst piecemeal protections of individual negative rights are an important judicial function, this form of prisoners' rights protection is more modest than that undertaken in Germany. The constitutional definition of the prisoner's legal status in Germany gives the FCC a platform from which to scrutinize the general aims and objectives of prison administration and the development of prison policy within the political arena. The European and English test, by contrast, is premised on a tacit understanding that courts should not enter into this political arena, a possibility described by one English judge as constitutional 'heresy'.[199] Rather, the test restricts courts to producing a set of rights which 'may impose some limits on prison regimes but does not fundamentally undermine the modern prison as we know it'.[200]

This modest definition of the prisoner's rights status in England, while signalling an absence of the German social constitutional rights tradition, reflects the orthodox constitutional division between the judicial concern with legality and the parliamentary control of the political. In this orthodox vision, it is the executive under Parliament which is afforded definitional power over the purpose and nature of prison administration, not the judiciary. Nevertheless, it is curious that English judges have rarely accepted this orthodox constitutional rationale when faced with limitations on their sentencing discretion, preferring to define for themselves the underlying rationale for punishment in each particular case.[201] It is a notable incongruity of the English context that judges guard jealously for themselves the definitional power over their sentencing discretion, whilst viewing the rationale for the administration of that sentence to be outside of their remit. Notwithstanding the introduction of the HRA 1998, the substantive basis of prison administration remains a question which English judges are reluctant to address. As Chapter 7 shows, this reluctance is both reflected in and entrenched by the judicial conception of prisoners' rights as negative rights and by a lack of close and principled attention to the prisoner's administrative rights. In short, whilst the English conception of the prisoner's rights status grounds itself in the protection of residual liberty, it tells us little about how such liberty is to be protected in conditions of confinement.

---

[198] *Golder v UK* (1975) 1 EHRR 524, para. 39.

[199] *R (Hargreaves) v Secretary of State* [1997] 1 All ER 397, 412 per Hirst LJ. See further 7.3.

[200] S. Livingstone, 'Prisoners' rights in the context of the European Convention on Human Rights' (2000) 2(3) *P&S* 309, 312.

[201] A. Ashworth. *Sentencing and Criminal Justice* (3rd edn, Butterworths, London, 2000) ch. 2.

6.3 Conclusion

This chapter highlights two important features distinguishing Germany and England: the differing weight of fundamental rights within contemporary constitutional culture and the divergent conception of the prisoner's fundamental rights status. As regards the former, the chapter argues that, in contrast to Germany's faith in fundamental rights and its systematic and comprehensive approach to fundamental rights protection, England experiences a cultural tension between an emergent rights culture and an established tradition of rights scepticism and respect for parliamentary sovereignty. In this environment the judiciary display ambivalence as to their role as guardians of fundamental rights and prisoners' rights in particular. As regards the latter, the chapter argues that, in contrast to Germany's ambitious conception, the English and European conception of the prisoner's fundamental rights status does not include any explicit articulation of the prisoner's administrative rights status or any positive conception of prisoners' rights. This is a more modest conception of the prisoner's fundamental rights status and one rooted in deeper constitutional sensibilities. The following and final chapter seeks to demonstrate the influence of these factors on the jurisprudence of prisoners' rights.

7

The Jurisprudence of Prisoners' Rights

If the courts were to entertain actions by disgruntled prisoners, the governor's life would be made intolerable. The discipline of the prison would be undermined. The Prison Rules are regulatory directions only. Even if they are not observed, they do not give rise to a cause of action.[1]

It is an axiom of our law that a convicted prisoner, in spite of his imprisonment, retains all civil rights which are not taken away expressly or by necessary implication . . . It will be a rare case in which it could be held that such a fundamental right was by necessary implication abolished or limited by statute. It will, we suggest, be an even rarer case in which it could be held that a statute authorised by necessary implication the abolition or limitation of so fundamental a right by subordinate legislation.[2]

Judicial attitudes to prisoners' rights in England have undoubtedly changed over the last thirty years. The difference above between the 'hands off approach' of Lord Denning in *Becker* and the interventionist tone of Lord Justice Steyn in *Leech* is dramatic. Yet while prisoners' rights cases are held up as evidence of a growing 'rights consciousness' in England,[3] others point out that progress has been limited.[4] In the English constitutional context both accounts of prisoners' rights jurisprudence are explicable. If we use orthodox English constitutionalism as our benchmark, the judicial development of prisoners' rights presents a victory for an emergent human rights consciousness. Alternatively, if we take an expansionist view of prisoners'

---

[1] *Becker v Home Office* [1972] 2 QB 407, 418 *per* Lord Denning.
[2] *R v Home Secretary, ex p Leech (No. 2)* [1994] QB 198, 209 and 212 *per* Lord Justice Steyn.
[3] M. Hunt, *Using Human Rights Law in English Courts* (Hart Publishing, Oxford, 1998) 175–81; S. Bailey, D. Harris, and B. Jones, *Civil Liberties: Cases and Materials* (3rd edn, Butterworths, London, 1991) 684.
[4] S. Livingstone, T. Owen, and A. MacDonald, *Prison Law* (3rd edn, OUP, Oxford, 2003) 551; G. Richardson, 'Prisoners and the Law: Beyond Rights' in C. McCrudden and G. Chambers (eds), *Individual Rights and the Law in Britain* (Clarendon Press, Oxford, 1994) 179, 201–3; C. Gearty, 'The Prisons and the Courts' in J. Muncie and R. Sparks (eds), *Imprisonment: European Perspectives* (Sage, London, 1991) 219; S. Livingstone, 'Prisoners have Rights, But What Rights?' (1988) *MLR* 525.

rights as Richardson does,[5] the judicial approach in England might equally be characterized as partial and uneven.

What happens if we view England through a German lens? Whilst individual areas of prisoners' rights protection would appear familiar, Germans would note the absence of an attempt to root the development of prisoners' rights within a constitutional conception of the purpose of imprisonment, a positive notion of the prisoner's fundamental rights status, and an explicit judicial commitment to the development of the prisoner's 'administrative rights'. From a German vantage point, judicial conceptions of rights in prisons do not include a broad-based commitment to shaping the nature of imprisonment and prison administration in line with deeper human rights principles. This chapter examines the judicial development of prisoners' administrative rights in England from this German perspective. It will explain the divergence between the German and English approaches in the light of the factors outlined in Chapters 5 and 6. An exhaustive analysis of the case law is not being attempted here,[6] rather, landmark cases will be picked out to illustrate general propositions.

7.1 THE ROAD TO *HAGUE*:
THE EMERGENCE OF RIGHTS DISCOURSE

In 1972 Lord Denning argued that courts would not intervene in prison administration.[7] This was a conservative position to take as, following the decision in *Ridge v Baldwin* in 1964,[8] there was potential for the courts to assume at least some supervisory jurisdiction, particularly as regards procedural fairness, over prison administration. Denning's categorical statement was, however, slowly eroded over the next two decades. The process began across the channel when the European Court of Human Rights (ECtHR) decided *Golder*.[9]

Golder had been wrongfully accused of taking part in a prison riot in Parkhurst prison. His correspondence concerning these allegations was

---

[5] G. Richardson, 'The Case for Prisoners' Rights' in M. Maguire, R. Morgan, and J. Vagg, *Accountability and Prisons* (Tavistock, London, 1985) 19; Richardson 1994 (n 4).

[6] For such an account, see Livingstone *et al.* (n 4); G. Richardson, *Law, Process and Custody: Prisoners and Patients* (Weidenfeld & Nicolson, London, 1993); S. Creighton and V. King, *Prisoners and the Law* (2nd edn, Butterworths, London, 2000).

[7] *Becker v Home Office* [1972] 2 QB 407, 418. See opening quotation.

[8] *Ridge v Baldwin* [1964] AC 40. Prior to this decision, judicial intervention on the grounds of natural justice was justified on the basis that the administrative decisions in question were either 'judicial' or 'quasi-judicial'. *Ridge v Baldwin* explicitly rejected these formalist restrictions on the courts' jurisdiction and argued that the courts' discretion to apply the principles of natural justice should be guided by the 'nature of the power exercised and its effect on the individual in question'. See P. Craig, *Administrative Law* (Sweet & Maxwell, London, 1999) 401–6; Richardson 1993 (n 6) 30.

[9] *Golder v UK* (1975) 1 EHRR 524.

stopped by the governor and his petition to the Home Secretary asking for transfer and permission to consult a lawyer in order to bring civil proceedings was rejected. The ECtHR, setting aside the 'inherent limitations doctrine', held that Golder's rights under the European Convention on Human Rights (ECHR), Articles 6 (fair trial) and 8 (privacy of correspondence), had been violated. The conception of the prisoner's Convention rights status applied in this case has already been discussed.[10] It achieved a clear statement of a prisoner's right of access to the courts and led to the amendment of the rule that prisoners must obtain permission from the Secretary of State in order to obtain legal advice.[11]

The impact of *Golder* on the domestic courts was symbolically powerful and a strong example of the globalization of English legal culture.[12] As Sedley argued, after this judgment 'the courts have consciously taken decisions on prisoners' rights designed at least in part to rescue the UK government from the prospect of further embarrassment in Strasbourg'.[13] It was not surprising then, that only a few years after *Golder* was decided, the domestic courts made their first break from the *Becker* position in *St Germain*.[14] Like *Golder*, this case dealt with disciplinary proceedings regarding involvement in a prison riot. The prisoners in question were found by the Board of Visitors to be in breach of Prison Rule 47 for 'concerted acts of indiscipline'. The procedures were cavalier and their sentences severe. In some cases the prisoners were awarded up to 720 days loss of remission without being able to present their case or cross-examine witnesses.[15] There was a clear argument for *certiorari* to lie against the decision on the grounds of breach of natural justice. The Court of Appeal was asked to settle whether it had jurisdiction to grant such an award.

The Court of Appeal asserted its jurisdiction on the basis of two alternative justifications: the one tentative, the other bold. The tentative position was presented by Lord Justice Megaw who stayed well within the confines of orthodox constitutionalism and applied formalist jurisdictional principles.[16] Justifying the Court's jurisdiction on the ground that the Board of Visitors was acting in a 'quasi-judicial' capacity,[17] he tried to hinder the extension of court supervision over prison administration generally. Consequently, he argued that the disciplinary functions of a prison governor were 'materially different' from those of a Board of Visitors:

[10] See 6.2.

[11] The new 'prior ventilation rule' required prisoners to obtain a decision from the Home Office concerning their grievance before being allowed to obtain legal advice. See further n 40 below.

[12] See 6.1.2.

[13] S. Sedley, 'Foreword to the First Edition' in Livingstone *et al.* (n 4), vii.

[14] *R v Board of Visitors of Hull Prison, ex p St Germain* [1978] 1 QB (CA) 425.

[15] M. Loughlin and P.M. Quinn, 'Prison Rules and Courts: A Study in Administrative Law' (1993) *MLR* 497, 508.

[16] See n 8 above.

[17] *R v Board of Visitors of Hull Prison, ex p St Germain* [1978] 1 QB (CA) 425, 447.

While the governor hears charges and makes awards, his position in so doing corresponds to that of the commanding officer in military discipline or the schoolmaster in school discipline. His powers of summary discipline are . . . intimately connected with his functions of day-to-day administration. To my mind both good sense and the practical requirements of public policy make it undesirable that his exercise of that part of his administrative duties should be made subject to certiorari . . . It may be difficult to define the distinction as a strict matter of logic. But I think that, as a matter of the proper practical application of the law in the general interest, not forgetting the legitimate interests of prisoners, that is where the line should be drawn.[18]

Megaw LJ's concern with the 'practical application of the law in the general interest', 'public policy', and his explicit admission that his drawing of jurisdictional boundaries had no logical foundation, could not have been more illustrative of the pragmatism rooted in orthodox English constitutional and legal culture. His brief allusion to the prisoner's 'legitimate interests' came more as an afterthought than as a principle upon which to ground the Court's jurisdiction.

   Megaw LJ's tentative pragmatic line was counterpoised by Lord Justice Shaw in the same case. Shaw LJ rooted jurisdiction in the prisoner's fundamental rights whilst paying, along the way, due respect to parliamentary intention. He noted of the Prison Act 1952 that 'in the scheme envisaged by the Act and shaped by those Rules, the courts have no defined place and no direct or immediate function' and that 'judicial intervention in the domestic management of a prison would generally be not merely *irrelevant* but also *intrusive* and *impolitic*'.[19] Notwithstanding, whilst the prisoner is subject to a special regimen and has a special status, he 'remains invested with residuary rights appertaining to the nature and conduct of his incarceration'. On this basis Shaw LJ presented the foundation of the prisoner's legal status in England:

Now the rights of a citizen, however circumscribed by a penal sentence or otherwise, must always be the concern of the courts unless their jurisdiction is clearly excluded by some statutory provision. The courts are in general the ultimate custodians of the rights and liberties of the subject whatever his status and however attenuated those rights and liberties may be as the result of some punitive or other process . . . Public policy or expediency as well as merits may be factors for relief; but to deny jurisdiction on the grounds of expediency seems to me . . . to be tantamount to abdicating a primary function of the judiciary.[20]

Accordingly, Shaw LJ saw no hindrance to the possible extension of the courts' jurisdiction:

I do not find it easy, if at all possible, to distinguish between disciplinary proceedings conducted by a Board of Visitors and those carried out by a prison governor . . . the

---

[18] At 447–8.   [19] At 454. Emphasis added.   [20] At 455.

essential nature of the proceedings as defined by the Prison Rules is the same. So, in nature if not in degree, are the consequences to the prisoner.[21]

St Germain displayed a tension between an established and an emergent constitutional culture. Lord Justice Megaw's tentative pragmatism resulted in a restrictive view of the courts' supervisory function in prisons, while Lord Justice Shaw delivered an expansionist view of prisoners' rights. These divergent positions laid the groundwork for two currents within judicial thinking that would shape the progress of prisoners' rights over the next decade.

Once given licence to review Board of Visitor disciplinary proceedings, the courts were quick to develop the principles of natural justice in this context. The process began with *St Germain (No. 2)*, which quashed all sixteen decisions of the Board.[22] Thereafter a number of decisions bolstered the requirements of natural justice, in particular fairness, with respect to the disciplinary proceedings of Boards of Visitors.[23] The most important decisions to arise in this respect dealt with the question of legal representation at Board of Visitor disciplinary hearings. Here the impetus was assisted, once again, by developments at the European level.

In *Campbell and Fell* the claimants had been involved in a protest of six prisoners and had been charged with the 'exceptionally grave' disciplinary offences of mutiny or incitement to mutiny.[24] The Board of Visitors had awarded 605 days and 570 days of loss of remission respectively. The European Commission on Human Rights decided that, due to the seriousness of the charges and the gravity of the penalties, the proceedings amounted to the determination of a 'criminal charge' under Article 6(3) ECHR (right to a fair trial). It also concluded that a Board of Visitors could not be classified as an 'independent and impartial tribunal' for the purposes of Article 6 ECHR. The Commission decision was referred to the ECtHR for final resolution. In the meantime the Home Secretary established the Prior Committee to review the operation of the prison disciplinary system.[25] Whilst the European Court decision was pending and the Prior Committee began its enquiries, the Divisional Court delivered its judgment in *Tarrant*.[26] This case dealt with Board of Visitors disciplinary proceedings in which similar charges were brought against prisoners involved in a riot in Albany prison.

In *Tarrant*, counsel invoked Article 6 ECHR and the Commission's decision in *Campbell and Fell* to argue for a prisoner's right to legal

---

[21] At 456.

[22] *R v Hull Prison Board of Visitors, ex p St Germain (No. 2)* [1979] 3 All ER 545.

[23] See in general S. Livingstone, 'The Changing Face of Prison Discipline' in E. Player and M. Jenkins (eds), *Prisons After Woolf* (Routledge, London, 1994) 97; Loughlin and Quinn (n 15) 497.

[24] *Campbell and Fell* (App. Nos 7819/77; 7878/77).

[25] Loughlin and Quinn (n 15), 517.

[26] *R v Secretary of the State Department, ex p Tarrant* [1985] 1 QB 251.

representation.[27] The Court declined to address Convention arguments on the grounds that it would not add anything to its decision and because it was 'bound by the settled jurisprudence of our law'.[28] Nevertheless, whilst stating that the prisoner's right to legal representation was discretionary, the Court indicated that the presumption in favour of such representation being granted in serious disciplinary proceedings was high. Thus, 'any reasonable tribunal, properly exercising their discretion, would have allowed those applicants legal representation'.[29] Reference was made to Lord Atkin's famous *dictum* that: 'administrative difficulties, simpliciter, are not in our view enough. Convenience and justice are often not on speaking terms'.[30] On this basis, the Court rejected a variety of government arguments based on 'administrative convenience', customary practice developed through 'ancient long-established usage', and 'threats to discipline within the prison'.[31] It concluded that there is 'nothing which takes away expressly or by necessary implication the discretion of a Board of Visitors to grant legal representation or, therefore, the right on the part of the prisoner to require the board to exercise it'.[32] Clearly, the *Tarrant* decision represented a local shift towards the recognition of rights and the invocation of principles. It was consequently described as the domestic 'high water mark of procedural standards' in disciplinary proceedings.[33]

After *Tarrant*, the ECtHR delivered its judgment in *Campbell and Fell*.[34] It held that whilst the Board of Visitors was sufficiently 'independent and impartial' to conduct disciplinary proceedings, the prisoners' rights under Article 6 ECHR had been violated because they were not 'entitled to obtain legal assistance prior to the Board's hearing or legal representation thereat'. The Court held that Article 6(3) applied despite the fact that disciplinary charges were not strictly speaking classified as 'criminal' offences within the English legal system. Rather the fact that the 'nature and severity of the penalties' were 'especially grave' was sufficient to allow their classification as 'criminal' for this purpose.[35] The case, while not binding as domestic law, served to reinforce the tone adopted in *Tarrant*.

Campbell and Fell and *Tarrant* had a significant impact on the shape of the prison disciplinary system.[36] Beyond the area of prison discipline, advances were being made on a number of different fronts both locally and at the European level. In *Silver* the European Commission and the ECtHR held that any restrictions of prisoner correspondence were only justifiable under Article 8(1) ECHR (privacy of correspondence) if they were 'prescribed by law' and 'necessary in a democratic society'. The Commission

---

[27] At 257–63.
[28] At 282 (*per* Webster J) and 296 (*per* Kerr LJ).
[29] At 293 *per* Webster J.
[30] *General Medical Council v Spackman* [1943] AC 627, 638 quoted at [1985] 1 QB 251, 281.
[31] At 279 and 281.
[32] At 282.
[33] Livingstone 1994 (n 23), 101.
[34] *Campbell and Fell v UK* (1984) 7 EHRR 165.
[35] Para. 73.
[36] Loughlin and Quinn (n 15), 497.

found that the stopping of letters on the grounds of Standing Orders and Instructions, which had not been published and made available to a prisoner, resulted in interference with his correspondence rights which were not 'foreseeable' and therefore not in 'accordance with the law'.[37] Whilst it was accepted that the 'prevention of disorder', 'the prevention of crime', 'the protection of morals', and /or 'the protection of the rights and freedoms of others' were 'legitimate aims' to be pursued under Article 8 ECHR and could justify monitoring and restrictions of prisoner correspondence, almost all of the restrictions in this case were viewed as disproportionate means of achieving such aims and thus not 'necessary in a democratic society'.[38] As a result of *Silver* the Government revised the directives on prisoner correspondence, published the orders relating to correspondence in their entirety,[39] and changed control practices regarding prisoner's legal correspondence.[40]

At the domestic level, courts continued to develop prisoners' rights which were a natural corollary of the admittance of court jurisdiction over Board of Visitors decisions in *St Germain*, namely rights of access to legal advice and to the courts. These decisions were heavily influenced by European human rights jurisprudence. In *Raymond v Honey* both Lords Wilberforce and Bridge made reference to *Golder*, alongside domestic authority,[41] in support of the prisoner's 'constitutional rights to have their legal rights and obligations ascertained and enforced by courts of law'.[42] Here the Court held that a prison governor's interception of a prisoner's correspondence to his solicitor was a violation of such a right and therefore a contempt of court. Summarizing the words of Shaw LJ in *St Germain* in the now famous *dictum* that 'a convicted prisoner, in spite of his imprisonment, retains all civil rights which are not taken away expressly or by necessary implication', both judges took the view that there was nothing in the Prison Act 1952 or the regulations thereunder which permitted the restriction of 'so basic a right' as the prisoner's right of access to the courts.[43] Lord Bridge stated outright that a 'basic principle' existed 'that a citizen's right to unimpeded access to the courts can only be taken away by express enactment'.[44] In *Anderson* the courts dealt a further blow to the control of a prisoner's legal correspondence and vindicated the prisoner's right of access to the courts and legal advice.[45] Lord Justice Goff applied *Golder* to show that access to

---

[37] *Silver v UK* (1983) 5 EHRR 347, para. 91.   [38] Para. 99.   [39] Para. 26.

[40] The 'prior ventilation rule' was amended to the 'simultaneous ventilation' rule whereby a prisoner had to state a grievance internally in order to seek outside legal advice, but would not have to wait for the outcome of the internal decision before seeking such advice. See n 11 above.

[41] *Attorney-General v Times Newspapers Ltd* [1974] AC 273, 310.

[42] *Raymond v Honey* [1983] AC 1.   [43] At 13.   [44] At 14.

[45] *R v Secretary of State for the Home Department, ex p Anderson* [1984] QB 778, which held the 'simultaneous ventilation rule' to be *ultra vires* the Home Secretary's rule making powers under the Prison Act, s. 47. The court was particularly concerned that the prisoner, in raising a complaint under the simultaneous ventilation rule, could be charged with the disciplinary

legal advice was an inseparable part of access to the courts,[46] and *Raymond v Honey* to argue that 'nothing in the Prison Act 1952 confers power to make regulations which would deny, or interfere with, the right of a prisoner to have unimpeded access to the court'.[47]

The decisions in the early 1980s could certainly be held up as evidence of an emergent rights consciousness within the English constitutional environment and of the growing influence of European human rights jurisprudence on the domestic judiciary. But the cumulative impact of these decisions was limited. The cases dealt with the particular areas of procedural rights within disciplinary proceedings, access to justice, and general correspondence rights. Judicial intervention was inspired by two concerns, namely to protect the prisoner's personal liberty where disciplinary penalties were particularly grave or to protect the prisoner's right of access to the courts. Court's were less inclined to intervene where disciplinary awards were lower, arguing that their role was to remedy 'substantial injustice' only.[48] Moreover, there was resistance to arguments which implied more fundamental reform of the Board of Visitors. In *Ex parte Lewis*,[49] where a prisoner had claimed a risk of bias on the part of the Board of Visitors, the Court refrained from using natural justice as a vehicle to eliminate the dual function of the Board of Visitors as both a disciplinary and complaints body. This dual function represented one of the major objections to the operations of Boards of Visitors, and significantly undermined their legitimacy as independent complaint forums. Only one year before the decision in *Lewis*, the Prior Committee had recommended the abolition of the Board's disciplinary functions and the creation of a Prisons Disciplinary Tribunal.[50] Notwithstanding this evident discontent, the Court declined to take such an activist step, preferring instead to let politicians undertake such reforms.

Beyond disciplinary procedures and access to justice, there was little close judicial scrutiny of the exercise of prison administrative power at the managerial level or with the further development of what the Germans would call prisoners' administrative rights. This resistance was manifest in *McAvoy*, where a remand prisoner challenged his transfer to a prison which

---

offence of making 'false and malicious allegations' against a prison officer. See n 11 and n 40 above.

[46] At 793.   [47] At 792.

[48] *R v Board of Visitors of Pentonville Prison, ex p Rutherford*, The Times, 21 February 1985; *R v Board of Visitors of Swansea Prison, ex p Scales*, The Times, 21 February 1985; *R v Board of Visitors of Wandsworth Prison, ex p Raymond*, The Times, 17 June 1985; *R v Board of Visitors of Winchester Prison, ex p Cartwright* QBD, 9 June 1981; *R v Board of Visitors of Dartmoor Prison, ex p Seray Wurie*, The Times, 5 February 1982; *R v Board of Visitors of Gartree Prison, ex p Sears*, The Times, 21 March 1985. See also Loughlin and Quinn (n 15), 508; M. Loughlin, 'The Underside of the Law: Judicial Review and the Prison Disciplinary System' (1993) CLP 23, 308.

[49] *R v Board of Visitors of Frankland Prison, ex p Lewis* [1986] 1 WLR 130.

[50] *Report of the Committee on the Prison Disciplinary System in England and Wales* (Cmnd. 9641) ch. 6. These changes were only made after the Woolf Report (see 5.4.2.2.).

neither his family nor lawyer could visit. Webster J refused to accept that a prisoners' right to be visited under the Prison Rules could be weighed against the Home Secretary's operational discretion:

The Secretary of State's powers . . . are . . . reviewable in exercise but they are also very wide. In my view it is undesirable—if not impossible—for this court to examine operational [and] security reasons for decisions made under that section . . . where the Secretary of State has security reasons for transferring a prisoner from one prison to another, the prisoner's rights to be visited . . . will rarely, if ever, be a factor of significance to be taken into account in making the decision whether that transfer should take place or not. In most cases, in my view, the same considerations apply to a prisoner's right to be visited by his legal adviser.[51]

Judicial reluctance to intervene in prison life was equally evident in *King*.[52] Here the court rejected the prisoners' application on the grounds that it did not have jurisdiction over the governor's disciplinary powers. All three judges in *King* took a highly orthodox and pragmatic view of the question. Lawton LJ argued that the courts were confined to controlling the powers of the Secretary of State who was obliged under section 4(2) of the Prison Act 1952 to ensure compliance with the prison rules.[53] He viewed the prison governor as 'nothing more than a manager appointed by and answerable to the Secretary of State' and the governor's disciplinary functions as an integral part of his 'managerial' function.

Lord Justice Browne-Wilkinson agreed with the view that Parliament had intended the courts to restrict their supervision to the powers of the Home Secretary.[54] He adopted a pragmatic approach, contradicting his own view in *Tarrant* that 'administrative difficulties simpliciter' were not enough to restrict the courts' jurisdiction:

I, too, can see no logical distinction between the disciplinary functions of prison governors and the disciplinary functions of boards of visitors which the House of Lords has held are subject to judicial review. On the other hand, the practical repercussions of holding that the disciplinary decisions of prison governors are subject to review by the courts are frightening. It would be to shut one's eyes to reality to ignore the fact that, if prisoners are able to challenge in the courts the disciplinary decisions of the governor, they are likely to try to do so in many unmeritorious cases and the maintenance of order and discipline in prisons is likely to be seriously undermined.[55]

Lord Justice Griffiths glorified the common law's pragmatic qualities. Being 'firmly of the opinion that the Court should not extend the boundaries of judicial review to embrace the decisions of prison governors', he rejected counsel's argument that the distinction between the Board of Visitors and the governor was 'absurd' and went on to reply:

[51] *R v Secretary of State for the Home Department, ex p McAvoy* [1984] 1 WLR 1408, 1417.
[52] *R v Deputy Governor of Camphill Prison, ex p King* [1985] QB 735
[53] At 749.   [54] At 753–4.   [55] At 753.

The common law of England has not always developed upon strictly logical lines, and where logic leads down a path that is beset with practical difficulties the courts have not been frightened to turn aside and seek the pragmatic solution that will best serve the needs of society. I can think of no more difficult task in contemporary society than that of managing and maintaining discipline in seriously overcrowded prisons . . . I am convinced that we should make it very much more difficult to carry out that task if the authority of the governor is undermined by the prospect of every disciplinary award being the subject of potential challenge in the court . . . I wish I could find a logical way in which to distinguish between governors and boards of visitors, but I have not been able to do so and I think at the end of the day I must content myself by pointing to some of the differences which justify a different approach.[56]

After balancing the so-called interests of society with the benefits of a strict logical application of the law, Griffiths LJ went on to 'content himself' with various analogous arguments as to the differences between the governor and the Board of Visitors and dismissed the appeal.[57]

This restrictive pragmatism, articulated by Lord Justice Megaw in *St Germain*, and glorified in *King* was to represent a block to the courts' jurisdiction over prisons in England until the highly principled *Leech* judgment.[58] The outcome in *Leech* was prompted by the decision of the Court of Appeal of Northern Ireland in *McKiernan* which held that there was no logical distinction between a Board of Visitors and a prison governor's disciplinary functions and that courts could exercise supervisory jurisdiction over such decisions.[59]

Aside from *McKiernan*, another decision predated *Leech* which indicated a small shift from the *King* position. This was the case of *Herbage* which related to the discovery proceedings of a prisoner who applied for judicial review of the decision to place him with mentally disturbed inmates in a hospital wing of a prison.[60] Herbage was of sound mind, although physically disabled, and he complained that his detention amounted to 'cruel and unusual' punishment contrary to the Bill of Rights 1688. The decision dealt with the narrower question of discovery, but the argument as to jurisdiction was raised by the respondents as a belated means of defeating the discovery action. On the basis of *King*, it was argued that the Court did not have jurisdiction to review the governor's decision and, in addition, that no decision on the part of the Home Secretary had been presented for review. The Court of Appeal was split on the question of jurisdiction. May LJ held that jurisdiction did not exist to review a governor's managerial decision taken in breach of the Prison Rules. Purchas LJ and Sir David Cairns held, however, that whilst no jurisdiction existed to review decisions taken by governors in

---

[56] At 750.　　　　　　　　　[57] At 751–3.
[58] *Leech v Deputy Governor of Parkhurst Prison* [1988] 1 AC 533.
[59] *R v Governor of The Maze Prison, ex p McKiernan* (1985) 6 NIJB 6.
[60] *R v Secretary of State for the Home Department, ex p Herbage (No. 2)* [1987] 1 QB 1077.

breach of Prison Rules, jurisdiction did exist where a breach of the Bill of Rights 1688 had been alleged. In this way the Court asserted its jurisdiction over the treatment of prisoners where such treatment was a clear case of 'cruel or unusual punishment'. This jurisdiction was exerted regardless of the status of the decision-maker or whether the decision was to be regarded as managerial or disciplinary. This was a broad view of jurisdiction rooted solely in the courts' role as the guardian of prisoner's rights.[61]

The *Leech* case dealt with the claims of two prisoners, Leech and Prevot. Leech applied for judicial review of the prison governor's refusal to change his prison record, despite having had his disciplinary award quashed by the Secretary of State. Prevot applied for judicial review of a governor's disciplinary award after unsuccessfully petitioning the Home Secretary. The Court of Appeal declined both applications on the ground that it had no jurisdiction to review governor's decisions after the *King* case. The case went on appeal to the House of Lords.

Counsel for the Home Office, Mr John Laws, used *King* to argue that courts should not directly interfere in the administration of prisons and implored the Court to adopt 'the pragmatic approach' in 'the judgment of Megaw LJ in *St Germain's* case'.[62] The case for the prisoners, presented by Stephen Sedley QC, was rooted in their right of access to the courts which had now been widely acknowledged by the case law with respect to decisions which had a bearing on the prisoner's personal liberty.[63] Sedley argued that, as a matter of logic and principle, supervisory jurisdiction should be extended to governor's disciplinary decisions and asked the Court not to 'allow pragmatism to become a ground for constricting jurisdiction'. He challenged the Court to reject the invitation 'not to take the single logical pace forward for fear of the steps which lie beyond it'.[64] In these arguments we see the battle between a prevailing culture of pragmatism and sovereignty and an insurgent culture of rights.

In marked contrast to the line taken in *King*, the House of Lords in *Leech* was highly receptive to the rights-based position. Lord Bridge rejected the arguments against the extension of court jurisdiction over governor's disciplinary decisions.[65] Crucially, he rejected the view that the extension of supervisory jurisdiction would have dire pragmatic consequences:

Mr. Laws held out the prospect, as one which should make our judicial blood run cold, that opening the door to judicial review of governors' awards would make it impossible to resist an invasion by what he called 'the tentacles of the law' of many other departments of prison administration. My Lords, I decline to express an

---

[61] The case was also a welcome departure from the courts previous position on conditions as evidenced in *Williams v Home Office (No. 2)* [1981] 1 All ER 1211 (which found 180 days' detention in a control unit to be neither cruel nor unusual punishment, nor a foundation for a claim for false imprisonment).

[62] *Leech v Deputy Governor of Parkhurst Prison* [1988] 1 AC 533, 543–5.

[63] At 539.   [64] At 547.   [65] At 561–4.

opinion on any of the illustrations advanced in support of this part of the argument. In a matter of jurisdiction it cannot be right to draw lines on a purely defensive basis and determine that the court has no jurisdiction over one matter which it ought properly to entertain for fear that acceptance of jurisdiction may set a precedent which will make it difficult to decline jurisdiction over other matters which it ought not to entertain. Historically, the development of the law in accordance with coherent and consistent principles has all too often been impeded, in diverse areas of the law besides that of judicial review, by the court's fear that unless an arbitrary boundary is drawn it will be inundated by a flood of unmeritorious claims.[66]

Moreover, Lord Bridge did not accept that supervisory jurisdiction should be limited because it might 'undermine the prison governor's authority and seriously aggravate the already difficult task of maintaining order and discipline in prisons'.[67] On the contrary, he argued in much the same way as the Woolf Report was later to argue,[68] that the absence of a sufficient remedy where a prisoner has a genuine grievance could just as easily damage order and discipline in prisons.[69] Lord Bridge acknowledged that his arguments were merely a more detailed exposition of the argument of Lord Shaw in *St Germain* and Lord Wilberforce in *Raymond v Honey* and finished by saying: 'I cannot help reflecting . . . that it would be a very remarkable state of affairs if he were denied access to the courts to challenge the proceedings of an inferior judicial authority empowered, in effect, to deprive him of liberty by extending the term of his imprisonment.'[70]

Lord Justice Oliver was in full agreement with Lord Justice Bridge, although perhaps more concerned initially to show his appreciation of the practical implications of affording prisoners' procedural rights: 'I am sensible of the inconvenience which may be occasioned in the administration of the prison system by over-frequent and possibly capricious applications for review by the court of decisions of prison governors.'[71] He nevertheless reasoned that, on the basis of *Ridge v Baldwin* and *O'Reilly v Mackman*,[72] any exercise of public power 'which affects the liberty and, to a degree, the status of the person affected by it' is 'subject to the general common law principle which imposes a duty of procedural fairness'.[73] He rejected the analogous arguments made in *King* to show the difference between the 'managerial' powers of the prison governor and the 'judicial' powers of the Board of Visitors, and argued that the governor's decision in disciplinary proceedings was one which is 'amenable to the courts' jurisdiction to review'. Moreover, he dismissed the notion that the prisoner's alternative remedy to petition the Secretary of State under section 4(2) of the Prison Act 1952 could oust the courts' jurisdiction, arguing that only a 'clear and unambiguous expression of the will of Parliament that the prima facie right

---

[66] At 566.   [67] At 566.   [68] See 5.2 and 5.3.   [69] At 568.
[70] At 568.   [71] At 574.
[72] *Ridge v Baldwin* [1964] AC 40; *O'Reilly v Mackman* [1983] 2 AC 237, 279.
[73] At 578.

to apply for judicial review should be removed' would be sufficient to dislodge the courts' inherent jurisdiction. Rather, the existence of alternative remedies should go to the exercise of the courts' discretion in granting a public law remedy rather than to the question of jurisdiction.[74] Finally, Lord Oliver rejected the assertion in *King* that the 'practical repercussions' of review by the courts would be 'frightening' and concluded:

I have, in the end of all, found myself unpersuaded not only that the position of a prison governor in relation to disciplinary adjudications can be logically distinguished from that of a Board of Visitors, but also that any sound or convincing reasons exist for holding that such adjudications should be treated so far as judicial review is concerned in any different way.[75]

There is little doubt that *Leech* was a landmark case. It significantly extended the courts' supervisory jurisdiction over prison life and marked a victory in the continuing tug-of-war between a culture of legal pragmatism and a culture of rights and principle. Nevertheless, the justification for judicial intervention remained rooted in the potential impact of disciplinary decisions on the prisoner's personal liberty. Although *Leech* was a step forward, in that it accepted jurisdiction over the governor's disciplinary powers, it did not go all the way to accepting that prisoners had rights worthy of judicial protection in the 'operational' or 'managerial' sphere. In short, there was still no full recognition of the German concept of prisoners' 'administrative rights'.

To sum up, the development of prisoners' rights during the late 1970s and 1980s was marked by the rights ambivalence present within legal and political culture in England generally. On the one hand, the courts grew more confident in their role as the guardians of the prisoner's constitutional rights and in founding their supervisory jurisdiction solely on this basis. They increasingly made recourse to European human rights jurisprudence in their development of prisoners' rights at common law. But alongside this insurgent rights discourse there was a concern that prison management remain firmly within the province of government and that courts retain a hands-off supervisory role. This was articulated in the alternative language of pragmatism and sovereignty. The conflict between prisoners' rights protection and the practical concern to protect administrative flexibility in prisons is not unusual nor is it absent from the German context. In contrast to Germany, however, no common language was used to reason out the balance between effective prison administration and rights protection. Rather the conflict manifested in a competition between two alternative discourses. English judges might adopt the language of rights when reasoning in support of the prisoner, but there was an equal negation of rights through the

---

[74] At 581.   [75] At 583.

discourse of pragmatism, sovereignty, and tradition. When *Hague* was decided in 1990 it was in a legal culture marked by these parallel discourses.

7.2 *HAGUE*: TURNING POINT OR DEAD END?

Hague is a central decision in prisoners' rights jurisprudence and remains authoritative today.[76] The case arose due to the following circumstances. Hague had been branded a 'trouble-maker' by the governor of Parkhurst Prison who had ordered his transfer to Wormwood Scrubs where he was held in segregation for 28 days. The governor had acted under Circular Instruction 10/1974 and Prison Rule 43, which permitted segregation for the purposes of good order and discipline. This was a common way of bypassing procedural safeguards attached to disciplinary procedures when dealing with 'subversive' prisoners. Hague argued that the procedure followed was unlawful and pursued a claim for judicial review, damages for false imprisonment and breach of statutory duty. Kenneth Weldon alleged that he had been beaten up by prison staff, dumped in a strip cell and left there naked overnight. He pursued a claim for assault and false imprisonment. Hague and Weldon's claims were considered separately until their appeals to the House of Lords were conjoined.

The decisions leading up to, and including, the House of Lords decision in *Hague* clarified three important questions, namely: the extent of the courts' supervisory jurisdiction over prison administration in public law, the legal status of the Prison Rules, and the rights which prisoners could claim in private law. The handling of these issues demonstrates important aspects of the English treatment of prisoners' rights and is worthy of separate consideration.

7.2.1 Supervisory Jurisdiction and Administrative Rights

In *Hague* the Divisional Court was asked to settle whether it had supervisory jurisdiction over the exercise of the prison governor's managerial or operational powers. The Court was being asked to break down the last jurisdictional barrier to judicial supervision over prison administration. It accepted that it had jurisdiction and that prisoners were not, as a rule, required to exhaust alternative remedies before turning to the court for assistance. It was argued that, although segregation was not strictly speaking a disciplinary sanction, in practice the prisoner experienced prolonged non-consensual segregation as a form of punishment. It therefore made no sense to restrict jurisdiction solely to measures formally classified as disciplinary.[77]

---

[76] *R v Deputy Governor of Parkhurst Prison, ex p Hague and Weldon* [1992] 1 AC 58.
[77] At 98.

The Court of Appeal was asked by Mr Laws, counsel for the respondents, to overturn the Divisional Court as to jurisdiction, or at least to restrict the level of scrutiny which might be applied by the courts to the exercise of the governor's managerial or operational powers. Taylor LJ accepted that the governor's non-disciplinary powers could be subject to review but, nevertheless, delivered a strong warning as to its use:

> The question whether any relief and what relief should be granted is a matter of discretion in each case. Consideration of public policy may well arise in relation to prison management which would not arise elsewhere. The need to maintain good order and discipline and the need to make speedy decisions often in an emergency are important considerations in the special context of prison management. I would therefore agree with Mr. Law's less bold proposition, that the court should approach the exercise of discretion with great caution. The well known proposition that managers should be left to manage applies a fortiori in regard to prisons save where a clear case is made out for relief *ex debito justitae*.[78]

Given this tentative proposition, Hague himself did not receive much in the way of relief. Although Taylor LJ accepted that Hague's transfer was unlawful on the technical ground that the governor at the receiving prison should have made the decisions relevant to the case, he held that Hague had not suffered any injustice.[79] Granting a declaration of illegality only, Taylor LJ denied that Hague had any right to be heard by the governor nor any right to reasons for the governor's decision.[80] He invoked 'reasons of public policy' to defeat the claims to both of these procedural rights, namely the necessity of making 'urgent' segregation decisions and the possibility of 'escalating trouble' if the prisoner had recourse to the reasons for his segregation.[81]

The Court of Appeal decision in *Hague* gave with one hand and took away with the other. While it extended supervisory jurisdiction to 'operational' and 'managerial' decisions, it argued that the discretion to grant relief in such circumstances was to be exercised with circumspection. Moreover, it was reluctant to impose exacting procedural standards to the decisions at hand.[82] All through the Court of Appeal decision in *Hague*, pragmatic concerns were used to defeat the potential rights of prisoners in the administrative sphere.

---

[78] At 116.   [79] At 114.

[80] At 109–14. Subsequent to this decision, however, the Prison Service changed its practice of giving reasons for segregation decisions in Circular Instruction 26/1990. It is also committed to giving reasons for decisions in the *Prison Service Framework Document* 1998 and Prison Service Order 2510. On this basis an argument for legitimate expectation of reasons may arise. See Livingstone *et al.* (n 4), 45.

[81] At 109–12.   [82] Richardson 1993 (n 6), 122.

7.2.2 Breach of Statutory Duty and the Prison Rules

In *Hague*, the House of Lords was asked to clarify whether a prisoner could claim for breach of statutory duty. The legal position, held consistently since *Arbon v Anderson* in 1943, was that the Prison Rules do not confer rights which can be vindicated through an action for breach of statutory duty.[83] The House was therefore being invited to overrule clearly established precedent on this question.

The possibility of a right to sue for breach of statutory duty was proposed by Sedley QC. He argued that a common law 'ground rule' applied that where a plaintiff belonged to a class of persons which the statutory provision was intended to protect, and no other statutory remedy was provided, he had a right to a remedy where a statutory breach had caused damage to him.[84] The question of legislative intent did *not* arise as there was no 'true remedy' expressly stipulated by Parliament for breach of the Prison Rules. On the already established fundamental principle that 'a convicted prisoner retains all civil rights which are not expressly or by necessary implication taken away' and on the assertion that there 'can and should be no special rule restricting the availability of relief in prison cases', Sedley invited the Court to overrule past precedent which had 'neither adequately considered nor correctly applied the established principles for determining whether an action for breach of statutory duty applied'.[85] Sedley rooted his argument in the right of the prisoner to an adequate remedy which he placed prior to any question of legislative intention in this regard. John Laws, acting on the respondent's behalf, started from the opposite constitutional premise. The only question to be considered, it was argued, was whether Parliament intended to confer under the Prison Act 1952 and the Prison Rules 1964 private rights to be vested in prisoners. The clear answer was that it did not, as section 47 of the Prison Act conferred no power on the Secretary of State to make rules which conferred such private rights on individuals.[86] Once again, in the competing arguments presented, we see a conflict between two visions of the English constitution.

The leading judicial arguments, presented by Lords Bridge and Jauncey, were imbued with respect for parliamentary intention. Both Lords agreed that:

... it must always be a matter for consideration whether the legislature intended that private law rights of action should be conferred upon individuals in respect of

---

[83] *Arbon v Anderson* [1943] 1 All ER 154, [1943] KB 252; *Becker v Home Office* [1972] 2 All ER 676, [1972] 2 QB 407.

[84] *R v Deputy Governor of Parkhurst Prison, Hague and Weldon* [1992] 1 AC 58, 149. Sedley relied on *Groves v Lord Wimborne* [1898] 2 QB 402; *Cutler v Wandsworth Stadium Ltd* [1949] 1 AC 398, 407; *Lonrho Ltd. v Shell Petroleum Co. Ltd (No. 2)* [1982] AC 173, 183; *London Passenger Transport Board v Upson* [1949] AC 155, 168.

[85] At 147–50.   [86] At 152.

breaches of the relevant statutory provision. The fact that a particular provision was intended to protect certain individuals is not of itself sufficient to confer private law rights of action upon them, something more is required to show that the legislature intended such conferment.[87]

Using this test, the House concluded:

The rules are wide ranging in their scope covering a mass of matters relevant to the administration and good government of a prison. Many of these do not directly relate to prisoners and I do not consider that those which do were ever intended to confer private law rights in the event of a breach. The rules are regulatory in character, they provide a framework within which the prison regime operates but they are not intended to protect prisoners against loss, injury and damage or to give them rights of action in respect thereof.[88]

The House of Lords decided *Hague* at a time when a number of the public law rights of prisoners were already recognized and established. Two judges deciding *Hague*, Lords Bridge and Ackner, had been highly instrumental in the development of these rights.[89] It could not be said that this was a court unsympathetic to the protection of prisoners' rights in principle. Moreover, *Hague* was in line with contemporary cases, dealing with non-prisoners, in looking to the intention of the legislature in order to establish the liability of public bodies to private law actions, or in its preference for public law remedies when dealing with the exercise of public discretion.[90] It could not be argued that the House of Lords treated prisoners in a patently different manner to non-prisoners on the question of breach of statutory duty. Notwithstanding, *Hague* is cited as evidence that English judges have not given any 'any real endorsement to a notion of prisoners having any rights which they might assert against the authorities, or rights which might shape or constrain the exercise of official power'.[91]

Whatever view we might have of the merits of this decision, its reasoning illustrates a deeper aspect of English constitutional culture. The House had two competing constitutional rationales to choose from. It could either follow a rights-based argument or it could defer to its interpretation of legislative intention. The court, clearly uncomfortable with the pragmatic implications of a decision in Hague's favour, opted for an orthodox line on the question. Instead of adopting as its starting premise the prisoner's right to an adequate remedy, the Court started from the alternative premise of parliamentary sovereignty. *Hague* thus symbolized a legal culture vacillating between opposing constitutional premises.

---

[87] At 170.   [88] At 172.
[89] *Leech v Deputy Governor of Parkhurst Prison* [1988] 1 AC 533; *Raymond v Honey* (1983) AC 1 (HL).
[90] Craig (n 8), 847–849.
[91] Livingstone *et al.* (n 4), 553. R. Morgan, 'Imprisonment: Current Concerns' in M. Maguire, R. Morgan and R. Reiner (eds), *Oxford Handbook of Criminology* (2nd edn, Clarendon Press, Oxford, 1997) 1138, 1164.

7.2.3 False Imprisonment and the Prisoner's Legal Status

The argument surrounding Hague and Weldon's case for false imprison-ment illustrates the malleability of the English conception of prisoners' rights, which is without any conceptual distinction between status and administrative decisions or any clear notion of positive administrative rights vested in prisoners.[92]

The argument was raised that a prisoner who was otherwise lawfully in prison could sue for false imprisonment in respect of a particular confine-ment which was unlawful. There were two arguments, based on nineteenth-century common law authority,[93] as to the possible unlawfulness of the confinement: a) that a prisoner unlawfully confined was capable of being falsely imprisoned; and b) that imprisonment could be rendered unlawful by reason of the conditions of detention. The House of Lords rejected both arguments. It argued that the tort of false imprisonment had two compo-nents, namely the fact of imprisonment and the absence of lawful authority to justify it. It then stated that section 12 of the Prison Act 1952 provided the governor and officers with lawful authority to restrain a prisoner within the defined bounds of any prison.[94] The reasoning flowing from this premise is deserving of closer attention.

On the question of Hague's case Lord Bridge asked:

Can the prisoner . . . complain that his legal rights are infringed by a restraint which confines him at any particular time within a particular part of the prison? It seems to me that the reality of prison life demands a negative answer to this question . . . the concept of the prisoner's 'residual liberty' as a species of freedom of movement within the prison enjoyed as a legal right which the prison authorities cannot law-fully restrain seems to me quite illusory. The prisoner is at all times lawfully restrained within closely defined bounds and if he is kept in a segregated cell, at a time when, if the rules had not been misapplied, he would be in the company of other prisoners in the workshop, at the dinner table or elsewhere, this is not the depriva-tion of his liberty of movement, which is the essence of the tort of false imprison-ment, it is the substitution of one form of restraint for another.[95]

On considering the arguments of the appellants, Lord Bridge went on to say:

Mr Harris (submits) that whenever there is a breach of the rules which is sufficiently 'fundamental' this converts an otherwise lawful imprisonment to an unlawful imprisonment. This, as I understand it, is quite a different concept from that of an infringement of residual liberty. The submission is that any breach of the rules which is sufficiently far reaching in its effects on the prisoner, for example the failure to supply him with clothing 'adequate for warmth and health' pursuant to r. 20(2),

---

[92] See 6.2.
[93] *Osborne v Angle* (1835) 2 Scott 500; *Yorke v Champman* (1839) 10 Ad 38, E 210; *Cobbet v Grey* (1850) 4 Exch 729; *Osborne v Milman* (1887) 18 QBD 471.
[94] *R v Deputy Governor of Parkhurst Prison, ex p Hague and Weldon* [1992] 1 AC 58, 162.
[95] At 162.

undermines the legality of his imprisonment. Logically this would lead to the conclusion that the prisoner who has not been supplied with proper clothing would be entitled to walk out of the prison, but Mr Harris understandably disclaims any such extravagant proposition. It follows that the authority given by s. 12(1) for lawful confinement of the prisoner cannot possibly be read as subject to any implied term with respect to compliance with the Prison Rules and this is fatal to any submission which seeks to make the lawfulness of the imprisonment depend in any sense on such compliance.[96]

Lord Bridge's proposition was supported by Lord Jauncey. He acknowledged that the *dictum* in *Raymond v Honey* meant that prisoners retain all civil rights not expressly or implicitly taken away. However, 'these observations . . . are highly relevant to the protection of such rights as a prisoner retains but they do not assist in determining what those rights are'.[97] On this basis he argued:

A prisoner is lawfully committed to a prison and while there is subject to the Prison Act 1952 and the Prison Rules 1964. His whole life is regulated by the regime. He has no freedom to do what he wants, when he wants. His liberty to do anything is governed by the prison regime. Placing Weldon in a strip cell and segregating Hague altered the conditions under which they were detained but did not deprive them of any liberty which they had not already lost when initially confined.[98]

Thus Lord Jauncey concluded that the prisoner cannot be deprived of liberty whilst in prison 'because he has none already'.[99]

The conclusions of Lords Bridge and Jauncey on the question of false imprisonment were arrived at on the basis of an indivisible view of the prisoner's liberty. This was a consequence of framing the question of residual liberty within the legal definition of false imprisonment. The proposition that the lawfulness of the detention could be called into question by the conditions of confinement or by breach of the Prison Rules was rejected on the basis that, once authority had been given to imprison a prisoner, the lawfulness of that authority could never be brought into question. Viewed from the perspective of the lawfulness of the restriction of the prisoner's personal liberty, this argument is unproblematic.

But were we to view this case from the German perspective of the prisoner's administrative rights, the reasoning becomes more problematic. It follows, as a matter of logic, from the *Raymond v Honey* principle that if the conception of residual liberty in prisons is to mean anything at all, it must, by definition, not be vitiated by the lawfulness of the prisoner's imprisonment. The argument cuts both ways, for on this divisible conception of the prisoner's liberty the lawfulness of detention cannot be called into question each time a prisoner wishes to challenge an administrative decision in the process of his imprisonment. It would indeed be an 'extravagant proposition' to call into question the lawfulness of the prisoner's detention if he

---

[96] At 163. [97] At 174. [98] At 176. [99] At 177.

was not supplied with adequate clothing. But, German commentators would argue that the prison officer's treatment of Hague and Weldon in changing the conditions of their detention did deprive them of further liberty than they had already lost when being placed in prison. They would question Lord Jauncey's assertions that the prisoner's 'whole life is regulated by the regime', that 'he has no freedom to do what he wants, when he wants' and that the prisoner has no liberty of which he could be deprived. They would question this, because it amounts to an almost total negation of the prisoner's liberty in the administrative sphere. Equally they would dismiss Lord Bridge's view of solitary confinement as the 'substitution of one form of restraint for another' but rather argue that measures such as solitary confinement be justified in each case as a necessary restriction of the prisoner's liberty in this sphere.

Hague also demonstrates a lack of clarity about what residual liberty really means within a prison's administrative framework. This was raised by Lord Jauncey when he noted that the proposition of residual liberty leaves us little guidance as to how to determine what prisoners' rights are. There is no legally defined benchmark presented in this case for determining what limitations of rights the prison administration may impose. Moreover, no principle has been recognized by the Court upon which to found positive administrative rights vested in prisoners which could compensate for the loss of personal liberty or act as a counter to the inherent limitations of imprisonment. In short, when read with German eyes, this aspect of the House of Lords decision in *Hague* is conspicuous for its indivisible view of the prisoners' liberty, it's negation of prisoners' administrative rights, and for the absence of any conceptual relationship between rights protections and the purpose of imprisonment.

7.2.4 *Hague* and Prison Conditions

Although the House of Lords eliminated the possibility of a prisoner suing for false imprisonment or breach of statutory duty, they did aver that certain alternative remedies might be available with regard to 'intolerable conditions'. The Court took the view that conditions 'seriously prejudicial to health' could be challenged in public law or, where a prisoner's health was materially affected by the conditions of his confinement, he could sue in negligence or seek a public law remedy.[100] The benchmark set in this instance was high. Nothing short of 'physical injury or an impairment of health' would suffice to qualify a prisoner for a claim in damages.[101]

Whilst this aspect of *Hague* displayed judicial concern with treatment inside prisons, it also reflected judicial reticence. The Court was only inter-

---

[100] R v Deputy Governor of Parkhurst Prison, ex p Hague and Weldon [1992] 1 AC 58, 166 and 177.
[101] At 166.

ested in protecting against extreme physical injury or damage to health. The decision did not advance the already well-established principle that prison authorities owe a duty of care with respect to the prisoner's health and physical well-being.[102] It certainly did not go as far as *Herbage*, which accepted a general jurisdiction to monitor 'cruel or unusual' treatment irrespective of the injury incurred. *Hague* added little to the judicial record of protection of prisoner treatment and conditions.

7.3 Prisoners' Rights in the 1990s: A Case of Snakes and Ladders?

Judicial protection of prisoners' administrative rights after the establishment of full supervisory jurisdiction in *Hague* was mixed. After *Brind*,[103] reference to Convention rights in prison cases became more common. But whilst reference to these rights occurred, the reasoning employed in their application or in the resultant development of common law rights and principles in prisons was diverse. Whilst quicker to intervene where a prisoner's access to the courts might be jeopardized (*Leech No. 2*, *Simms*), courts were slow to recognize protections flowing from other Convention rights (*O'Dhuibhir*). Moreover, the legal test applying to limitations of the prisoners' access to justice was challenged in the Court of Appeal in *Simms*. With respect to the development of prisoners' rights in the administrative sphere, judicial scrutiny was far from exacting and the tentative tone demonstrated in *Hague* was manifest. Courts were disinclined to check the substance of prison governors' or Home Secretaries' powers where these related to internal prison administration (*Hargreaves*, *Hepworth*, *Mehmet*). Rather the judiciary were more likely to intervene where the Home Secretary's decision affected the sentence duration, thereby threatening the personal liberty of the prisoner (*Duggan*). This general reticence was starkly counterpoised by judicial activism in the 1990s with respect to the early release of life sentenced prisoners (*Doody*, *Pierson*, *Thompson and Venables*).[104] In short,

---

[102] *Ellis v Home Office* [1953] 2 QB 135.

[103] *Brind v Secretary of State for the Home Department* [1991] 1 All ER 720, HL accepted that the ECHR had an impact on domestic law through the presumption in the interpretation of statutes that Parliament did not intend to legislate against it and that the courts could pay attention to it in the development of the common law. See also 6.1.2.

[104] *R v Home Secretary, ex p Doody* [1993] 1 All ER 151; *R v Secretary of State for the Home Department, ex p Pierson* [1997] 3 All ER 577; *R v Secretary of State for the Home Department, ex p Thompson and Venables* [1997] 3 All ER 577. These decisions combined to place strict procedural obligations on the Home Secretary in tariff setting and extended court control over the substantive exercise of the Home Secretary's discretion in this regard. The domestic movement here was inspired by the ECtHR decisions in *Weeks v UK* (1988) 10 EHRR 293; *Thynne, Wilson and Gunnell* (1991) 13 EHRR 666; and later in *Hussain v UK* (1996) 22 EHRR 1.

we see a pattern of judicial bifurcation between the protection of prisoners' personal liberty and the forestalling of administrative rights.

The judicial concern to avoid interfering with prison policy, and the absence of any clear purpose of prison administration, was evident in *Hargreaves*.[105] Here the Court of Appeal denied that a prisoner had a substantive legitimate expectation where the Home Secretary had changed his policy on eligibility for home leave.[106] The applicants, convicted in 1994, were serving sentences of between six and eight years and had been told in a notice that they could apply for the home leave privilege after serving one-third of their sentences. They had also signed a 'compact' with the prison authorities under which consideration for home leave was promised in return for their good behaviour. In 1995 the Home Secretary, Michael Howard, changed the home leave system so that prisoners would only become eligible to apply after serving one-half of their sentences. The Home Secretary, responding to a number of prisoners who had absconded or committed further crimes while on leave, and to the escapes at Whitemoor and Parkhurst prisons more generally,[107] claimed to be improving public confidence in the administration of justice as well as public safety. The prisoners, who now had to wait for a much longer period of time before they could apply for home leave, argued that their legitimate expectation had been violated by the Home Secretary's change in policy. Relying on *Hamble Fisheries*, the prisoners argued that they had a substantive legitimate expectation which could hamper the policy-making power of government, suggesting that judges should balance the interests of the individual against the 'constitutional importance of ministerial freedom to formulate and reformulate policy'.[108]

The Court of Appeal maintained that the ambiguity in the wording of the notice and compact meant that no legitimate expectation arose. It also rejected the possibility of using the action of legitimate expectation to restrict the Home Secretary's policy-making power. The most a prisoner could legitimately expect was that 'his case would be examined individually in the light of whatever policy the Secretary of State saw fit lawfully to adopt'.[109] Hirst LJ emphasized that courts were not 'as close, or as sensitive, to public opinion as a minister responsible to Parliament and the electorate [who] has to . . . determine the policies needed to maintain public confidence in the criminal justice system'.[110] He argued that the relevant test was

[105] *R v Secretary of State, ex p Hargreaves* [1997] 1 All ER 397.

[106] Contrast with statutory and constitutional protection of rights to home leave in Germany. See 4.2.1.1, 4.3.2, and 4.4.1.

[107] See 5.3.

[108] *R v Ministry for Agriculture, Fisheries and Food, ex p Hamble (Offshore) Fisheries Ltd* [1995] 2 All ER 714. See Craig (n 8), 611–28.

[109] At 398.

[110] At 412. Contrast *Hargreaves* with the German approach to legitimate expectations in prisons; see 4.4.4.4.

whether the policy was irrational in the *Wednesbury* sense, branding as constitutional 'heresy' the notion that courts should undertake a balancing exercise between the minister's policy-making freedom and the legitimate interests of individuals.[111] Applying the *Wednesbury* standard, the Court found that the decision had been properly considered and that the Home Secretary could 'not be faulted' in consideration of the factors of 'public safety and restoration of public confidence in the administration of justice'.[112]

The hands-off approach in *Hargreaves* was replicated with respect to the prison governor's operational discretion in *Hepworth*.[113] This case dealt with whether a governor's power could be reviewed under Prison Rule 4(4) which requires governors to indicate at each prison what system of privileges is in operation and includes procedures for determining when a prisoner is entitled to a higher level of privileges, when a privilege previously granted may be removed, as well as a duty on the governor to give reasons why a privilege has been removed. Laws LJ, in the Divisional Court, took a very restrictive view of the possibilities for review:

. . . I have some misgivings in principle as regards the privilege cases. They are attempts to review executive decisions arising wholly within the context of internal prison management, having no direct or immediate consequences for such matters as the prisoner's release. While this court's jurisdiction to review such decisions cannot be doubted, I consider that it would take an exceptionally strong case to justify its being done. There are plain dangers and disadvantages in the courts maintaining an intrusive supervision over the internal administrative arrangements by which the prisons are run, including any schemes to provide incentives for good behaviour, of which the system in question here is in my judgment plainly an example. I think that something in the nature of bad faith or what I may call crude irrationality would have to be shown, which is not suggested here. I accept that the qualitative difference (from the prisoner's point of view) between the privileges scheme and, for example, the system of re-categorisation may be said to be a difference of degree; but the difference is very considerable. Re-categorisation touches much more closely the prisoner's aspiration to liberty.

In stressing the link between judicial intervention and the protection of personal liberty, Laws LJ undermined the protection of administrative rights in prisons.

This link between personal liberty and judicial intervention was evident in *Duggan*, where the Divisional Court took the view that there was 'no material practicable difference' between the decision to categorize a prisoner

---

[111] At 412.

[112] At 414. The law on legitimate expectations has since shifted outside the prison context in *R v North and East Devon Health Authority, ex p Coughlan* [2001] QB 213.

[113] *R v Secretary of State for the Home Department, ex p Hepworth* QBD (unreported) 25 March 1997 (Lexis transcript, Smith Bernal). For two further unsuccessful challenges of the prison privilege systems see *R (Bowen) v Home Secretary* CA (unreported) 26 January 1998 (Lexis transcript, Smith Bernal); *R (Bowen) v Featherstone Prison* [1999] CLY 4106.

as category A (high security) and the decision to release on parole, in that the former decision had a significant impact on the latter.[114] As a result it held that fairness required that the gist of the reports, on which categorization decisions were made, should be revealed to the prisoner and that reasons for the decision should subsequently be given.[115] A later attempt to use *Duggan* to support a claim to procedural fairness in allocating prisoners to closed supervision centres (CSCs) failed, however. The Court, in *Mehmet*, was unconvinced that 'the mere fact of allocation' to CSCs would 'adversely impact on the prospects of parole' and thus rejected the application.[116] The reasoning in this case reinforced Laws LJ's argument in *Hepworth*, that common law protection would normally be linked to clear infringements of the prisoner's personal liberty.

Alongside the protection of the prisoner's personal liberty, courts were concerned to protect the prisoner's rights of access to justice. But even with respect to this well-established right, the courts are not always rigorous. In *Wynne*, a prisoner applied for judicial review of the Home Secretary's requirement that he bear the cost of his own production to court.[117] As the prisoner had refused to fill out the relevant application form for transportation at his own cost, the House of Lords held that there was no decision to be reviewed. But the Court did indicate how it might require the Home Secretary to exercise his discretion on such matters. Lord Goff argued that the tension between the prisoner's right of access to the courts and the countervailing public interest in the prisoner's secure containment should be resolved by 'practical means' on a case-by-case basis. He highlighted the pragmatic undercurrents of Convention jurisprudence. He argued that the admissions in *Golder* that 'the right of access to the courts was not absolute', and 'that it is not the function of the court to elaborate a general theory of limitations to the right admissible in the case of convicted prisoners', provided 'support for the view that a search for practical solutions may be desirable'.[118] In his cursory examination of this issue,[119] Lord Goff made no mention of the extent of the possible protections of the prisoner's Convention rights in this context, nor did he indicate which considerations or standards might be taken into account when resolving this tension.

---

[114] *R v Secretary of State, ex p Duggan* [1994] 3 All ER 277.

[115] Fairness does not extend to providing the prisoner with full reports. In *McAvoy*, the CA reaffirmed that fairness requirements had to be balanced against the 'proper running of the prison' and would be fulfilled by providing the gist of the reports in question. *R v Secretary of State, ex p McAvoy* [1997] 1 WLR 790.

[116] *R v Home Secretary, ex p Mehmet* (1999) 11 Admin LR 529. Despite this outcome, the decision was clearly critical of the procedures regarding CSCs and noted the Prison Service's own decision to afford a right to representation in their Operating Standards.

[117] *Wynne v Secretary of State for the Home Department* [1993] 1 All ER 574.

[118] At 581.

[119] The consideration of the European Convention took nine lines at 581.

This pragmatic approach to human rights interpretation was starkly contrasted in *Leech (No. 2)*.[120] This case dealt with Prison Rule 33(3) which authorized prison governors to censor and stop legal correspondence where future actions were being contemplated. The Court of Appeal, led by Lord Justice Steyn, recognized that the actions under this rule restricted a number of the prisoner's common law rights, namely: the citizen's right to confidentiality of letters, the right to confidentiality of communications between solicitors and their clients, the right of unimpeded access to a court, and, to this end, the right of unimpeded access to a solicitor for the purpose of receiving advice and assistance. The Court accepted that under section 47(1) of the Prison Act 1952 the Home Secretary was authorized to make 'rules for the regulation of prisons' which, by 'necessary implication', allowed 'some interference' with these rights.[121] Nevertheless, the Court insisted that 'it will be a rare case in which it could be held that such a fundamental right was by necessary implication abolished or limited by statute' and 'an even rarer case in which it could be held that a statute authorised by necessary implication the abolition or limitation of so fundamental a right by subordinate legislation'. Instead, Steyn LJ argued that 'an objective need' must be 'demonstrated' that such interferences could be shown to be 'in the interests of the regulation of prisons'. He stated that 'the question is whether there is a self-evident and pressing need for an unrestricted power to read letters between a prisoner and a solicitor and a power to stop such letters'.[122] The court did not accept that the Home Secretary had demonstrated an objective need for 'an unrestricted power to read and examine letters and for a qualified power to stop letters on the grounds of objectionability'.[123] Thus, the Court concluded that Rule 33(3) was *ultra vires* in so far as it applied to correspondence between prisoners and their legal advisers. Whilst it recognized that section 47(1) of the Prison Act 1952 by 'necessary implication' authorized some screening of correspondence passing between a prisoner and a solicitor, it stipulated that 'the authorised intrusion must, however, be the minimum necessary to ensure that the correspondence is in truth bona fide legal correspondence'.[124]

Leech (No. 2) represented a breakthrough in prisoners' rights reasoning in England and human rights reasoning more generally. The 'minimum interference' test had potential to increase judicial scrutiny by providing a standard against which to evaluate whether administrative measures are acceptable limitations of negative rights:

... the Court was not standing back and asking the traditional question 'could a decision-maker acting reasonably have reached this decision?' Rather it was placing the burden on the executive to persuade it, as a matter of evidence as much as legal

---

[120] *R v Home Secretary, ex p Leech (No. 2)* [1994] QB 198, 217.
[121] At 209.   [122] At 212.   [123] At 213.   [124] At 217.

principle, that in an area not expressly authorised by Parliament a fundamental right is to be curtailed or burdened in its exercise via a process of necessary implication.[125]

This was clearly an advance on previous English reasoning on prisoners' rights in the administrative sphere. But the decision was not without its limits. As discussed in Chapter 6, it did not give us a broader purposive framework within which to evaluate the limitation of rights in prisons.[126] Perhaps for this reason, courts, when confronted with the claims of other categories of prisoners or the vindication of other civil and political rights, are not consistent in their application of the *Leech* test or with the standard and rigour with which it was initially applied. When put to the test, where prison security or public protection is at stake, courts are tempted to retreat from the *Leech* approach.[127] This was evident in the Court of Appeal decisions of *O'Dhuibhir* and *Simms and O'Brien*.

O'Dhuibhir concerned two prisoners who had been categorized as exceptional risk category A and were required to have glass screens placed between them and all their visitors (including close family and lawyers).[128] The prisoners argued that closed visits interfered with the free flow of communication between prisoner and lawyer and violated the principles which had been established in *Raymond v Honey*, *Anderson* and *Leech (No. 2)*. Moreover, it was argued that 'prisoners retained the residual right to a degree of physical contact with their immediate families and that to deny such contact, potentially for years on end, was calculated to result in family break up and to increase the risk of mental illness in prisoners'.[129] Instead, it was argued that the requisite level of security could be achieved by less intrusive methods such as screening and searching or by the application of the closed visit policy on a case-by-case basis.[130]

In the Court of Appeal, Kennedy LJ argued that glass screens do not impede the free flow of communication between solicitors and clients.[131] Moreover, he denied that there is a fundamental right of physical contact between prisoner and family under Article 8 ECHR (right to family life). Citing *X v UK* as evidence that risks to security could justify limitations of this right and be shown to be 'necessary in a democratic society', he averred that 'it would be an impossible position if judges, not prison service officials, become the ultimate arbiters of what security demands'. As a result, Kennedy LJ distinguished *Leech (No. 2)*, arguing that 'it was doubtful whether the *Leech* test of "self-evident and pressing need" could be applied

---

[125] T. Owen, 'Prisoners and Fundamental Rights' (1997) *JR* 81, 83.   [126] See 6.2.

[127] See J. Schone, 'The Short Life and Painful Death of Prisoners' Rights' (2001) 40 *Howard Journal* 70.

[128] *R v Home Secretary, ex p O'Dhuibhir* [1997] COD 315, 316. Contrast approach of the German FCC on glass screens, see 4.4.4.5.

[129] Owen (n 125), 84.   [130] Owen (n 125), 84.

[131] *R v Home Secretary, ex p O'Dhuibhir* [1997] COD 315, 317.

in the instant case'.[132] Instead the question turned on whether the direction could be shown to be *Wednesbury* unreasonable.

In *Simms and O'Brien* two questions arose. First, whether a blanket prohibition on journalists using material gleaned from prisoners which was justified in the interests of security, discipline, and control was lawful. Secondly, whether arrangements for cell searching that allowed the examination of the prisoner's legal correspondence in the prisoner's absence constituted an obstruction of the right to privileged legal correspondence. With respect to the first question, the Home Secretary used *O'Dhuibhir* to argue that the decision turned on whether the policy was reasonable on 'conventional' *Wednesbury* grounds.[133] The prisoners argued that the question turned on the prisoner's right to freedom of expression under both common law and Article 10 ECHR and on whether the policy passed the 'minimum interference' test.[134] Kennedy LJ did not wish to 'dwell' on either domestic or European authorities on the prisoner's behalf and negated the application of the 'minimum interference test'.[135] He held that the prisoner 'had no right to communicate orally with a journalist' as 'the loss of that right . . . is part and parcel of the sentence of imprisonment'.[136] In a short justification of one paragraph and in a tone reminiscent of the discussion on false imprisonment in the House of Lords in *Hague*,[137] Kennedy LJ employed an indivisible conception of the prisoner's liberty:

. . . the loss of such a 'right', if it can properly be so described, is part and parcel of the sentence of imprisonment. He [the prisoner] can no longer go where he wishes. He is confined. He can no longer speak to those outside prison or receive visits from anyone other than his lawyer and his relatives and friends . . . I entirely accept that, in the language of article 10, the freedom 'to receive and impart information and ideas without interference by public authority' is curtailed by imprisonment but that is what imprisonment is all about, and that too is recognised by the European Convention.[138]

At no point did Kennedy LJ indicate how limitations of a prisoner's Convention rights might be measured in such circumstances. He declined to comment on whether the 'minimum interference test' or the *Wednesbury* test should apply. He simply rejected, at the outset, the existence of the right to communicate orally with a journalist by recourse to a vague notion of imprisonment.

With respect to the second question in *Simms*, which dealt directly with legal correspondence, Kennedy LJ accepted that the *Leech* test at least applied. He acknowledged that legal professional privilege attached to legal correspondence in a prisoner's cell and thus that the policy of searching

---

[132] At 317.   [133] *R v Secretary of State, ex p Simms* [1998] 2 All ER 491, 499–500.
[134] At 500–1.   [135] At 501.   [136] At 501.
[137] See 7.2.3. above.
[138] *R v Secretary of State, ex p Simms* [1998] 2 All ER 491, 501.

letters without the prisoner present was an 'impairment of the privilege'. But, in the light of the recent escapes from Whitemoor and Parkhurst prisons, he was convinced that there was a 'self evident and pressing need' for such a policy and that the activities taken thereunder constituted 'no more than the minimum interference with the prisoner's rights which are necessary to ensure that security is maintained'.[139]

Kennedy LJ's limitation of the *Leech* test to the right of access to the court and legal advice was confirmed by Lord Justice Judge, who argued that the *Leech* test 'cannot be used by straightforward analogy to evaluate the rights of the prisoner to communicate with those who are not his legal advisers'.[140] Consequently, this aspect of the judgment suggested that the test for establishing how limitations of fundamental rights in prisons should occur would differ depending on the right in question and the weight accorded to it by the judiciary.

Further, aspects of Judge LJ's reasoning are of particular importance. Whilst setting out the *Raymond v Honey dictum* at the outset of his argument, Judge LJ went on to subtly reformulate the test in terms less rigorous than those of *Leech*. He averred that restrictions of rights were the 'automatic' and 'inevitable' consequence of incarceration and that 'it was not the Secretary of State, nor the operation of powers granted by s 47 of the 1952 Act which deprives prisoners of their rights to liberty and freedom of movement and association' but 'a consequence of the order of a court'.[141] On this basis, Judge LJ argued that when evaluating limitations of prisoners' rights, 'the starting point is to assume that a civil right is preserved unless it has been expressly removed or its loss is *an inevitable consequence of lawful detention in custody*'.[142] He was thus anxious to stress that rights may be limited under European Convention jurisprudence by the 'ordinary and reasonable requirements of imprisonment',[143] and that both European and domestic precedent had either upheld or acknowledged the 'inevitable restrictions on ordinary rights which follow incarceration'.[144] Moreover, in rejecting the right of a prisoner to communicate orally with a journalist, he stated that: 'the starting point is simple. Communications by prisoners . . . are seriously curtailed . . . these are most serious deprivations consequent on the order of imprisonment'.[145]

Thus, only a few months after Labour announced its intention to incorporate the ECHR into domestic law, the Court of Appeal sought to limit its potential impact on prisoners. First, it confined the *Leech* test to the prisoner's right of access to justice and questioned its general application to further Convention rights. Secondly, it developed an alternative 'inevitable consequence' test, reminiscent of the 'inherent limitations of imprisonment' doctrine overturned in *Golder*.[146] This subtle reformulation was a step back

---

[139] At 505.   [140] At 507.   [141] At 506.   [142] At 506. Emphasis added.
[143] At 508.   [144] At 509.   [145] At 509.   [146] See 6.2.

from the stringency of the 'minimum interference test' in *Leech (No. 2)*. Moreover, it conflated restrictions of rights pursuant to the 'court's order of imprisonment' with those which flow as a result of the daily exercise of state power in the administration of the prison. Just as England was embarking on one of its most fundamental shifts towards a culture of rights, the Court of Appeal was seeking to minimize the protections of Convention rights in prisons.

The House of Lords in *Simms and O'Brien* did not entirely remedy the problems raised by the Court of Appeal.[147] The appeal in *Simms* dealt with the single question of whether a blanket prohibition on journalists using material gleaned from prisoners, in the interests of security, discipline, and control, was lawful. On many levels the decision was a leading example of human rights jurisprudence. Lord Steyn, who first formulated the *Leech* test in 1994, argued that limitations of the right to freedom of expression in general should be shown to be 'necessary in a democratic society' and that 'necessary' requires the existence of a pressing social need, and that the restrictions should be no more than is proportionate to the legitimate aim pursued'.[148] In addition, he asserted that any general words in the Prison Rules which might be used to justify a blanket policy would be subject to the principle of legality.[149] The principle of legality was further elucidated by Lord Hoffman who stated that 'in the absence of express language or necessary implication to the contrary, the courts therefore presume that even the most general words were intended to be subject to the basic rights of the individual'.[150] Applying these principles in his evaluation of the limitations of the prisoner's right to free speech, Lord Steyn concluded that blanket prohibition on communications between prisoners and journalists was not lawful.[151]

But the judgment is not without its problems. Lord Steyn's central justificatory link was between the prisoner's right to free speech and the protection of the prisoner's personal liberty and access to justice. He laid much weight on the fact that the prisoners were seeking in their communications with the journalist 'to have the safety of their convictions further investigated and to put forward a case in the media for the reconsideration of their convictions'.[152] These interviews were central to the avoidance of a possible miscarriage of justice. Lord Steyn conceded that the prisoner's right to free speech was 'outweighed by the deprivation of liberty by the sentence of a court, and the need for discipline and control in prisons'.[153] He did not, therefore, think that a prisoner could 'claim to join a debate on the economy

---

[147] *R v Secretary of State for the Home Department, ex p Simms and another* [2000] AC 115.

[148] At 122.   [149] At 127.   [150] At 128.   [151] At 127.

[152] At 117. See also Lord Steyn 'Human Rights: The Legacy of Mrs Roosevelt' (2002) *PL* 473, 474.

[153] At 124.

or on political issues by way of interviews with journalists'.[154] But he maintained that the free speech in question in the *Simms* case was 'qualitatively of a very different order', namely that 'the prisoners are in prison because they are presumed to have been properly convicted. They wish to challenge the safety of their convictions. In principle it is not easy to conceive of a more important function which free speech might fulfil'.[155] As a consequence, Lord Steyn narrowly formulated the prisoner's right to free speech as 'the right of a prisoner to seek through oral interviews to persuade a journalist to investigate the safety of the prisoner's conviction and to publicise his findings in an effort to gain access to justice for the prisoner'.[156]

Moreover, Lord Steyn confirmed, in conjunction with the *Raymond v Honey dicta*, Judge LJ's statement that 'the starting point is to assume that a civil right is preserved unless it has been expressly removed or its loss is an inevitable consequence of lawful detention in custody'.[157] It was only later in his judgment when explicating the general limitations permissible of the right to freedom of speech under the Convention that he referred to the proportionality test of 'necessary in a democratic society'. Whilst this might simply have been an oversight, there is a strong difference, in terms of the protection of prisoners' administrative rights, between viewing rights limitations as 'the inevitable consequence of lawful detention in custody' and viewing all rights limitations in prison in terms of the 'minimum interference test'. Lord Steyn was not clear on this point. In short, from the perspective of the prisoner's administrative rights, the damage done to the 'minimum interference' principle in the Court of Appeal in *Simms* had not been entirely remedied by Lord Steyn in the House of Lords.

7.4 THE HUMAN RIGHTS ACT AND PRISONERS' RIGHTS

Given the extent to which prisoners have relied on Convention rights in England over the last two decades, it should come as no surprise that the Human Rights Act (HRA) 1998 has not marked a watershed in the jurisprudence on prisoners' rights. The primary victories for prisoners since the Act came into force remain, with some notable exceptions,[158] in familiar judicial territory. Prisoners have successfully used Convention rights to challenge the Home Secretary's tariff-fixing powers for mandatory lifers (*Anderson*);[159] expedite Parole Board hearings on the completion of the

---

[154] At 124.   [155] At 124.   [156] At 126.   [157] At 118.

[158] *R (P and Q) v Secretary of State for the Home Department* [2001] 1 WLR 2002; *R (Howard League for Penal Reform) v Secretary of State for the Home Department (No. 2)* [2002] EWHC 2497; *R (Hirst) v Secretary of State for the Home Department* [2002] 1 WLR 2929; *R (Amin) v Secretary of State for the Home Department* [2003] UKHL 51.

[159] *R (Anderson) v Secretary of State for the Home Department* [2002] 4 All ER 1089. Invoking Art. 6 ECHR (right to fair trial).

tariff period of life sentences (*Noorkoiv*);[160] challenge procedures concerning the release of lifers reviewed by Mental Health Review Tribunals (*D*);[161] ameliorate the interpretation of section 2 of the Crime (Sentences) Act 1997 and avoid grossly disproportionate automatic life sentences being imposed on offenders (*Offen*);[162] secure risk assessments for placement on witness protection programmes where a risk to life can be shown (*DF*);[163] and protect the confidentiality of their legal correspondence (*Daly*).[164] A number of the victories with respect to life sentenced prisoners and the protection of the right to life can be linked to recent breakthroughs in the ECtHR.[165] But, as argued above, the domestic judiciary has always been more likely to protect prisoners' rights where personal liberty is at stake. Likewise, the cases extending prisoners' right of access to justice and confidentiality of legal correspondence are no less consistent with judicial attitudes prior to the introduction of the HRA 1998.

It is instructive to contrast these cases with those where prisoners have failed to improve their position through recourse to the Convention. Gavin Mellor, a life-sentenced prisoner, failed to obtain judicial support in his attempt to have a child with his wife by artificial insemination.[166] Pearson and Martinez were defeated in their attempts to secure the right to vote whilst in prison.[167] Neville Waite, who had been recalled to prison from release on life-licence following a drugs charge, failed to secure housing benefit allowance available to remand prisoners.[168] Ponting, a dyslexic prisoner

---

[160] *Noorkoiv v Secretary of State for the Home Department* [2002] 4 All ER 515. Invoking Art. 5(4) ECHR (right to proceedings to test lawfulness of deprivation of liberty).

[161] *D v Secretary of State for the Home Department* [2002] EWHC 2805. Invoking Art. 5(4) ECHR.

[162] *R v Offen (No.2)* [2001] 2 All ER 154. Invoking Arts 5 (right against arbitrary deprivation of liberty) and 3 ECHR (right to protection from torture and inhuman and degrading treatment).

[163] *R (DF) v Chief Constable of Norfolk* [2002] EWHC 1738. Invoking Art. 2 ECHR (right to life).

[164] *R (Daly) v Secretary of State for the Home Department* [2001] 3 All ER 433. Invoking Art. 6 ECHR.

[165] *Stafford v UK* (2002) 35 EHRR 32 (absence of possibility for mandatory lifers to have the lawfulness of continued detention determined by a court was in violation of Art. 5(4) ECHR—contradicting *R (Stafford) v Secretary of State for the Home Department* [1999] 2 AC 38); *Benjamin v UK* (2002) 36 EHRR 1 (Mental Health Review Tribunals inability to order the release of discretionary lifers detained on grounds of mental disorder is in violation of Art. 5(4) ECHR); *Keenan v UK* (2001) 33 EHRR 38 (Art. 2 ECHR gives rise to positive obligations on prison authorities to protect life of prisoners); *Edwards v UK* (2002) 35 EHRR, 19 (Art. 2 protects the right of the family to participation in a full and public inquiry into the death of a prisoner murdered by a fellow prisoner).

[166] *R (Mellor) v Secretary of State for the Home Department* [2001] 3 WLR 533. Invoking Arts 8 (right to private and family life) and 12 ECHR (right to heterosexual marriage and to found a family).

[167] *R (Pearson and Martinez) v Secretary of State for the Home Department* [2001] HRLR 39. Invoking Art. 3 of Protocol 1 ECHR, which establishes implied right to vote in democratic elections.

[168] *Waite v Hammersmith and Fulham LBC* [2002] EWCA Civ 482. Invoking Arts 8 and 14 ECHR (right to freedom from discrimination in enjoyment of Convention rights).

who required a computer in order to prepare a legal application, unsuccessfully challenged the Governor's restrictions of his use of IT facilities.[169] Gilbert, one of thirty-seven prisoners detained in a Close Supervision Centre, was refused a transfer to a lower security prison in order to receive a number of family visits.[170] Prisoner 'N' failed to assert his right to privacy in order to stop a prison governor's disclosure of his prior conviction for gross indecency with a child.[171] John Broom's challenge of his regular transfers between unsanitary cells without modesty screens, was sharply dismissed.[172] Sunder, a lifer, failed in challenging his recategorization to a higher security level.[173] Similarly, Burgess was unsuccessful in challenging the Home Secretary's refusal to accept the Parole Board's recommendation that he be reclassified from category C to category D conditions.[174] Finally, Mathew William's argument that the Category A Review Committee's consistent refusal to recategorize him violated his right to a fair hearing before the Discretionary Lifer Panel failed.[175] These cases suggest a continuing judicial resistance to extending Convention rights protections to what Germans would term the 'administrative' sphere.

Even where personal liberty is at stake, courts have not always been sympathetic to innovative human rights arguments. Lichniak and Pyrah were unsuccessful in their use of Articles 3 and 5 ECHR to challenge the mandatory life sentence.[176] The House of Lords, having just decided in *Anderson* that the life sentence would be under full judicial control, were not convinced that the mandatory life sentence could be characterized as either arbitrary or disproportionate. In *Giles*, the Court rejected the proposition that Article 5(4) ECHR (right to proceedings to test lawfulness of deprivation of liberty) applied to determinate sentences imposed solely on the grounds of public protection under section 80(2)(b) of the Powers of Criminal Court Sentencing Act.[177] The argument of two lifers, Martin Clough and John Spence, that the Home Secretary should not be entitled to determine the periods between Parole Board assessments or to override the Board's recommendations in this regard, on the basis of '*inter alia*' Articles

[169] *R (Ponting) v Governor of Whitemoor Prison* [2002] EWCA Civ 224. Invoking Art. 6 ECHR.
[170] *R (Gilbert) v Home Secretary for the Home Department* [2002] EWHC 2832. Invoking Art. 8 ECHR.
[171] *N v Governor of Dartmoor Prison* [2001] EWHC Admin 93. Invoking Art. 8 ECHR.
[172] *Broom v Governor of Wakefield Prison* [2002] EWHC 2041. Invoking Art. 3 ECHR (right to protection from torture and inhuman and degrading treatment).
[173] *R (Sunder) v Secretary of State for the Home Department* [2001] EWHC Admin 252; [2001] EWCA Civ 1157. Invoking Arts 5(4) and 6 ECHR.
[174] *R (Burgess) v Secretary of State for the Home Department, Daily Telegraph* (5 December 2000). Invoking Art. 5(4) ECHR.
[175] *R (Williams) v Secretary of State for the Home Department* [2002] 4 All ER 872. Invoking Art. 5(4) ECHR.
[176] *R (Lichniak and Pyrah) v Secretary of State for the Home Department* [2001] 4 All ER 934, [2002] 4 All ER 1122.
[177] *R (Giles) v Parole Board* [2002] 3 All ER 1123.

5 and 6 ECHR, were dismissed.[178] These decisions were a retreat from the progressive approach in *Anderson* which, along with the ECtHR decision in *Stafford*, was distinguished by the Court of Appeal in *Spence*. Again in the parole context, Justin West's argument that Parole Board proceedings determining the release of a life sentenced prisoner amounted to a 'criminal' proceeding in the meaning of Article 6 ECHR, was rejected.[179] The Court of Appeal left open the possibility, however, that the proceedings may still be classified as 'civil' for the purposes of Article 6 ECHR and result in the prisoner being granted an oral hearing and legal representation. It stressed that 'the common law has always regarded the right to freedom from physical coercion, sometimes referred to as the right to bodily integrity, as the most important of civil rights'.[180] In *Uttley*, the Court rejected the argument that the imposition of a one-year licence after completion of a twelve-year custodial sentence violated Article 7 ECHR because it resulted in a heavier sentence being imposed than would have been applicable at the time the offence was committed.[181] Finally, in *Carroll*, the Court of Appeal rejected the argument that governor disciplinary proceedings resulting in the imposition of 'additional days' should be classified as 'criminal' for the purposes of Article 6(3) ECHR and subject to certain procedural safeguards.[182] These decisions were later overturned in the ECtHR judgment of *Ezeh* which,[183] like *Stafford*, displayed the breach between the domestic and European approach to prison matters.

Local commentators argue that there is the potential for change in the future, and that we can look forward to breakthroughs as courts become more familiar with human rights discourse.[184] Whilst there is some evidence to support this optimism, fundamental issues remain to be resolved if prisoners are to be successful in using the Convention to further their administrative rights.

7.4. 1 Approaching the European Convention on Human Rights

The advancement of prisoners' rights in England will depend to a large extent on the approach which domestic courts take to the jurisprudence of the ECtHR.

---

[178] *R (Clough) v Secretary of State for the Home Department* [2003] EWHC 597; *R (Spence) v Secretary of State for the Home Department* [2002] EWHC 2717, [2003] EWCA Civ 732.

[179] *R (West) v Parole Board* [2002] EWCA Civ 1641.   [180] Para. 49.

[181] *R (Uttley) v Secretary of State for the Home Department* [2003] EWHC 950.

[182] *R (Carroll, Al-Hasan, Greenfield) v Secretary of State for the Home Department* [2002] 1 WLR 545.

[183] *Ezeh and Connors v UK* (2002) 35 EHRR 28 (holding denial of legal representation in violation of Art. 6(3) ECHR).

[184] Livingstone *et al.* (n 4) 563.

The HRA 1998 is opaque as regards the status and weight of Convention jurisprudence in domestic judicial reasoning. Although section 2 of the HRA 1998 states that courts must take Convention jurisprudence into account, it does not hold that they are bound by these decisions.[185] The opacity of section 2 gives rise to a number of possibilities with respect to prisoners' rights. On the one hand, domestic courts can now rely on ECtHR jurisprudence to bolster prisoners' claims, particularly where no precedent exists at common law. But equally, judges are able to minimize the importance of this body of decisions where they wish to defeat such claims. Nevertheless, whilst there is nothing in the HRA 1998 to bind the domestic courts to ECtHR decisions, there is nothing to stop domestic courts from going beyond the rights protections already developed by the ECtHR.[186] Presently the ECtHR, despite its consciousness of its supra-national status, is proving to be more progressive in its approach to prisoners' rights than domestic courts. But, as indicated in Chapter 6, the approach of the ECtHR to prisoners' rights is not without its limits.[187] The future judicial development of prisoners' administrative rights will not only be determined by the extent to which domestic courts follow the more progressive aspects of Convention reasoning, it will also depend on whether they are prepared to go beyond the decisions of the ECtHR.

Recent prisoner cases under the HRA 1998 display a range of approaches to ECtHR decisions. One approach to Strasbourg jurisprudence, evident prior to the 1998 Act in cases like *Wynne*,[188] is that of restrictive pragmatism. In this approach a minimalist view of Convention rights protections is justified by characterizing Strasbourg jurisprudence not as a corpus of human rights principles, but as piecemeal, flexible, and pragmatic solutions to the facts of each case. The most compelling example of this is found in the Court of Appeal judgment in the *Amin* case where the family challenged the Home Secretary's refusal to hold a full and public inquiry into the death of a prisoner in which they could fully participate.[189] The ECtHR has developed an 'adjectival' procedural obligation under Article 2 ECHR (right to life) to conduct an independent and effective investigation into the death of persons in state care, including prisoners. In *Jordan* it set out a number of

---

[185] Lord Lester and David Pannick (eds), *Human Rights Law and Practice* (Butterworths, London, 1999) 22.

[186] The German FCC takes the view that European Convention law is simple federal law as opposed to 'Basic Law'. The Convention binds neither the state nor federal legislatures unless the rights thereunder go further, in their protective potential, than those rights under the Basic Law. K. Hesse, 'Bestand und Bedeutung der Grundrechte in der Bundesrepublik Deutschland' (1978) *EuGRZ* 427, 428.

[187] See 6.2.

[188] *Wynne v Secretary of State for the Home Department* [1993] 1 All ER 574. See 7.3 above.

[189] *R (Amin and Middleton) v Secretary of State for the Home Department* [2002] EWCA Civ 390.

requirements for the conduct of such an enquiry.[190] These had been applied in *Edwards*, where the right of the deceased prisoner's family to involvement in the inquiry into his death at the hands of a fellow prisoner was upheld.[191]

In *Amin* the Court of Appeal dismissed the family's challenge, taking the view that their argument could not 'be satisfactorily resolved by a process of reasoning which sticks like glue to the Strasbourg texts'. Rather, the Court averred that 'what is required is a flexible approach, responsive to the dictates of the facts case by case'.[192] The Court argued that Strasbourg jurisprudence generally is 'essentially pragmatic', that the Jordan requirements are 'by no means set in stone' and concluded: 'the task of our courts is to develop a domestic jurisprudence of fundamental rights, drawing on the Strasbourg cases of which by HRA s.2 we are enjoined to take account, but by which we are not bound'.[193] Here, Convention law principles were weakened by viewing Strasbourg jurisprudence through the lens of the pragmatic common law tradition.

An alternative judicial approach to the Convention might be characterized as restrictive formalism. Here the Court justifies a minimalist view of Convention rights protections by adopting a technical and narrow view of Strasbourg authority. Paradoxically, this usually entails that domestic courts 'stick like glue' to Strasbourg authority. Such an approach was evident in *Williams* and *Burgess* where the courts' fidelity to *Ashingdane* prevented the extension of Article 5(4) ECHR to categorization and transfer decisions which had a deleterious impact on the prisoners' prospects of release.[194] The line in *Ashingdane*, that Article 5(4) ECHR had no application to the manner in which detention is executed, was maintained by the domestic courts despite the close relationship in these cases between the prisoners' categorization, transfer, and release.

A very different approach to the Convention is characterized by the pursuit of principle. In *Amin*, the House of Lords overturned the decision of the Court of Appeal as regards a family's right to participation in a public inquiry into the death of a prisoner. Lord Bingham led the court in arguing that the Court of Appeal had failed to recognize that *Jordan* and *Edwards* had established an 'irreducible, minimum, standard of review' which 'could be met only by an appropriate level of publicity and an appropriate level of

---

[190] *Jordan v UK (App. No. 24746/94)* 4 May 2001.

[191] *Edwards v UK* (2002) 35 EHRR 19.

[192] *R (Amin and Middleton) v Secretary of State for the Home Department* [2002] EWCA Civ 390, para. 62.

[193] Paras 60–61.

[194] Art. 5(4) ECHR states: 'everyone who is deprived of his liberty by arrest or detention shall be entitled to take proceedings by which the lawfulness of his detention shall be decided speedily by a court and his release ordered if the detention is not lawful'. *R (Burgess) v Secretary of State for the Home Department*, Daily Telegraph, 5 December 2000; *R (Williams) v Secretary of State for the Home Department* [2002] 4 All ER 872; *Ashingdane v UK* (1985) 7 EHRR 528.

participation by the next of kin'. He insisted that the Court of Appeal's approach had 'diluted' the minimum standards developed by Strasbourg 'so as to sanction a process of inquiry inconsistent with domestic and Convention standards'.[195] Here is a judgment, expressly critical of the pragmatic restrictive approach, which views Strasbourg jurisprudence as establishing principles and minimum standards in the protection of Convention rights.

Another variant of the principled approach takes a broader view of the Convention, placing it firmly within a framework of international human rights principles. Here we see a reading of the Convention with the potential to develop a human rights vision of imprisonment. Thus, in *Howard League*,[196] which dealt with the obligations owed to detainees of young offender institutions (YOIs), Munby J interpreted the Convention in the light of the United Nations Convention on the Rights of the Child (1989) as well as the Charter of Fundamental Rights of the European Union (2000). He explained his approach thus:

'The European Convention is, of course, now part of our domestic law by reason of the Human Rights Act 1998. Neither the UN Convention nor the European Charter is at present legally binding in our domestic law and they are therefore not sources of law in the strict sense. But both can, in my judgment, properly be consulted insofar as they proclaim, reaffirm or elucidate the content of those human rights that are generally recognised throughout the European family of nations, in particular the nature and scope of those fundamental rights that are guaranteed by the European Convention'.[197]

Taking this broadly based approach, and on the basis of a careful examination of the Convention rights in question, Munby J concluded that 'human rights law imposes on the Prison Service enforceable obligations' namely, 'the "welfare" principle encapsulated in the UN Convention and the European Charter' and the protection of children in young offenders institutions 'from any ill-treatment, whether at the hands of Prison Service staff *or of other inmates*, of the type which engages either article 3 or article 8 of the European Convention'.[198] Here was a broad and purposive reading of the Convention, breaking with the tradition of judicial reticence in England with respect to shaping the objects of prison administration.

The future of prisoners' rights in England depends to a large extent on which of these contrasting approaches prevails. If we are to see progress, courts would need to move beyond a pragmatic or formalist approach to Convention interpretation, and exploit the potential of section 2 of the HRA 1998 to develop a distinctive domestic human rights vision of imprison-

---

[195] R (Amin) v Secretary of State for the Home Department [2003] UKHL 51, paras 28 and 32.

[196] R (Howard League for Penal Reform) v Secretary of State for the Home Department (No. 2) [2002] EWHC 2497.

[197] Para. 51.   [198] Para. 68.

ment. In addition to this, however, domestic courts will have to break with the historically entrenched approach to the prison administrative sphere. This entails a rigorous application of the proportionality doctrine to matters relevant to prison administration and, necessarily, a fresh appreciation of judicial deference in this context.

7.4.2 Defining the Test for Limitations of Convention Rights in Prisons

As recognized in the run up to the German Prison Act and beyond, the impact of human rights in the prison context is interlocked with the legal test for defining the application of human rights in prisons. Inspired by the ECtHR in *Golder*, the English courts developed a test for the restriction of prisoners' rights early on in the cases of *St Germain* and *Raymond v Honey*. As this chapter has shown, this test has been developed under the common law with cases such as *Leech (No. 2)* departing from the *Wednesbury* reasonableness approach and allowing for the application of a proportionality test to the restriction of prisoners' rights. However, the test for the restrictions of prisoners' rights was not consistently applied, with cases like *O'Dhuibhir* and the Court of Appeal in *Simms* seeking to limit the *Leech (No. 2)* test to the restriction of rights of access to justice and legal advice. Furthermore, these cases developed an alternative test which rested on an indivisible conception of the offender's liberty, and conflated the rights restrictions pursuant to the legal imposition of a prison sentence with those which flow from the administration of the prison sentence. As argued, on the eve of the entry into force of the HRA 1998 the House of Lords failed to rescue the test for prisoners' rights developed in *Raymond v Honey* and *Leech (No. 2)* in the *Simms* decision. This was because it conceded the Court of Appeal's formulation in *Simms* that rights restrictions could flow as 'an inevitable consequence of lawful detention in custody' and, rather than asserting the right *per se*, it linked the protection of freedom of speech in this case to the right of access to justice which, in turn, was necessary to protect the prisoners' personal liberty.[199] What has happened to the test for prisoners' rights since the Act has come into force?

7.4.2.1 Distinguishing personal liberty and administrative rights

The test for prisoners' rights developed in *Raymond v Honey* asserts that prisoners retain certain rights whilst in prison. In other words, the prison sentence does not automatically authorize the restriction of prisoners' rights whilst they serve their sentence. Nevertheless, this chapter has shown that no clearly articulated distinction between personal liberty and administrative rights exists in English case law, despite the judicial tendency to give preference to the protection of personal liberty in practice. Certainly, recent

---

[199] See 7.3 above.

case law under the HRA 1998 has shown that judges are more likely to intervene where personal liberty is at stake. Despite this evident trend, tacit judicial recognition of a divisible conception of liberty and commitment to the protection of administrative rights is tentatively re-emerging. It is too soon, however, to talk of a strong consensus in this regard.

Our analysis must begin with the case of *Mellor* which dealt with a life sentenced prisoners' claim, on the basis of Articles 8 (right to private and family life) and 12 ECHR (right to marry and found a family), that he should be allowed to conceive a child with his wife by artificial insemination at their own cost. The Secretary of State had a longstanding policy to refuse such requests in the absence of exceptional circumstances because 'it is an explicit consequence of imprisonment that prisoners should not have the opportunity to beget children whilst serving their sentences', and 'serious and justified public concern would be likely if prisoners continued to have the opportunity to conceive children while serving sentences, it was better for children to be able to have contact with both parents.[200] The Court of Appeal, led by Lord Phillips MR, rejected Mellor's appeal, arguing that Home Secretary's policy was a legitimate restriction of the prisoners' rights under Articles 8 and 12. This conclusion was reached partly by recourse to Convention jurisprudence which was held not to provide strong authority for a prisoner's right to have a child through artificial insemination.[201] More fundamentally, however, it rested on an indivisible view of the prisoner's liberty.

The opposing arguments of counsel in the case highlighted the indistinctness of the House of Lords decision in *Simms* on the question of the test for evaluating restrictions of prisoners' liberty. David Pannick QC, representing Mellor, argued that *Simms* 'demonstrated that a prisoner was entitled to exercise any of the rights that he would have been able to exercise if at liberty unless they were incompatible with the exercise of good order and discipline in the prison'.[202] Here was a bold assertion of the prisoner's administrative rights status. The question here was whether the measure was proportionate to the specific aims of prison administration. Miss Rose, counsel for the Home Secretary, argued otherwise. She elided rights restrictions which flowed from the administration of prisons with restrictions of the prisoners' personal liberty through the sentence of imprisonment. Hence, she submitted that the House of Lords in *Simms* had held that 'the restriction on freedom of expression was part of the deprivation of liberty that imprisonment was designed to achieve'.[203] This had implications for how proportionality was to be applied when evaluating restrictions of prisoners' rights. According to Miss Rose, the prisoner's 'special reason' for

---

[200] *R (Mellor) v Secretary of State for the Home Department* [2001] 3 WLR 533, paras 60–67.

[201] Paras 22–39. [202] Para. 50. See end of 7.3 above. [203] Para. 51.

gaining access to journalists in *Simms*, namely to obtain a review of their convictions, resulted in the restriction of their freedom of expression being 'disproportionate to the social need that justified imprisonment'.[204] So the question here was not whether the rights restriction was proportionate to the aim of maintaining 'good order and discipline in prisons' but rather whether it was proportionate to the broader social aim of imprisoning offenders. Moreover, for Miss Rose, the factor in *Simms* which tilted the balance in favour of the prisoners was the link between the prisoners' freedom of speech and their access to justice in order to safeguard their personal liberty.

Lord Phillips accepted the latter submission, arguing that *Simms* had 'recognised that a degree of restriction of the right of expression was a justifiable element in imprisonment, not merely in order to accommodate the orderly running of a prison, but as part of the penal objective of deprivation of liberty'.[205] He devoted close attention to the judgments in *Simms* showing that Lords Steyn, Hoffmann and Millett all accepted that limitations on the freedom of speech were part of 'the punitive object of deprivation of liberty'.[206] Noting that *Simms* had interpreted 'English law in accordance with the Convention' he formulated the test for the restrictions of prisoners' rights as follows:

'The approach under the Strasbourg jurisprudence and under English domestic law is the same. The consequences that the punishment of imprisonment has on the exercise of human rights are justifiable provided that they are not disproportionate to the aim of maintaining a penal system designed both to punish and to deter. When the consequences are disproportionate, special arrangements may be called for to mitigate the normal effect of deprivation of liberty'.[207]

In viewing restrictions of Convention rights as the consequence of 'the penal objective of the deprivation of liberty', and in suggesting that 'special arrangements could be made to mitigate the normal effects of deprivation of liberty', Phillips asserted an indivisible view of the offenders' liberty. On this basis, rights restrictions were legitimate unless disproportionate to the 'aim of maintaining a penal system designed both to punish and to deter' and the possibility for judicial scrutiny was thereby weakened under the proportionality test. Rather than applying a targeted and differentiated proportionality test of 'minimum interference' to rights restrictions in prisons where the measure in question required justification in terms of its specific administrative aim, this test asked the judge to embark upon a broad-brush balancing exercise in order to assess whether the measure resulted in the sanction of imprisonment *per se* being disproportionate to the broader social aim of punishing the offender. This decision had the potential seriously to undermine the prisoners' legal status under the European Convention.

---

[204] Para. 51.   [205] Para. 52.   [206] Para. 54.   [207] Para. 58.

This potential was quickly realized in the first instance decision in *P and Q* which dealt with the compatibility of the Prison Service's policy on mothers and children with Article 8 ECHR (right to private and family life). Lord Woolf, who argued that 'prisoners are sent to prison as a punishment, a deterrence and for rehabilitation', relied on *Mellor* to argue that 'the impairment of the right of family life is a consequence of the deprivation of liberty which prison involves'.[208] As a consequence of this assertion, and in the light of his view of relevant Convention jurisprudence, Lord Woolf rejected the argument that Article 8 imposed stringent requirements on the prison administration as regards welfare considerations and family ties:

What is required of the Prison Service is to adopt a reasonable balance between the various considerations involved. As it appears to us this is what they have sought to do. Their conclusion is not flawed and in those circumstances the courts should not intervene. It is not for the courts to run the prisons.[209]

Despite the setback in *Mellor* (which has yet to be overruled), we have seen the re-emergence of a differentiated view of the prisoners' liberty in a number of recent and important cases. The most important decision in this regard is *Daly*,[210] which dealt with the surveillance of the prisoners' legal correspondence. Outside of the area of prisoners' rights, this decision represents the leading authority on how rights restrictions are to be assessed under the HRA 1998 generally.[211] Whilst Lord Steyn's now well-known speech on the application of the proportionality doctrine under the HRA 1998 is examined further below,[212] it is the language of Lord Bingham that is of central importance to the protection of the prisoner's administrative rights. In the opening stages of his speech, he set out his conception of prisoners' legal status:

Any custodial order inevitably curtails the enjoyment, by the person confined, of rights enjoyed by other citizens. He cannot move freely and choose his associates as they are entitled to do. It is indeed an important objective of such an order to curtail such rights, whether to punish him or to protect other members of the public or both. But the order does not wholly deprive the person confined of all rights enjoyed by other citizens. Some rights, perhaps in an attenuated or qualified form, survive the making of the order. And it may well be that the importance of such surviving rights is enhanced by the loss or partial loss of other rights. Among the rights which, in part at least, survive are three important rights, closely related but free standing, each of them calling for appropriate legal protection: the right of access to a court; the right of access to legal advice; and the right to communicate confidentially with a legal adviser under the seal of legal professional privilege. Such rights may be curtailed

---

[208] *R (P and Q) v Secretary of State for the Home Department* [2001] EWHC Admin 357, para. 37.
[209] Para. 57.
[210] *R (Daly) v Secretary of State for the Home Department* [2001] 2 AC 532.
[211] See 6.1.3.1.   [212] See 7.4.2.3 below.

only by clear and express words, and then only to the extent reasonably necessary to meet the ends which justify the curtailment.[213]

In Lord Bingham's conception of the prisoner's legal status, the recognition that personal liberty is restricted by the imposition of a prison sentence stands, clearly, alongside the assertion that prisoners retain certain rights whilst in prison. It also recognizes that the rights which prisoners retained could only be limited 'to the extent reasonably necessary to meet the ends which justify the curtailment'. This was an unambiguous restatement of the common law test developed in *St Germain, Raymond v Honey* and *Leech (No. 2)* all of which Bingham quoted at length as justification for his position.[214] In addition to this, Bingham recognized that some rights require more vigilant protection precisely because of the restrictions inherent in imprisonment. This represents the beginnings of a legal foundation for additional positive rights to be vested in prisoners due to their particular vulnerability and dependence in prisons.[215] Whilst Lord Bingham's focus on the prisoners' rights of access to justice and legal advice takes a rather narrow view of the rights prisoners retain in prisons, there is nevertheless a principled distinction here between restrictions of personal liberty and the existence of residual liberty in the administrative sphere, a restatement of the application of the proportionality test to assessments of restrictions of this residual liberty, and a potential justification for what Germans would view as the prisoner's positive rights status.

That *Daly* stemmed the regressive trend in the conception of the prisoner's legal status was evident from the shift in tone between the Divisional and Appeal Court decisions in *P and Q*.[216] Lord Phillips MR, accepted that careful scrutiny of the compatibility of the Prison Service's policy on mothers and children with Article 8 ECHR was possible under the HRA 1998 as a consequence of *Daly*, holding that the policy had to be applied on a case-by-case basis with careful evaluation of the rights of those affected if it was to be Convention compliant. He confirmed as 'authoritative' Lord Bingham's conception of the prisoner's legal status and emphasized the point that certain rights in imprisonment are 'enhanced by the loss or partial loss of other rights'.[217] More recently, however, the Divisional Court decision of Elias J in *Hirst* has gone beyond Lord Bingham's words by delivering the most extensive consideration yet undertaken in English courts of the necessity for the distinction between restrictions of personal liberty and those restricting residual liberty in the administrative sphere in prisons.[218]

[213] Para. 5.   [214] Paras 6–12.   [215] See ch. 1, n 13.

[216] Although courts are not always true to the Bingham formulation. In *Nilsen*, for example, the 'inevitable consequence' test was reasserted. Perhaps unsurprisingly, it was accompanied by a rather cursory consideration of whether the governor's refusal to hand over a prisoners' autobiography violated Arts 8 and 10 ECHR. *R (Nilsen) v Governor of Whitemoor Prison* [2002] EWHC 668.

[217] *R (P and Q) v Secretary of State for the Home Department* [2001] 1 WLR 2002.

[218] *R (Hirst) v Secretary of State for the Home Department* [2002] 1 WLR 2929.

Hirst dealt with the Convention compatibility of the policy of denying prisoners contact with the media except in exceptional circumstances. Elias J held that a blanket ban of this kind was unlawful and could not be justified under Article 10 ECHR (freedom of speech). Elias argued that, when evaluating the proportionality of a restrictive measure permissible under Article 10(2), it was first necessary to decide whether the rights restriction in question was 'an inherent part of the sentence of imprisonment itself or whether it is a restriction which is simply the result of the fact that rules have to be made for the good order and discipline of the prisons, together with other related objectives'.[219] He went on to explain the implications of the two approaches. On the former approach, which he took to be the approach in *Mellor*, 'the right is removed as the deliberate and considered response to the need to provide an effective penal policy'.[220] In this case, he argued, the courts are unlikely to interfere with the decision in question as 'there is in truth no room for the court to apply the principle of minimum response'.[221] On the latter approach, which he took to be the approach in *Daly*, the courts position is very different. Where the prisoner retains the right 'notwithstanding the sentence', Elias J argued, the proportionality doctrine applied in a very 'different way'. Whilst interference may still be justifiable under Article 10(2) ECHR, 'the government must show that the means used to impair the right go no further than is necessary to accomplish those legitimate objectives'. As a result:

... the courts can with more confidence exercise a tighter review of the restriction to ensure that it does not unnecessarily interfere with Convention rights. There is not simply a general striking of a balance between individual rights and the public interest with deference being shown to the views of the state authorities; the starting point is the Convention right, which it is accepted in principle remains in play. The authority must demonstrate a proper basis for interfering with it, and show that nothing short of the particular interference will achieve the avowed objective.[222]

Consequently, the question which Elias J sought to answer was whether the ban on communication between prisoners and journalists was part of the sentence of imprisonment or was a necessary part of the prison administrative regime. On his view, *Simms* was authority for the fact that some restrictions of freedom of speech formed part of the sentence of imprisonment, while others were viewed as part of the prison regime. In Elias J's view, restrictions on the right to communicate orally with journalists in certain circumstances did not form part of the sentence of imprisonment. This was, *inter alia*, because no democratic society should seek wholly to silence prisoners through eliminating contact with journalists.

Elias J's judgment in *Hirst*, in demonstrating the necessity of distinguishing restrictions of personal liberty from those within the administrative sphere when applying the proportionality doctrine in prisons, makes a

---

[219] Para. 32.   [220] Para. 33.   [221] Para. 32.   [222] Para. 40.

seminal contribution to the conception of the prisoner's legal status in England. Whether the higher courts will come to recognize this contribution remains to be seen. But, there is also the danger lurking in the reasoning of *Hirst*, that the questions central to the evaluation of prisoners' administrative rights will be subverted by an ongoing fixation with whether the restriction in question constitutes part of the sentence of imprisonment or whether it can be characterized as a prison administrative measure. This is made all the more difficult in England by the absence of any legal or fixed political consensus as to the nature and purpose of the sanction of imprisonment or, for that matter, of prison administration.[223] Finally, there is the associated danger that judicial deference will be hidden behind the claim that rights restrictions belong to the sentence of imprisonment. In this context, the German experience of the longstanding and highly articulated distinction between administrative rights and status liberty, may be of some relevance.[224] Certainly, the future of prisoners' rights in England hangs together with the extent to which administrative rights are recognized and protected in prisons.

7.4. 2.2 Proportionality and judicial deference in prisons

Lurking behind the judicial approach to prisoners' administrative rights is the broader question as to the extent of deference to be paid to administrative decision-makers and the Home Secretary in determining what goes on inside prisons. Chapter 6 showed that the language of deference permeates much of human rights reasoning under the HRA 1998, although the meaning of deference differs according to judges' views of the place of human rights in the English constitution. The issue is a live one for prisons, for it is evident from the instant chapter that, outside clearly defined areas, the English judiciary has a strong proclivity to defer to decision makers inside prisons and their scrutiny of prison discretionary powers is often cursory.

Not long after the HRA 1998 came into force, we were given a salutary demonstration of how deference to Parliament can impact on prisoners' rights claims in *Pearson*.[225] The case dealt with the Convention compatibility of restrictions on the prisoners' right to vote under section 3(1) of the Representation of the People Act 1983. The prisoners invoked Article 3 of Protocol 1 ECHR, which holds that elections should be held 'under conditions which will ensure the free expression of the opinion of the people in the choice of the legislature'. The Divisional Court rejected the prisoners' application. Its reasoning relied heavily on the doctrine of judicial deference as articulated in domestic authorities such as *Kebeline*, *Lambert*, and *Brown v Stott*.[226] Kennedy LJ stressed that the right to vote was not absolute, being

---

[223] See 5.4.3.   [224] See chs 2 and 4.
[225] *R (Pearson and Martinez) v Secretary of State for the Home Department* [2001] EWHC Admin 239.
[226] See 6.1.3.1.

inferred from Article 3 of Protocol 1 ECHR, and that disenfranchisement was permissible. He noted that 'if an individual is to be disenfranchised that must be in pursuit of a legitimate aim', but also acknowledged that 'in the case of a convicted prisoner serving his sentence the aim may not be easy to articulate'.[227] The 'true nature of the disenfranchisement' was, Kennedy LJ argued, 'best left to the philosophers' to discern 'whilst recognizing that the legislature does different things'.[228] Whilst the Convention required that limitations of the right should be 'proportionate', Kennedy LJ noted:

> . . . that is the point at which, as it seems to me, it is appropriate for this court to defer to the legislature . . . Parliament in this country could have provided differently in order to meet the objectives which it discerned . . . I would accept that the tailoring process seldom admits of perfection, so the courts must afford some leeway to the legislator . . . there is a broad spectrum of approaches among democratic societies, and the United Kingdom falls into the middle of the spectrum . . . its position in the spectrum is plainly a matter for Parliament not for the courts.[229]

Kennedy LJ's approach to this question has been met with widespread domestic criticism.[230] His excessive caution negated any engagement with the justification for the disenfranchisement in question or, for that matter, any general discussion of the nature of the right to vote. There can be no better case example of an elision of 'deference' with 'submission', or of a judicial argument less willing to engage with the principles at stake. The judgment was all the more problematic in the light of the fact that Parliament has not considered the issue of prisoner disenfranchisement in over a century.[231] Given the chorus of disapproval in England, it is worth noting that Germany's Prison Act protects the prisoner's right to vote and requires prison administrators to assist the prisoner in exercising that right.[232]

Whilst *Pearson* was a sobering example of how prisoners' rights can be undermined by deference to Parliament, the risk is also present in judicial deference to prison administrators and the Home Secretary. At the centre of this discussion lies the speech of Lord Steyn in *Daly*.[233] As discussed in Chapter 6, Lord Steyn was fully aware of the attempts in early human rights cases to subvert the rigours of the proportionality doctrine by recourse to a language of reasonableness. He used his short judgment for one purpose: to ensure that 'cases involving Convention rights must be analysed in the

---

[227] Para. 40.   [228] Para. 40.   [229] Para. 41.

[230] H. Lardy, 'Prisoner Disenfranchisement: Constitutional Rights and Wrongs' (2002) *Public Law* 524; Livingstone *et al.* (n 4) 200–1; S. Foster, 'Prisoners, the HRA and the Right to Vote' (2001) 151 *NLJ* 560.

[231] Lardy (n 230) 546.

[232] Prison Act 1976, § 73. At the very least this must involve informing prisoners of the use of the postal vote and facilitating this use. This provision may also serve as an additional reason to grant leave from prison, in the absence of a risk of 'danger of misuse'. R.-P. Calliess and H. Müller-Dietz, *Strafvollzugsgesetz* (Beck, Munich, 2002) § 73, mn 2.

[233] *R (Daly) v Secretary of State for the Home Department* [2001] 2 AC 532, paras 24–8.

correct way'.[234] He set out the differences between the *Wednesbury* and proportionality approaches with a view to showing that 'the intensity of review is somewhat greater' under the latter.[235] Unlike the traditional approach to judicial review, courts can 'assess the balance which the decision maker has struck, not merely whether it is within the range of rational or reasonable decisions' as well as 'require attention to be directed to the relative weight accorded to interests and considerations'.[236] The greater intensity of review under proportionality was sustained, according to Lord Steyn, by 'the twin requirements that the limitation of the right was necessary in a democratic society, in the sense of meeting a pressing social need, and the question whether the interference was really proportionate to the legitimate aim being pursued'.[237]

With these words Lord Steyn heralded the 'unequivocal embrace of proportionality' under the HRA 1998 and 'the abandonment of the deferential *Wednesbury* standard in all cases involving Convention rights'.[238] But, as Chapter 6 indicated, he went on to make one crucial concession to a doctrine of judicial deference:

The differences in approach between the traditional grounds of review and the proportionality approach may therefore sometimes yield different results . . . This does not mean that there has been a shift to merits review. On the contrary . . . the respective roles of judges and administrators are fundamentally distinct and will remain so. To this extent the general tenor of the observations in *Mahmood* [2001] 1 WLR 840 are correct. And Laws LJ rightly emphasised in *Mahmood*, at p 847, para 18, 'that the intensity of review in a public law case will depend on the subject matter in hand'. That is so even in cases involving Convention rights. In law context is everything.[239]

There are few 'contexts' in public law more prone to incite judicial deference than that of internal prison operations and management, especially where security is at stake. Lord Steyn's reference to 'context' need not necessarily be viewed as restricting judicial competence to assess rights limitations in prisons.[240] Nevertheless, these few words had the potential to reinforce what remains the greatest hurdle to the recognition of prisoners' administrative rights. This was confirmed in *Ponting*, which dealt with the access of a dyslexic prisoner to computer facilities for the preparation of his trial. Here the Court of Appeal rejected the application, stressing 'the margin of discretion' that must be left to prison administrators and the Home Secretary who have greater 'expertise' in determining issues of prison administration.[241] Moreover, in *Waite* the failure of a recalled lifer to secure housing benefit allowance available to remand prisoners by relying on

---

[234] Para. 28.   [235] Para. 27.   [236] Para. 27.   [237] Para. 27.
[238] M. Hunt, 'Sovereignty's Blight: Why Contemporary Public Law Needs the Concept of "Due Deference"' in N. Bamforth and P. Leyland (eds), *Public Law in a Multi-Layered Constitution* (Hart, Oxford, 2003) 337, 341
[239] Para. 28.   [240] See 6.1. 3.1.
[241] *R (Ponting) v Governor of Whitemoor Prison* [2002] EWCA Civ 224.

Articles 8 and 14 ECHR (right to freedom from discrimination in enjoyment of Convention rights),[242] was due in large part to reliance on deference. Laws LJ noted that 'the distribution of state benefit lies particularly within the constitutional responsibility of elected Government',[243] and concluded 'that the Government have reached an overall judgment here as to the distribution of housing benefit, taking account of the special needs of prisoners, and it is a judgment which lay well within the margin of discretion available to the decision-maker'.[244]

The future of prisoners' rights under the HRA 1998 is thus inextricably linked with the future of judicial deference. If this doctrine successfully sustains constitutional orthodoxy and a view of deference as submission,[245] then the impact of the 1998 Act on the prisoners' administrative status will be negligible. However, if this doctrine is reconciled with a culture of justification, in which prison officials and the Home Secretary are pressed to demonstrate the necessity and proportionality of the measures in question, then the future is more optimistic for prisoners' administrative rights.

7.5 RECENT PRISONERS' RIGHTS CASES AT COMMON LAW

Beyond the HRA 1998, recent decisions regarding common law rights display continuing evidence of an entrenched judicial resistance to intervention in the administrative sphere. Certainly, in the absence of a significant and consequent threat to the offender's personal liberty or access to justice, judges are slow to develop exacting standards of review.

The emphasis on personal liberty is particularly evident in the case law regarding categorization. In *Hirst*,[246] the Home Secretary ordered that a long-serving lifer be recategorized and transferred to a category B prison on the grounds of security. This went against the recommendation of the discretionary lifer panel that he be classified as category C and sent to open prison. The prisoner argued that he should have been given reasons and a chance to make representations before his transfer. Laws LJ distinguished *Duggan*,[247] stressing that decisions regarding prisoners in categories B, C, and D were distinct from those concerning category A prisoners in that they did not have a 'direct bearing upon the prisoner's prospects of release'.[248] He made it plain that the:

---

[242] *Waite v Hammersmith and Fulham LBC* [2002] EWCA Civ 482.
[243] Para. 37.   [244] Para. 39.   [245] See 6.1.3.1.
[246] *R (Hirst) v Secretary of State for the Home Department* 2000 WL 976102 (QBD).
[247] *R (Duggan) v Secretary of State* [1994] 3 All ER 277. See 7.3 above.
[248] Para. 10.

. . . court should be very slow to impose strict procedural standards upon the internal workings of the prison system in so sensitive a context as transfers between prisons and categories where to do so might create very real prejudice, not just to the efficacy but to the security of the system and in circumstances where the court cannot itself confidently judge the degree of prejudice that might arise.[249]

For Lord Justice Laws, the court's intervention hinged on the extent to which the challenged decision impacted on the likelihood of the prisoners' release. On his view of the facts of the case, intervention was not justified.

The Court of Appeal in *Hirst* disagreed with Laws LJ's view of the impact of the categorization decision, emphasizing that the prisoner's regressive categorization in this case would have a 'material effect on the prisoner's eventual release date'.[250] It thus argued that a flexible concept of fairness, which was capable of 'meeting proper operational requirements',[251] should be applied in these circumstances. It noted, however, that it would be improper for courts to 'prescribe to the prison authorities precise details as to how a proper balance should be achieved between fairness to the individual prisoner and operational necessity'.[252] Despite acknowledging the court's potential to assess internal prison administrative decisions against a benchmark of fairness, the court remained hesitant in its approach, justifying its intervention by reference to the threat to the prisoner's personal liberty.

The threat to the offender's release prospects was also determinative of the reasoning in *Williams*.[253] Despite rejecting the possibility that Article 5(4) ECHR might apply to categorization proceedings, it was nevertheless conceded that in the exceptional circumstance that a category A review committee took a differing approach to a discretionary lifer panel on the question of an offender's risk to the public, a category A prisoner seeking recategorization was entitled to an oral hearing and full disclosure of the reports on which his categorization was based.[254] The Court was concerned by the fact that the DLP and category A committee were working from different material, it was also concerned to avoid the prisoner being caught in an unending process in which the two bodies came to opposing conclusions and the prisoner was unable to further his chances of release. In none of these cases, however, was any link made to the fact that the prisoner's personal experience of his day-to-day incarceration is materially affected by categorization and transfer decisions. This was simply not an issue of legal relevance.

---

[249] Para. 10.

[250] *R (Hirst) v Secretary of State for the Home Department* [2001] EWCA Civ 378, para. 29.

[251] Para. 25.   [252] Para. 25.

[253] *R (Williams) v Secretary of State for the Home Department* [2002] 4 All ER 872.

[254] Para. 31.

Finally, the common law approach to the administrative sphere was recently discussed in the case of *Potter*.[255] In this case a number of sexual offenders had been refused enhanced status under the Incentives and Earned Privileges Scheme (IEPS) because the Prison Service would not allow prisoners who deny their guilt to take part in a sexual offender's treatment programme. Their challenge, which had received a favourable response from the Prisons Ombudsman, went straight to the question of the extent to which courts could intervene in internal prison administrative schemes in the absence of a direct threat to personal liberty. The prisoners had argued that the approach taken by the courts in this context should be guided by the *Daly* decision, whilst the respondents relied on Laws LJ in *Hepworth* to restrict the court's intervention in this sphere.[256] Mr Justice Moses, quoting the Court of Appeal in *Hirst*, accepted that 'requirements of fairness which are of sufficient flexibility to encompass operational difficulties and problems do provide a standard against which to test the quality of decisions in relation to IEPS'.[257] He nevertheless stressed that 'those who manage prisons are better placed to take a wider view of the demands of fairness than an aggrieved prisoner, who must necessarily have a confined perspective'.[258] Moses J returned to the words of Laws LJ in *Hepworth* and *Hirst* as well as the Court of Appeal decision in *Hague*, to emphasize that the chances of a prisoner gaining success in a case regarding internal administrative schemes were slight:

I do not regard the decision of Laws J as ruling out a challenge on such a basis. His decision is, however, of importance in emphasising that the chances of success in relation to challenges to decisions in relation to the IEPS will be rare and that the courts should be slow to interfere with decisions which relate to the management of prisons (see *R v Deputy Governor of Parkhurst Prison, ex parte Hague* [1992] 1 AC 101 at 115H to 116B). 'The well-known proposition that managers should be left to manage applies a fortiori in regard to prisons, save where a clear case is made out for relief *ex debito justitae*.'[259]

Whilst it is accepted that the first instance *Potter* decision 'should not be taken to be the last word on this subject',[260] it is nevertheless illustrative of the extent to which the *Hague* approach still prevails in the judicial conception of the prisoner's legal status. It displays well how the breakthroughs in *Daly* may yet be watered down in the prevailing culture of deference to prison administrative decision-makers.

[255] *R (Potter) v Secretary of State for the Home Department* [2001] EWHC Admin 1041.
[256] See 7.3 above.   [257] Para. 41.   [258] Para. 41.   [259] Para. 38.
[260] Livingstone *et al.* (n 4) 196.

7.6 Conclusion

When viewed from a German perspective, judicial development of prisoners' administrative rights in England has been partial and uneven. Judges are tentative in their supervision of prison administration and concerned not to interfere in prison life. Unless the issue at hand impacts on the prisoner's personal (i.e. status) liberty or their access to the courts, or results in serious damage to their health, judges are inclined to take a hands-off approach. The judiciary resist developing rights, principles, and standards to guide the activities of those working inside prisons. Thus, Livingstone *et al.*, echoing the majority of prison law observers, have argued that 'while courts have ensured that prisoners are no longer treated as slaves of the state, they have yet to recognise them as citizens behind bars'.[261]

This judicial record in England is rooted in a broader context. Unlike their German counterparts, English judges are without a clear legislative invitation to intervene in internal prison life. No matter how activist, judges have always had to tread a fine line between the protection of prisoners' rights and respect for a legislative regime aimed at ensuring political control and accountability. Even when asserting the foundation of the prisoner's legal status in *St Germain*, Lord Justice Shaw warned that 'judicial intervention in the domestic management of a prison would generally be not merely *irrelevant* but also *intrusive* and *impolitic*'.[262] At the very moment when prisoners' rights were recognized under English law, there was concern with parliamentary sovereignty and the practical implications of judicial intervention.

Whilst walking the tightrope between judicial deference to Parliament and the protection of prisoners' rights, English judges have vacillated between a language of rights and principles and a language of pragmatism and sovereignty. The struggle between these two discourses reflects the controversy in English constitutional culture generally about the place of fundamental rights. It hindered the advancement of judicial jurisdiction over prisons until the early 1990s, and has remained implicit in the judicial bifurcation between the protection of prisoners' personal liberty and negation of administrative rights. Notwithstanding the HRA 1998, there is ongoing evidence of the traditional attitude of deference to prison policy and administration. In short, judicial development of prisoners' administrative rights in England has always been tentative, resting on an uncertain statutory and constitutional footing.

---

[261] Livingstone *et al.* (n 4) 552.   [262] [1978] 1 QB (CA) 425, 454. Emphasis added.

8

Conclusion

Cultural analysis is intrinsically incomplete. And, worse than that, the more deeply it goes the less complete it is. It is a strange science whose most telling assertions are its most tremulously based, in which to get somewhere with the matter at hand is to intensify the suspicion, both your own and that of others, that you are not quite getting it right.[1]

This book set out to explore the conception of the prisoner's legal status in England and Germany. In doing so, it hoped to provoke a reflection on alternative legal orders and to identify the broader social, political, and cultural dynamics which have shaped the conception of prisoners' rights. But this exploration is best viewed as 'explanatory rather than conclusory'.[2] It ends, as it began, with the suspicion that there is more to discover in the maze of meanings, attitudes, and beliefs which we identify as culture. In this sense, this study can be viewed as a 'preliminary to more specific questions' about the legal conception of prisoners' rights and the social context in which it has been formed.[3]

To sum up the arguments, in Germany prisoners' rights were formed in a political and legal culture shaped by constitutional rights, characterized by faith in fundamental rights and dominated by rights rhetoric. This fidelity to constitutional rights sprang out of a 'deep revulsion against a distasteful past'.[4] It is the signal of a culture 'finely tuned to the dark side of political expression'.[5] In this wary political culture, Germans seek refuge in an idealist and rationalist constitutional project which gives them the certainty that their organic political traditions have never delivered. In Germany we witness a vision of a constitutional State which derives the rationale for its existence in its capacity to safeguard and protect fundamental rights. We see too, an ambitious and powerful Federal Constitutional Court (FCC), confident in its role as the guardian of the constitutional State. This faith in fundamental rights shapes legal and political relations generally and in turn

[1] C. Geertz, 'Thick Description: Toward an Interpretive Theory of Culture' in C. Geertz (ed.), *The Interpretation of Cultures* (Basic Books, New York, 1973) 3, 29.

[2] J. Allison, *A Continental Distinction in the Common Law* (OUP, Oxford, 2000) 235.

[3] R. Cotterell, 'The Concept of Legal Culture' in D. Nelken (ed.), *Comparing Legal Cultures* (Dartmouth, Aldershot, 1996) 13, 29.

[4] P. Merkl, *The Origin of the West German Republic* (OUP, New York, 1963) 176.

[5] J. Steinberg, 'Constitutional Court can take cue from foreign experiences' *Business Day*, 11 November 1999.

has led to the dominance of 'rights rhetoric' when invoking arguments concerning social, legal, and political change.

The imperatives of the German Basic Law, and the dynamics of German political and legal culture, meant that talk of legal or penal reform was unlikely to occur without evidence of its accordance with constitutional rights and principles. In this climate, the symbolic and institutional power of the German FCC was significant. The Court was in a unique position to effect penal reform through the invocation of constitutional rights and principles. It built upon the pre-existing arguments of the penal reform lobby and, through its decisions in the early 1970s, gave these arguments legal and political legitimacy of the highest order.

The constitutional arguments for penal reform presented during the late 1970s and adopted by the FCC, were intertwined with the concept of fundamental rights developed in Germany post-1945. The protection of prisoners' negative rights was prompted by the imperatives of the *Rechtsstaatsprinzip*, whilst the development of the prisoners' positive rights status and the 'constitutional resocialization principle' formed part of a re-emergent social rights movement in Germany. This movement originated in nineteenth-century social democratic activism, found expression in the Weimar Constitution and the work of Hermann Heller, and drew on the Social State principle and right to human dignity enshrined under the Basic Law.

The entrenchment of prisoners' rights was also linked to the depth of the codification impulse in Germany. This had been present since the early nineteenth century and the political pressure for this to be achieved by the 1970s was intense. Codification was founded on the 'internal relationship' between prison law and criminal law and centred on the definition of the prisoners' legal status. The commitment to codification was bound up in a broader historical context. Crucial here were the aspiration towards the achievement of legal unity (*Rechtseinheit*) across the German states brought about by German unification in the 1870s, the social-liberal reformism of the Weimar period, the aspiration towards the 'rehumanization' of prison law after 1945 and the energetic reformism of the social liberal alliance in the 1970s. By this time, the political climate was ripe for fundamental penal reform. It was in this atmosphere of imminent change that the German FCC declared existing prison law unconstitutional and required the legislature to deliver a new Prison Act. This Act had to define prisoners' positive rights, limitations of prisoners' basic rights, and substantive principles of prison administration in line with the imperatives of the *Rechtsstaatsprinzip* and the 'constitutional resocialization principle'. It was to be infused with the ideals of the Constitution from start to finish.

In this reforming environment the penal academy enjoyed conspicuous influence. It initiated calls for codification and dominated the substance of arguments associated with penal reform. Its influence was key in the achievement of a unitary statutory purpose of prison administration and the 'constitutional resocialization principle'. That this was achieved when the 'rehabilitation' ideal was declining internationally was testimony to the continuing faith in the resocialization ideal within the academy, the dominance of domestic academic opinion, and the deeper relationship between social liberal politics and the resocialization ideal. The survival of resocialization can also be attributed to the academy's effective use of constitutional arguments in advancing and entrenching this ideal, in turn signalling the efficacy of 'rights rhetoric' as a penal reform strategy in Germany.

But the Prison Act was marked by the consensus style of German politics and the imperatives of German-style federalism. The changes made in the final stages of legislative drafting led to the creation of what many called a 'compromise Act' (*Kompromißgesetz*). Since the Act entered into force, the prisoner's legal status has been undermined by the broad discretion under the Act, the initial resistance of state administrations to the fundamental ideals of the Act, the refractory behaviour of prison administrators, the prisoners' lack of access to legal support, the slowness of the Higher Regional Courts to develop substantive principles of prison administration and the failure of the special Prison Courts to develop into informal and constructive conflict resolution forums for prisoners and prison administrators.

These obstacles, while not insignificant challenges to the development of prisoners' rights, are countered by an active and critical penal academy whose opinions have fed into the judgments of the FCC. This relationship between judges and academics in sustaining and creating the law, a central facet of German legal culture, has underpinned the continuing protection of the Prison Act's ideals. This pursuit of principle has not manifested itself in a constitutional jurisprudence of prisoners' rights rooted purely in abstract argument. Neither the members of the penal academy, who are trained in penology and law, nor the FCC, which is guided by its critical opinion, is oblivious to the institutional dynamics of prison institutions or the complexity of prison life. Rather they have both sought to further the development of specialized principles of prison administration, to simplify the processes of prisoners' rights enforcement and to find the elusive balance between protecting prisoners' negative rights, realizing the 'constitutional resocialization principle', and maintaining security and order and administrative flexibility. In short, German prison law can be viewed as a site of struggle between the fulfilment of an ambitious conception of the prisoner's legal status and the imperatives of penal politics and administrative practice. Whilst much remains to be achieved, constitutional and penological principle has acted as a normative compass in a time of increasing hostility to the welfare-oriented and liberal ideals of the 1970s.

It is difficult to find clear legal principles guiding the exercise of prison administration and defining prisoners' rights in English law. Germans would note the absence of any attempt to root the development of prisoners' rights within a constitutional conception of the purpose of imprisonment, an articulated notion of the prisoners' administrative rights status, or recognition of prisoners' positive rights. Part II of this book seeks to explore this divergence.

Unlike Germany, the statutory regime governing prisons in England is concerned, not with the definition of the prisoners' legal status or the creation of legally enforceable rights, but with clarifying lines of political control and accountability. The statutory regime places the Home Secretary in a central position, giving him the power to make and amend Prison Rules. These are broadly drafted, give prisoners minimum entitlements, and afford prison authorities broad discretion. There are no overarching judicially recognized principles of prison administration to assist in the interpretation of these rules or to structure the exercise of administrative discretion. The Rules are complemented by a plethora of performance indicators and managerial standards monitored by processes of self and external audit. These managerial structures, if backed by sympathetic political will, financial resources, and a commitment to substantive 'outcomes' rather than 'outputs', have strong potential to enhance prisoner interests and prison life. But, they do not vest prisoners with individual entitlements. Like the statutory regime, the broadly drafted Prison Rules, and the limited remit and competence of complaints and inspection bodies, managerial strategies remain complementary to the pivotal role of the Home Secretary in the definition of prison policy and prisoners' rights. They are part of the broader project of maintaining a flexible and politically responsive prison system.

Consequently, neither the general statutory framework, nor the rules governing the administration of prisons 'purport to provide a code of directly legally enforceable rights in prisoners'.[6] In contrast to Germany, there is no legislative invitation to the courts, to take an active role in the administration of prisons. Rather, English courts have chipped away at administrative discretion and carved out their own role in the prison accountability network. Encouraged by the activism of the European Court of Human Rights, domestic courts have developed individual prisoners' rights, using general principles of public law as well as Convention rights (furthered more recently by the Human Rights Act (HRA) 1998). But judicial supervision of prison life is tentative, resting on a tremulous statutory footing, and prisoners' legal protections vary, being dependant on the subject matter involved and the extent to which prisoners' personal liberty is at stake.

Calls for the reform and modernization of the statutory regime governing prisons, and the better definition of prisoners' rights, have been present in England for over thirty years. This domestic reform movement is part of,

---

[6] G. Richardson, 'Prisoners and the Law: Beyond Rights' in C. McCrudden and G. Chambers (eds), *Individual Rights and the Law in the UK* (Clarendon Press, Oxford, 1993) 179, 183.

and gains support from, a broader international concern with prisoners' rights which has intensified since the early 1970s and led to the development of what might be termed an international law of prisoners' rights. Many hard fought victories have been attained by this movement, including a highly critical and activist Prisons Inspectorate and Prisons Ombudsman. But domestic reform initiatives have not yet been successful in achieving the legislative reform of prisoners' rights. With little political capital to be gained from instituting a bill of prisoners' rights, successive English governments have protected the administrative and policy discretion afforded them by current legislative arrangements. Over the last thirty years this political control has become central to, and facilitative of, the politicization of penal policy and criminal justice generally. In this penal environment, 'rights rhetoric' struggles for influence in the face of the powerful competing discourses of 'instrumental managerialism', 'populist punitivism' and 'public protection'. Prisoners' interests are represented in a broader political climate of fiscal restraint, declining social sympathy, and increased anxiety about crime.

But prisoners' administrative rights in England are not only weakened by the absence of statutory protection. Of equal importance is the broader constitutional environment in which judges are operating. In contrast to Germany's highly-articulated rights culture, England experiences an ambivalent cultural relationship to fundamental rights. This ambivalence is grounded in the historical continuity and relative success of organic democratic traditions, conventions, and institutions. The rationalist project of fundamental rights protection within German legal and political culture, which is inextricably entwined with the self-doubt of the country's political memory, is not present in England. Constitutional rights do not hold the same symbolic significance. Rather, orthodox and radical English constitutional traditions place faith in the flexibility and evolutionary nature of the political constitution and view Parliament, rather than the judiciary, as the ultimate protector of individual liberty. The traditional belief in parliamentary sovereignty is interlocked with a broad division between 'the judicial control of legality and the parliamentary control of the political' and accompanied by the deep pragmatic traditions of the common law.

The rise of a constitutional rights discourse in England, culminating in the HRA 1998, represents a cultural shift in political and legal culture. It signals a reinvention of the organic and pragmatic approach to the protection of liberty. This shift to a rights consciousness, both within internal legal culture and political culture more generally, is a response to concern that traditional constitutional arrangements cannot keep up with the threats to liberty posed by modern government. Moreover, it is a sign of the impact of a global rights discourse on domestic English legal and political culture. The HRA 1998 is the product of a concern to balance this incipient rights approach with the profound constitutional attachment to parliamentary sovereignty.

It is the legislative symbol of the ambivalence towards fundamental rights which lies at the heart of English constitutional culture. Unlike the Basic Law, which signalled a clean break with Germany's past, the 1998 Act is legitimized by its continuity with England's constitutional traditions. Consequently, the extent of the human rights project in England remains a matter of deep controversy and, as the recent discourse of judicial deference demonstrates, judges are ambivalent in their role as guardians of constitutional rights. This has complex implications for prisoners, for while the development of prisoners' rights has been intertwined with an incipient rights discourse, it has also been shaped by the competing and entrenched discourses of sovereignty and pragmatism.

In this complex and ambivalent constitutional environment, the English judiciary have developed a modest conception of the prisoner's legal status. In contrast to Germany's ambitious definition, the English notion of the prisoner's legal status is without an explicit division between the prisoner's personal liberty and administrative rights, any positive conception of prisoners' rights or any broader constitutional conception of the purpose of imprisonment. This modest conception, which is closely allied to that of the European Court of Human Rights, focuses on the protection of the prisoner's negative liberty through the assertion of a general principle of proportionality. It does not provide any institutionally specific, overarching principles by which to evaluate what limitations of fundamental rights imprisonment should represent. At best, the conception of the prisoner's fundamental rights status provides piecemeal protection of a prisoner's rights in the individual case. It reflects judicial hesitancy in encroaching on the political terrain of prison administration as well as an absence of any social constitutional rights tradition in England.

The legislative and constitutional context within which judges are operating, and the modest conception of fundamental rights which has been developed in this context, constitute the backdrop against which the jurisprudence of prisoners' rights in England must be viewed. It explains why, from a German perspective, the judicial development of prisoners' rights appears tentative, partial, and uneven. Resting on an uncertain legislative and constitutional footing, judicial development of prisoners' rights vacillates between a language of rights and a language of pragmatism and sovereignty (articulated more recently as judicial deference). It remains attached to an indivisible conception of prisoners' liberty, focusing primarily on the assertion and protection of what Germans would view as prisoners' status rights whilst neglecting prisoners' administrative rights and the broader purposes of prison administration. Consequently, while the English conception of prisoners' rights, as developed by a common law judiciary, now seeks to protect the personal liberty of the offender it has yet to produce an ambitious conception of the exercise of fundamental rights in conditions of confinement.

Bibliography

BOOKS AND ARTICLES

Abel, R., 'Comparative Law and Social Theory' (1978) 26 *AJCL* 219.

Alexy, R., 'Grundrechte als subjektive Rechte und als objektive Normen' (1990) *Der Staat* 49.

—— *A Theory of Constitutional Rights* (trans. Julian Rivers, OUP, Oxford, 2002).

Allan, T., 'Legislative Supremacy and the Rule of Law: Democracy and Constitutionalism' (1985) *CLJ* 111.

—— 'Dworkin and Dicey: the Rule of Law as Integrity' (1988) 8(2) *OJLS* 266.

—— 'Pragmatism and Theory in Public Law' (1988) 104 *LQR* 422.

—— 'Constitutional Rights and Common Law' (1991) 11(4) *OJLS* 453.

—— *Law, Liberty and Justice* (Clarendon Press, Oxford, 1993).

Allison, J., *A Continental Distinction in the Common Law* (OUP, Oxford, 2000).

Argent, G., 'I don't want this human rights waffle—and I'm a lawyer' *Mail on Sunday*, 1 October 2000.

Arloth, F., 'Der Angleichungsgrundsatz des § 3 Abs. 1 StVollzG: Gestaltungsprinzip oder Leerformel?' (1987) *ZfStrVo* 328.

—— 'Strafzwecke im Strafvollzug' (1988) *GA* 403.

—— 'Aufgaben des Strafvollzugs' (1990) *ZfStrVo* 329.

Aschrott, P., 'Die neuen Grundsätze über den Vollzug von Freiheitsstrafen in Deutschland' (1898) 18 *ZStW* 384.

Ashworth, A., *Sentencing and Criminal Justice* (3rd edn, Butterworths, London, 2000).

—— 'Sentencing' in Maguire, M. *et al.* (eds), *Oxford Handbook of Criminology* (OUP, Oxford, 2002) 1077.

—— *Human Rights, Serious Crime and Criminal Procedure* (53rd Hamlyn Lecture, Sweet & Maxwell, London 2002).

Atiyah, P.S., *Pragmatism and Theory in English Law* (Hamlyn Lectures 39th Series, Stevens & Sons, London 1987).

Badura, P., 'Das Prinzip der sozialen Grundrechte und seine Verwirklichung im Recht der Bundesrepublik Deutschland' (1975) 14 *Der Staat* 17.

Bailey, S., Harris, D. and Jones, B., *Civil Liberties: Cases and Materials* (3rd edn, Butterworths, London, 1991).

Baldwin, R., 'The Next Steps: Ministerial Responsibility and Government by Agency' (1998) *MLR* 622.

Bamforth, N., 'The True "Horizontal Effect" of the Human Rights Act 1998' (2001) 117 *LQR* 35.

Barnum, D., Sullivan, L. and Sunkin, M., 'Constitutional and Cultural Underpinnings of Political Freedom in Britain and the United States' (1992) 12(3) *OJLS* 362.

Barron, A. and Scott, C., 'The Citizen's Charter Programme' (1992) 55 *MLR* 526.

Baumann, J. *et al.* (eds), *Alternativ-Entwurf eines Strafgesetzbuches (Allgemeiner Teil)* (Arbeitskreis deutscher und schweizerischer Strafrechtslehrer, Tübingen, 1966).

——*Alternativ-Entwurf eines Strafvollzugsgesetzes* (Arbeitskreis deutscher und schweizerischer Strafrechtslehrer, Tübingen, 1973).

Bayer, W. *et al.*, 'Tatschuldausgleich und vollzugliche Entscheidungen' (1987) *MschrKrim* 167.

BBC News, 'League Tables Shame Worst Prisons', 24 July 2003. http://news.bbc.co.uk/2/hi/uk_news/3091949.stm.

—— 'Numbers pressure causing prison suicides', 17 August 2003. http://news.bbc.co.uk/2/hi/uk_news/3157873.stm.

Beatson, J. (ed.), *Constitutional Reform in the United Kingdom: Practice and Principles* (Hart, Oxford, 1988).

Beckmann, H., 'Anmerkung Zu BVerfGE 64, 261' (1984) *StV* 165.

Beirne, P., 'Cultural Relativism and Comparative Criminology' (1983) 7 *Contemporary Crises* 371.

Bell, J., 'Comparative Law and Legal Theory' in Summers, R., Krawietz, W., MacCormick, N. and von Wright, G.H. (eds), *Prescriptive Formality and Normative Rationality in Modern Legal Systems* (Duncker and Humblot, Berlin, 1994) 19.

——*French Legal Cultures* (Butterworths, London, 2001).

—— 'Comparing Public Law' in in Harding, A. and Örücü, E. (eds), *Comparative Law in the 21st Century* (Kluwer, London, 2002) ch. 13.

Bemman, G., 'Im Vollzug der Freiheitsstrafe soll der Gefangene fähig werden, künftig in sozialer Verantwortung ein Leben ohne Straftaten zu führen' (1988) 12 *StV* 549.

—— 'Strafvollzug im sozialen Rechtsstaat' in Bemman, G. and Manodelakis, I. (eds), *Probleme des Staatlichen Strafens unter besonderer Berücksichtigung des Strafvollzugs* (Nomos, Baden-Baden, 1989) 35.

Benda, E., Maihofer, W. and Vogel, H.-J. (eds), *Handbuch des Verfassungsrechts* (De Gruyter, Berlin, 1983).

Bengoetxea, J. and Jung, H., 'Towards a European Criminal Jurisprudence?' (1991) 11 *LS* 239.

Bennett, R., 'Britain may opt out of human rights convention' *The Times*, 20 February 2003.

Bennion, F., 'What interpretation is possible under section 3 of the HRA (2000) *PL* 77.

Bingham, Lord, 'Incorporation of the ECHR: The Opportunity and the Challenge' (1998) 2 *Jersey Law Review* 257.

Bingham, Sir Thomas, 'The European Convention of Human Rights: Time to Incorporate?' (1993) 109 *LQR* 390.

Bitburger Gespräche, Jahrbuch 1986/2 (Trier Rechtspolitik, Beck, Munich, 1986) 1.

Blackbourn, D., *The Fontana History of Germany: The Long Nineteenth Century, 1780–1918* (Fontana, London, 1997).

Blankenburg, E., 'Civil Litigation Rates as Indicators for Legal Cultures' in Nelken, D. (ed.), *Comparing Legal Cultures* (Dartmouth, Aldershot, 1996) 69.

Blau, G., 'Aufgaben und Grenzen der Kriminalpädagogik' in Busch, M. and Edel,

G. (eds), *Erziehung zur Freiheit durch Freiheitsentzug* (Luchterhand, Neuwied, 1969) 383.

—— 'Die Kriminalpolitik der deutschen Strafrechtsreformgesetze' (1977) *ZStW* 511.

—— (ed), *Die Reform des Strafvollzugs im Lichte internationaler Reformtendenzen* (Brockmeyer, Bochum, 1981).

Böckenförde, E.-W., 'Grundrechte als Grundsatznormen' (1990) *Der Staat* 1.

—— *Staat, Verfassung, Demokratie* (Suhrkamp, Frankfurt am Main, 1991).

—— 'Die Überlastung des Bundesverfassungsgerichts' (1996) *ZRP* 281.

——, Jekewitz, J. and Ramm, T., *Soziale Grundrechte* (Müller, Heidelberg, 1980).

Böhm, A., 'Vollzugslockerungen und offener Vollzug zwischen Strafzwecken und Vollzugszielen' (1986) *NStZ* 201.

—— 'Strafzwecke und Vollzugsziele' in Busch, M. and Krämer, E. (eds), *Strafvollzug und Schuldproblematik* (Centaurus, Pfaffenweiler, 1988) 129.

—— 'Zur "Verrechtlichung" des Strafvollzugs' (1992) *ZfStrVo* 37.

Börne, B. *et al.* (eds), *Einigkeit und Recht und Freiheit—Festschrift für Karl Carstens* (Heymanns, Cologne, 1984).

Bottomley, A., *Criminology in Focus: Past Trends and Future Prospects* (Martin Robertson, Oxford, 1979) ch. 4.

—— 'The Justice Model in America and Britain: development and analysis' in Bottoms, A. and Preston, R. (eds), *The Coming Penal Crisis: a criminological and theological explanation* (Scottish Academic Press, Edinburgh, 1980).

Bottoms, A., 'The Philosophy and Politics of Punishment and Sentencing' in Clarkson, C. and Morgan, R. (eds), *The Politics of Sentencing Reform* (Clarendon Press, Oxford, 1995) 17.

—— 'Theoretical Reflections on a Penal Policy Initiative' in Zedner, L. and Ashworth, A. (eds), *The Criminological Foundations of Penal Policy* (OUP, Oxford, 2003) 107.

Bradley, A., 'The Sovereignty of Parliament—In Perpetuity' in Jowell, J. and Oliver, D. (eds), *The Changing Constitution* (3rd edn, OUP, Oxford, 1994).

—— 'The Sovereignty of Parliament—Form or Substance?' in Jowell, J. and Oliver, D. (eds), *The Changing Constitution* (4th edn, OUP, Oxford, 2000) 23.

Britz, G., 'Leistungsgerechtes Arbeitsentgelt für Strafgefangene?' (1999) *ZfStrVo* 195.

Browne-Wilkinson, Lord, 'The Infiltration of a Bill of Rights' (1992) *PL* 397.

Caldwell, P.C., *Popular Sovereignty and the Crisis of German Constitutional Law* (Duke University Press, Durham, 1997).

Calliess, R.-P., *Strafvollzugsrecht* (Beck, Munich, 1992).

—— and Müller-Dietz, H., *Strafvollzugsgesetz* (9th edn, Beck, Munich, 2002). **(Abbreviation: Calliess/Müller-Dietz)**

Campbell, T., Ewing, K. and Tomkins, A., *Sceptical Essays on Human Rights* (OUP, Oxford, 2001).

Casale, S., 'Conditions and Standards' in Player, E. and Jenkins, M. (eds), *Prisons After Woolf: Reform through Riot* (Routledge, London, 1993) 66.

—— and Plotnikoff, J., *Minimum Standards for Prisons: A Programme of Change* (NACRO, London, 1989).

Cavadino, M. and Dignan, J., *The Penal System* (2nd edn, Sage, London, 1997).

Cavadino, M. and Dignan, J. (eds), 'Reparation, Retribution and Rights' in von Hirsch, A. and Ashworth, A. *Principled Sentencing—Readings on Theory and Policy* (2nd edn, Hart, Oxford, 1998) 351.

——, Crow, I. and Dignan, J., *Criminal Justice 2000: Strategies for a New Century* (Waterside Press, Winchester, 1999).

Christians, 'Die Sicherung gerechter Behandlung der Gefangen im deutschen Recht' (1935) 66 *BlGefk* 232, 242.

Clarkson, C. and Morgan, R. (eds), *The Politics of Sentencing Reform* (Clarendon Press, Oxford, 1995).

Clayton, R. and Tomlinson, H., *The Law of Human Rights* (OUP, Oxford, 2000).

Constantinesco, L.-J., 'Die Kulturkreise als Grundlage der Rechtskreise' (1981) 22 *ZfRV* 161.

Cotterell, R., 'The Concept of Legal Culture' in Nelken, D. (ed.), *Comparing Legal Cultures* (Dartmouth, Aldershot, 1996) 13.

—— 'Seeking Similarity, Appreciating Difference: Comparative Law and Communities' in Harding, A. and Örücü, E. (eds), *Comparative Law in the 21st Century* (Kluwer, London, 2002).

Craig, G., *The Germans* (Penguin, London, 1991).

Craig, P., *Public Law and Democracy in the United Kingdom and the United States of America* (Clarendon Press, Oxford, 1990).

—— 'Formal and Substantive Conceptions of the Rule of Law: An Analytical Framework' (1997) *PL* 467.

—— 'Ultra Vires and the Foundations of Judicial Review' (1998) *CLJ* 63.

—— *Administrative Law* (4th edn, Sweet & Maxwell, London, 1999).

—— 'Competing Models of Judicial Review' (1999) *PL* 428.

—— 'Public Law, Political Theory and Legal Theory' (2000) *PL* 211.

—— 'The Courts, The Human Rights Act and Judicial Review' (2001) 117 *LQR* 589.

Creifelds, C., *Rechtswörterbuch* (Beck, Munich, 2000).

Creighton, S. and King, V., *Prisoners and the Law* (2nd edn, Butterworths, London, 2000).

Cressey, D. (ed.), *The Prison: Studies in Institutional Organisation and Change* (Holt, Rinehart and Winston, New York, 1961).

Curran, V.G., 'Cultural Immersion, Difference and Categories in US Comparative Law' (1998) 46 *American Journal of Comparative Law* 43.

Cygan, A., *Constitutional Civil Liberties in Germany and the United Kingdom* (Civil Liberties Research Unit, Kings College and Goethe-Institut, London, 1998).

Darnstädt, T., 'Die enthauptete Republik' *Der Spiegel*, 25 June 2003.

—— and Kloth, M., 'Die Konsens-Falle' *Der Spiegel*, 25 June 2003.

Daum, W., 'Soziale Grundrechte' (1968) *RdA* 81.

De Cruz, P., *Comparative Law in a Changing World* (2nd edn, Cavendish, London, 1999).

De Smith, S. and Brazier, R., *Constitutional and Administrative Law* (Penguin, London, 1998).

Degenhart, C., *Staatsrecht I* (13th edn, Müller, Heidelberg, 1997).

Dicey, A.V., *The Law of the Constitution* (8th edn, Macmillan, London, 1927).

—— *The Law of the Constitution* (10th edn, Macmillan, London, 1959).

Dine, J., 'European Community Criminal law?' (1993) *CLR* 163.

Dopslaff, U., 'Abschied von den Entscheidungsfreiräumen bei Ermessen und unbestimmten Rechtsbegriffen mit Beurteilungsspielraum im Strafvollzugsgesetz' (1988) *ZStW* 567.

Douglas, G. and Moerings, M., 'Prisoners' Rights in the Netherlands and England and Wales' in Harding, R. *et al.*, *Criminal Justice in Europe: A Comparative Study* (Clarendon Press, Oxford, 1995) 341.

Downes, D., *Contrasts in Tolerance* (Clarendon Press, Oxford, 1988).

—— 'The *macho* penal economy' (2001) 3(1) *P&S* 61.

—— and Morgan, R., 'Dumping Hostages to Fortune' in Maguire, M. *et al.* (eds), *Oxford Handbook of Criminology* (2nd edn, OUP, Oxford, 1997) 87.

—— and Morgan, R., 'The skeletons in the cupboard: the politics of law and order at the turn of the millennium' in Maguire, M. *et al.* (eds), *Oxford Handbook of Criminology* (3rd edn, OUP, Oxford, 2002) 286.

Drewry, G., 'Revolution in Whitehall: The Next Steps and Beyond' in Jowell, J. and Oliver, D. (eds), *The Changing Constitution* (3rd edn, OUP, Oxford, 1994) 155.

Duff, A., *Punishment* (Dartmouth, Aldershot, 1993).

Dünkel, F., 'Die Rechtsstellung von Strafgefangenen und Möglichkeiten der rechtlichen Kontrolle von Vollzugsentscheidungen in Deutschland' (1996) *GA* 518.

—— 'Germany' in Dünkel, F. and van Zyl Smit, D. (eds), *Prison Labour: Salvation or Slavery? International Perspectives* (Dartmouth, Aldershot, 1999) 77.

—— and Kunkat, A., 'Zwischen Innovation und Restauration. 20 Jahre Strafvollzugsgesetz—eine Bestandsaufnahme' (1997) *NK* 24.

Dünkel, H., 'Die Strafvollstreckungskammer—weiterhin ein unbeliebter Torso?' (1992) *Bewährungshilfe* 196.

Dworkin, R., *Taking Rights Seriously* (Duckworth, London, 1978).

Dyzenhaus, D., *Legality and Legitimacy* (OUP, Oxford, 1997).

Eagleton, T., *The Idea of Culture* (Blackwell, Oxford, 2000).

Ebke, W. and Finkin, M. (eds), *Introduction to German Law* (Kluwer, The Hague, 1996).

Editorial, 'Gefangene müssen bei Pflichtarbeit besser entlohnt werden' *Frankfurter Allgemeine Zeitung*, 2 July 1998, 1.

—— 'Bringing Rights Home' *The Economist*, 26 August 2000.

—— 'Judges as Politicians' *Daily Telegraph*, 13 December 2000.

—— 'Prisons and the Law' (2002) 142 *Prison Service Journal* 1.

—— 'Human Rights Need Bite' *The Guardian*, 16 May 2003.

Edwards, R., 'Judicial Deference under the Human Rights Act' (2002) 65 *MLR* 859.

Elliot, M., 'The Demise of Parliamentary Sovereignty? The Implications for Justifying Judicial Review' (1999) 115 *LQR* 119.

—— 'The Ultra Vires Doctrine in a Constitutional Setting: Still the Central Principle of Administrative Law' (1999) *CLJ* 129.

Erichsen, H.-U., *Allgemeines Verwaltungsrecht* (10th edn, Walter de Gruyter, Berlin, 1995).

—— 'Die Drittwirkung der Grundrechte' (1996) *Jura* 527.

Ericson, R. K Carriere, K., 'The Fragmentation of Criminology' in Nelken, D. (ed.), *The Futures of Criminology* (Sage, London, 1994) 89.

Eschke, D., *Mängel im Rechtsschutz gegen Strafvollstreckungs-und Strafvollzugsmaßnahmen* (R. v. Decker's Verlag, Heidelberg, 1993).

Eser, A., 'Resozialisierung in der Krise' in Baumann, J. and Tiedemann, K. (eds), *Einheit und Vielfalt des Strafrechts: Festschrift für Karl Peters:* (Mohr, Tübingen, 1974) 505.

—— 'The Importance of Comparative Legal Research for the Development of Criminal Sciences', Paper at World Law Conference, Brussels, 9–12 September 1996.

—— and Huber, B., *Strafrechtsentwicklung in Europa* (Max Planck Institute for Foreign and International Criminal Law, Freiburg, 1993).

Evans, M, and Morgan, R., 'The CPT: An Introduction' in Morgan, R. and Evans, M. (eds), *Protecting Prisoners: The Standards of the European Committee for the Prevention of Torture in Context* (OUP, Oxford, 1999) 3.

Ewing, K., 'Social Rights and Constitutional Law' (1999) *PL* 104.

—— 'The Human Rights Act and Parliamentary Democracy' (1999) 62 *MLR* 79.

—— and Gearty, C., *Freedom under Thatcher: Civil Liberties in Modern Britain* (Clarendon Press, Oxford, 1990).

—— and Gearty, C., *The Struggle for Civil Liberties* (OUP, Oxford, 2000).

Feest, J., *Imprisonment and the Criminal Justice System in the Federal Republic of Germany* (Arbeitspapiere des Forschungsschwerpunktes, Soziale Probleme: Kontrolle und Kompensation, Nr. 8, Bremen, 1982).

—— (ed.), *Kommentar zum Strafvollzugsgesetz* (3rd edn, Luchterhand, Neuwied, 1990).

—— (ed.), *Kommentar zum Strafvollzugsgesetz* (4th edn, Luchterhand, Neuwied, 2000).

(Abbreviation: Feest)

—— and Selling, P., 'Rechtstatsachen über Rechtsbeschwerden—Eine Untersuchung zur Praxis der Oberlandesgerichte in Strafvollzugssachen' in Kaiser, G. *et al.*, *Kriminologische Forschung in den 80er Jahren* (MPI, Freiburg, 1988) 259.

——, Lesting, W. and Selling, P., *Totale Institution und Rechtsschutz* (Westdeutscher Verlag, Opladen, 1997).

Feldman, D., *Civil Liberties and Human Rights in England and Wales* (Clarendon Press, Oxford, 1993).

Feldman, E., 'Patients' Rights, Citizens' Movements and Japanese Legal Culture' in Nelken, D. (ed.), *Comparing Legal Cultures* (Dartmouth, Aldershot, 1997) 215.

Ferracuti, F., 'Possibilities and Limits of Comparative Research in Criminology' in Jescheck, H.H. and Kaiser, G. (eds), *Die Vergleichung als Methode der Strafrechtswissenschaft und der Kriminologie* (Duncker and Humblot, Berlin, 1980).

Field, S. and Jörg, N., 'Corporate Liability and Manslaughter: Should We Be Going Dutch?' (1991) *CLR* 156.

Finnis, J., *Natural Law and Natural Rights* (Clarendon Press, Oxford, 1982).

Forsyth, C., 'Of Fig Leaves and Fairy Tales: The Ultra Vires Doctrine, the Sovereignty of Parliament and Judicial Review' (1996) 55(1) *CLJ* 122.

Foster, S., 'Prisoners, the HRA and the Right to Vote' (2001) 151 *NLJ* 560.

Fox, L.W., *The English Prison and Borstal Systems* (Routledge & Kegan Paul, London, 1952).

Fowles, A., 'Monitoring Expenditure on the Criminal Justice System: The Search for Control' (1990) 29 *Howard Journal* 82.

Frankenberg, G., 'Critical Comparisons: Re-thinking Comparative Law' (1985) 26(2) *Harvard Intl Law J* 411.

Frehsee, D., 'Neuere Tendenzen in der aktuellen Kommentar- und Lehrbuchliteratur zum Strafvollzug' (1993) *NStZ* 165.

Freudenthal, B. 'Der Strafvollzug als Rechtsverhältnis des öffentlichen Rechts' (1911) *ZStW* 222.

——'Die staatsrechtliche Stellung des Gefangenen', Rektoratsrede Jena 1910, printed in (1955) *ZfStrVo* 157.

Friedman, L., *The Legal System: A Social Science Perspective* (Russell Sage Foundation, New York, 1975).

—— 'Is There a Modern Legal Culture?' (1994) 7(2) *Ratio Juris* 117.

—— 'The Concept of Legal Culture: A Reply' in Nelken, D. (ed.), *Comparing Legal Cultures* (Dartmouth, Aldershot, 1997).

Friedrich, M., 'Die Grundlagendiskussion in der Weimarer Staatsrechtslehre' (1972) 13 *Politische Vierteljahresschrift* 582.

Friesenhahn, E., 'Der Wandel des Grundrechtsverständnisses' in *Verhandlungen des 50. Deutschen Juristentages* (Beck, Munich, 1974).

Fulbrook, M., *The Fontana History of Germany: 1918–1990—The Divided Nation* (Fontana, London, 1991).

Gadamer, H.G., *Truth and Method* (Sheed & Ward, London, 1975).

Gamble, A., 'Privatisation, Thatcherism, and the British State' (1989) 16 *JLS* 1.

Garland, D., *Punishment and Welfare* (Gower, Aldershot, 1985).

——*Punishment and Modern Society* (Clarendon Press, Oxford, 1990).

—— 'Punishment and Culture: Cultural Forms and Penal Practices' in Garland, D., *Punishment and Modern Society* (Clarendon Press, Oxford, 1990).

—— 'The Limits of the Sovereign State' (1996) 36 *BJC* 445.

—— 'The Culture of High Crime Societies' (2000) 40 *BJC* 347.

——*The Culture of Control* (OUP, Oxford, 2001).

—— and Sparks, R., 'Criminology, Social Theory and the Challenge of Our Times' (2000) 40 *BJC* 189.

Gearty, C., 'The Prisons and the Courts' in Muncie, J. and Sparks, R. (eds), *Imprisonment: European Perspectives* (Sage, London, 1991) 219.

—— (ed.), *European Civil Liberties and the European Convention of Human Rights: A Comparative Study* (Martinus Nijhoff Publishers, The Hague, 1997).

—— 'Reconciling Parliamentary Democracy and Human Rights' (2002) *LQR* 118, 248.

Geerds, F., 'Berthold Freudenthal' (1969) *ZfStrVo* 251.

Geertz, C., *The Interpretation of Cultures* (Basic Books, New York, 1973).

—— 'Thick Description: Toward an Interpretive Theory of Culture' in Geertz, C., *The Interpretation of Cultures* (Basic Books, New York, 1973) 3.

——*Local Knowledge: Further Essays in Interpretive Anthropology* (Basic Books, New York, 1983).

Gessner, V., 'Global Legal Interaction and Legal Cultures' (1994) 7 *Ratio Juris* 132.

——, Hoeland, A. and Varga, C. (eds), *European Legal Culture* (Dartmouth, Aldershot, 1996) 66.

Gewirth, A., 'The Epistemology of Human Rights (1984) I *Social Philosophy and Policy* 1.

Ghestin, J. and Boubeaux, G., *Traité de Droit Civil: Introduction Générale* (3rd edn, Libr. Gen. de Droit et du Jurisprudence, 1990).

Gilbride, P., 'More Killers are being released under Euro law' *The Express*, 4 June 2003.

Glenn, H., *Legal Traditions of the World* (OUP, Oxford, 2000).

Goffmann, E., 'On the Characteristics of Total Institutions: the Inmate World' in Cressey, D. (ed.), *The Prison: Studies in Institutional Organisation and Change* (Holt, Rinehart and Winston, New York, 1961) 16.

Goldsworthy, J., *The Sovereignty of Parliament, History and Philosophy* (OUP, Oxford,1999).

Goodridge, P., *Languages of Law* (Weidenfeld & Nicolson, London, 1990).

Gordon, R., 'Critical Legal Histories' (1984) 36 *Stanford LRev* 57.

Gray, J., *Enlightenment's Wake: Politics and Culture at the Close of the Modern Age* (Routledge, London, 1995).

Griffiths, J., 'The Political Constitution' (1979) 42 *MLR* 1.

—— *The Politics of the Judiciary* (4th edn, Fontana, London, 1991).

—— 'Brave new world of Sir John Laws' (2000) 63 (2) *MLR* 159.

—— 'The Political Constitution' (2001) 117 *LQR* 42.

Großfeld, B., *Kernfragen der Rechtsvergleichung* (Mohr/Siebeck, Tübingen, 1996).

Grosz, S., Beatson, J. and Duffy, P., *Human Rights: The 1998 Act and the European Convention* (Sweet & Maxwell, London, 2000).

Grunau, T. and Tiesler, E., *Strafvollzugsgesetz* (Heymanns, Cologne, 1977).

Gusy, C., 'Freiheitsentziehung und Grundgesetz' (1992) *NJW* 457.

Häberle, P., 'Grundrechte im Leistungsstaat' (1972) 30 *VVDStRL* 75.

—— 'Das Bundesverfassungsgericht im Leistungsstaat' (1972) *DÖV* 729.

Habermas, J., *Faktizität und Geltung* (Suhrkamp, Frankfurt am Main, 1992).

Haberstroh, D., 'Grundlagen des Strafvollzugsrechts' (1982) *Jura* 617.

Haffke, B., 'Gibt es ein verfassungsrechtliches Besserungsverbot' (1975) *MschrKrim* 246.

Hailsham, Lord, *The Dilemma of Democracy: Diagnosis and Prescription* (Collins, London, 1978).

Harden, I., *The Contracting State* (Open University Press, Buckingham, 1992).

—— and Lewis, J., *The Noble Lie: The British Constitution and the Rule of Law* (Hutchinson, London, 1986).

Harding, A. and Örücü, E. (eds), *Comparative Law in the 21st Century* (Kluwer, London, 2002).

Harding, C., Fennell, P., Jorg, N. and Swart, B. (eds), *Criminal Justice in Europe: A Comparative Study* (Clarendon Press, Oxford, 1995).

Harlow, C. (ed.), *Public Law and Politics* (Sweet & Maxwell, London, 1986).

—— 'Changing the Mindset: The Place of English Administrative Law' (1994) 14(3) *OJLS* 419.

—— and Rawlings, R., *Law and Administration* (2nd edn, Butterworths, London, 1997).

Hart, H.L.A., 'Are there any natural rights?' in Quinton, A. (ed.), *Political Philosophy* (OUP, Oxford, 1967) 53.

—— *Punishment and Responsibility: Essay in the Philosophy of Law* (Clarendon Press, Oxford, 1970).

—— *The Concept of Law* (2nd edn, Clarendon Press, Oxford, 1994).

Hassemer, W., 'Resozialisierung und Rechtsstaat' (1982) *KrimJ* 161.

—— 'Aktuelle Perspektiven der Kriminalpolitik' (1994) *StV* 333.

—— '"Zero tolerance"—Ein neues Strafkonzept?' in Albrecht, H. (ed.), *Internationale Perspektiven in Kriminologie und Strafrecht: Festschrift für Günther Kaiser* (Duncker and Humblot, Berlin, 1998) 793.

Hastrup, K. (ed.), *Legal Cultures and Human Rights* (Kluwer, The Hague, 2001).

Heghmanns, M., 'Die neuere Rechtsprechung des Bundesverfassungsgerichts zur gerichtlichen Überprüfung der Versagung von Vollzugslockerungen—eine Trendwende?' (1999) *ZStW* 647.

Heidensohn, F. and Farrell, M. (eds), *Crime in Europe* (Routledge, London, 1991).

Hesse, K., 'Bestand und Bedeutung der Grundrechte in der Bundesrepublik Deutschland' (1978) *EuGRZ* 427.

Hill, J., 'Comparative Law, Law Reform and Legal Theory' (1989) 9 *OJLS* 101.

Hill, W., 'Tatschuld und Strafvollzug: Analyse eines Beschlusses des Bundesverfassungsgerichts' (1986) *ZfStrVo* 139.

Hirsch, H.J. *et al.* (eds), *Gedächtnisschrift für Hilde Kaufmann* (Scherper Verlag, Berlin, 1981).

Hirschberg, L., *Der Grundsatz der Verhältnismäßigkeit* (Schwarz, Göttingen, 1981).

Hoffmann, Lord, 'The Separation of Powers' (2002) 7(3) *JR* 137.

Hofmann, H., 'Zur Herkunft der Menschenrechtserklärungen' (1988) *JuS* 841.

—— 'Die Grundrechte 1789–1949–1989' (1989) *NJW* 3177.

Hohfeld, W., *Fundamental Legal Conceptions as Applied in Judicial Reasoning* (Yale University Press, New Haven, 1919).

Honderich, T., *Punishment: The Supposed Justifications* (3rd edn, Polity Press, Cambridge, 1989).

Hood, R., 'Penal Policy and Criminological Challenges in the New Millennium' (2001) 34 *The Australian and New Zealand Journal of Criminology* 1.

Huber, B., 'Safeguarding of Prisoners' Rights Under the New West German Prison Act' (1978) *SAJC* 229.

Hudson, B., *Justice Through Punishment: A Critique of the 'Justice' Model of Corrections* (Macmillan, London, 1987).

Hug, W., 'The History of Comparative Law' [1931/32] XLV *Harvard L Rev* 1027.

Hunt, M., *Using Human Rights Law in English Courts* (Hart Publishing, Oxford, 1998).

—— 'The Horizontal Effect of the Human Rights Act' (1998) *Public Law* 423.

—— 'The Human Rights Act and Legal Culture: The Judiciary and the Legal Profession' (1999) *JLS* 86.

—— 'Judicial Review after the Human Rights Act (1999) 2 *QMWLJ* 14.

—— 'Sovereignty's Blight: Why Contemporary Public Law Needs the Concept of 'Due Deference' in Bamforth, N. and Leyland, P. (eds), *Public Law in a Multi-Layered Constitution* (Hart, Oxford, 2003) 337.

Irvine, Lord, 'Constitutional Reform and a Bill of Rights' (1997) 5 *EHRLR* 483.

—— 'The Development of Human Rights in Britain under an Incorporated Convention on Human Rights' (1998) *PL* 221, 225.

—— 'The Impact of the Human Rights Act: Parliament, the Courts and the Executive' (2003) *PL* 308.

Isensee, J. and Kirchhoff, P. (eds), *Handbuch des Staatsrechts der Bundesrepublik Deutschland, Band IV: Allgemeine Grundrechtslehren* (Müller, Heidelberg, 1992).

Jacobs, F. and White, R., *The European Convention on Human Rights* (2nd edn, Clarendon Press, Oxford, 1996).

Jacobsen, A. and Schlink, B. (eds), *Weimar: A Jurisprudence of Crisis* (University of California Press, Berkeley, 2000).

Jarass, H.-D., 'Grundrechte als Wertentscheidungen bzw. objektivrechtliche Prinzipien in der Rechtsprechung des Bundesverfassungsgerichts' (1985) *AöR* 363.

—— and Pieroth, B., *Grundgesetz für die Bundesrepublik Deutschland* (4th edn, Beck, Munich, 1997).

Jenkins, S., *Accountable to None: The Tory Nationalization of Britain* (Penguin, London, 1995).

Jennings, I., *Law and the Constitution* (University of London Press, London, 1938).

Jescheck, H., *Recht und Staat in Geschichte und Gegenwart: Entwicklung, Aufgaben und Methoden der Strafrechtsvergleichung* (Mohr, Tübingen, 1955).

—— and Kaiser, G. (eds), *Die Vergleichung als Methode der Strafrechtswissenschaft und der Kriminologie* (Duncker and Humblot, Berlin, 1980) 129.

—— and Weigend, T., *Lehrbuch des Strafrechts: Allgemeiner Teil* (5th edn, Duncker and Humblot, Berlin, 1996).

Johnston, P. and Jones, G., 'Blair to take on judges over asylum' *The Daily Telegraph*, 20 February 2003.

Jones, C., 'Auditing Criminal Justice' (1993) 33 *BJC* 187.

Jones, P., *Rights* (Macmillan, London, 1994).

Jowell, J., 'Of Vires and Vacuums: The Constitutional Context of Judicial Review' (1999) *PL* 448.

—— 'Beyond the Rule of Law: Towards Constitutional Judicial Review (2000) *PL* 671.

—— and Lester, A., 'Beyond Wednesbury: substantive principles of administrative law' (1987) *PL* 368.

—— and Lester, A., 'Courts and Administration in Britain: Standards, Principles and Rights' (1988) *Israel Law Review* 409.

—— and Oliver, D. (eds), *The Changing Constitution* (OUP, Oxford, 1994).

Jung, H., 'Behandlung als Rechtsbegriff' (1987) *ZfStrVo* 38.

Justen, D., *Unbestimmte Rechtsbegriffe mit 'Beurteilungsspielraum' im Strafvollzugsgesetz* (Doctoral Dissertation, Mainz, 1995).

Kahn-Freund, O., *Comparative Law as an Academic Subject* (Clarendon Press, Oxford, 1965).

Kaiser, G., 'Begriff, Ortsbestimmung und Entwicklung des Strafvollzugs' in Kaiser, G. *et al.*, *Strafvollzug* (Müller, Karlsruhe, 1974) 1.

—— 'Resozialisierung und Zeitgeist' in Herren, R. *et al.* (eds), *Kultur-Kriminalität-Strafrecht: Festschrift für Thomas Würtenberger* (Duncker and Humblot, Berlin, 1977) 359.

—— 'Strafvollzug im internationalen Vergleich' in Hirsch, H.J. *et al.* (eds), *Gedächtnisschrift für Hilde Kaufmann* (Scherper Verlag, Berlin, 1981) 599.

—— *Strafvollzug im europäischen Vergleich* (Wissenschaftliche Buchgesellschaft, Darmstadt, 1983).

—— and Albrecht, H.-J., *Crime and Criminal Policy in Europe: Proceedings of the Second European Colloquium* (MPI, Freiburg, 1990).

——, Kerner, H.-J. and Schöch, H., *Strafvollzug* (Müller, Heidelberg, 1992).

—— *et al.*, *Kleines Kriminologisches Wörterbuch* (Müller, Heidelberg, 1993).

——and Schöch, H., *Strafvollzug* (Müller, Heidelberg, 2002).

Kammann, U., *Gerichtlicher Rechtsschutz im Strafvollzug: Grenzen und Möglichkeiten der Kontrollen vollzuglicher Maßnahmen am Beispiel der Strafvollstreckungskammer beim Landgericht Arnsberg* (Centaurus, Pfaffenweiler, 1991).

——'Der Richter als Mediator im Gefängnis: Idee, Wirklichkeit und Möglichkeit' (1993) *KrimJ* 13.

——'Die Erweiterung des Renitenzbegriffs im Strafvollzug (1993) *ZfStrVo* 206.

——'Der Beurteilungsspielraum und sein Einfluß auf die Ver-un-rechtlichung des Strafvollzuges' (1994) *ZRP* 474.

——'Die Blindheit der Justitia oder: die reaktionäre Entwicklung im Strafvollzug' (1996) *NK* 14.

——'Das Urteil des Bundesverfassungsgerichts vom 1.7.1998 (StV 98, 438) zur Gefangenenentlohnung, ein nicht kategorischer Imperativ für den Resozialisierungsvollzug' (1999) *StV* 438.

——*Handbuch für die Strafvollstreckung und den Strafvollzug* (Verlag für Rechts- und Anwaltspraxis Recklinghausen, 2002).

Karpen, U. (ed.), *The Constitution of the Federal Republic of Germany: Essays on the Basic Rights and Principles of the Basic Law* (Nomos, Baden-Baden, 1988).

Kennedy, E., 'The Politics of Toleration in Late Weimar' (1985) 5 *HPT* 109.

King, R. and Morgan, R., *The Future of the Prison System* (Gower, Aldershot, 1980).

King, R. and McDermott, K., 'British Prisons 1970–1987: The Ever Deepening Crisis' (1989) 29 *BJC* 107.

Klare, K., 'Legal Culture and Transformative Constitutionalism' (1988) 14 *SAJHR* 146.

Klug, F., *Values for a Godless Age* (Penguin, London, 2000).

——'A Law Fit for a Prince' *The Guardian*, 3 October 2002.

——'Judicial Deference Under the Human Rights Act 1998' (2003) 2 *EHRLR* 125.

——and K Starmer 'It's all about cultural change' *The Times*, 1 August 2000.

Knowles, D., 'Punishment and Rights' in Matravers, M. (ed.), *Punishment and Political Theory* (Hart, Oxford, 1999) 28.

Koepsel, K., 'Das Vollzugskonzept des Strafvollzugsgesetzes und seine Veränderung durch Verwaltungsvorschriften und Erlasse der Landesjustizverwaltungen' (1992) *ZfStrVo* 46.

——*Strafvollzug im Sozialstaat* (Doctoral Dissertation, Hamburg, 1985).

Kommers, D., *The Constitutional Jurisprudence of the Federal Republic of Germany* (Duke University Press, Durham, 1997).

Krohne, K., *Die gesetzliche Regelung des Strafvollzugs im Deutschen Reiche* (Schulze, Oldenburg, 1875) 2.

Kruis, K. and Cassardt, G., 'Verfassungsrechtliche Leitsätze zum Vollzug von Straf- und Untersuchungshaft' (1995) *NStZ* 521.

——and Cassardt, G., 'Fortschreibung der verfassungsrechtlichen Leitsätze zum Vollzug von Straf-und Untersuchungshaft' (1998) *NStZ* 593.

Kühne, J.-D., 'Die französische Menschen- und Bürgerrechtserklärung im Rechtsvergleich mit den Vereinigten Staaten und Deutschland' (1990) *Jahrbuch des öffentlichen Rechts der Gegenwart* 1.

Kunig, P., 'The Principle of Social Justice' in Karpen, U. (ed.), *The Constitution of the Federal Republic of Germany: Essays on the Basic Rights and Principles of the Basic Law* (Nomos, Baden-Baden, 1988) 187.

Lacey, M., and Haakonssen, K. (eds), *A Culture of Rights* (CUP, Cambridge, 1990).

Lacey, N., *State Punishment: Political Principles and Community Values* (Routledge, London, 1988).

—— 'Government as Manager, Citizen as Consumer' (1994) 57 *MLR* 534.

—— 'Principles, Politics and Criminal Justice' in Zedner, L. and Ashworth, A. (eds), *The Criminological Foundations of Penal Policy* (OUP, Oxford, 2003) 79.

—— and Zedner, L., 'Community in German Criminal Justice: A Significant Absence?' (1998) 7 *S&LS* 7.

Lange, K., 'Soziale Grundrechte in der deutschen Verfassungsentwicklung und in den derzeitigen Länderverfassungen' in Böckenförde, E.-W., Jekewitz, J. and Ramm, T. (eds), *Soziale Grundrechte* (Müller, Heidelberg, 1980).

Lardy, H., 'Prisoner Disenfranchisement: Constitutional Rights and Wrongs' (2002) *Public Law* 524.

Laubenthal, K., *Strafvollzug* (2nd edn, Springer, Berlin, 1998).

Laughland, J., 'British Law Should not be undermined by these Euro outsiders; Human Rights Ruling Destroys our Freedom' *The Express*, 7 May 2001.

Laws, J., 'Is the High Court the Guardian of Fundamental Constitutional Rights?' (1993) *PL* 59.

—— 'Law and Democracy' (1995) *PL* 72.

—— 'The Constitution: Moral and Rights' (1996) *PL* 622.

—— 'The Limitations of Human Rights' (1998) *PL* 254.

Legrand, P., 'Comparative Legal Studies and Commitment to Theory' (1995) 58(2) *MLR* 262.

—— 'European Systems are not Converging' (1996) 45 *ICLQ* 52.

—— 'How to Compare Now' (1996) 16(2) *LS* 232.

—— *Fragments of Law-as-Culture* (W.E.J. Tjeenk Willink, Deventer, 1999).

—— 'John Merryman and Comparative Legal Studies: A Dialogue' (1999) 27(3) *American Journal of Comparative Law* 50.

Liebling, A., Muir, G., Rose, G. and Bottoms, A., 'Incentives and Earned Privileges for Prisoners: An Evaluation', *Home Office Research Findings No. 87* (Home Office, London, 1999).

Leigh, I., 'Taking Rights Proportionately: Judicial Review, the Human Rights Act and Strasbourg' (2002) *PL* 265.

Lester, A., 'European Human Rights and the British Constitution' in Jowell, J. and Oliver, D. (eds), *The Changing Constitution* (3rd edn, OUP, Oxford, 1994) 57.

—— 'Human Rights and the British Constitution' in Jowell, J. and Oliver, D. (eds), *The Changing Constitution* (4th edn, OUP, Oxford, 2000) 89.

Lester, Lord and Pannick, D. (eds), *Human Rights Law and Practice* (Butterworths, London, 1999).

Lesting, W., *Normalisierung im Strafvollzug: Potential und Grenzen des §3 Abs. 1 StVollzG* (Centaurus, Pfaffenweiler, 1988).

—— 'Normalität im Gefängnis? Zum Umgang der Gerichte mit sozialwissenschaftlichen Erkenntnissen' (1988) *ZfRSoz* 259.

—— and Feest, J., 'Renitente Strafvollzugsbehörden. Eine rechtstatsächliche Untersuchung in rechtspolitischer Absicht' (1987) *ZRP* 390.

Leyland, P., 'Oppositions and Fragmentations: In Search of a Formula for Comparative Analysis?' in Harding, A. and Örücü, E. (eds), *Comparative Law in the 21st Century* (Kluwer, London, 2002).

Light, R., 'Pressure Groups, Penal Policy and the Gaols' (1995) 100 *Prison Service Journal* 27.

Limbach, J., 'Das Bundesverfassungsgericht als politischer Machtfaktor' (1996) *Humboldt Forum Recht*, Beitrag 12.

Lipkke, R., 'Toward a theory of prisoners' rights' (2002) 15(2) *Ratio Juris* 122.

Livingstone, S., 'Prisoners have Rights, But What Rights' (1988) *MLR* 525.

—— 'The Changing Face of Prison Discipline' in Player, E. and Jenkins, M. (eds), *Prisons After Woolf* (Routledge, London, 1994) 97.

—— 'Prisoners' rights in the context of the European Convention on Human Rights' (2000) 2(3) *P&S* 309.

——, Owen, T. and MacDonald, A., *Prison Law* (3rd edn, OUP, Oxford, 2003).

Loader, I. and Sparks, R., 'Contemporary Landscapes of Crime' in Maguire, M. *et al.* (eds), *Oxford Handbook of Criminology* (OUP, Oxford, 2002) 83.

Loucks, N., *Prison Rules: A Working Guide* (Prison Reform Trust, London, 2000).

Loughlin, M., *Public Law and Political Theory* (Clarendon Press, Oxford, 1992).

—— 'The Underside of Law: Judicial Review and the Prison Disciplinary System' (1993) *CLP* 23.

—— 'Courts and Governance' in Birks, P. (ed.), *Frontiers of Liability* (OUP, Oxford, 1994) 91.

—— 'Rights Discourse and Public Law Thought in the United Kingdom' in Anderson, G. (ed.), *Rights and Democracy: Essays in UK-Canadian Constitutionalism* (Blackstone, London, 1999) 193.

—— and Quinn, P.M., 'Prison Rules and Courts: A Study in Administrative Law' (1993) *MLR* 497.

Maguire, M., Morgan, R. and Vagg, J. (eds), *Accountability and Prisons: Opening up a Closed World* (Tavistock, London, 1985).

——, Morgan, R. and Reiner, R. (eds), *Oxford Handbook of Criminology* (2nd edn, OUP, Oxford, 1997).

——, Morgan, R. and Reiner, R. (eds), *Oxford Handbook of Criminology* (3rd edn, OUP, Oxford, 2002).

Mansfield, M., *Presumed Guilty: The British Criminal Justice System Exposed* (Mandarin, London, 1994).

Markesinis, B. (ed.), *The Gradual Convergence* (OUP, Oxford, 1994).

Marshall, G., *Constitutional Conventions* (Clarendon Press, Oxford, 1984).

—— 'Interpreting Interpretation in the Human Rights Bill' (1998) *PL* 167.

—— 'Two kinds of compatibility: more about section 3 of the Human Rights Act 1998' (1999) *PL* 377.

Martinson, R., 'What works?—questions and answers about prison reform' (1974) *The Public Interest* 22.

Matravers, M. (ed.), *Punishment and Political Theory* (Hart, Oxford, 1999).

Matthews, R. and Francis, P. (eds), *Prisons 2000: An International Perspective on the Current State and Future of Imprisonment* (Macmillan, Basingstoke, 1996).

Maurer, H., *Allgemeines Verwaltungsrecht* (11th edn, Beck, Munich, 1997).

Newburn, T., 'Youth, Crime, and Justice' in Maguire, M. *et al.* (eds), *The Oxford Handbook of Criminology* (2nd edn, OUP, Oxford, 1997) 613.

McConville, S., *A History of English Prison Administration* (Routledge, London, 1981).

McCormick, J., 'The Crisis of Constitutional Social Democracy in the Weimar Republic' (2002) 1(1) *European Journal of Political Theory* 121.

McCrudden, C., 'Northern Ireland and the British Constitution' in Jowell, J. and Oliver, D. (eds), *The Changing Constitution* (3rd edn, OUP, Oxford, 1994) 323.

—— and Chambers, G., *Individual Rights and the Law in Britain* (Clarendon Press, Oxford, 1994).

McDermont, M., 'The Elusive Nature of the "Public Function": Poplar Housing and Regeneration Community Association Ltd v Donoghue' (2003) 66 *MLR* 113.

McDermott, K. and King, R., 'A Fresh Start: The Enhancement of Prison Regimes' (1989) 28 *Howard Journal* 161.

McDonald, D., 'Public Imprisonment by Private means' (1994) 34 *BJC* 29.

Meier-Beck, P., 'Schuld und Generalprävention im Vollzug der Freiheitsstrafe' (1984) *MDR* 447.

Merkl, P., *The Origin of the West German Republic* (OUP, New York, 1963).

Merten, D., 'Grundrechte und besonderes Gewaltsverhältnis' in Börne, B. *et al.* (eds), *Einigkeit und Recht und Freiheit—Festschrift für Karl Carstens* (Heymanns, Cologne, 1984) 721.

Miller, S., 'Soziale Grundrechte in der Tradition der deutschen Sozialdemokratie' in Böckenförde, E.-W., Jekewitz, J. and Ramm, T. (eds), *Soziale Grundrechte* (Müller, Heidelberg, 1980) 35.

Minogue, K., 'What is Wrong with Rights' in Harlow, C. (ed.), *Public Law and Politics* (Sweet & Maxwell, London, 1986).

Mitsch, C., *Tatschuld im Strafvollzug* (Doctoral Dissertation, Frankfurt am Main, 1990).

Morgan, R., 'Prison Accountability Revisited' (1993) *PL* 314.

—— 'Learmont: Dangerously Unbalanced' (1996) 35 *Howard Journal* 346.

—— 'Imprisonment: Current Concerns' in Maguire, M. *et al.* (eds), *Oxford Handbook of Criminology* (2nd edn, OUP, Oxford, 1997) 1137.

—— 'Imprisonment' in Maguire, M. *et al.* (eds), *Oxford Handbook of Criminology* (3rd edn, OUP, Oxford, 2002) 1113.

—— and Evans, M. (eds), *Protecting Prisoners: The Standards of the European Committee for the Prevention of Torture in Context* (OUP, Oxford, 1999).

Morris, N. and Rothman, D. (eds), *The Oxford History of the Prison* (OUP, Oxford, 1998).

Müller, C. and Staff, I. (eds), *Der soziale Rechtsstaat: Gedächtnisschrift für Hermann Heller 1981–1933* (Nomos, Baden-Baden, 1984).

Muller, J., 'Carl Schmitt, Hans Freyer and the radical conservative critique of liberal democracy in the Weimar republic' (1991) 12(4) *HPT* 695.

Müller, T., 'Offener Vollzug und Vollzugslockerungen (Ausgang, Freigang)' (1999) *ZfStrVo* 3.

Müller-Dietz, H., *Strafvollzugsgesetzgebung und Strafvollzugsreform* (Heymanns, Cologne, 1970).

—— *Probleme des modernen Strafvollzuges* (vol. 45 Schriftenreihe der Juristischen Gesellschaft e.V., Berlin, 1974).

—— *Strafvollzugsrecht* (Walter de Gruyter, Berlin, 1977).

—— 'Die Rechtsprechung der Strafvollstreckungskammern zur Rechtsgültigkeit der VVStVollzG' (1981) *NStZ* 409.

—— 'Schuldschwere und Urlaub aus der Haft' (1984) *JR* 353.

—— 'Die Aufgaben des Strafvollzugs—kritisch gesehen' (1985) *ZfStrVo* 212.

—— 'Strafvollzug, Tatopfer und Strafzwecke' (1985) *GA* 147.

—— 'Die Strafvollstreckungskammer als besonderes Verwaltungsgericht' in Präsident des Landgerichts Saabrücken (ed.), *150 Jahre Landgericht Saarbrücken* (Heymanns, Cologne, 1985) 335.

—— 'Der Strafvollzug in der Weimarer Zeit und im Dritten Reich' in Busch, M. and Krämer, E. (eds), *Strafvollzug und Schuldproblematik* (Centaurus, Pfaffenweiler, 1988) 15.

—— 'Entwicklungstendenzen des Strafvollzugs im internationalen Vergleich' (1989) 6 *ZfStrVo* 323.

—— '20 Jahre Strafvollzugsgesetz—Anspruch und Wirklichkeit' (1998) *ZfStrVo* 12.

Muncie, J. and Sparks, R. (eds), *Imprisonment: European Perspectives* (Harvester Wheatsheaf, Hemel Hempstead, 1991).

Munro, C., *Studies in Constitutional Law* (Butterworths, London, 1999).

Nelken, D. (ed.), *Special Issue on 'Legal Culture, Diversity and Globalization'* (1995) 4(4) *S&LS*.

—— (ed.), *Comparing Legal Cultures* (Dartmouth, Aldershot, 1997).

—— 'Comparing Criminal Justice' in Maguire, M. *et al.* (eds), *Oxford Handbook of Criminology* (3rd edn, OUP, Oxford, 2002) ch. 6.

Newburn, T., 'Youth, Crime, and Justice' in Maguire, M. *et al.* (eds), *Oxford Handbook of Criminology* (2nd edn, OUP, Oxford, 1997) 613.

Niebler, E., 'Die Rechtsprechung des Bundesverfassungsgerichts zum Strafvollzug' in Fürst, W., Herzog, R. and Umbach, D. (eds), *Festschrift für Wolfgang Ziedler* (Walter de Gruyter, Berlin, 1987) 1567.

Noaks, L., Levi, M. and Maguire, M. (eds), *Contemporary Issues in Criminology* (University of Wales Press, Cardiff, 1995).

Northoff, R., 'Strafvollstreckungskammer: Anspruch und Wirklichkeit' (1987) *ZfStrVo* 207.

Norton, P., *The Constitution in Flux* (Blackwell, Oxford, 1986).

O'Brien, P., 'The Prison on the Continent: Europe, 1865–1965' in Morris, N. and Rothman, D. (eds), *The Oxford History of the Prison* (OUP, Oxford, 1998) 178.

Ogus, A., 'The Economic Basis of Legal Culture: Networks and Monopolization' (2002) 22 *OJLS* 419.

Olechinski, B., 'Strafvollzug in Deutschland vor und nach 1945' (1992) 2 *Neue Justiz* 65.

Oliver, D., 'Is the Ultra Vires Rule the Basis of Judicial Review' (1987) *PL* 543.

—— 'The Frontiers of the State: Public Authorities and Public Functions under the HRA' (2000) *PL* 476.

Örücü, E., 'Unde Venit, Quo Tendit Comparative Law?' in Harding, A. and Örücü, E. (eds), *Comparative Law in the 21st Century* (Kluwer, London, 2002) 1.

Ossenbühl, F., 'Rechtsbindung der Verwaltung' in Erichsen, H.-U. (ed.), *Allgemeines Verwaltungsrecht* (10th edn, Walter de Gruyter, Berlin, 1995) 172.

Ostendorf, H., *Kommentar zum Jugendgerichtsgesetz* (Luchterhand, Neuwied, 1987).

Owen, T., 'Prisoners and Fundamental Rights' (1997) *JR* 81.

Pannick, D., 'Principles of interpretation of Convention rights under the Human Rights Act and the discretionary area of judgement' (1998) *PL* 545.

Parkes, S., *Understanding Contemporary Germany* (Routledge, London, 1997).

Pascoe-Watson, G., 'The human rights laws that could bring chaos to every area of our lives' *The Sun*, 2 August 2000.

Peters, K., 'Beurlaubung von zu lebenslanger Freiheitsstrafe Verurteilten' (1978) *JR* 177.

Pfister, W., 'Freistellung des Gefangenen von der Arbeitspflicht (§ 42 StVollzG)' (1988) *NStZ* 117.

Phillips, G., 'Still waiting for the outrageous and bizarre' *The Times*, 1 October 2002.

Pieroth, B., 'Geschichte der Grundrechte' (1984) *Jura* 568.

——and Schlink, B., *Grundrechte: Staatsrecht II* (2nd edn, Müller, Heidelberg, 1986).

——and Schlink, B., *Grundrechte: Staatsrecht II* (13th edn, Müller, Heidelberg, 1997).

Player, E. and Jenkins, M. (eds), *Prisons After Woolf: Reform through Riot* (Routledge, London, 1994).

Postema, G., *Bentham and the Common Law Tradition* (Clarendon Press, Oxford, 1986).

Power, M., *The Audit Society* (OUP, Oxford, 1999).

Preusker, H., 'Erfahrungen der Praxis mit dem Strafvollzugsgesetz' (1987) *ZfStrVo* 11.

Prison Reform Trust, *Prison Incentives Schemes: Briefing Paper* (Prison Reform Trust, London, 1999).

Prowse, R., Weber, H. and Wilson, C., 'Rights in Prisons in Germany: Blueprint for Britain?' (1992) 20 *IJSL* 111.

Puchalska-Tych, B. and Salter, M., 'Comparing Legal Cultures of Eastern Europe: The Need for a Dialectical Analysis' (1996) 16(2) *LS* 157.

Quinton, A. (ed.), *Political Philosophy* (OUP, Oxford, 1967).

Radbruch, G., *Rechtsphilosophie* (Koehler, Stuttgart, 1950).

Radzinowicz, L., *A history of English criminal law and its administration from 1750, Volume 1, The Movement for Reform* (Stevens, London, 1948).

——*The Roots of the International Association of Criminal Law and their Significance* (MPI, Freiburg, 1991).

——and Hood, R., *A history of English criminal law and its administration from 1750, Volume 5, The Emergence of Penal Policy* (Stevens, London, 1986).

Ramm, T., 'Die sozialen Grundrechte im Verfassungsgefüge' in Böckenförde, E.-W., Jekewitz, J. and Ramm, T., *Soziale Grundrechte* (Müller, Heidelberg, 1980) 17.

Raz, J., *The Morality of Freedom* (Clarendon Press, Oxford, 1986).

——'On The Nature of Law' (1996) 82(1) *Archives for Philosophy of Law and Social Philosophy* 1.

Redecker, K., 'Der moderne Fluch der Versuchung zur Totalität' (1995) *NJW* 3369.

Redwood, J., 'Freedom to confuse' *The Independent*, 7 October 2000, 9.

Reiner, R. and Cross, M. (eds), *Beyond Law and Order: Crime and Criminology into the 1990s* (Macmillan, Basingstoke, 1991) 1.

Rheinstein, M., *Einführung in die Rechtsvergleichung* (2nd edn, Beck, Munich, 1987).

Richardson, G., 'The Case for Prisoners' Rights' in Maguire, M., Morgan, R. and Vagg, J., *Accountability and Prisons* (Tavistock, London, 1985) 19.

——*Law, Process and Custody: Prisoners and Patients* (Weidenfeld & Nicolson, London, 1993).

—— 'Prisoners and the Law: Beyond Rights' in McCrudden, C. and Chambers, G. (eds), *Individual Rights and the Law in the UK* (Clarendon Press, Oxford, 1993) 179.

—— 'From Rights to Expectations' in Player, E. and Jenkins, M. (eds), *Prisons After Woolf: Reform through Riot* (Routledge, London, 1994) 78.

—— and Genn, H. (eds), *Administrative Law and Government Action* (Clarendon Press, Oxford, 1994).

Riles, A. (ed.), *Rethinking the Masters of Comparative Law* (Hart, Oxford, 2001).

Rivers, J., 'Stemming the flood of constitutional complaints in Germany' (1993) *PL* 553.

Robson, W.A., *Justice and Administrative Law* (Macmillan, London, 1928).

Rodley, N., *The Treatment of Prisoners under International Law* (2nd edn, Clarendon Press, Oxford, 1999).

Rogall, K., 'Stillstand oder Fortschritt der Strafrechtsreform' (1982) *ZRP* 124.

Rotthaus, K., 'Die Zusammenarbeit zwischen Justizvollzugsanstalt und Strafvollstreckungskammer' in Schwind, H. (ed.), *Festschrift für Günter Blau* (Walter de Gruyter, Berlin, 1985) 327.

—— 'Die Bedeutung des Strafvollzugsgesetzes für die Reform des Strafvollzugs' (1987) *NStZ* 1.

—— 'Der Schutz der Grundrechte im Gefängnis' (1996) *ZfStrVo* 1.

Roxin, C., 'Sinn und Grenzen staatlicher Strafe' (1966) *JuS* 377.

—— 'Zur Entwicklung der Kriminalpolitik seit den Alternativ-Entwürfen' (1980) *JA* 545.

Rupp, H.-H., 'Vom Wandel der Grundrechte' (1976) *AöR* 161.

Ryan, A., 'The British, the Americans, and Rights' in Lacey, M. and Haakonssen, K. (eds), *A Culture of Rights* (CUP, Cambridge, 1991).

Ryan, M., 'Penal Policy Making Towards the Millennium: Elites and Populists; New Labour and New Criminology' (1999) 27 *IJSL* 1.

—— *Penal Policy and Political Culture in England and Wales* (Waterside, Winchester, 2003).

Sack, P., 'Law and Custom: Reflections on the Relation between English Law and the English Language' in Gessner, V., Hoeland, A. and Varga, C. (eds), *European Legal Culture* (Dartmouth, Aldershot, 1996) 66.

Saladin, P., 'Die Funktion der Grundrechte in einer revidierten Verfassung' (1968) 87 *Zeitschrift für sozialrefurnn (Neue Fassung)* 531.

—— and Wildhaber, L., *Der Staat als Aufgabe, Gedenkenschrift für M. Imboden* (Helbing & Lichtenhahn, Basle and Stuttgart, 1972).

Sajó, A., *Limiting Government: An Introduction to Constitutionalism* (CEU Press, Budapest, 1999).

Savage, S. and Nash, M., 'Law and Order under Blair' in Savage, S. and Atkinson, R. (eds), *Public Policy Under Blair* (Palgrave, Basingstoke, 2001).

Schaaf, B., 'Anklopfen an Haftraumtür vor Betreten durch Vollzugsbedienstete' (1994) *ZfStrVo* 145.

Scheuner, U., 'Die Funktion der Grundrechte im Sozialstaat.' (1971) *DÖV* 505.

Scheuerman, B., 'The rule of law under siege: Carl Schmitt and the death of the Weimar Republic' (1993) 14(2) *HPT* 265.

Schluchter, W., *Entscheidung für den sozialen Rechtsstaat* (Nomos, Baden-Baden, 1983).

Schmidt, C., 'Schwitzen statt sitzen' *Der Spiegel*, 21 July 2003.

Schmidt, W., 'Soziale Grundrechte im Verfassungsrecht der Bundesrepublik Deutschland' (1981) 5 *Der Staat* (Beiheft) 9.

Scholz, R., '10 Jahre Strafvollzugsgesetz (1986) *Bewährungshilfe* 361.

Schone, J., 'The Short Life and Painful Death of Prisoners' Rights' (2001) 40 *Howard Journal* 70.

Schönke, A. and Schröder, H., *Strafgesetzbuch, Kommentar* (25th edn, Beck, Munich, 1997).

Schuler-Springorum, H., *Strafvollzug im Übergang* (Schwartz Verlag, Göttingen, 1969).

—— 'Tatschuld im Strafvollzug' (1989) *StV* 262.

Schwarze, H.-U., *European Administrative Law* (Sweet & Maxwell, London, 1992).

Schwind, H., 'Zum Sinn der Strafe und zum Ziel (Zweck) des (Straf-) Vollzugs' (1981) 23 *Bewährungshilfe* 351.

—— and Blau, G., *Strafvollzug in der Praxis* (Walter de Gruyter, Berlin, 1976).

—— and Blau, G., *Strafvollzug in der Praxis* (2nd edn, Walter de Gruyter, Berlin, 1988).

—— et al., *10 Jahre Strafvollzugsgesetz: Resozialisierung als alleiniges Vollzugsziel?* (Kriminalistik Verlag, Heidelberg, 1988).

—— and Böhm, A., *Strafvollzugsgesetz* (Walter de Gruyter, Berlin, 1999). (Abbreviation: Schwind/Böhm)

Scott, C., 'Accountability in the Regulatory State' (2000) 79 *JLS* 38.

—— and Barron, A., 'The Citizen's Charter Programme' (1992) 55 *MLR* 526.

Sedley, S., 'Governments, Constitutions, and Judges' in Richardson, G. and Genn, H. (eds), *Administrative Law and Government Action* (Clarendon Press, Oxford, 1994) 35.

—— 'Human Rights—A Twenty First Century Agenda' (1995) *PL* 386.

Seneviratne, M., 'The Prisons Ombudsman' (2001) 23(1) *Journal of Social Welfare and Family Law* 93.

Shaw, S., 'The CPT's Visits to the United Kingdom' in Morgan, R. and Evans, M. (eds), *Protecting Prisoners: The Standards of the European Committee for the Prevention of Torture in Context* (OUP, Oxford, 1999) 265.

—— 'The Right to Liberty and Humanity' (2001) 136 *Prison Service Journal* 39.

Shrimpton, M., 'Legal Status of Human Rights Act' *The Times*, 7 September 2000.

Sieber, U. (ed.), *Europäische Einigung und Europäisches Strafrecht* (Carl Heymanns Publishers, Cologne, 1993).

Siekmann, H. (ed.), *Der Staat des Grundgesetzes* (Heymanns, Cologne, 1993).

Singh, R., Hunt, M. and Demetriou, M., 'Is there a Role for the "Margin of Appreciation" in National Law under the Human Rights Act?' (1999) 1 *EHRLR* 15.

Sofsky, W., *Die Ordnung des Terrors: Das Konzentrationslager* (Fischer, Frankfurt am Main, 1993).

Sontheimer, K., 'Zur Grundlagenproblematik der deutschen Staatsrechtslehre in der Weimarer Republik' (1960) 46 *ARSP* 39.

—— 'Principles of Human Dignity in the Federal Republic' in Stern, K. (ed.), *Germany and its Basic Law* (Nomos, Baden-Baden, 1993) 213.

Sparks, R., 'Penal 'Austerity': The Doctrine of Less Eligibility Reborn?' in Matthews, R. and Francis, P. (eds), *Prisons 2000: An International Perspective on the Current State and Future of Imprisonment* (Macmillan, Basingstoke, 1996) 74.

Starck, C., 'Die Grundrechte des Grundgesetzes' (1981) *JuS* 237.

—— 'Menschenwürde als Verfassungsgarantie im modernen Staat' (1981) *JZ* 457.

Starmer, K. (ed.), *European Human Rights Law* (Legal Action Group, London, 1999).

—— 'Two years of the Human Rights Act' (2003) 1 *EHRLR* 14.

Stellungnahme zum Entwurf eines Strafvollzugsgesetzes (Bund der Strafvollzugsbediensteten Deutschlands e.V., 1974).

Steinberg, J., 'Constitutional Court can take cue from foreign experiences' *Business Day*, 11 November 1999.

Stern, K., 'Der Rechtsstaat' in Siekmann, H. (ed.), *Der Staat des Grundgesetzes* (Heymanns, Cologne, 1993) 3.

—— 'Menschenwürde als Wurzel der Menschen-und Grundrechte' in Siekmann, H. (ed.), *Der Staat des Grundgesetzes* (Heymanns, Cologne, 1993) 224.

—— 'Sozialstaat' in Siekmann, H. (ed.), *Der Staat des Grundgesetzes* (Heymanns, Cologne, 1993) 123.

—— 'Staatsrecht und Verfassungsrecht in ihrer Wechselbezüglichkeit' in Siekmann, H. (ed.), *Der Staat des Grundgesetzes* (Heymanns, Cologne, 1993) 133.

—— (ed.), *Germany and its Basic Law* (Nomos, Baden-Baden, 1993).

Stern, V., *Bricks of Shame* (Penguin, Harmondsworth, 1987).

—— *A Sin Against the Future* (Penguin, London, 1998).

Stevens, R., *Law and Politics: The House of Lords as a Judicial Body 1800–1976* (Weidenfeld & Nicolson, London, 1983).

—— 'A Loss of Innocence? Judicial Independence and the Separation of Powers' (1999) 19(3) *OJLS* 365.

Stewart, J. and Walsh, K., 'Change in the Management of Public Services' (1992) 70 *Public Administration* 499, 504.

Steyn, Lord, 'The New Legal Landscape' (2000) 6 *EHRLR* 549.

—— 'Human Rights: The Legacy of Mrs Roosevelt' (2002) *PL* 473.

—— 'Democracy through Law' (2002) 6 *EHRLR* 723.

Stirk, P., 'Hugo Preuss, German political thought and the Weimar constitution' (2002) 23(3) *HPT* 497.

Stone-Sweet, A., *Governing With Judges: Constitutional Politics in Europe* (OUP, Oxford, 2000).

Straw, J., 'Parliament Decides' *Daily Telegraph*, 15 December 2000.

—— and Boateng, P., *Bringing Rights Home: Labour Plans to incorporate the ECHR into UK law*, December 1996 (published in (1997) 1 *EHRLR* 71).

Summers, R., Krawietz, W., MacCormick, N. and von Wright, G.H. (eds), *Prescriptive Formality and Normative Rationality in Modern Legal Systems* (Duncker and Humblot, Berlin, 1994).

Tait, N., 'Judges Exercise Human Rights Powers "Conservatively"' *Financial Times*, 7 March 2003.

Taylor, Lord, 'The Judiciary in the 1990s' 1992 Dimbleby Lecture (30 November 1992).

Ten, C., *Crime, Guilt and Punishment* (Clarendon Press, Oxford, 1987).

Thorton, P., Mallalieu, A. and Scrivener, A., *Justice on Trial: Report on the Independent Civil Liberty Panel on Criminal Justice* (Civil Liberties Trust, London, 1992).

Tomkins, A., 'Inventing Human Rights Law and Scholarship' (1996) 16 *OJLS* 153.

Train, C., 'Management Accountability in the Prison Service' in Maguire, M., Vagg, J. and Morgan, R. (eds), *Accountability in Prisons: Opening Up a Closed World* (Tavistock, London, 1985) 177.

Travis, A., 'Chief justice clashes with Straw on jail policy' *The Guardian*, 1 February 2001, 6.

—— 'A look inside' *The Guardian*, 12 July 2003.

—— 'Jail Numbers to top 80,000' *The Guardian*, 16 July 2003.

Treacy, V., 'Prisoners' Rights Submerged in Semantics' (1989) *Howard Journal* 27.

Uchida, M., 'Chalk and Cheese' (1998 February) *Prospect* 24.

Ullenbruch, T., 'Vollzugsbehörde contra Strafvollstreckungskammer' (1993) *NStZ* 517.

Vagg, J., *Prison Systems: A Comparative Study of Accountability in England, France, Germany, and the Netherlands* (Clarendon Press, Oxford, 1994).

Van Bueren, G., 'Including the Excluded: the Case for an Economic, Social and Cultural Human Rights Act' (2002) *Public Law* 456.

Van Caenegem, R., *Judges, Legislators and Professors: Chapters in European Legal History* (CUP, Cambridge, 1987).

Van Hoecke, M. and Warrington, M., 'Legal Cultures, Legal Paradigms and Legal Doctrine: Towards a New Model for Comparative Law' (1998) *ICLQ* 47.

Van Zyl Smit, D., 'Leave of Absence for West German Prisoners' (1988) 28 *BJC* 1.

—— 'Is Life Imprisonment Constitutional: The German Experience' (1992) *PL* 263.

—— and Dünkel, F. (eds), *Imprisonment Today and Tomorrow* (Kluwer, Deventer, 1991).

Verhandlungen des 48. Deutschen Juristentages (Beck, Munich, 1970).

Verhandlungen des 50. Deutschen Juristentages (Beck, Munich, 1974).

Verkaik, R., 'Civil Liberties: Shortage of new cases confounds critics of the nutters' charter' *The Independent*, 27 May 2003.

Vogel, H.-J., '10 Jahre sozialliberale Rechtspolitik' (1980) *ZRP* 1.

Vogelgesang, E., 'Kleintierhaltung im Strafvollzug' (1994) *ZfStrVo* 67.

Volckart, B., 'Anmerkung zu BGHSt 30, 320' (1982) *NStZ* 174.

Von Engelberg, 'Zur Frage des Strafvollzugs' (1898) 3 *DJZ* 195.

Von Feuerbach, A. (ed.), *Feuerbach's biographischer Nachlass* (2nd edn, Ludwig Feuerbach Weber, Leipzig, 1853).

Von Hirsch, A., *Doing Justice: The Choice of Punishments* (Hillang Wang, New York, 1976).

—— *Censure and Sanctions* (Clarendon Press, Oxford, 1993).

—— and Ashworth, A. (eds), *Principled Sentencing* (Edinburgh University Press, Edinburgh, 1992).

—— and Ashworth, A., *Principled Sentencing—Readings on Theory and Policy* (2nd edn, Hart, Oxford, 1998) 351.

Von Kyaw, D., 'Germany's problem is federalism' *Financial Times*, 29 July 2003.

Von Mangoldt, H., 'Grundrechte und Grundsatzfragen des Bonner Grundgesetzes' (1949) *AöR* 273.

Von Schewick, H., 'Verfassungsrechtliche Grenzen der Resozialisierung' (1985) *Bewährungshilfe* 3.

Wade, W., 'The Basis of Legal Sovereignty' (1955) *CLJ* 172.

—— 'The United Kingdom's Bill of Rights' in Beatson, J. (ed.), *Constitutional Reform in the United Kingdom: Practice and Principles* (Hart, Oxford, 1998) 61, 66.

—— 'Horizons of Horizontality' (2000) 116 *LQR* 48.

—— and Forsyth, C., *Administrative Law* (7th edn, Clarendon Press, Oxford 1994).

Wadham, J. and Mountfield, H., *Human Rights Act 1998* (Blackstone, London, 1999).

Wagner, J., 'Die Neuregelung der Zwangsernährung' (1976) *ZRP* 1.

Waldron, J. (ed.), *Theories of Rights* (OUP, Oxford, 1984).

Walter, M., *Strafvollzug* (Boorberg, Stuttgart, 1991).

—— *Strafvollzug* (2nd edn, Boorberg, Stuttgart, 1999).

Weigend, T., 'Neoklassisismus—ein transatlantisches Mißverständnis' (1982) *ZStW* 801.

Wirth, 'Beiträge zur Frage über die gesetzliche Regelung des Strafvollzugs' (1873) 8 *BlGefk* 36.

—— 'Soll der Strafvollzug auf dem (im) Wege der Gesetzgebung geregelt werden?' (1875) *BlGefk* 359.

Woolf, Lord, 'Droit Publique—English Style' (1995) *PL* 57.

—— 'We still fail our prisoners' *The Times* 2, 1 February 2001, 4.

Würtenberger, T., 'Reform des Strafvollzuges im sozialen Rechtsstaat' (1967) *JZ* 233.

—— 'Freiheit und Zwang im Strafvollzug' (1969) *NJW* 1747.

—— *Kriminalpolitik im sozialen Rechtsstaat* (Enke, Stuttgart, 1970).

Young, J., 'The Politics of the Human Rights Act' (1999) 26(1) *JLS* 27.

—— 'Crime and Social Exclusion' in Maguire, M. *et al.* (eds), *Oxford Handbook of Criminology* (3rd edn, OUP, Oxford, 2002) 459.

Zedner, L., 'Comparative Research in Criminal Justice' in Noaks, L., Levi, M. and Maguire, M. (eds), *Contemporary Issues in Criminology* (University of Wales Press, Cardiff, 1995) 13.

—— 'In Pursuit of the Vernacular: Comparing Law and Order Discourses in England and Germany' (1995) 4(4) *S&LS* 517.

—— 'Dangers of Dystopia' (2002) 22(2) *OJLS* 341.

—— and Ashworth, A., *The Criminological Foundations of Penal Policy* (OUP, Oxford, 2003).

Zellick, G., 'The Prison Rules and the Courts' (1981) *CLR* 602.

Ziekow, J., 'Deutsche Verfassungsentwicklung und sozialer Liberalismus' (1989) *JuS* 107.

Zweigert, K., 'Rechtsvergleichung als universale Interpretationsmethode' (1949/50) 54 *Rabels Zeitschrift für Ausländisches und Internationales Privatrecht* 203.

—— and Kötz, H., *An Introduction to Comparative Law*, vol. 1 (North-Holland Publishing Co, Amsterdam, 1977).

ENGLISH OFFICIAL PUBLICATIONS

Annual Report 1997–98 of HM Chief Inspector of Prisons (HMSO, London, 1998).

Annual Report of HM Chief Inspector of Prisons for England and Wales 1999–2000 (HMSO, London, 2001).

Annual Report of HM Chief Inspector of Prisons for England and Wales 2001–2002 (HMSO, London, 2002).

Auld, Lord Justice, *A Review of the Criminal Courts of England and Wales* (HMSO, London, 2001).

The Citizen's Charter (Cm. 1599).

Custody, Care and Justice (Cm. 1647).

The Framework Document for the Prison Service (HMSO, London, 1993).

Halliday, J., *Making Punishment Work: Report of a Review of the Sentencing Framework for England and Wales July 2001* (HMSO, London, 2001).

HM Prison Service, *Operating Standards* (HMSO, London, 1994).

—— *Framework Document* (HMSO, London, 1998).

—— *Performance Standards Programme* (HMSO, London, 1999).

—— *Standards Manual 2002* (HMSO, London, 2002).

—— *What Works in Prison Strategy* (Home Office Communications Directorate, February 2002).

—— *Annual Report and Accounts April 2002–March 2003* (HC 885 HMSO, London, 2003).

Justice for All (Cm. 5536).

Learmont, General Sir John, *Review of Prison Service Security in England and Wales and the Escape from Parkhurst Prison on Tuesday 3rd of January 1995* (Cm. 3020).

Leigh L.H. and Zedner, L., *The Royal Commission on Criminal Justice: A Report on the Administration of Criminal Justice in the Pre-trial Phase in France and Germany* (HMSO, London, 1992).

Lloyd, Sir Peter, *Review of the Boards of Visitors: A Report of the Working Group* (HMSO, London, 2001).

Modernising the Management of the Prison Service: An Independent Report by the Targeted Performance Initiative Working Group (Chaired by Lord Laming of Tewin CBE) (HMSO, London, 2000).

Park, I., *Review of Comparative Costs and Performance of Privately and Publicly Operated Prisons 1998–99*, Statistical Bulletin 6/00 (Home Office, London, 2000).

Prison Disturbances April 1990: Report of an Inquiry by the Rt. Hon. Lord Justice Woolf (part I and II) and His Honour Judge Stephen Tumin (Part II) (Cm. 1456).

Private Sector Involvement in the Remand System (Cm. 434).

Report of the Committee of Inquiry into the United Kingdom Prison Services (May Committee) (Cm. 7673).

Report of the Committee on the Prison Disciplinary System in England and Wales (Cmnd. 9641).

Rights Brought Home: The Human Rights Bill (Cm. 3782).

Review of Prison Service Security in England and Wales and the Escape from Parkhurst Prison on Tuesday 3rd of January 1995 (The Learmont Report) (Cm. 3020).

The Royal Commission on Criminal Justice Report (Cm 2263).

Through the Prison Gate: A Joint Thematic Review by HM Inspectorates and Probation (HMSO, London, 2001).

Towards Resettlement: Prisons and Probation Ombudsman for England and Wales Annual Report 2002–2003 (HMSO, London, 2003).

Woodcock, Sir John, *Report of the Enquiry into the Escape of Six Prisoners from the Special Security Unit at Whitemoor Prison, Cambridgeshire, on Friday 9th September 1994* (Cm. 2741).

German Official Publications

Bericht und Antrag des Sonderausschusses für die Strafrechtsreform zu dem von der Bundesregierung eingebrachten Entwurf eines Gesetzes über den Vollzug der Freiheitsstrafe und der freiheitsentziehenden Maßregeln der Besserung und Sicherung–Strafvollzugsgesetz (BT-Dr. 7/3998).

Bundesministerium der Justiz, *Entwurf eines Gesetzes über den Vollzug der Freiheitsstrafe und der freiheitsentziehenden Maßregeln der Besserung und Sicherung–Strafvollzugsgesetz* (Müller, Karlsruhe, 1971).

Gesetzesvorschlag des Bundesrates 1973 (BT-Dr. 7/918).

Jung, H. and Müller-Dietz, H. (eds), *Vorschläge zum Entwurf eines Strafvollzugsgesetzes* (2nd edn, Fachausschuß I 'Strafrecht und Strafvollzug' des Bundeszusammenschlusses für Straffälligenhilfe 1974).

Konferenz der Justizminister und -senatoren, Beschlußprotokoll von 4.6.1987 (Bt-Dr 7/3218).

Materialien zur Strafrechtsreform: rechtsvergleichende Gutachten zur Strafvollzugsreform (Bundesministerium der Justiz, Bonn, 1969) vol. 8.

Protokolle der Sitzungen des Bundestags-Sonderausschusses für die Strafrechtsreform (Deutscher Bundestag, 7. Wahlperiode, Stenographischer Dienst, 1975).

Regierungsentwurf eines Strafvollzugsgesetzes (BT-Dr. 7/918, 1972/73).

Index